Let's Program It...
in True BASIC

By

Avery Catlin

True BASIC Press

Let's Program It ... in True BASIC

By
Avery Catlin

ISBN 0-939553-34-1

True BASIC, Inc.
www.truebasic.com

Contents

Preface

Let's Program It... in True BASIC is designed to teach you how to write programs in True BASIC. This language is one of the first commercial versions of BASIC that conforms in most details to the American National Standard for the Programming Language Full BASIC (ANS BASIC). Since its conception at Dartmouth College in 1964, BASIC has become one of the most widely used computer languages. Unfortunately, many different implementations of BASIC have been developed and they vary considerably in scope and syntax. This book was created as a valuable supplement to the reference manual you receive with the True BASIC Language System. This guarantees that all program statements in this book and the reference manual will be the same, and save unnecessary confusion.

This is not a book on computer literacy, but rather a book on programming. While it covers many aspects of True BASIC syntax, it is not meant to replace the *True BASIC Reference Manual*. The latter publication is available in different versions for different computers. This textbook teaches you how to write practical programs in a modern, fully structured version of standard BASIC that is known as True BASIC.

Even though the subject matter is programming, most users of this book are not likely to become professional programmers. Almost all of them will, however, use personal computers in their business or professional lives. They will run application programs much of the time, but will also occasionally find a need to write small programs, probably in BASIC. While designed primarily to teach programming, the book is also designed to give users a better understanding of the capabilities of modern computers.

The material is suitable for self study or a one-semester or two-quarter course in a school curriculum. By omitting several chapters (for example, the chapters on graphics, matrices, and indexed databases), the book is a suitable text for a one-quarter course. A knowledge of high school level mathematics is assumed. While the book is written for the student with general interests, its advanced examples come mostly from the business world and are based on the everyday use of computers in business.

Several areas receive special emphasis:

- Careful adherence to ANS BASIC standards.

- An early introduction to modular program development using independent procedures, functions and subroutines.

- Extensive display of example programs to show how BASIC statements are used.

- The importance of good program style, or how to write programs that are easy to read and understand, and thus easy to maintain.

- An early explanation of program debugging techniques.

- Examples of techniques for storing and retrieving information using data files and databases, probably the most important commercial use of computers.

A textbook is designed to teach, to explain those small but difficult points that may not be understood by a student, even after attending lectures. Every effort was made to write clear and complete explanations. After years of experience teaching students, I have found that there are certain ideas that students have difficulty understanding, and these ideas are explained in detail.

The following points are given special attention and explanation:

- The difference between a variable name and a variable value.

- Just how do variables store information.

- The difference between a number and a string of digits.

- The use of indexed variables, especially for students with a limited mathematical background.

- The concept of program files and data files, how they are alike and how they differ.

- What happens when a disk file is over-written or erased.

- The concept and scope of local variables.

- The different methods for passing information to functions and subroutines.

Programming cannot be learned just by reading. The book assumes that you have access to a computer and will write programs. It presents material in such a way that you can start writing programs soon after you begin this course of study. A list of important points, a dozen or more self-test questions, and several practice programs are included at the end of all chapters except Chapter 1. All example programs and test data for many of the practice programs are on a disk which comes with this book.

This textbook covers both PC and Macintosh computer systems. In Chapters 1 and 2, machine-specific material appears in separate sections. Other differences between the two computer systems are noted throughout the text. Every example program in the book runs on both PCs and Macs.

In addition to the changes required by newer versions of True BASIC, the text was modified in many places to improve explanations and discussions. One significant change is an explanation early in the book (and in the course) of how to write programs that can read simple text files. Students feel that the programs they write are more realistic if data is read from files and in many cases, time is not wasted entering data from the keyboard. This change allows test data for student programs to be placed in files that are made available on floppy disks or on a computer network.

Over the past several years, suggestions have come from students and teachers. I appreciate these suggestions and have incorporated many of them into the new edition. All example programs were reviewed and modified if I could find a way to improve their clarity. Sample computer output is included for most example programs in the text. A section on common programming errors was added at the end of each chapter. This latest edition attempts to keep pace with the almost unbelievable increase in small computer performance.

Desktop computer systems are now many times faster than before; the Pentium has become the CPU of choice in new PCs while the PowerPC has become the CPU of choice in new PowerMacs and their clones. Windows has largely replaced DOS (or more correctly, supplemented DOS) as an operating system and the latest version, Windows 95 is just starting to be installed on PCs. System 7.5 of MacOS is the current system on Macs with System 8 maybe a year away.

Many computer systems now have CD-ROMs and increasingly good sound systems with external or internal speakers. With the rapid drop in hard disk prices, the 1 gigabyte disk is rapidly becoming the standard on desktop machines. The price of memory has not dropped as rapidly, but more and more computers are now sold with 16 megabytes of RAM already installed.

Notebook computers were just starting to appear five years ago; you now see lots of business travellers carrying their notebook computers through airports. These computers are still significantly more expensive than the desktop models, primarily because of the cost of color LCD screens. Color monitors are quickly becoming the standard on all types of small computers, and software publishers are now taking advantage of that fact by using color in the latest versions of application programs.

During this period of time, there have been few changes in True BASIC which attests to its excellent original design. Newly released editions for both PCs and Macs provide an excellent working environment for developing large programs. These versions run under Windows as DOS programs and their Macintosh editions have been updated to run on the PowerMac.

With Microsoft discontinuing QuickBasic on the Macintosh, True BASIC remains the premier beginner's language that runs on almost all brands of small computers. This amazing technical feat means that little or no conversion of your source code is needed when you move your program from one type of computer to another.

In preparation for this latest edition, every chapter and appendix has been carefully reviewed, errors have been corrected, and some less-than-clear passages have been completely rewritten. I believe the clarity of the book has been improved.

A few of the original Practice Programs have been rewritten to state a problem more clearly, one Practice Program has been removed and one added. Three new help files are included on the example program disk which now comes with each book.

Acknowledgements

Many people contributed to the development of this book. The first edition was used by four classes in draft form before publication. It has been used by dozens of classes at the University of Virginia since its original publication. The students in these classes made many contributions through their questions and comments, and graduate teaching assistants and instructors helped find and correct errors in both text and programs. Comments and corrections have come in from schools and colleges throughout the country. My thanks go to all who have helped make it a better textbook.

Critical reviewers are an important asset when writing a textbook. I was fortunate to have the help of five dedicated and experienced teachers who were responsible for turning my draft of the first edition into a much better book. A Russian edition appeared in 1990 and I thank those faculty at the University of Moscow who wrote me with comments and suggestions. I am grateful also to the three reviewers of the second edition draft. The editors at True BASIC, Inc. and especially the president, John Lutz, have provided strong support as the third edition was prepared for publication by that firm.

Writing a book in ones spare time means that not enough time is left for other things. My special thanks to my wife, Edie, for her support and understanding during all those weekends and vacations when I spent so many hours in front of my computer.

— Avery Catlin

PART 1

Fundamentals of Structured Programming

CHAPTER

1

Getting Started

1.1 INTRODUCTION

Before starting to write computer programs, you must decide what language to use. I explain why True BASIC (a version of American National Standard BASIC) is your best choice. You must learn how to operate your computer, which I assume is either an IBM PC-compatible or an Apple Macintosh computer. You also learn how to use this book as you study the True BASIC language.

Figure 1.1 *Typical personal computer system*

1.2 WHY LEARN BASIC?

Most of the people who use personal computers are not professional programmers. They use a computer as a tool to help them accomplish some particular task. They need to learn programming to become more familiar with computers and to write small programs for particular jobs. Their computer language requirements are different from those of the professional programmer.

True BASIC is an ideal language for their use, being both easy to learn and powerful enough to handle difficult jobs. Moreover, the same True BASIC program runs on almost every one of the desktop and laptop computers that a non-professional programmer might use.

Writing a computer program can be fun, it stimulates your mind. It's a little like doing crossword puzzles, an intellectual exercise. But writing programs can also produce real benefits. Most importantly, you learn more about your computer and how it works.

Many professional programmers and computer scientists will tell you that BASIC is not a suitable language for writing large programs. They may be correct if they refer to one of the early, unstructured versions of the BASIC language. The True BASIC language, however, is an advanced version of BASIC. It combines the simplicity and ease of use of original BASIC with the structure and power of more sophisticated languages.

Here are some of the advantages of almost every version of BASIC:

- It is easy to learn.
- It is easy to use.
- It uses a simple grammar or statement syntax.
- Its programs are easy to modify.
- It runs without modifying programs on most small computers.

For these and other reasons, BASIC has become the most popular programming language on personal computers. Today more people write programs in BASIC than in any other computer language.

There are some disadvantages to the original version of BASIC:

- It produces slow programs.
- It lacks varied and effective control statements.
- It is easy to create unstructured programs.
- Its syntax varies from one type of computer to another.

True BASIC eliminates these disadvantages, making it a suitable language for both casual users and writers of large programs.

1.3 FIRST STEPS

This book will show you how to write programs in the True BASIC language. All of the example programs run on both IBM PC and Macintosh computers. There are many personal computers on the market that are compatible with an IBM PC to varying degrees and **I denote these machines by the generic term PC**. These computers are sometimes called DOS or Windows computers based on their operating system. The example programs also run on the various Apple Macintosh models and **I denote these by the generic term Mac**.

The book concentrates on teaching computer programming, not on covering every detail of the BASIC language. You should supplement this textbook with the *True BASIC Reference Manual* published by True BASIC, Inc. The language reference manual is the final authority on correct syntax of True BASIC statements and commands. You should refer to it for detailed information that is not covered in the textbook. Each *Reference Manual* also contains sections of information devoted to your particular computer system.

I assume you have access to a personal microcomputer that supports the True BASIC language. Computer programming can be learned only by doing, not just by reading. As you read the text, type in the example programs on your computer or load them from disk that accompanies this book.

You have probably noticed that I am already starting to use some computer terms like *program*, *floppy disk*, and *hard disk*. These terms are defined in the next chapter and if they sound strange to you, look ahead now and read the definitions. New terms are printed in italic face as they are introduced.

You must learn first how to turn on your computer, insert a floppy disk (if necessary), and start the True BASIC system. If your computer has a hard disk or is connected to a network, you may not need to use a floppy disk, but there are probably other procedures to follow. There should be a switch that turns on your computer, located on the front, side, or back of its case. Your monitor may have a separate switch as well as knobs to adjust brightness and contrast.

One of the most frustrating initial steps in learning to write computer programs is learning to use your computer. Get help from your computer manual, your instructor, or a fellow student. Only after you become familiar with your computer equipment can you concentrate on learning to write BASIC programs.

In the next two sections, you learn how to start up the True BASIC system, and how to exit that system when you are finished. Ask someone to help you the first time and remember, the second time you use the computer is much easier than the first time.

A set of general specifications for True BASIC on PC and Mac computers is given in Appendix A. Some of these specifications will make little sense to you until you learn more about the language. You should know, however, that this appendix exists and is available for reference.

1.4   USING YOUR IBM PC-COMPATIBLE (PC) COMPUTER

I assume in this section that you have an IBM Personal Computer or one of the many different IBM PC-compatible computers. It should have at least one *floppy-disk drive* that accepts removable disks and probably has a fixed or *hard-disk drive*. It uses the MS-DOS (or PC-DOS; they are essentially the same) operating system, version 2.0 or later, **commonly called DOS for disk operating system.**

Starting from a Hard Disk

Turn on your computer and let the disk come up to speed. If a menu is displayed, select True BASIC from the menu. If there is no menu, type HELLO after the C:\> (or C>) prompt and press the Return key ↵ sometimes marked Enter. Here is how that entry might look, user input is shown in italic face to distinguish it from the computer prompt:

```
C:\> HELLO
```

The True BASIC system is loaded, and when it is ready, it displays the Ok. prompt. You can now write a True BASIC computer program.

Starting from a Floppy Disk

Insert a disk containing the operating system and True BASIC into drive A, close the drive door, and turn on your computer. After the computer does some checking, it may ask you for the date, which you must enter using the MM-DD-YY format. It will then ask you for the time, and you enter it using the HH:MM format. Note that a colon is required to separate hours and minutes. Most PC computers have a built-in clock that automatically sets the date and time.

The computer next displays the prompt A>, which indicates that drive A is the selected drive and that it is waiting for instructions. Type HELLO (in either uppercase or lowercase characters) and press the Return key. You may now write a True BASIC computer program.

Stopping True BASIC

When you have finished writing programs, you can leave the True BASIC system by typing BYE in response to the Ok. prompt and pressing the Return key, as shown:

    Ok. BYE

You will see the A> or C:\> prompt again, and if you are through using the computer, remove any floppy disk from its drive and turn off the machine.

1.5   USING YOUR WINDOWS COMPUTER

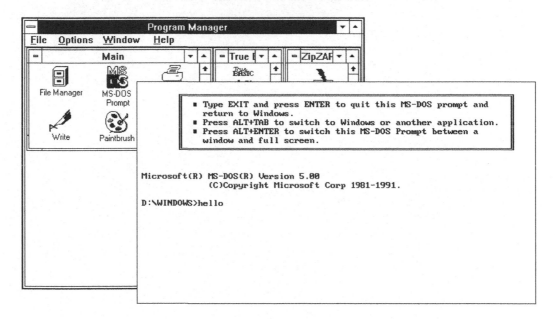

Figure 1.2 *Use the MS-DOS Prompt to run True BASIC under Windows.*

More and more PC computers now use a version of Microsoft Windows. If that is your case, you may want to run True BASIC under Windows as a non-Windows application. Windows requires that your computer have a hard disk. If you are familiar with Windows, you will know how to install True BASIC to operate in this mode; if not, you should get someone to install it for you.

Newly released versions of True BASIC, designed specifically to run under Windows 3.1 and Windows 95, are also available if you are using these operating systems on your PC in addition to DOS.

To run True BASIC, start your computer and eventually a window will appear containing groups and icons. Find the icon (a small picture) representing True BASIC and double-click on it to start the application. You may have to open a group to find the icon. Read the next section if you are unfamiliar with these terms. True BASIC will open in a window and the screen will look exactly as it does when running under DOS. Your mouse is active and can be used as discussed in Chapter 2, Section 2.8.

Stopping True BASIC is done in the same way as described for a Mac in the next section. Move the mouse to place the mouse cursor on the title File in the menu bar at the top of the screen, hold down the mouse button, drag the cursor down to the command Quit, and release the mouse button.

1.6   USING YOUR APPLE MACINTOSH (MAC) COMPUTER

I assume in this section that you have an Apple Macintosh computer, anything from the simple Macintosh 512K to the latest Power Mac. True BASIC does not run on the original 128K Macintosh. Your computer should be using version 6 or later of the operating system, **called MacOS**. As a Mac user, I assume you are familiar with a mouse and how to use it.

As I hope you know already, the term *double-click* means to position the mouse cursor (an arrow-shaped symbol) on top of an icon or other object and press the mouse button twice in rapid succession. This action opens the file or folder represented by the icon.

Starting from a Hard Disk

Turn on your computer and its software components should start to load. When loading is complete, you will see an icon (a small picture) on the screen representing your hard disk. Double-click with the mouse on this icon and additional icons representing applications should appear. Identify the icon for True BASIC and double-click on it to start that program. An untitled window called the *editing window* will appear with a menu bar at the top. You are now ready to write a True BASIC program.

Figure 1.3 *True BASIC on a Mac with Edit, Command, and Output windows open.*

Starting from a Floppy Disk

If you have only one removable or *floppy-disk drive* and no fixed or *hard disk drive,* you must create a working disk. This floppy disk should contain a copy of the operating system (also called the System folder) and a copy of True BASIC. Detailed information on how to create this disk is contained in the *True BASIC Macintosh User's Guide.* The user's guide also tells you how to proceed if you have two floppy-disk drives, a hard-disk drive, or a networked computer. If you have not had much experience with the Mac, try to get help from a more experienced user.

Place your working disk in the floppy-disk drive (the bottom drive if there are two drives) and turn on your computer. If the Mac starts successfully, you should see a floppy-disk icon (a small picture of a floppy disk) in the upper righthand corner of the screen. Double-click on this icon and the True BASIC icon should become visible.

The next step is to double-click on the True BASIC icon and an untitled window with a menu bar at the top should appear. This window is called the *editing window*. You are now ready to write a True BASIC program.

Stopping True BASIC

When you have finished writing programs, you can leave True BASIC by using the File pull-down command menu. Move the mouse to place the mouse cursor on the title File in the menu bar, hold down the mouse button, drag the cursor down to the command Quit, and release the mouse button. *Dragging* means to move the mouse while the mouse button is held down. These procedures are complicated to describe but easy to execute.

Any program statements that you have written will now disappear and a new menu bar will be displayed. Move the mouse to place the mouse cursor on the title Special in the menu bar, hold down the mouse button, drag the cursor down to the command Shut Down, and release the button. After a few seconds, any disks in floppy-disk drives will be ejected and a message appears telling you that it is safe to turn off the computer. You can now turn off the power switch.

1.7 HOW TO USE THIS BOOK

The first six chapters of the book constitute Part I and should be read in sequence. They give you enough knowledge of True BASIC to write many programs. The next three chapters are Part II and cover three important advanced topics in BASIC programming. I expand on the use of text files in Chapter 7, introduce the concept of separate program units or procedures in Chapter 8, and explain how to use arrays in Chapter 9. I recommend that the chapters in Part II be read in the order in which they are presented. The last six chapters cover specialized features of the True BASIC language and make up Part III. This part of the book uses many concepts introduced in earlier chapters as well as introducing some new concepts. The emphasis is on designing and writing larger application programs in True BASIC.

Examples of True BASIC statements and example programs are located throughout each chapter. As mentioned earlier, these example programs are available on a floppy disk for either PC or Mac computers. Instructions on how to read these programs are printed in Appendix F.

I urge you to run all the example programs, typing them in from the book if you do not have them on disk. Don't be afraid to modify them; even if you make mistakes, you will learn more about programming. Several programming assignments are listed at the end of every chapter except Chapter 1. These assignments can and should be used for further practice and to help you evaluate your progress.

Summary of Important Points

- True BASIC is an expanded version of American National Standard BASIC.

- BASIC is an ideal programming language for most personal computer users who are not professional programmers.

- The term PC is used to describe any IBM PC or compatible computer.

- The term Mac is used to describe any Apple Macintosh computer.

- True BASIC runs on many different personal computers, including PCs and Macs.

- Be sure to run the example programs that are on the floppy disk provided with this book.

Common Errors

- Not reading the instructions for your specific computer before trying to use it.

- Trying to start the computer by inserting a startup disk in the wrong disk drive.

- Trying to start the computer by inserting a floppy disk that is not a startup disk — that is, does not contain a copy of the operating system.

PC Users

- Not pressing the Return key after entering a command like HELLO or BYE.

- Failing to type a colon between the hours and minutes when entering the current time.

Mac and Windows Users

- Double-clicking the mouse button too slowly when opening a drive or the True BASIC system.

- Not continuing to hold down the mouse button while dropping down a menu.

Self-Test Questions

1. Where can you find additional information on the True BASIC language, beyond what is covered in this book?

2. Should True BASIC commands be entered using uppercase characters or lowercase characters?

PC Users

3. What operating system is used by your computer?

4. Should the startup disk (used to start or "boot" your computer) be inserted in drive A or drive B?

5. What is the correct format for entering the date when requested by the operating system?

6. What is the correct format for entering the time?

7. If the prompt B> is displayed on the screen, which disk drive is the active or selected drive?

8. What command is entered to start the True BASIC system?

9. What command is entered to stop the True BASIC system?

10. What prompt is displayed by the True BASIC system?

Mac Users (some questions apply also to Windows Users)

11. What is the procedure for opening or starting True BASIC when the True BASIC icon is displayed on the screen?

12. What is the name of the window where True BASIC programs are written?

13. How do you exit True BASIC?

14. What is the proper procedure for turning off your Mac?

CHAPTER 2

Writing and Editing Simple Programs

2.1 INTRODUCTION

Computer users have developed their own special vocabulary so I begin by defining several computer terms. After some definitions, I show you how to write a simple computer program in True BASIC and how to make the computer execute the program instructions — that is, run the program. Program statements are introduced that accept information typed on the keyboard and display this information on the screen.

I next discuss the editing facilities available in True BASIC for writing computer programs on both PC and Mac computers. Several commands that create, run, and save new programs — and retrieve old programs — are introduced.

2.2 DEFINITIONS

A *computer system* consists of a computer, the electronic unit that executes program statements, and its associated equipment. This system requires one or more programs to make the computer do anything useful. The computer and its associated equipment are called *hardware*, while the programs are called *software*.

Hardware Definitions

Here are definitions of some of the hardware objects you will use, shown in Fig. 2.1. The diagram does not include all possible peripheral units — computer owners are continually looking for and testing new computer accessories.

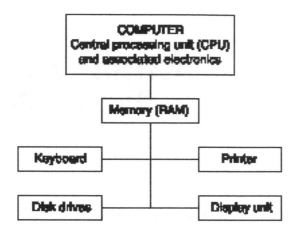

Figure 2.1 *Diagram of a computer system.*

Before learning the definitions of computer hardware items, you must learn the meaning of the terms "bit" and "byte."

Bit. A binary digit usually denoted by 1 or 0. It also means the smallest unit of memory which can store only one of two values: 1 or 0, "on" or "off," "true" or "false."

Byte. A byte is 8 bits. It is a common unit for specifying memory size. The term *kilobyte* (KB) equals 1024 bytes; the term *megabyte* (MB) equals one thousand bytes, the term gigabyte (GB) equals one thousand megabytes.

Computer. This term refers properly to the central processing unit (CPU) — a small but complex silicon chip which performs actions based on program instructions — and its associated electronics. The term is often used, however, to refer to a complete computer system.

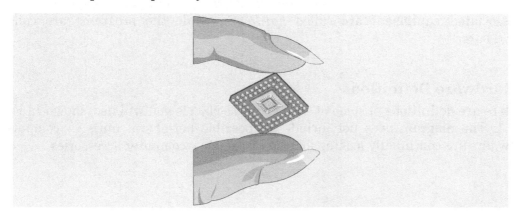

Figure 2.2 *A very small silicon chip contains your computer's CPU.*

Disk drive. This is a device, similar in operation to a compact disk (CD) player, that stores information on magnetic disks. The information is stored in a relatively permanent form and may be quickly retrieved. Information stored on a disk is not lost when you turn off your computer system. If a disk is physically damaged, however, its stored information may be destroyed.

There are two general categories of disk drives, one for fixed or *hard disks* and one for *floppy disks* (also called *diskettes*). Hard disks are usually not removable from the drive (there is at least one well-known exception) and have large storage capacities. A typical hard disk may store a gigabyte or more of data. Floppy disks are removable, are available in different sizes and capacities, and generally store about a megabyte of data.

Memory is much faster than a disk — about 10,000 times faster — which means that it takes longer to write information on a disk than into memory. It also takes more time to read information from a disk. A hard-disk drive is much faster than a floppy-disk drive.

Figure 2.3 *Reasonably priced hard disks can now store over one billion characters.*

Display unit. The televisionlike screen where characters are displayed. These characters may be sent to the screen from the keyboard or from the computer. This unit is often called a *monitor*.

Modern monitors usually display images in color, the most common version displaying 256 different colors. Older monitors and screens on small laptop computers may be monochromatic, displaying only black and white.

A special character on the screen called a *cursor*, often a bright and blinking underline, shows where the next character will appear.

Keyboard. The typewriterlike device with keys that you press to enter characters into the computer. When you press most keys, a character also appears on the display unit screen.

Memory. Memory is an array of electronic devices or *memory chips* where the computer stores information. **When you turn off your computer, it loses all information stored in memory.** Memory is sometimes called RAM, short for "random access memory."

Memory location. This is the address of a place in memory where the computer stores a particular item of information.

Mouse. A small device, about the size of your hand, that can be rolled across the desk top and moves an arrow cursor or large rectangular cursor on the screen. This cursor is called the *mouse cursor*. A mouse has one to three buttons on its top that can be pressed to perform different functions — you will use the left button most of the time if there is more than one button. This device is a useful supplement to the keyboard.

Printer. This is a device connected to your computer, directly or through a computer network, that prints characters on paper as they are received from the computer. *Ink jet* printers create characters from small printed dots, produced by tiny nozzles that squirt ink on the paper. They are inexpensive, produce good-quality characters, and print about one page a minute. *Laser* printers produce high-quality characters using a technology similar to that used in office copiers. They are more expensive and print 4 to 12 pages per minute.

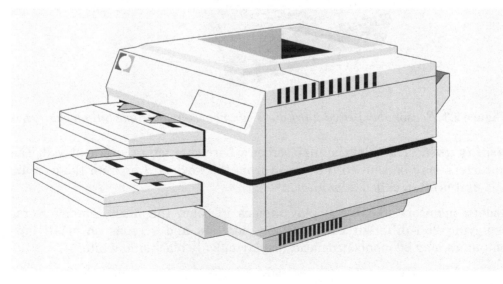

Figure 2.4 *A laser printer.*

Software Definitions

Software is an equally important part of any computer system. Here are definitions for several computer software terms.

File. A file is a collection of characters or other information, usually stored on a computer disk. Each file is identified by name and a directory of all files is maintained automatically on the disk. The concept of storing a BASIC computer program in a file on disk has already been mentioned. Any other collection of text characters, such as a term paper or even a letter to a friend, may be stored in a file. Any file that is a collection of characters is called a *text file* and can be displayed on the screen.

On the other hand, a file may contain noncharacter information, and it is then called a *binary file*. This kind of file cannot be displayed on the screen. The True BASIC system itself is a binary file.

Operating system. This is a special program (see the following definition) that controls the operation of the computer. A major task of the operating system is to maintain the directory of all files on disk and supervise the reading and writing of disk files. The most common operating system for PCs is DOS or Windows. The Mac uses a proprietary operating system called MacOS.

Note that the True BASIC language system is just one of several software systems that can operate under the control of the operating system. Figure 2.5 shows the relationship between an operating system and two application systems.

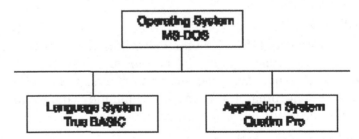

Figure 2.5 *Operating and application systems in a directory.*

Program. A program is a sequence of instructions to the computer, telling it how to carry out a specific task. For example, the task might be to sort a list of names and print out the sorted list on a printer. The individual instructions are called *program statements* (see the following definition). In this example, a program statement might be used to print a single name. The program itself may be in memory and operating as the *current program,* or stored in a file on a computer disk.

Statement. Program statements are instructions in a computer program that tell the computer to carry out a certain action. For example, the statement PRINT "ABC" instructs the computer to print or display the letters ABC on the screen. The computer does not display these letters until the program containing the statement is executed or run (see next definition).

True BASIC is not case-sensitive, you may write statements and commands in either lowercase or uppercase letters.

Command. Direct instructions given by the user to the computer are called commands. Whereas a statement is an instruction that is part of a computer program, a command is an instruction that is given directly to the computer and usually done immediately. More accurately, the instruction is given to a software program such as the operating system or the True BASIC system. For example, the command Run tells the computer to execute the program statements in memory. Written commands are executed when the Return key is pressed.

2.3   WRITING PROGRAMS

While seated at a personal computer, a user can type in program statements and then execute or run the resulting program. The mode of operation for a PC can be quite different from that for a Mac. I discuss these two modes in the following paragraphs.

Writing on PCs

When you enter the True BASIC system, you will notice that the screen divides into two parts. The smaller part at the bottom of the screen is the history or *command window.* It is here that you enter commands and see the results when a program is run. The prompt Ok. in the command window means that the system is waiting for you to enter a command.

The top part of the screen is the source window or program window or *editing window.* I tend to use the latter term. Pressing the F1 function key on the keyboard moves the cursor — a flashing underline or box character — from the command window to the editing window. Pressing the F2 function key moves the cursor back to the command window. All function keys are grouped together, usually across the top of the keyboard.

Figure 2.6 *The F1 and F2 keys.*

You can write or edit program statements only when the cursor is in the editing window. A nonflashing, dark box on the left margin is called a *line tag* and shows where a statement has been or can be written. A line tag appears at the beginning of each statement line.

To run a program after you have finished writing the statements, press the F2 function key. You will return to the command window and see the Ok. prompt again. Type the True BASIC command Run and your program will execute, often displaying output on the screen. You can enter commands only when the cursor is in the command window and the prompt Ok. is displayed on a line by itself.

To write a new program, you must first erase the existing or *current program*. Return to the command window (if you are not already there) by pressing the F2 key and enter the New command to erase screen and memory. The old program disappears from the editing window and at the same time it is erased from memory. After entering the New command, the cursor moves automatically to the editing window and you can begin writing a new program.

If you are using version 3 or later of True BASIC, you can use a mouse and pull-down menus to replace or supplement the preceding commands. I discuss this technique in Section 2.8.

Writing on Macs

When you enter the True BASIC system, the entire screen consists of a single window — the *editing window* — with the usual Mac menu bar at the top of the screen. You simply start writing program statements.

To run a program after you have finished writing the statements, use the mouse to execute the Run command. As described earlier, use the mouse to pull down the Run menu and release the mouse button when the cursor is on the Run command. A faster way to execute this command is to hold down the Command key (also called the Apple key) and press the letter R key. Your program runs or executes, displaying output on a separate window called the *output window*.

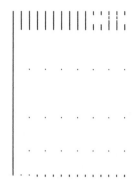

Figure 2.7 *Pull-down Run menu on a Mac.*

After you have finished examining the output, you must press the mouse button or any key to return to the editing window.

Unless you specify otherwise, your output window is a full-screen window. It is possible to select a smaller output window, using the Output command in the Windows pull-down menu. However, if the output window overlaps the editing window, you will see the output only momentarily and then the editing window returns. When using a small output window, it is better to locate it so it does not overlap the editing window and then it maintains its display until a key is pressed.

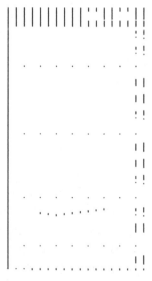

Figure 2.8 *Pull-down Windows menu on a Mac.*

To write a new program, you must first erase the existing or *current program* — use the mouse to select the command New from the File pull-down menu. I assume at this point that you do not want to keep the current program but if you do, I will show you in a later section how to save True BASIC programs on disk.

Figure 2.9 *Pull-down File menu on a Mac.*

If the current program has not been saved, you will see a separate window, called a *dialog box*, containing the message "Do you want to save this file?" and three *buttons*. The button marked Yes lets you save the old program. The button marked No deletes the old program. The button marked Cancel cancels the last command (the New command). Place the mouse cursor on the No button and press the mouse button. The old program disappears from the editing window and is erased from memory. An empty editing window appears on your screen.

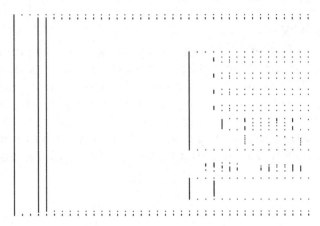

Figure 2.10 *Dialog box for saving a file on a Mac.*

2.4   A SIMPLE PROGRAM

Here is your first True BASIC program, containing three statements. I show it now so you can see what a program looks like and discuss it later in this section:

```
! Example Program 2-1

PRINT "Hello!"
END
```

As you might expect, this program displays the message

```
Hello!
```

on the screen.

A BASIC program consists of one or more program statements. You may write statements in either uppercase or lowercase letters. You may insert a blank line any place in a True BASIC program to make the program easier to read.

No Line Numbers

Many versions of BASIC require that you write a numeric label, called a *line number*, at the beginning of each statement. **Line numbers are not required in True BASIC** and will not be used in this book. Here is a line with a line number:

```
110 PRINT "Hello!"
```

The Return Key

You type in each line of your program by pressing the appropriate keys on the keyboard. The cursor shows where the next character will be displayed. You must end each line by pressing the Return key on your keyboard. On the IBM PC keyboard, a bent-arrow symbol (⏎) often denotes the Return key. On some other PC keyboards, the Return key is labeled the Enter key. Note that the Mac keyboard has both a Return key and an Enter key. **The key marked Return, not the key marked Enter, must be pressed to end a program line**.

Figure 2.11 *Return key on an IBM keyboard.*

When writing a program, pressing the Return key tells the computer that you have finished typing a statement. Unlike a word processor, you must press the Return key after each program statement or at the end of each line. The computer then accepts that statement and the cursor moves to the beginning of the next line, indicating that the computer is ready for you to type in another statement.

When you press the Return key, you generate a nonprinting character called a *carriage return* and the cursor moves to the left edge of the screen. When the computer receives a carriage return, it generates another nonprinting character called a *line feed* and the cursor moves to the next line. This pair of characters, the carriage return and line feed, marks the end of each program statement.

All this explanation can be condensed into one simple instruction: Press the Return key when you have finished typing a BASIC statement or command.

The ! or REM Statement

Here is the first example program again:

```
! Example Program 2-1

PRINT "Hello!"
END
```

The first line contains a remark statement or *comment*. A comment appears in a program for the convenience of the programmer and anyone else who reads the program. The exclamation point (!) and any words that follow it are ignored by the computer. The word REM (for remark) can be used instead of an exclamation point.

The PRINT and END Statements

The PRINT statement displays the characters within quotation marks on the screen. In computer terminology, this set of characters is called a *string constant* and must be enclosed in quotation marks. The END statement is used to indicate the end of the program. **It is required in all True BASIC programs.**

Let's now look at a similar but slightly different program:

```
REM Example Program 2-2

PRINT 22.5  ! print a number
END
```

This program displays the number

```
22.5
```

on the screen. Note that the number is not enclosed in quotation marks. The value now displayed (22.5) is a *numeric constant*, not a string constant, and is never enclosed in quotation marks.

True BASIC statements use spaces to separate words and numbers, just as spaces are used in ordinary sentences. Extra spaces between words and numbers usually cause no harm. You can also leave one or more blank lines between program statements. Notice that the key words of the example program statements are shown in uppercase, a practice I will follow throughout the book.

The first comment statement is rewritten using the word REM in place of the exclamation point, and another comment beginning with an exclamation point comes after the PRINT statement. Remarks may be included in programs as separate lines or as comments at the end of program statement lines. In the latter case, you must use an exclamation point rather than the word REM.

2.5   ANOTHER PROGRAM

Here is another, slightly longer program. Before writing a new program, you should erase the old program from the screen and from memory. If you don't, you will get a mixture of old and new program statements. Its easy to do — just press F2 to go to the command window and enter the command New after the Ok. prompt.

The INPUT Statement with a Prompt

This new program asks the user to type in his or her name and displays it on the screen.

```
! Example Program 2-3
! Program to display a name.

INPUT prompt "Type in your name...": Name$
PRINT Name$
END
```

The fourth line (first executable program line) introduces a new statement, an INPUT statement with an optional prompt. This statement does two things. First, it displays on the screen the words within quotation marks — the prompt — and then it waits for the user to type a reply of one or more characters. After typing the characters, the user must press the Return key. All characters typed before the Return key is pressed are associated with the word Name$, which is called a *variable*.

I will discuss variables at some length in the next chapter. For the time being, you can think of Name$ as the name of a mailbox (it is really a memory location) where a string or collection of characters can be stored. This string of characters is called the *value* of the variable Name$. **The characters typed in from the keyboard are stored in the variable Name$.** The PRINT statement in the fifth line then displays this stored value on the screen.

Program 2-3 produces the following screen dialog:

```
Type in your name...Frances Compton
Frances Compton
```

Note that characters entered by the user are identified by italic type-face, another practice I shall follow throughout the book. You, of course, don't type italic characters, that's just a trick I use in the book so you can tell which characters are typed by the user and which are created and displayed by the program.

```
Francis Compton
```
— typed by the user

```
Francis Compton
```
— created by the program

The Plain INPUT Statement

An INPUT statement can also be written without a prompt. In this case, the statement displays a single question mark on the screen to indicate that input is expected. Most programs are easier to use and understand if INPUT statements include prompts.

If an INPUT statement does not include a prompt, you may want to use a separate PRINT statement to prompt the user. Here is an example:

```
! Example Program 2-4
! Input statement without a prompt.

PRINT "Type in your name after the question mark:"
INPUT EmployeeName$
PRINT EmployeeName$
END
```

The following screen display is produced with user-entered characters again identified by italic type-face:

```
Type in your name after the question mark:
? Tom Jackson
Tom Jackson
```

Line Continuation (Version 3)

The technique in Example Program 2-4 is often used if inclusion of the prompt in the INPUT statement would make that statement too long to be displayed on the screen. It is perfectly correct to have statements longer than the screen width, but these statements are difficult to read because the screen must be scrolled horizontally. True BASIC, version 3, avoids the need for scrolling by allowing you to extend a long program statement over more than one screen line. The ampersand character (&) is used as a marker. Here is a program fragment that demonstrates line continuation:

```
INPUT prompt "Type in your name after this prompt": &
& EmployeeName$
```

Note that an ampersand must appear as the last character on the first line and as the first character on the continuation line. The break between lines cannot occur in the middle of a word or in the middle of a constant. For example, the break in the preceding statement cannot occur within the prompt string. One or more continuation lines are allowed — see the *True BASIC Reference Manual* for details.

How to Print a Blank Line

You might want Example Program 2-3 to display a blank line before it prints the user-entered name. Insert the statement PRINT on a line by itself, just above the statement PRINT Name$. See the discussion on editing for your particular computer (in a subsequent section) to find out how to insert a new line in the current program. The program, now named Example Program 2-5, will then read as follows:

```
! Example Program 2-5
! Program to display a blank line and a name.

INPUT prompt "Type in your name...": Name$
PRINT
PRINT Name$
END
```

This modified program produces the following output:

```
Type in your name...John Peters

John Peters
```

The PRINT statement, used by itself, produces a blank line in the output displayed by the program. If you want to produce two blank lines, you must include two PRINT statements, each statement on a separate line.

2.6 EDITING PROGRAMS ON THE PC

To edit a program means to change it, most often by modifying or deleting existing statements or by inserting new statements. True BASIC allows you to edit the current program in the editing window.

The original method of editing, discussed in this section, uses the arrow keys for editing and expects you to enter commands from the command line. A newer method, discussed in Section 2.10, uses a mouse for editing and for selecting commands from pull-down menus. I recommend that you at least try using a mouse if one is available, especially for editing.

Cursor Movement Keys

A number of special keys on the PC keyboard, located on the right side in the numeric keypad, are used for editing. Fig. 2.3 lists several keys used for moving the cursor. If these keys produce numbers instead of the actions listed here, press the Num Lock key to deactivate the numeric keypad and allow the cursor movement functions to work.

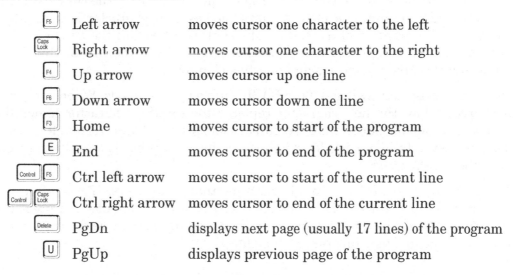

F5	Left arrow	moves cursor one character to the left
Caps Lock	Right arrow	moves cursor one character to the right
F4	Up arrow	moves cursor up one line
F6	Down arrow	moves cursor down one line
F3	Home	moves cursor to start of the program
E	End	moves cursor to end of the program
Control F5	Ctrl left arrow	moves cursor to start of the current line
Control Caps Lock	Ctrl right arrow	moves cursor to end of the current line
Delete	PgDn	displays next page (usually 17 lines) of the program
U	PgUp	displays previous page of the program

Figure 2.12 *Cursor movement keys on the PC keyboard.*

An enhanced keyboard that is supplied with some PCs has an additional set of cursor movement keys. This set is located between the main keyboard and the numeric keypad, and can be used if you find it more convenient.

The designation "Left arrow" means to press the key marked with a left arrow.

It is confusing because there are several such keys close together on the keyboard. I mean the keypad key that also has a digit 4 on the keycap. The designation "Ctrl left arrow" means to hold down the Control key (usually marked Ctrl or Control) and simultaneously press the left arrow key.

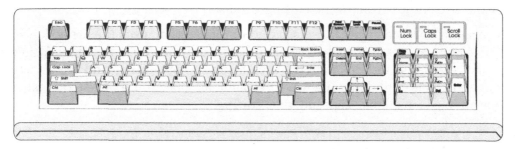

Figure 2.13 *A typical IBM PC keyboard.*

The Insert Key

The Ins or Insert key switches the mode of typing between the insert mode and the overwrite mode. When you start True BASIC, if you move the cursor to some point in your program and press a character key, that character is inserted in the text at the position of the cursor. The character beneath the cursor and all characters to the right move one position to the right. You are in the insert mode and the cursor symbol is an underline character.

Pressing the Ins key switches True BASIC into overwrite mode. When you press a character key, the new character replaces the existing character under the cursor. You should notice that the cursor changes to a large rectangle or box. The Ins key acts like a toggle switch; each time you press it you change from one mode to the other.

You may want to insert a new line rather than characters. If you place the cursor on a line tag when in either the insert or overwrite mode and press the Return key, a new blank line appears in your program just above the cursor. You can then type in a new program statement.

The Delete Key

The Del or Delete key deletes the character under the cursor. If you want to delete several characters, hold the key down and it repeats automatically. To delete a statement line, place the cursor on the line tag and press the Del key. The entire line disappears.

Function Keys

I have already discussed two of the function keys, the F1 key and the F2 key, that move the cursor between the command window and the editing window. Another important function key is the F10 key, the help key. You can press this key at any time to get help on a specific topic. When the prompt "Help:" is displayed, you should enter the name of the command on which you want help. If you don't know, enter the word "topics" and the computer displays a list of topics for which help is available, as shown in Fig. 2-14. Note that help is provided only for commands, not for statements.

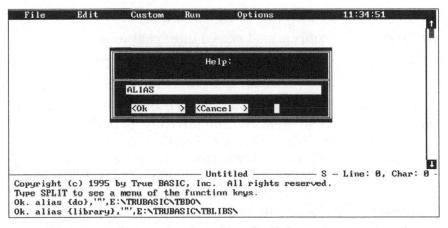

Figure 2.14 *Screen produced by the Help topics command.*

The other function keys are discussed in Chapter 6 and are listed in Appendix B. When you have time, start to learn about the function keys and use them as you write programs. You will find that they simplify many editing tasks.

2.7   COMMANDS ON THE PC

True BASIC commands are direct instructions to the computer telling it to do something immediately. On a PC, they are entered from the command window in response to the Ok. prompt. Commands can be entered using either uppercase or lowercase characters or a combination of both.

You will need to use many of the commands in this section when you write your first computer programs. As you type the commands, you will gradually find yourself memorizing them. A complete list of all True BASIC commands and command keys appears in Appendix B.

DOS File Names and Path Names

The DOS operating system limits file names to an eight-character name, plus an optional suffix consisting of a period followed by three characters. You will be safe if you use only letter or digit characters in the file name. **Remember that a blank space is considered a character and it cannot be used in a DOS file name.**

Examples of legal file names are as follows:

```
CHAP12.TRU
QUIZ5.DOC
GRAPHLIB.TRU
```

The following names are examples of illegal file names:

QUIZ5.TEXT   (suffix cannot exceed three characters)

GRAPHLIBR   (name cannot exceed eight characters)

HW ONE.TRU   (blank characters not allowed)

Every disk drive has a DOS name consisting of a single letter. Every disk, either floppy or hard, contains at least one file directory. A backslash character (\) identifies this directory, called the *root directory*. A hierarchy of additional directories can be created, all under the root directory, so that different kinds of files can be stored in different directories. Figure 2.14 shows the directory structure of a disk with multiple directories. Most floppy disks have only a root directory, while hard disks usually have multiple directories.

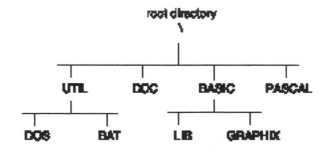

Figure 2.14 *Structure of file directories on a disk.*

The complete identifier for a file, called its *path name*, consists of the disk drive letter followed by a colon (:), the hierarchy of directory names (separated by backslash characters), and the file name (including its optional suffix). The structure of this path name can sometimes be confusing because the backslash character is used both as the name of the root directory and as a separator between other directory names. There can be no blank spaces anywhere in a

DOS path name. Figure 2.15 is a list of some example path names.

`A:\MYFILE.TRU`	Program MYFILE.TRU in the root directory of the disk in drive A
`A:MYFILE.TRU`	Same as above; the backslash is not required but recommended
`C:\WEEK05\TEST.TRU`	Program TEST.TRU in directory WEEK05 of disk drive C
`C:\BIN\DOS\TYP.COM`	Program TYP.COM in directory DOS under directory BIN of disk drive C
`B:\TBOOK\TOC.DAT`	Data file TOC.DAT in directory TBOOK of the disk in drive B

Figure 2.15 *List of example path names.*

Simple Commands

Only a few of the many True BASIC commands are described in the following paragraphs:

Help. This command displays information on the screen. You are given general information and told how to get more specific information on individual topics.

Bye. You exit the True BASIC system with the command Bye, returning to the DOS operating system. If a current program exists and has not been saved, you are asked if you wish to do so before exiting. An answer of "No" erases the program and exits True BASIC. An answer of "Cancel" just cancels the BYE command. An answer of "Yes" saves the program on disk before exiting. If you have not already named the current program, you are asked to name it.

New. This command clears the editing window and erases the current program from the user workspace. It should always be used before writing a new program. The user workspace is a section of memory where the current program resides. Again, you have an opportunity to save the current program before clearing the window and erasing the program.

Files. The names of all True BASIC program files in the current directory on the disk in your current disk drive are listed. These files always have the suffix TRU. The *current disk drive* is the one from which you started True BASIC. On a computer with a hard-disk drive, it is usually drive C. On a computer with only floppy-disk drives, it is usually drive A.

Save. A program that you have just written may be saved on disk by using this command followed by the path name. **If you specify no suffix for the file name, the usual program suffix of TRU is added automatically.**

Every program is stored on disk in a file that has a name identifying that particular program. For example, a program you wrote earlier might be stored in a file named MYFILE.TRU in the directory named DOCS on the disk in drive B, using the command SAVE B:\DOCS\MYFILE.

You can use the Save command without a file name to save the current file if it has already been named — that is, if it has been saved previously. You are asked if you want to replace the existing file on disk. If you want to keep the existing file as a backup file, answer "no" and then enter the Save command again with a different file name.

Old. This command, followed by a path name, retrieves the named file (often a program file) from disk and loads it into the user workspace. The suffix TRU is assumed if not specified. For example, the command OLD B:\HWORK\HW07 loads the file HW07.TRU from directory HWORK on the disk in drive B. The path name specified is called the *current path name*.

If you intended to load a file named HW07 that has no suffix, use the command OLD B:\HWORK\HW07. (note the period) where the trailing period indicates that the file name has no suffix.

The current program is erased automatically when you load a program into the user workspace from disk. If you want to keep the current program, you must be sure to save it on disk before loading another program.

Run. This command instructs the computer to execute the current program. A program must be in memory in the user workspace — displayed in the editing window — before it can be executed.

The Run command causes two actions to take place. First, the program is translated from True BASIC into a sequence of instructions understood by the computer, a process called *compilation*. After compilation, the compiled program is executed by the computer. With large programs, there may be a noticeable delay while the program is being compiled.

The Interrupt Key

You may want to stop the execution of a program before it reaches its normal end. DOS provides an Interrupt key. Hold down the Ctrl key and simultaneously press the Break key in the upper right-hand corner of the keyboard. Program execution stops and the normal Ok. prompt is displayed.

Other Commands

There are other True BASIC commands that are used less frequently and four of them are introduced in this section.

Unsave. This command, followed by a path name, deletes that file from disk. Use this command with caution because **once a file has been deleted, it cannot be recovered**.

List. The command List prints your current program on a printer connected directly to your computer. If no such printer exists, however, the List command may lock up your computer and require you to reset it, causing the loss of any program code stored only in memory. This is an example of how you can lose program code when programs are not saved frequently on disk. **Always save a program on disk before trying to list it on a printer.**

Include. It is sometimes convenient to merge or insert a disk file into your current program. The command Include, followed by a file or path name, inserts the named file into your program immediately after the program statement designated by the cursor.

As an example, you might keep a standard program heading in a disk file called HEADING.TRU, consisting of the following remark lines:

```
! PROGRAM:  First Program
! AUTHOR:   John Williams
! DATE:     March 15, 1992
! DESCRIP:  Displays a name on the screen
!
```

Assume that this file is stored in directory TEMPLATES of drive C.. You can include the heading file in your current program by moving the cursor to the editing window and creating an empty line at the beginning of the program (see Section 2.5). Place the cursor on the line tag of this new line, press the F2 key to move to the command window, and enter the command

```
Include C:\TEMPLATES\HEADING
```

The file HEADING.TRU will be inserted into your program immediately below the new empty line. If you wish, you can then delete the empty line.

Split. Another command allows the boundary between the editing window and the command window to be moved. The command syntax is Split N where N is the number of lines in the editing window. The value N cannot be less than 6 or greater than 24. Figure 2.16 shows some examples of the use of this command.

Split 6	Command window fills most of screen
Split 24	Leaves a command window of one line
Split 17	Default value, 8-line command window and 17-line editing window

Figure 2.16 *Use of the Split command.*

2.8   MENU BAR AND MOUSE SUPPORT ON THE PC

True BASIC, version 3, introduced mouse support on PCs. The operation of these computers then becomes similar in many ways to that of Macs — discussed in subsequent sections. Two cursors are visible on the screen: the *mouse cursor* is a large, non-flashing rectangle while the *text cursor* remains a flashing underline. There is a menu bar across the top of the screen and a vertical scroll bar along the right edge of the editing window.

Using the Mouse

A mouse designed for PCs has two or three buttons. **True BASIC recognizes only the left button.** To change the position of the text cursor, move the mouse cursor to the desired position and click the mouse button. The term *click* or *clicking* is often used to denote this action of pressing and quickly releasing the mouse button. The text cursor now appears at the new position.

You can move between the editing and command windows by clicking the mouse when the mouse cursor is in the desired window. In the editing window, you can change the position of the text cursor by clicking the mouse when the mouse cursor is at the desired position in the program.

As you begin to write longer programs, you may find that the program becomes too long for the editing window. Look at Fig. 2.17 and the vertical *scroll bar* on the right edge of the screen. The scroll bar consists of a dark background, a highlighted rectangle called a *slider* in the middle of that background, and an arrow at each end.

Figure 2.17 *Screen displayed by True BASIC, version 3, with mouse.*

Clicking on the top arrow moves the window up one line, displaying the preceding line. Clicking on the dark area between the arrow and the slider moves the window up one page, a distance that is a little less than the editing window height. Clicking on the bottom arrow moves the window down one line, while clicking on the dark area below the slider moves the window down one page.

Instead of clicking on the arrows or the dark area, you can move the window by *dragging* the slider up or down with the mouse cursor. Dragging means moving the mouse to place the mouse cursor on top of the slider (the cursor may change appearance or color), pressing the mouse button and holding it down, moving the cursor and slider to the desired position on the scroll bar, and then releasing the mouse button. The editing window should move in the same direction as the slider.

The Menu Bar

The menu bar lists the titles of five command menus: File, Edit, Run, Custom, and Options, as shown in Fig. 2.17. There is a standard procedure to execute a command from these menus. Move the mouse to place the mouse cursor on the menu title and press the mouse button to pull down the menu. While holding down the button, move the cursor to the desired command, which is then highlighted, and release the mouse button to execute that command.

These five command menus can also be pulled down by pressing a combination of the Alt key and a digit key. Alt-1 pulls down the File menu, Alt-2 the Edit menu, Alt-3 the Run menu, and so forth. The Alt-0 key closes any command menu that is currently open.

Note that a single letter appears after many of the command names. The shortcut to execute a command is to press simultaneously the Alt key and the letter key. For example, the key combination Alt-R has the same effect as selecting the Run command from the Run menu.

Appendix B has a complete list of all PC pull-down menus and commands and equivalent shortcut keys.

The File Menu

This menu contains commands related to file handling. You should learn these commands and are referred to the *PC User's Guide* from True BASIC for detailed information on any commands not covered here.

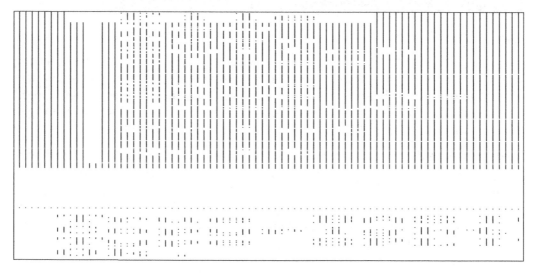

Figure 2.18 *Pull-down File menu on a PC.*

New.   The New command creates a new and empty editing window, and at the same time moves the current program, if any, to a temporary background window. You are asked to name the current program if it does not already have a name. Several programs can be kept open at the same time in this manner, using the editing window and one or more temporary background windows.

You probably will want to keep only one window open when you start programming. To disable this multiple-window capability, enter the command Switch from the command line. If you are using a STARTUP.TRU file, place the command Switch in that file.

Once switching is disabled, executing the New command erases any current program as it creates a new and empty editing window. **Be careful not to erase any text that you want to save.** In a new editing window, the line tag for the first program line is displayed with the text cursor right next to it. A new program can now be typed in. This new program is not assigned a name until it is saved with the Save As command.

Open. This command allows a user to select a program on disk and load it into memory as the current program. A *selection dialog box* appears, asking you to identify the desired program file. If you see the program file name that you want, click on that name to highlight it and then click on the <Ok> button to open the file.

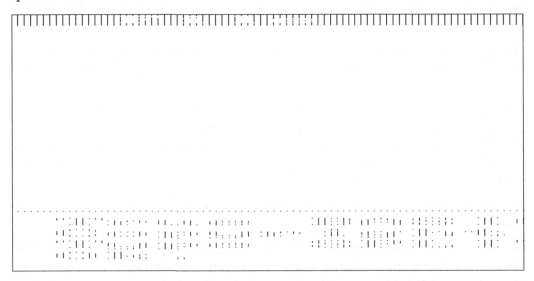

Figure 2.19 *Dialog box for opening a file.*

If the desired program file is on another disk drive, click on the "Change drives" option, enter the proper drive letter, and then click on the <Ok> button. In a similar manner, you can select the parent directory of the current directory by clicking on the ".." option.

For example, assume your current directory is named HOMEWORK and is under the root directory on drive B. You want to open the program file QUIZ1.TRU in directory EXAMS (also under the root directory) on the same drive.

Select the ".." option and you should see a list of all files and subdirectories in the parent directory, which is also the root directory in this case. Select the subdirectory named EXAMS (by clicking on its name) and a list of the files in that subdirectory appears. Select the desired program named QUIZ1.TRU. If at any time you wish to back out of the selection dialog box, click on the <Cancel> button one or more times.

The process of selecting a file from a disk directory is a little confusing when described in words but not so difficult in practice. If you have trouble, ask an experienced user for help. You may find the Alt-O shortcut key especially useful when opening a program file.

Close. This command closes the current program file. Click on the "Current file" option to close the current file and as before, click on the <Ok> button to execute this option. If the program has not already been saved, you are asked if you wish to do so and to specify its name.

Save As. Use the Save As command when saving a new program for the first time, or when you want to save an old program under a different name.

Again a selection dialog box is displayed and you can specify the drive letter and directory where the program should be saved. After these parameters are specified, you are asked to specify the program file name.

Remember that True BASIC automatically adds the extension TRU to any file name whose extension is not specified. **If you wish to specify a file name without an extension, put a trailing period at the end of the file name.** For example, write a file name as MYFILE. — note the trailing period — rather than as MYFILE to save it without an extension.

The Save As command gives you an opportunity not only to save your current program but also to change its name.

Save. The Save command saves the current program under its current name. You cannot use this command to save a new program that has not been named; you must use the Save As command the first time to specify a name.

After a program has been named, develop the habit of using the shortcut Alt-S key frequently while writing or editing program code. If anything happens to your computer, everything you have typed up to the last save is stored on disk and is relatively safe.

Print. You can produce a paper copy of your program with the Print command. This command is equivalent to the List command entered from the command line. The current program is printed on an attached printer which must be turned on and connected to your computer. You may need special instructions if you are using a networked printer.

Quit. I have already discussed this command. If you have made changes in the current program, you are given an opportunity to save it before leaving the True BASIC system.

The Edit Menu

Editing with a mouse is very simple. Most editing depends on the use of a clipboard to hold text temporarily, and the application of the three editing commands, Cut, Copy, and Paste, to selected text.

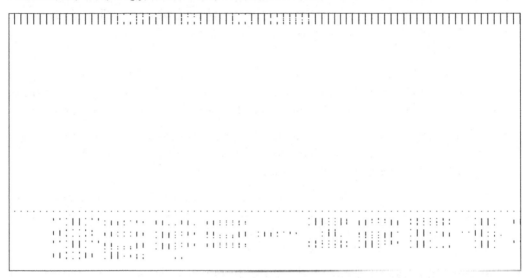

Figure 2.19 *Pull-down Edit menu on a PC.*

Use the mouse to select text. Move the mouse to place the mouse cursor at the beginning of any text to be selected, hold down the left mouse button, drag the cursor to the end of the text to be selected, and release the mouse button. The selected text or line tags are highlighted.

Note that there is a difference between selecting one or more program lines and selecting individual characters, words, or sections in a single line. If you place the mouse cursor on a program line and drag down to the next line, the first line is selected. A selected line is denoted by a highlighted line tag. If you drag down from the first line to the fifth line, the first four lines are selected. If you hold down the Shift key and click on a program line, everything from that line to the end of the program is selected. This means that you can select an entire program by clicking on the first line with the Shift key depressed.

If you drag the mouse cursor horizontally on a single program line, part of the line is selected and highlighted. Don't worry if you select the wrong block of text: Move the mouse cursor off the text area, click the mouse button again, and the highlighting will disappear. You can then try again to select the correct block of text. You can also select a single word by placing the mouse cursor on that word and then *double-clicking* the mouse. The term double-clicking means to press the mouse button twice in rapid succession.

Once text has been selected, it can be edited using the following Cut, Copy, and Paste commands.

Cut. The Cut command in the Edit menu deletes a selected text block. The deleted text is saved in a special section of memory called the *clipboard*, **erasing any text that currently resides in the clipboard**. The Alt-X key — pressing the Alt and X keys simultaneously — provides a shortcut for executing the Cut command.

A selected text block can also be deleted by pressing the Del or delete key. In this case, the last text deleted can be recovered by pressing the F7 key. **If more than one block of text is deleted, only the last deletion can be restored.**

Copy. The Copy command (also in the Edit menu) saves a copy of the selected text block in the clipboard but does not delete the block. The Alt-C key provides a shortcut for executing the Copy command.

Paste. Text saved in the clipboard can be inserted into any part of the program by using the Paste command. Click the mouse at the desired point of insertion and then execute the Paste command from the Edit menu. The Alt-V key provides a shortcut for this command.

Remember that the clipboard can hold only one text selection at any time. If another text selection is placed in the clipboard, even a single character, the current contents of the clipboard are erased and cannot be recovered.

The Run Menu

The one command in the Run menu that is important to know at this time is the **Run** command. This command is identical to the same command executed from the command line. As you know, the Run command compiles and executes the current program.

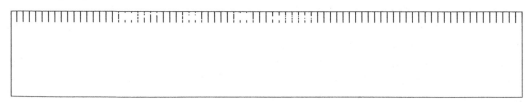

Figure 2.20 *Pull-down Run menu on a PC.*

2.9   EDITING PROGRAMS ON THE MAC

To edit a program means to change it, most often by modifying or deleting existing statements or by inserting new statements. True BASIC allows you to edit the current program in the editing window.

Moving the Cursor

The cursor can be moved with either the mouse or the arrow keys but the mouse is usually more convenient on a Mac, a mouse-oriented computer. **When you are using a mouse, there are two different types of cursors displayed in the editing mode.** The *mouse cursor* appears as an I-beam symbol when it is within the editing window. It appears as an arrow or pointer when it is outside that window on the menu bar or a scroll bar. The *text cursor*, which shows where the next typed character will appear, is a blinking vertical line.

To change the position of the text cursor, move the mouse cursor to the desired position and click the mouse button. As you probably know, the term *click* or *clicking* means pressing and quickly releasing the mouse button. The text cursor now appears at the new position.

As you begin to write longer programs, you will notice that the program becomes too long to fit inside the editing window. You will also see a vertical *scroll bar* with a dark or dotted background on the right edge of the editing window. The scroll bar contains a light rectangle called a *slider* in the middle of the bar and an arrow head at each end.

Clicking on the top arrow head moves the window up one line, displaying a previously-written program line. Clicking on the dark area between the arrow head and the slider moves the window up one page, a distance that is a little less than the window height. Clicking on the bottom arrow head moves the window down one line, while clicking on the dark area below the slider moves the window down one page.

Instead of clicking on the arrow heads or the dark area, you can move the window by dragging the slider up or down with the mouse cursor. Place the mouse cursor (the cursor is now an arrow) on the slider, press the mouse button and hold it down, move the slider to the desired position along the scroll bar, and then release the button.

If some program statements are too long to fit within the width of the window, a similar scroll bar appears at the bottom of the screen. This scroll bar is used to move the window horizontally.

Selecting Text

The mouse is used to select text for editing. You can select part of a line, an entire line, several lines, or the whole program. The selected text is *highlighted* with light characters on a dark background.

An easy way to select text is to drag the mouse cursor over part of the program. To select part of a statement, press the mouse button when the mouse cursor is at the beginning of the desired part and drag the cursor to the right to select that part. If you want to select several statements, drag the mouse cursor down over these statements. Practice this technique on an example program. You can always remove selection highlighting by clicking the mouse when the mouse cursor is at any point outside the selected block.

Another way to select a single word in a statement is to *double-click* — two clicks, one right after the other — on the word. The entire statement can be selected by using the mouse to *triple-click* on any character in the statement line.

Sometimes you may want to change the size of a selected text block. Hold down the shift key and click at the beginning of a line inside the block to reduce the block size. Use the same technique on a line outside the block to increase the block size. You can add or delete one or more statements, but you cannot add or delete part of a statement.

There is also a method for selecting the entire program. Select the first statement of the program and use the scroll bar to move the window to the end of the program. Then position the mouse cursor at the end of the last statement and press the mouse button while holding down the shift key. The entire program is selected and highlighted.

Editing Commands

Once text has been selected, it can be edited. Mac editing is based on the use of the Cut, Copy, and Paste commands.

Cut. The Cut command in the Edit menu deletes a selected text block. The deleted text is saved in a special section of memory called the *clipboard*, **erasing any text that currently resides in the clipboard**. The Cmd-X key (pressing the Command and X keys simultaneously) provides a shortcut for the Cut command.

Figure 2.21 *Pull-down Edit menu on a Mac.*

A selected text block can also be deleted by pressing the Delete key (sometimes called and labeled the Backspace key). **In this case, the deleted text is lost and cannot be recovered**; it is not placed in the clipboard.

Copy. The Copy command (also in the Edit menu) saves a copy of the selected text block in the clipboard but does not delete the block. The Cmd-C key provides a shortcut for the Copy command.

Paste. The Paste command inserts text saved in the clipboard into any part of the program. Click the mouse at the desired point of insertion and then execute the Paste command from the Edit menu. The Cmd-V key provides a shortcut for this command.

You will find that these techniques of cutting, copying, and pasting provide a powerful editing environment. Moreover, the same editing method is used by almost every Mac application, so you should quickly become familiar with it.

There are three special True BASIC editing keys that can be used to edit a selected block of text. These character keys are listed and described in Fig. 2.22. Try these keys yourself — they can save you time.

!   This key adds an exclamation point to the beginning of every line in a selected block, turning these lines into comments. If a line already starts with an exclamation point, that exclamation point is removed.

>   This key indents the selected block by adding one space to the beginning of each line.

<   This key un-indents the selected block by deleting one space from the beginning of each line.

Figure 2.22 *Special True BASIC editing keys on the Mac.*

2.10   COMMANDS ON THE MAC

True BASIC commands are direct instructions to the computer telling it to do something immediately. On the Mac, commands are selected, usually by mouse, from the various menus whose titles appear on the menu bar at the top of the screen. To execute a command, carry out the following steps:

- Move the mouse to point the mouse cursor at the desired menu title.

- Press the mouse button to pull down the menu

- While holding down the mouse button, move the cursor to the desired command, which is then highlighted

- Release the mouse button to execute that command.

Appendix B has a complete list of all Mac pull-down menus and commands, and the equivalent shortcut keys.

The File Menu

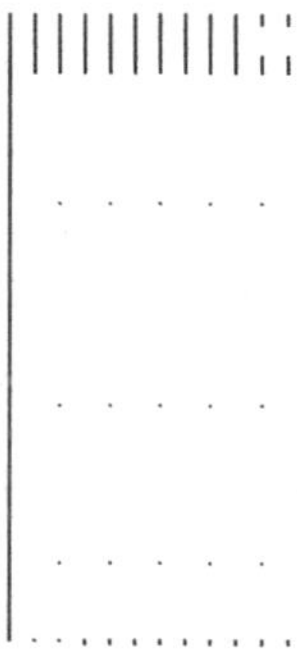

Figure 2.23 *Pull-down File menu on the Mac.*

This menu contains several of the most important commands. Notice that many of these commands have command-key equivalents that are listed along the right edge of the menu. For example, the Cmd-S key saves the current program on disk.

New. This command creates a new and empty editing window, erasing any text that may be present. The new window has the name of "Untitled." Before creating a new window, you have an opportunity to save an existing program that has not been saved previously.

Open. This command copies a program on disk into the editing window, and loads the equivalent program source statements into memory. A dialog box appears, asking you to identify the desired program file in a *folder*, equivalent to a directory in DOS. You locate the desired program file by using the mouse, starting at the icon and name of the disk containing the program. First you double-click on the disk icon to open that disk. Then you double-click on each folder icon or name in the hierarchical path leading to the desired program, finally double-clicking on the program itself. The icon or name of each selected disk, folder, or file is highlighted as it is selected. Instead of double-clicking (which opens the object), you can single-click on each object (this only selects or highlights it) and then click on the Open button.

For example, the program file you want might be named "test 25.tru" and might be located in a folder named "True BASIC" that is in another folder named "Applications" on a disk named "boot disk." Place the mouse cursor on the folder icon appearing at the top of the dialog box, pull down the hierarchical menu, and release the mouse button on the disk icon named "boot disk." All the folders on "boot disk" are displayed and you double-click on the folder named "Applications." Another list of the folders and files within "Applications" is displayed and you double-click on the folder named "True BASIC." Finally, you see the names of files and folders within "True BASIC" and double-click on our desired file, "test 25.tru."

The process of selecting a file from a disk directory is hard to describe in words but easy to do on the computer. If you have problems, get some help from a more experienced user the first time that you try it.

There is a significant difference in the syntax of disk, folder (or directory), and file names on a Mac and on a PC. **A legal name on the Mac may contain one or more blank space characters.** The maximum length of a name is 31 characters.

Save As. Use the Save As command when saving a new program for the first time, or when you want to save an old program under a different name. Again, a dialog box is displayed and you can name your program, using up to 31 characters in the file name.

You must specify where you want the program saved, in which folder on which disk. The procedure is very similar to that used with the Open command. When you have highlighted the desired folder, click on the Save button and the program will be saved. Notice that the program is not erased from the screen.

The Save As command gives you an opportunity not only to save your current program, but also to change its name.

Save. The Save command saves the current program under its current name. You cannot use this command to save a program with the name "Untitled"; you must first use the Save As command to change that name before saving.

Develop the habit of using the shortcut Cmd-S key frequently when writing a named program. If anything happens to stop your computer, everything you have typed up to the last save is stored on disk and is relatively safe.

Print. You can produce a paper copy of your program with the Print command. The current program is printed on an attached printer. You have the opportunity to set several printer parameters depending on the type of printer you are using. You will need special instructions if you are using a networked printer.

Quit. I have already discussed this command in the previous chapter. As with the New command, you have an opportunity to save the current program before leaving the True BASIC system.

File and Path Names

There is a significant difference in the way PCs and Macintoshes handle program file names without a suffix. **On a Mac, if you want to open or save a file with a suffix of TRU, you must explicitly specify the suffix.** If you write a program file name with no suffix, the TRU suffix is not automatically added.

Path names are defined for Mac files that are similar to the path names used with DOS files. On the Mac, a path name consists of the disk name, followed by each folder name in hierarchical order, followed by the file name. Colons are used as separators between the various parts of the path name.

In the preceding discussion of the Open command, I used an example file named "test 25.tru." The complete path name for this file is as follows:

```
boot disk:Applications:True BASIC:test 25.tru.
```

Most of the time you access Mac files by clicking on icons and so don't use the path names. You may need to use path names, however, when accessing information files from True BASIC programs. Remember that blank spaces are allowed in Mac file and path names, but do not add extra spaces just before or after the colon separators.

The Edit Menu

I have already discussed the most important commands in the Edit menu, namely the Cut, Copy, and Paste commands, and shown the menu in Fig. 2.21. Here is another useful command from that menu:

Include. This command allows a disk file to be included within the current program file. Select the Include command and a dialog box opens. Highlight the name of the include file (see the Open command) and then click on the Include button. The include file is inserted at the location of the text cursor.

As an example, you might keep a set of standard program heading statements in a disk file named "heading.tru." It might consist of the following remark lines:

```
! PROGRAM:  First Program
! AUTHOR:   John Williams
! DATE:     March 15, 1992
! DESCRIP:  Displays a name on the screen
!
```

To include the heading file in your current program, go to the editing window and create an empty line at the beginning of the program. Do this by placing the text cursor at the beginning of the first line and pressing the Return key. The text cursor is now at the beginning of the first empty line. Execute the Include command, select the file named "heading.tru," and click on the Include button The desired file is inserted at the beginning of your program.

The Run Menu

There are two important commands in the Run menu, as shown several pages earlier in Fig. 2.7.

Run. This is the command that executes or runs the current program. Results appear in the output window.

Stop. This command halts a running program that has not reached the END statement. It is often used when a mistake in programming has put a program into an endless or *infinite loop*. This problem is discussed in later chapters, but it is important to learn at an early stage how to stop a program that seems to be running out of control. The shortcut Cmd-Period (pressing the Command and Period keys simultaneously) is the equivalent of an interrupt key.

The Help Menu

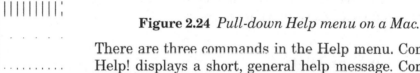

Figure 2.24 *Pull-down Help menu on a Mac.*

There are three commands in the Help menu. Command Help! displays a short, general help message. Command Help Topics lists the various topics for which help is available. Command Help... displays a dialog window from which you can select help on any of the True BASIC commands. The Help menu provides no help on program statements or functions.

Using the Command Line

It is perfectly possible to use commands entered from the command line on a Mac computer, using a window called the *command window*. This method of operation is similar to that used with a PC. It is useful for some commands that can be executed only from the command line.

Select the command named Command from the Windows menu to open a command window. The familiar Ok. prompt appears, indicating that you can enter a command. The command window is closed by selecting the Close Command command from the Windows menu (see Fig. 2.8). If you want to enter commands from the command line, read Section 2.7.

2.11   BACKUP AND PRINTING

It is important to develop the habit now of making copies of all your work and we have two specific suggestions. It is also important to know how to produce paper copies of a program and its output.

Saving Your Program During Development

Remember to pause and save your program on disk each 15 minutes or so as you type in a new program. Use the Save command if the program has a name, otherwise use the Save As command. If anything happens to stop your computer, such as a power failure or some mistake on your part that locks up the operating system, everything you have written will not be lost. **Programs saved on disk are relatively safe, whereas programs in memory can be easily erased.**

As you continue writing a new program or modifying an existing program, execute the Save command frequently to preserve the latest changes on disk.

When modifying a program, it is a good idea to keep a separate copy of the original program on disk. You can save it on disk with a different name. If your modifications are unsuccessful and the modified program does not run, you can always delete it and go back to your original version.

Backing Up Your Disk

Another good habit is to keep backup copies of all important programs on another floppy disk. You can use an appropriate copying command (as described in your operating system manual) to transfer programs to a backup disk. You can also use the Save As command from True BASIC, specifying where you want the backup copy saved. Remember that floppy disks are easily damaged and they do wear out. **Eventually, you will be unable to access a program stored on your program disk. A backup disk then becomes invaluable.**

Many programmers keep two backup copies when working on an important project. One copy is often kept in a separate room or building in case a major disaster such as a fire occurs at the computer site.

Printing a Program Listing and Program Output

When a printer is attached to your computer, the List or Print command produces a paper listing of your current program. Only a single block of text is printed if that block has been selected. You must make certain that the printer is connected to your computer, turned on, and set for on-line operation. If you fail to do so, you may lock up your computer and anything you have not saved on disk may be lost.

A paper copy of program output can be printed if you are using version 2.0 or later of True BASIC. One method is to add the parameter >> to the Run command. Here is how that command will look on the command line following the Ok. prompt:

```
Ok. Run >>
```

Note that a space is required between the word Run and the >> symbol. The characters you type in are in italic face.

Another method uses the Echo command in the following sequence of commands:

```
Ok. Echo
Ok. Run
Ok. Echo off
```

The command Echo copies whatever output is displayed on the screen to the printer. The Echo Off command stops the process. You can use this sequence of commands on a PC or from the command line on a Mac computer.

If all the information you want to capture on paper is displayed in one window, you can use the PrtSc key on a PC to transfer an image of the screen to your printer. Hold down the Shift key and press the PrtSc key. Extended keyboards may have a Print key instead of the PrtSc key and the Shift key may not be required. Before printing the screen image, you can increase the size of the command window by entering the Split 0 command.

A similar procedure works on a Mac computer if your active window is the output window. Hold down the Command and Shift keys and press the digit 4 key in the top row of keys. Your attached printer should start to print an image of the active window. To produce an image of the entire screen, press the Caps Lock key and then follow the preceding procedure. Remember to press the Caps Lock key again when you are through printing. These printing procedures do not work with an Apple LaserWriter or with any printer connected through an AppleTalk network.

If no printer is attached to your computer but it is connected to a network that includes printers, see the local authorities for specific printing instructions.

Summary of Important Points

- When you turn off your computer, all information stored in memory is lost.

- Line numbers are not required with True BASIC statements.

- Always press the Return key when you finish typing a BASIC statement or command.

- When writing programs on a Mac computer, the Return key, not the Enter key, must be pressed to end a program line.

- A blank space is a character and can never be used in a DOS file name, but may be used in a Mac file name.

- When a program is saved or opened on a PC, a suffix of TRU is added automatically to any program file name that does not end with a period. On a Mac, no suffix is added.

- The New command erases the current program from the user workspace.

- Be sure to save your current program before using the command Old to load another program.

- Once a file has been "unsaved" or deleted from your disk, it cannot be recovered.

- Two different types of cursors are displayed on the screen when you are using a mouse: a text cursor and a mouse cursor.

- When text is cut or copied to the clipboard, any text that was previously in the clipboard is erased.

- A block of text that is deleted with the Del key on a PC can be recovered by pressing the F7 key. A block deleted with the Delete key on a Mac cannot be recovered. A block that is cut on either machine (and thus written in the clipboard) can usually be recovered.

- Develop the habit of frequently saving your current program while you are writing it.

- Keep backup copies of all important programs on one or more separate disks. Eventually, you will be unable to access a program stored on your program disk. A backup disk then becomes invaluable.

Common Errors

- Confusing the terms *bit* and *byte*.

- Failing to distinguish between operating system commands and True BASIC commands.

- Failing to save a program on disk before turning off the computer.

- Forgetting to keep your backup disk in a safe place or, even worse, not having a backup disk.

- Forgetting to write an END statement as the last statement in a program.

- Deleting a program file from your disk by mistake and then immediately writing a new file on the disk, thus eliminating almost any possibility of recovering the deleted file.

- Failing to save your program on disk during two hours of difficult programming, only to have the lights flicker and hear the computer rebooting, erasing all the program code that you had stored in memory.

- Trying to use the printer when it is turned off or not connected to your computer, sometimes resulting in locking up your computer and losing all information in memory.

- Failing to save a program before trying to print it on paper.

- Failing to enclose a string constant in quotation marks.

- Saving a new version of a program with the same name as the old version, thus overwriting and erasing the old version. It is safer to save each version of a program with a different name.

PC Users

- Including a space in a path name, especially between the colon after the drive letter and the first letter of the file name.

- Saving a program with the file name MYPROG and then being unable to access it with a DOS command, forgetting that the suffix TRU was added automatically by True BASIC.

- Using the forward slash (/) instead of the backslash (\) as a separator in a DOS path name.

- Forgetting that a suffix of TRU is added automatically to any program file name if a suffix is not specified.

Mac Users

- Pressing the Enter key after typing a command when you should have pressed the Return key.

- Cutting two items in succession from your program and moving them to the clipboard, thus overwriting and erasing the first item.

- Forgetting to click the mouse button to relocate the text cursor after moving the I-beam mouse cursor to a new location, resulting in any new text being inserted at the old location of the text cursor.

- Expecting to have the suffix TRU added automatically to a program file name.

Self-Test Questions

1. What is RAM?

2. Is information stored on a floppy disk lost when the computer is turned off?

3. Is information stored in memory lost when the computer is turned off?

4. What is a disk file?

5. Are line numbers at the beginning of program statements required in True BASIC?

6. After you type the letters of a command, which key should you press to tell the computer to execute the command?

7. Which character or characters are used to denote the beginning of a REMARK statement?

8. What statement is required in every True BASIC program?

9. What program statement is used to accept characters typed in from the keyboard?

10. How do you indicate to the computer that you are finished typing information in response to a prompt?

11. How do you print an image of the computer screen?

12. How do you redirect program output to an attached printer?

PC Users

Some of these questions may apply to Macs when commands are entered from the command line.

13. Which part of the screen is the command window, the upper part or the lower part?

14. Which function key do you press to move the cursor to the editing window?

15. What is the name of the small nonflashing box at the left margin of each program statement?

16. Which key or keys should you press (when in the editing window) to move the cursor to the start of the current line?

17. When in the editing window, what happens when you press the key marked Home?

18. When you enter the True BASIC editor (move to the editing window), are you in the insert mode or the overwrite mode?

19. Which key do you press to move the cursor to the command window?

20. When the cursor is a flashing underline character, are you in the insert mode or overwrite mode?

21. What happens when the cursor is on a program line tag and you press the Return key?

22. What action results when a statement consisting of the single word PRINT is executed?

23. How do you delete an entire line of your program?

24. Which function key do you press to get help?

25. When you enter the NEW command from the command line, what happens to your current program?

26. What command lists the names of all True BASIC program files on the disk in drive B?

27. What command do you use to load the program file HW3.TRU from the disk in drive B into the user workspace?

28. What command do you use to save a new version of an old program file?

29. You are writing programs in True BASIC and have just saved a new program file named PROJECT.TRU on the disk in drive B. Explain how you would save a backup copy of this program file on another disk.

30. What command do you use to enlarge the command window and make it fill the entire screen?

Mac Users

Some of these questions may apply to PCs when using a mouse and pull-down menus.

31. What are the names of the command menus in the menu bar?

32. What are the two types of cursors visible in the editing window?

33. Describe the technique of clicking the mouse.

34. Describe the technique of dragging the mouse.

35. How do you move the text cursor to a new location?

36. What is the purpose of the scroll bar slider on the right side of the screen?

37. How do you select three lines from the current program?

38. How do you select a single word in a program line?

39. What is the key combination equivalent to the Cut command?

40. What is the key combination equivalent to the Copy command?

41. What is the key combination equivalent to the Paste command?

42. Can a file name contain the blank space character?

43. What key combination can be used to save the current program on disk?

Practice Programs and Exercises

In each of the following problems, write a True BASIC program that will produce the specified results.

1. Display the following lines on the screen:

    ```
    True BASIC, Inc.
    12 Commerce Avenue
    West Lebanon, NH 03784-1669
    ```

2. Display your name, local address, and telephone number on separate lines on the screen.

3. Ask a user — the person who runs the program — to enter his or her name and then display that name again on the screen.

    Test your program using the name William P. Blank.

4. Ask a user to enter three numbers in response to three prompts. Display these numbers again on the screen, one above the other, in reverse order (the opposite order from entry).

    Test your program using the numbers -7, 2, and 13.

5. Display the names of four of your friends on the screen. Display these names in double-spaced format (names separated by blank lines).

    Test your program using the following list of names:

    ```
    Mary F. Jones
    Hannah G. Forbes
    Bill Bradley
    Peter C. Johnson
    ```

The following exercises are designed to give you practice using some of the True BASIC and DOS commands.

6. Use the True BASIC editor to write a series of REMARK statements, similar to those in the file HEADING.TRU on the example program disk or as specified by your instructor. Name this series of statements HEADING.TRU and save it on your program disk.

    Then load one of your other True BASIC programs into memory from disk. Use the INCLUDE command to insert HEADING.TRU at the beginning of your current program. Save the new program on disk, and if a printer is available, list the new program on paper.

7. Copy a True BASIC program from your program disk to a separate
    backup disk. Look up the DOS COPY command and use this command
    to make the copies.

    If your program disk is in drive B and your backup disk is in drive A, the
    proper command to backup file HW01.TRU is

    ```
    COPY B:\HW01.TRU A:\
    ```

8. Use the COPY command of DOS to make a copy of one of the program
    files on your program disk. Give the copy a different name from the
    original program. Look up the DIR command of DOS and use it to
    display the directory of files saved on your program disk.

    Enter the True BASIC system and use the FILES command to look
    again at the program disk directory. Use the UNSAVE command to
    delete the copied file that you have just created.

9. This exercise is designed to give you practice using a mouse with True
    BASIC. Select Example Program 2-5 as your current program. Use the
    Copy and Paste commands to replace the single PRINT statement in line
    5 with two PRINT statements, thus adding a line to the program.
    Change the prompt string in the INPUT statement to the string "Enter
    your full name..." Save the modified program on your program disk
    under the file name EX02-05A.TRU.

CHAPTER
3

Assigning Values to Variables

3.1 INTRODUCTION

True BASIC uses labeled mailboxes — actually memory locations — called variables to store information that can be accessed from a program. Two types of variables are identified; those that store numbers (numeric variables) and those that store characters (string variables). I explain how to assign values to variables and how to manipulate variables.

Information may be stored in a separate disk file or in a section of memory used by DATA statements. I show you how to read information from these two sources and use it in a program. You can enhance your ability to display information by learning new statements that provide more control over the format of screen displays.

3.2 ASSIGNMENT STATEMENT

A variable name in a computer program is the name of a memory location where information is stored. You might think of a variable name as the label of a mailbox for storage of information. This mailbox is, of course, really just a small area of memory. A typical variable for storing a number might be named Cost. The rules for forming variable names are discussed in the next section.

Numeric Variables

The information stored in a variable is called its *value*. You can assign the value 29 to the variable Cost or store the value 29 in the mailbox whose label is Cost. True BASIC allows you to use the variable name Cost for only one memory location or mailbox — this name should not be used for any other purpose in your program.

The assignment or LET statement is used to assign a value to a variable. As an example, this statement could be

```
LET Cost = 29
```

Note that the equal sign (=) is used here as an assignment symbol, not as an equality symbol. The distinction will become clear later.

The word LET is required in True BASIC unless the modifying statement

```
OPTION NOLET
```

has been placed near the beginning of the program. I use the word LET in most of the example programs but in a few cases (see Example Program 3-2) have used the OPTION NOLET statement so you can see how it works.

This mythical mailbox has certain unusual properties. When another value is placed in the mailbox — or a new value is assigned to the variable — the original value is overwritten and destroyed. It cannot be recovered. Thus the statement

```
LET Cost = 86
```

replaces the original value of 29 with the new value of 86.

To remind you that the equal sign is not an equality symbol when used in this manner, look at the following example:

```
LET Cost = Cost + 10
```

This statement tells the computer to take the value now in the mailbox Cost — a value of 86, add 10 to it, and place the resulting value back in the mailbox. The variable Cost now has a value of 96. As you study this example, you see that it is obviously not a mathematical equality.

Please read over this section again if you have any questions about the difference between a variable and its value. There are two main points to remember:

- **A variable can have only one value at a time.**
- **Assigning a new value to a variable destroys the old value.**

Here is a simple program that uses the assignment statements just discussed to assign different values to a variable:

```
! Example Program 3-1
```

```
! Use of assignment statements.

LET Cost = 29
PRINT Cost
LET Cost = 86
PRINT Cost
LET Cost = Cost + 10
PRINT Cost
LET Cost = Cost - 25
PRINT Cost
END
```

This program displays the following list of numbers:

```
29
86
96
71
```

Do you agree with these results? Do you understand how each of the numbers is calculated? If not, go through the program again line by line.

Here is a similar program containing the OPTION NOLET statement:

```
! Example Program 3-2
! Use of assignment statements
! and the OPTION NOLET statement.

OPTION NOLET
Cost = 29
PRINT Cost
Cost = 86
PRINT Cost
Cost = Cost + 10
PRINT Cost
Cost = Cost - 25
PRINT Cost
END
```

This program produces the same output as Example Program 3-1.

Initial Values

What happens if you execute a program statement like

```
PRINT Cost
```

and you have not yet assigned a value to Cost? True BASIC assigns an initial value of zero to a numeric variable and thus a zero will be printed. It is good programming practice, however, always to assign an initial value to a variable, even though True BASIC does not require this step.

3.3   VARIABLE NAMES

A variable name must begin with a letter of the alphabet. It may contain an unlimited number of characters in version 3, but only 31 characters in earlier versions. I recommend that you use no more than 31 letter and digit characters. **A blank or space character is not allowed in variable names.**

The lowercase and uppercase versions of a letter are treated as the same character in variable names. My usual practice is to use an uppercase letter for the first character and lowercase letters for the other characters. A reserved word in True BASIC, such as PRINT (see Appendix D for a list of reserved words), cannot be used as a variable name.

You should choose appropriate variable names that describe the physical entities that they reference. For example, a variable used to hold the sum of several numbers might be named Sum, while a number used to hold the balance in a bank account might be named Balance or even better, BankBalance.

True BASIC has two types of variable names. The variable you have been using, Cost, is the name of a numeric variable. This type of variable can have only numeric values, such as 29 or 109.23 or -1300 or 0.000025.

String Variables

The other type of variable name is used for string variables. A string variable name differs from a numeric variable name by having a dollar sign ($) as the last character. I recommend a maximum length of 31 characters, including the dollar sign. Remember that a string is any sequence of characters (even a sequence of digits) and that this sequence of characters is the value of the string variable. In many cases, the value must be enclosed in quotation marks, as in the following example:

```
LET Phrase$ = "a test string"
```

The initial value of a string variable in True BASIC is the null string, meaning that it contains no characters. Thus a string variable may have a value of "covered boxes" or "abc" or "12345" or even a null value denoted by two quotation marks ("") with no character between them.

Here are two program statements that illustrate the difference between numeric and string values:

```
LET Cost = 225.75
LET Cost$ = "225.75"
```

In the first statement, the variable is a numeric variable and its value can be used in arithmetic calculations. This value is stored in memory as a number. In the second statement, the variable is a string variable and its value consists of six characters: five digits and a decimal point. This value can be displayed on the screen with a PRINT statement but cannot be used in calculations. It is stored in memory as six characters.

Note especially that these two variables, Cost and Cost$, are not the same and are not equal to each other, even though their values look similar. **A numeric variable is never equal to a string variable.**

3.4 NUMBERS

True BASIC defines only one type of number. It makes no distinction between whole numbers, which mathematicians call *integers*, and numbers containing a decimal part, which are called *real numbers*.

Exponential Notation

Numbers may be written or displayed in decimal format, such as 13.375, or in exponential format. The latter format is especially useful for very large or very small numbers. Thus the number 1,475,000,000,000 can be written as 1.475e+12 or 1.475E+12. This format is shorthand notation for 1.475 multiplied by 10 raised to the 12th power (or 1.475 multiplied by a number consisting of a one followed by 12 zeroes). The plus sign is optional; the number can also be written as 1.475E12. Small numbers can be represented in a similar fashion, the number .0000228 being written as 2.28e-5, which is 2.28 divided by 10 raised to the 5th power.

Sometimes when you write large numbers in other applications, you insert a comma before every third digit, as shown:

```
2,125,000,000
```

This format cannot be used when you assign a numeric value to a variable, **the commas are not allowed**. Other common formats for numbers, such as $19.95 or 75%, are **not** allowed when entering numeric values.

Depending on the size of a number, True BASIC will make an automatic choice to display the number in either decimal or exponential format. When you use a number in a program, as a constant or as the value of a variable, you can write it in either format. A user can enter a number in response to the INPUT statement in either format. Appendix E gives further information on how True BASIC displays numbers.

3.5   ARITHMETIC OPERATIONS

Arithmetic expressions are used in BASIC to make numeric calculations. These expressions may contain arithmetic operators, numeric constants, and numeric variables. Here are the arithmetic operators and their symbols:

> +   addition
> -   subtraction
> *   multiplication
> /   division
> ^   exponentiation

The symbols for addition and subtraction are familiar. Some examples follow:

```
LET Sum = Sum + 1
LET N1 = N2 - N3
LET Ans = A - (B - C)
```

The symbol for multiplication is an asterisk (*) and must always be used. While the expression 2X in mathematics means 2 times X, in BASIC it must be written 2 * X. The symbol for division is the familiar forward slash (/).

For example, the program

```
! Example Program 3-3
! Use of arithmetic operators

LET X = 3
LET Result = ((X * 7) - 2) / 5
PRINT "The result is"; Result
END
```

displays the output

```
The result is 3.8
```

Note the use of a semicolon as a separator in the PRINT statement. This technique is frequently used to print both a label and a numeric result. I discuss separators in more detail in Section 3.9.

In another example, you can calculate the total cost of an item that has both a sales tax and a handling charge:

```
! Example program 3-4
! Calculate total price for an item

OPTION NOLET
Price = 13.90
TaxRate = 0.1  ! 10 percent
Handling = 1.00
Total = Price + (TaxRate * Price) + Handling
PRINT "Total price is"; Total; "dollars"
END
```

Note the explanatory comment after the statement that assigns a value to TaxRate. This program displays the following output line:

```
Total price is 16.29 dollars
```

In this example, the OPTION NOLET statement eliminates the need for the word LET in subsequent assignment statements. I normally use LET in all assignment statements but thought I would show you one more example program where the word LET is not used.

Exponentiation means "raising to a power." The variable X multiplied by itself is called "X squared" and is written X^2. The exponentiation symbol is displayed as a caret (^). Here is an example program:

```
! Example Program 3-5
! Use of exponentiation

LET X = 5
PRINT "The cube of"; X; "is"; X^3
END
```

It displays the following line of output:

```
The cube of 5 is 125
```

By the way, most desktop computers can multiply numbers much faster than they can raise numbers to a power. If you have a choice, multiply. For example, on my computer the quantity X*X*X is calculated in one-third the time required to calculate X^3.

A similar program can be used to calculate the area of a circle. The function Pi is a system function with a constant value of approximately 3.14159:

```
! Example Program 3-6
! Calculate the area of a circle

LET Radius = 12.2
LET Area = Pi * (Radius ^ 2)
PRINT "Area of circle is"; Area
END
```

This program displays the following result:

```
Area of circle is 467.595
```

Order of Precedence

There is a rule called the order of precedence for arithmetic operators. It says that operators are evaluated from left to right, first exponentiation, then multiplication and division, then addition and subtraction. Expressions within parentheses are always evaluated first. By using this rule, you can determine just how True BASIC will evaluate an expression.

For example, in the statement

```
LET X = 2 * 5 + (9 / 3) ^ 2 - 7
```

the first scan evaluates the expression in parentheses (9/3) and produces a value of 3, resulting in the equivalent statement

```
LET X = 2 * 5 + 3 ^ 2 - 7
```

The second scan performs the exponentiation, raising 3 to the second power and producing a value of 9. The equivalent statement then becomes

```
LET X = 2 * 5 + 9 - 7
```

The third scan multiplies 2 by 5, giving a result of 10 and an equivalent statement of

```
LET X = 10 + 9 - 7
```

The final scan performs the addition and subtraction and assigns a value of 12 to X.

The use of many parentheses provides an alternative way to write arithmetic expressions. For example, you could write the original statement as

```
LET X = (2 * 5) + ((9 / 3) ^ 2) - 7
```

Follow the rule of evaluating the contents of inner parentheses first and quickly calculate the value of the expression. If you use parentheses wherever possible — as in the example programs — you seldom need to worry about the order of precedence.

As an example of how parentheses can change the value of an expression, look at the following program:

```
! Example Program 3-7
! Use of parentheses

LET A = 5
LET B = 7
PRINT A - 2 / B + 3
PRINT (A - 2)/(B + 3)
PRINT A - (2/B) + 3
PRINT A - (2/(B + 3))
END
```

This program displays the following results:

```
7.71429
.3
7.71429
4.8
```

You can see that placing the parentheses at different locations produces different results.

True BASIC arithmetic expressions can be used with numbers of widely different sizes. Expressions are calculated to at least 10 digits. The largest number is about 1.8E+308 and the smallest number is about 5.6E-309. Exact values for the largest and smallest numbers are given in Appendix A.

If a number is too large in absolute size (greater than 1.8E+308 or less than

-1.8E+308), an overflow error occurs. On the other hand, if a number is too small (closer to zero than 5.6E-309 or -5.6E-309), True BASIC substitutes zero for the number.

3.6 STRINGS

As explained earlier, string variable names must end with a dollar sign. These variables contain string values that are character sequences of varying length. The maximum length of a string in True BASIC is at least 32,000 characters (the length is much larger for a Mac), so you seldom need to worry about exceeding the maximum length.

In addition to its maximum length, every string has a current or *dynamic length*, the actual number of characters currently stored in the string variable. Information on dynamic length is also stored in the string variable and can be accessed with a standard function — the Len function which is described in Chapter 5.

The assignment statement may be used to assign a value to a string variable, as in the following example:

```
LET Phrase$ = "What is your name?"
```

Remember that the string value or constant must be enclosed in quotation marks.

Including Quotation Marks in String Constants

If you want to include quotation marks within the string, use a double set of quotation marks. For example, the program fragment

```
LET Phrase$ = "He said ""Hello""."
PRINT Phrase$
```

displays the sentence

```
He said "Hello".
```

The Null String

A string with a dynamic length of zero is called a *null string* because it has a no value. It can be created by the statement

```
LET Example$ = ""
```

where no character — not even a space — is enclosed by the two quotation marks. Note that the null string is different from a string containing a single blank or space character. Remember that every string variable is set initially to a null string.

Using Substrings

True BASIC allows you to access *substrings*, sequences of contiguous characters within string variables. An expression in square brackets, like [a:b], when added to a string variable name, designates a substring that starts at the character in position "a" and ends at the character in position "b." Note that "a" and "b" are numbers and the first character in a string is at position 1.

If the variable Phrase$ has a value of "What is your name?", then the substring Phrase$[6:7] has a value of "is" and the substring Phrase$[14:17] has a value of "name."

The notation Phrase$[a:b] makes it easy to refer to a substring of the string variable Phrase$. The limits "a" and "b" must be integers or numeric expressions. If "a" has a value of less than 1, the value 1 is used instead. If "b" has a value greater than the length of the entire string, the string length is used instead. If the value of "a" is greater than the value of "b", a null substring is created.

The substring notation can also be used in an assignment statement. For example, the program

```
! Example Program 3-8
! Assign a value to a substring and thus
! change the value of a string variable.

LET Trip$ = "travel in town"
LET Trip$[8:9] = "to"
PRINT Trip$
END
```

displays the phrase

```
travel to town
```

You can actually insert a new substring that is of different length from the original substring. For example, if the statement

```
LET Trip$[8:9] = "into"
```

is placed in the above program as a replacement for the second line, the modified program now displays the phrase "travel into town."

You can also use substrings to separate a string into two or more parts. Consider the case where you have a string containing both an account number and a name, such as "163259,John Ivory."

Assume that the number always contains six digits and is separated from the name by a comma. This string value is assigned to the string variable Line$.

```
LET Line$ = "163259,John Ivory"
```

You can separate the account number from the name and display it by using the statement

```
PRINT Line$[1:6]
```

which displays the string value 163259.

If we assume that the string Line$ is no longer than 100 characters, the name can be extracted by using the statement

```
PRINT Line$[8:100]
```

which displays the string value "John Ivory." It makes no difference if the original string is less than 100 characters long.

This ability to separate strings into substrings has many important uses in True BASIC programs.

Concatenation of Strings

A useful operation with strings, similar to the addition operation with numbers, is *concatenation*. This means adding one character string to the end of another character string. The ampersand (&) is used to indicate string concatenation in True BASIC.

For example, the program

```
! Example Program 3-9
! Concatenate three strings

OPTION NOLET
FirstName$ = "Mary"
LastName$ = "White"
Name$ = FirstName$ & " " & LastName$
PRINT Name$
END
```

displays the name

```
Mary White
```

Note that a one-character string consisting of a single blank is placed between the strings FirstName$ and LastName$.

The LINE INPUT Statement

If you are using the INPUT statement to enter a string value from the keyboard, the characters typed in cannot include a comma because the INPUT

statement interprets a comma as the end of input. The general form of the
INPUT statement is

```
INPUT Var1, Var2, Var3,...
```

where the variables may be either numeric or string. A user must use commas to separate the several values that are assigned to variables. For example, the program

```
! Example Program 3-10
! Entering multiple values with INPUT statements

PRINT "Enter two names separated by a comma:"
INPUT Name1$, Name2$
INPUT prompt "Salaries? ": Salary1, Salary2
PRINT "The salary of "; Name1$;
PRINT " is"; Salary1; "dollars."
PRINT "The salary of "; Name2$;
PRINT " is"; Salary2; "dollars."
END
```

produces the following sample dialog between user and program:

```
Enter two names separated by a comma:
John H. Smith, Mary Johnson
Salaries? 23500, 24000
The salary of John H. Smith is 23500 dollars
The salary of Mary Johnson is 24000 dollars
```

If you need to enter a string of characters containing one or more commas, you must either enclose the entire string in quotation marks or use the LINE INPUT statement. The latter statement can be used only with string variables. In many applications, only a single string variable is used in the LINE INPUT statement to simplify the program structure.

A prompt can be included in the LINE INPUT statement, as it is in the INPUT statement:

```
! Example Program 3-11
! Enter and display a name

LINE INPUT prompt "Type in your name...": Name$
PRINT "Your name is "; Name$
END
```

The following dialog is typical of a case where the LINE INPUT statement is needed:

```
Type in your name...James Brown, Jr.
Your name is James Brown, Jr.
```

A name containing a comma, such as James Brown, Jr., is accepted by the LINE INPUT statement and assigned to the variable Name$. This name would not be accepted by a plain INPUT statement.

The LINE INPUT statement has another useful property. It accepts a null string value (the user just presses the Return key) and assigns that value to a string variable. This type of entry is often used in programs to signal a particular user response. The regular INPUT statement will not accept a null string value.

3.7   READING VALUES FROM MEMORY

The programs you have written up to this point require string or numeric values to be entered from the keyboard. An alternative form of input is to read values from a reserved section of computer memory where they have been stored by the program.

The DATA Statement

DATA statements are used to store string or numeric values in memory. String values must be enclosed in quotation marks if you wish to include minus signs, leading or trailing blanks, internal spaces, or other punctuation marks. In particular, a string containing a comma must be placed in quotation marks. Individual values are separated from each other by commas in the DATA statement.

Here are some typical DATA statements:

```
DATA 10, Computer, 15, Disk Drive
DATA 8, Chair, 2, "Table, 3 ft. by 8 ft."
```

DATA statements may be placed anywhere in a program before the END statement. When you run a program, the computer first examines all DATA statements and stores their values in a reserved section of memory. Note that the last string in the second statement, the string starting with the word Table, is enclosed in quotation marks because it contains a comma.

The READ Statement

One or more READ statements are used to read these stored values into variables. Variables in a READ statement are also separated from each other by commas. For example, the following READ statement can be used with either of the preceding DATA statements:

```
READ Quantity1, Name1$, Quantity2, Name2$
```

The computer keeps track automatically of which values have been read and which is the next value to read. Reading starts with the first value in the first data statement. In the preceding examples, when the first DATA statement is read, the first value 10 is assigned to the first variable Quantity1, the string value Computer to variable Name1$, and so forth.

The single READ statement can be replaced by several READ statements and the results will be identical, as shown in the following program fragment:

```
READ Quantity1
READ Name1$, Quantity2
READ Name2$
```

If you try to put a nonnumeric string in a numeric variable, you get an error message. You can, of course, put digit characters in a string variable but you must remember that these digits represent a string value, not a numeric value.

If the number of variables in READ statements is greater than the number of values in DATA statements, you get an error when you try to read a value that does not exist. No error occurs if the number of values is greater than the number of variables, although the extra values are not read.

Here is an example program that reads three numbers from a DATA statement, calculates their sum, and prints it on the screen:

```
! Example Program 3-12
! Use of the DATA statement

READ First, Second, Third
LET Sum = First + Second + Third
PRINT "The sum of three data values is"; Sum

DATA 15.3, -181.7, 225
END
```

This program displays the following output:

```
The sum of three data values is 58.6
```

READ and DATA statements are introduced here and subsequently used in programs where the READ statement is in a loop, as discussed in the next chapter.

3.8   READING VALUES FROM TEXT FILES

You already know how to use the INPUT and LINE INPUT statements to read values from the keyboard. Let's now expand the use of these statements to read values from text files. Before reading from files, you must learn how to open files and prepare them for reading.

Our initial discussion of text files is limited to their simplest attributes. Text files will be discussed in greater detail in Chapter 9. All I want to do in this chapter is show you how a text file can be used as a source of data for a True BASIC program.

Text Files

You may remember that a file is defined as a collection of characters or other information, usually stored on a computer disk. Up to this point, your files have contained True BASIC program statements. You have saved your programs in files on a disk.

There is no reason, however, to restrict files to program statements. Any kind of information may be placed in a file. Thus some files may contain values or data or manuscripts, while other files contain programs.

You are familiar with the concept of reading or inputting values from the keyboard and writing or printing values on the screen. These values may be numbers or strings. In a similar manner, you can read values from a disk file and write values on a disk file.

In this chapter, you will work only with files containing characters. These files are called *text files*. They are further identified as *sequential text files*, meaning that the information they contain can only be read sequentially, from beginning to end.

A sequential file has its information stored one item after another. In the examples you will use, each item consists of a separate line of text. This means that two nonprinting characters, the carriage return and the line feed, are used together to separate one data item from another. This pair of characters, carriage return and line feed, is called a *line delimiter*.

Thus a simple type of sequential text file has *lines* or items of information consisting of characters, these lines are stored sequentially, and they are separated from one another by line delimiters. A line may contain numeric characters and represent a numeric value, or it may contain any characters and represent a string value.

There is no other structure inherent in the file itself — it is nothing more than a sequence of lines of text characters. Here is a list showing the contents of a short text file containing names:

```
Mark C. Kitchin
Judy Wright
G. Helen Lee
Frederic Taylor
J. Andrew Koontz
```

Here is another list showing the contents of a text file containing numbers:

```
22903
22945
22932
24521
23607
```

A computer program can read information from files of this type. **Reading text from a sequential text file always starts at the beginning of the file** and continues as long as requested by the program or until the end of the file is reached. You cannot start reading somewhere in the middle of the file, only at the beginning.

Opening a Text File

To use a file in a True BASIC program, it must first be opened. The process of opening a file makes it available for use. A True BASIC file or *channel number* is associated with the file name used by the operating system. A BASIC program cannot read information from a file until the file has been opened.

Every file used in a program must be identified by a channel number. Thus the fundamental statement to open a file is

```
OPEN #N: NAME PathName$
```

where N is a numeric variable or constant representing the channel number and PathName$ is a string variable, expression, or constant representing the path name. In some cases, the path name will just be the file name. Once the file has been opened, it is known from then on in the program by its channel number N, not as a file named PathName$.

For example, the statement

```
OPEN #1: name "NUMBERS.DAT"
```

opens the file named NUMBERS.DAT (assuming it is in the current directory or folder) and assigns it to channel number 1. From this point on in the program, you refer to file NUMBERS.DAT as file #1.

The channel number must be an integer from 1 to 1000. File #0 is reserved for reading from the keyboard or writing on the screen; this channel is always open. If N has a noninteger value, it is rounded to the nearest integer. You can use a numeric constant like 2 or a numeric expression instead of a numeric variable. I usually open the first file in a program as file #1, the second as file #2, and so forth, but any number up to 1000 is valid. Check the *True BASIC User's Guide* for your particular computer to determine how many files you can have open at the same time, that number is usually five or more.

The rest of the OPEN statement consists of one or more optional phrases, separated from each other by commas. These phrases are discussed in detail in Chapter 9. For the time being, you can assume that any file you want to read already exists. In that case, the preceding, simple OPEN statement is sufficient and no optional phrases are needed.

Reading from a Text File

A modified form of the INPUT or LINE INPUT statement is used to read information from a file. When reading string values from a text file, I recommend that you use the LINE INPUT statement because it will read all characters up to the end of the line, including commas. Here is the statement used to read a line of text from a file opened as file #1:

```
LINE INPUT #1: Line$
```

The identifier Line$ must be a string variable. After reading a line of text, the program is ready to read the next line.

You can also use the LINE INPUT statement with two or more variables. If you assume that the file was written with a single string value on each line, the values of sequential lines in the file will be assigned to variables in the LINE INPUT statement, one line per variable. An example statement might look as follows:

```
LINE INPUT #1: Line1$, Line2$, Line3$,...
```

The first line value is assigned to variable Line1$, the second to Line2$, the third to Line3$, and so forth.

If a line in your file contains characters representing a number, you can read the line as a string and convert it to a number with the Val function (see Chapter 5). You can also use an INPUT statement (not LINE INPUT) and assign the value directly to a numeric variable.

```
INPUT #1: Number
```

A fatal error results if one of the characters you are converting or reading is not allowed in a numeric expression. You can use the error-handling techniques discussed in Chapter 6 to trap this type of error.

An Example Program

Let's look now at a previous example program, but change it slightly to read information from a text file rather than from DATA statements. Assume a text file exists containing the following numeric values, one per line:

```
15.3
-181.7
225
```

Assume further that this file is named NUMBERS.DAT and resides in the current directory or folder — that is, the same directory that contains the example program. Here is a listing of the program, a revision of Example Program 3-12:

```
! Example Program 3-13
! A revision of Example Program 3-12
! that reads data from a text file
! with one number value per line.

OPEN #1: name "NUMBERS.DAT"
INPUT #1: First
INPUT #1: Second
INPUT #1: Third
LET Sum = First + Second + Third
PRINT "The sum of three file values is"; Sum
END
```

The revised program displays this output:

```
The sum of three file values is 58.6
```

Other example programs that use files appear in subsequent chapters. After you learn about loops in Chapter 4, you can use simple True BASIC programs to read the contents of large text files.

3.9   MORE ON PRINTING

You have used the PRINT statement in Example Programs to display a single
expression value. This statement can also be used to display several expression values by using comma and semicolon separators between expressions.
Remember that an expression can be a constant, a variable, or a combination
of constants and variables connected by operators.

The Comma Separator

Commas are used to separate the variables First, Second, and Third in the following example program. These separators tell the PRINT statement to display the three values in separate print zones, where a *print zone* is defined as
a subdivision of the screen width. The default width of a print zone in True
BASIC is 16 columns, but this width can be changed as you will see later. Each
variable value is displayed at the beginning of a print zone:

```
! Example Program 3-14
! Use of print zones

LET First = 5
LET Second = 10
LET Third = -20
PRINT First, Second, Third
END
```

The example program displays its output in the following format:

```
    5               10              -20
```

The print zone width and effective screen width can be determined and
changed by program statements. The statement

```
ASK ZONEWIDTH Width
```

assigns the value of the current print zone width to the variable Width. The
program fragment

```
LET NewWidth = Width / 2
SET ZONEWIDTH NewWidth
```

reduces the print zone width by 50% after assigning a value to NewWidth
that is half the value of Width. The expression following ZONEWIDTH must
be numeric, usually a numeric variable or constant. Print zone width cannot
be less than one column or greater than the screen width.

Here is a modified version of the previous print zone example:

```
! Example Program 3-15
! Changing the print zone width

LET First = 5
LET Second = 10
LET Third = -20
PRINT "Original print zone width is 16"
PRINT
PRINT First, Second, Third
PRINT
SET ZONEWIDTH 8
PRINT "New print zone width is 8"
PRINT
PRINT First, Second, Third
END
```

It produces a slightly different output, as shown:

```
Original print zone width is 16

 5               10              -20

New print zone width is 8

 5      10      -20
```

Note that after printing the first sequence of numbers in standard-width print zones, the second sequence is printed in reduced-width zones that are eight columns wide.

Two similar statements

```
ASK MARGIN Width
SET MARGIN NewWidth
```

determine and change the right margin of the display screen. The default margin value for most display units is 80, giving a screen width of 80 columns. The screen width cannot be less than one column and must be at least as wide as the current print zone width. These two statements are introduced at this point because they are related to the ZONEWIDTH statements, but you will not use them in programs until a later chapter.

The Semicolon Separator

As you read earlier in this chapter, semicolons are also used to separate expressions. For example, the statement

```
PRINT First; Second; Third
```

produces the display

```
 5  10 -20
```

A semicolon separator tells the PRINT statement to put the numbers as close together as possible. You will note that a space is left in front of the 5 and the 10. This space is for the numeric sign that is not displayed if the number is positive but is displayed if the number is negative. Another space is always left after each number.

String expressions are displayed in much the same way as numeric expressions. The semicolon separator leaves no space either before or after each string expressions. If you want a space, you must add it:

```
! Example Program 3-16
! Use of semicolons with strings

LET First$ = "Mary"
LET Last$ = "White"
PRINT First$; " "; Last$
END
```

This program displays the output

```
Mary White
```

Compare the output of this program with that of Example Program 3-9. Both programs display the same phrase but use different methods. Example Program 3-9 uses string concatenation, while Example Program 3-16 uses semicolon separators in a PRINT statement. There is, however, an important difference in the results of the two operations. Concatenation produces a new string expression; using a PRINT statement does not.

The Trailing Semicolon

A semicolon at the end of a PRINT statement — called a trailing semicolon — has a different meaning; it suppresses the carriage return and line feed that normally follow a PRINT statement. For example, the statements

```
PRINT "A"
PRINT "B"
```

display

```
A
B
```

while the statements

```
PRINT "A";
PRINT "B"
```

display

```
AB
```

You can use a PRINT statement with a trailing semicolon in place of an INPUT statement with a PROMPT clause. If you want to suppress the question mark normally displayed automatically by an INPUT or LINE INPUT statement without a prompt, add a prompt consisting of a null string. Here is another way to write Example Program 3-11:

```
! Example Program 3-17
! Use of trailing semicolon and null prompt

PRINT "Type in your name...";
LINE INPUT prompt "": Name$
PRINT Name$
END
```

It produces the same output as Example Program 3-11. This technique might be used if you have such a long prompt string that the LINE INPUT statement is longer than the screen width.

Simple PRINT USING Statement

Another way to control the format of information displayed on the screen is to use a special print statement called the PRINT USING statement. I introduce a simple form of that statement here and discuss additional forms and capabilities in Chapter 10.

The PRINT USING statement uses a format string to control the appearance of items displayed on the screen or printed on paper. You will use this statement to display only a single numeric value.

The format string in this simple version is a string constant, consisting of a sequence of numeric format characters — the sharp sign character (#) — and an optional decimal point. Enough format characters must be included in the string to accommodate the largest numeric value that might be displayed.

The number of format characters after the decimal point specifies the number of decimal digits that are displayed. The term *decimal digit* means any digit written after the decimal point. The numeric value is *right-justified* in the format string field, meaning that the number is placed as far to the right as possible in the field. If there are not enough zeroes after the decimal point to create the specified format, additional zeroes are added. This technique is called "padding with zeroes on the right." On the other hand, if the value contains too many decimal digits, the excess digits are deleted and the remaining right-most digit is rounded.

Count the number of digits plus any minus sign before the decimal point in the number. Count the number of format characters before the decimal point in the format string. If there are more digits than format characters, the number cannot be properly formatted. In this case, an error message consisting of a string of asterisks (*) is displayed.

Here is an example program showing how this simple version of the PRINT USING statement works:

```
! Example Program 3-18
! Use of the PRINT USING statement

PRINT using "####": 125
PRINT using "####": 1285.9
PRINT using "####": 34562
PRINT
PRINT using "###.##": 12.5
PRINT using "###.##": -12.521
PRINT using "###.##": -133.33
END
```

This program produces the following display:

```
 125
1286
****

 12.50
-12.52
******
```

In summary, the comma and semicolon characters provide a limited formatting capability with PRINT statements. The simple PRINT USING statement adds slightly more capability. Chapter 10 introduces other ways to achieve greater format control. In the meantime, use these simple techniques to give you some control over the output display format.

Summary of Important Points

- A variable can have only one value at a time.
- Assigning a new value to a variable destroys the old value.
- A numeric variable is never equal to a string variable.
- Commas are not allowed in numbers.

- The LINE INPUT statement can only be used with a single string variable.

- Reading text from a sequential text file always starts at the beginning of the file.

- Do not use the INPUT # statement with multiple variables; it cannot read the normal text file structure.

- Be sure to include enough format characters in a format string; if you don't, the PRINT USING statement displays a row of asterisks.

Common Errors

- Assigning a string value to a numeric variable; that is, to a variable whose name does not end with a dollar sign.

- Including a blank or space character in a variable name.

- Using a True BASIC reserved word as a variable name.

- Trying to use a string variable in an arithmetic expression.

- Typing in a numeric value containing commas or a dollar sign.

- Pressing just the Return key in response to an INPUT statement prompt. This reply is accepted only by the LINE INPUT statement.

- Using a numeric variable in a LINE INPUT statement.

- Failing to put enough parentheses in a complicated arithmetic expression and then getting the wrong answer because the correct operator precedence was not recognized.

- Trying to READ more values than are stored in the program's DATA statements.

- Including too few formatting characters in the format string of a PRINT USING statement.

- Choosing a DOS file name that contains a space character.

- Failing to use the complete path name when opening a file that is not in the current directory or folder.

Self-Test Questions

1. What is the assignment operator or symbol in True BASIC?

2. Is the keyword LET required in an assignment statement?

3. How do you differentiate between a numeric variable name and a string variable name?

4. Is the statement LET B = B/2 a valid True BASIC statement? If not, why not?

5. What happens to the old value stored in a variable when a new value is assigned to the variable?

6. What is the initial value of
    - (a) a numeric variable?
    - (b) a string variable?

7. Can a space be included as part of a variable name?

8. How many characters are allowed in a variable name?

9. Which of the following expressions are valid variable names?
    - (a) Ending
    - (b) 2ndEnding
    - (c) Spare Tire
    - (d) NoSuchLuck

10. If the variable Value$ is assigned a value of "12", is it possible to evaluate the expression (Value$ + 2)? If not, why not?

11. What, if anything, is wrong with each of the following statements?
    - (a) LET Value = 1,230,000
    - (b) LET Value = 1.23e6
    - (c) LET Value = 15%
    - (d) LET Value = $12.95

12. Evaluate the following expressions.
    - (a) LET X = 1 - 2 / 2
    - (b) LET X = 2 ^ 3 - 1 / 2
    - (c) LET X = 1 + 2 - 3 * 4 / 2
    - (d) LET X = 2 + 2 / 2 + 2

13. Can a string variable named Long$ be assigned a string value containing 500 characters?

14. The string variable Name$ has been assigned the value "Bill Wilson".
    (a) What is the value of the substring Name$[6:11]?
    (b) What is the proper substring notation for the first name "Bill"?

15. If Prefix$ has the value "for" and Suffix$ has the value "ever", what is the value of the expression (Prefix$ & Suffix$)?

16. Is the statement LINE INPUT Cost a valid True BASIC statement? If not, why not?

17. Can a DATA statement be
    (a) the first statement in a program?
    (b) the last statement?

18. If the first READ statement in a program is READ A and the first DATA statement in the same program is DATA 3, -2, 7, what value is assigned to the variable A?

19. (a) If a program has one READ statement and one DATA statement, what happens if the number of variables in the READ statement is greater than the number of values in the DATA statement? (b) What happens if the opposite situation exists?

20. When reading information from a file, do you refer to the file by its
    (a) file name?
    (b) file number?
    (c) path name?

21. If there are five lines in a text file, can you write a program that reads only
    (a) the third line?
    (b) the first line?
    (c) the last line?

22. What is the correct program statement to open a text file named VALUES, in the current directory or folder on the current disk, as file #3?

23. What is the correct program statement to read a line of text from a file that has been opened as file #2 and then assign this string value to the variable Line$?

24. Given the program
    ```
    LET Star$ = "*"
    PRINT Star$, Star$
    END
    ```

in which column will

   (a) the first asterisk be displayed?

   (b) the second asterisk be displayed?

25. What statement is used to change the print zone width from its current value to 10 columns?

26. What is the effect of a trailing semicolon at the end of a PRINT statement?

27. What display is produced by the statement

```
PRINT using "##.##": Number
```

when Number has

   (a) a value of 17.2?

   (b) a value of -17.2?

Practice Programs

1. Assign the value 10259 to the variable First and the value 137321 to the variable Second. Display the sum of these two variables on the screen.

2. A DATA statement contains three numeric values. Display the average of these three values on the screen.

Test your program using the statement

```
DATA 1001, 12.3, 2.59
```

3. The text file VALUES.DAT, on the current directory of the current disk, contains three numbers on separate lines. Read these three numbers from the file and display their average value on the screen.

4. Ask a user to enter his or her first name, middle initial, and last name, all on separate lines. Store these values in three separate variables. Then display the complete name on the screen, with a single space before the initial and a period and space after the initial.

Test your program by entering these three values:

```
Constance
W
Green
```

5. Ask a user to enter a number and then display the cube of that number on the screen. Your screen should look like this (entered number is in italic face):

```
Number? 5
Cube of 5 is 125
```

Test your program using the numbers 5 and -7.

6. The text file NAMES.DAT, on the current directory of the current disk, contains five string values, each on a separate line. These values represent a member's first name, middle initial, and last name. Read these three string values from the file and display the complete name on the screen, with a single space before the initial and a period and space after the initial.

7. Ask a user to enter three numbers and store them in variables A, B, and C. Calculate and display the value of the expression (B*B - 4*A*C).

Test your program using the values A = 4, B = 7, and C = 3.

8. Ask a user to enter two numbers and then display their sum and difference on the screen. The screen display should look as follows:

```
Enter two numbers: 13.2, 7.5
Sum is 20.7  Difference is 5.7
```

Test your program using these number pairs:

```
13.2, 7.5
128.3, 301.7
56, 7
```

9. A temperature in degrees Fahrenheit (F) can be converted to degrees Celsius (C) by using Equation 3.1.

$$C = \frac{5 \times (F - 32)}{9} \qquad\qquad [3.1]$$

Ask a user to enter a temperature in degrees Fahrenheit and display the corresponding temperature in degrees Celsius. The screen display should appear as shown here:

```
Fahrenheit temperature? 59
Celsius temperature is 15 degrees
```

Test your program using Fahrenheit temperature values of 59, 32, and 212 degrees.

10. A farmer has a 14-foot diameter silo that is 60 feet high. Ask a user to enter the height of silage that has been stored in this silo. Display the number of tons of silage in storage. Assume corn silage that has an average weight of 45 pounds per cubic foot.

Test your program using a silage height of 46 feet.

11. Ask a user to enter the size of a room (width and length, in feet) and the price of carpet per square yard. Add a charge of $2.00 per square yard for delivery and installation. Display the total cost of carpeting the room. Use the PRINT USING statement to display dollar amounts to the nearest cent. Your screen display should look as follows:

```
Length of room in feet? 18
Width of room in feet? 12
Price of carpet per square yard? 12.50
Cost of installed carpeting is 348.00
```

Test your program using data in the following table:

Length	Width	Price
18	12	$12.50
11	11	$14.35
10	8	$9.75

12. The present value (P) of an amount (A) produced by compounding interest annually for N years at a percentage interest rate of I, is given by Equation 3.2.

$$P = \frac{A}{\left(1 + \dfrac{I}{100}\right)^N} \qquad\qquad [3.2]$$

Ask a user to enter the amount of money in dollars, the interest rate in percent, and the number of years. Display the present value of this amount. Use the PRINT USING statement to display dollar amounts to the nearest cent. The screen should display the following input and output:

```
Amount? 10000
Interest in percent? 11.5
Number of years? 12
Present value is 2708.33
```

Test your program using data in the following table:

Amount	Interest	Years
10,000	11.5%	12
5,000	8.3%	9

13. Ask a user to enter the amount of an initial deposit in a savings account. Assuming an interest rate of 8 percent, compounded annually, calculate and display the amount of money in the account at the end of 10 years. Use the PRINT USING statement to display dollar amounts to the nearest cent.

Test your program using initial deposits of $100, $1200, and $5000.

CHAPTER
4

Program Control Statements

4.1 INTRODUCTION

Computer programs become more powerful and useful when they are capable of making decisions (branching) and repeating actions (looping). Chapter 4 introduces both concepts and explains how to use the different branching and looping statements.

You also learn about relational operators and logical expressions, fundamental concepts in any discussion of computer decision making. I show you how to use logical expressions to control the reading of text files and DATA statements. You then use these concepts to study two common types of computer programs; one type counts and sums a sequence of numbers, while the other type identifies the largest and smallest numbers in a sequence.

4.2 FLOW OF PROGRAM CONTROL

Statements are executed sequentially, one after another, in a simple BASIC program. In the example program that follows, first a PRINT statement is executed, then three INPUT statements, then another PRINT statement, and finally an END statement. The result of the program is to print the sum of three numbers entered from the keyboard.

```
! Example Program 4-1
! Print sum of three numbers.

PRINT "Enter number when prompted by '?'"
INPUT A
INPUT B
INPUT C
PRINT "The sum is"; A + B + C
END
```

This program produces the following user interaction:

```
Enter a number when prompted by '?'
? 7
? 10
? 4
The sum is 21
```

Writing the program in this manner becomes unsatisfactory if you want to find the sum of many numbers — say 500 numbers. Computer programs often need to repeat the same statement or sequence of statements over and over again. The technique used to accomplish this repetition is called *looping*.

The DO and LOOP Statements

Looping requires two kinds of statements: one to tell the program to repeat a block or group of statements and the other to tell it when to stop repeating. I first list a program containing a loop and then explain how it works.

```
! Example Program 4-2
! Print sum of positive numbers.

LET Sum = 0
PRINT "Enter one or more positive numbers."
PRINT "Enter a negative number to stop."
INPUT Number
DO while Number >= 0
   LET Sum = Sum + Number
   INPUT Number
LOOP
PRINT "The sum is"; Sum
END
```

Here is an example of user interaction and program output:

```
Enter one or more positive numbers.
Enter a negative number to stop.
? 7
? 10
? 4
? -1
The sum is 21
```

Two new statements are introduced, DO and LOOP. These statements enclose a block of one or more adjoining statements — often called the *loop body* — that are executed over and over again. Note the use of indentation to set off the block of statements in the loop.

Whenever the LOOP statement is reached, program control is transferred back to the DO statement. At this point, a check is made to see whether the value of Number is greater than or equal to zero and if so, the loop continues. On the other hand, if Number is negative, control is transferred out of the loop and the statement following the LOOP statement (the "PRINT Sum" statement) is executed. The variable Number is called a *control variable*.

The first INPUT statement, outside the loop, accepts the first number entered by the user. If this number is negative, no sum is calculated and a zero is displayed.

The INPUT statement inside the loop is used for subsequent entries. As an example, consider the case where a value of -1 is entered for Number. In this case, the DO statement transfers control to the PRINT statement following the LOOP statement and the value of Sum is displayed.

The IF and ELSE Statements

Another type of statement is used by a computer program to decide which of two blocks of statements to execute. This process is called decision making or *branching*.

Here is an example program that illustrates branching:

```
! Example Program 4-3
! Branching example.

INPUT prompt "Answer Y or N...": Reply$
IF Reply$ = "Y" then
    PRINT "The answer is yes."
ELSE
    PRINT "The answer is no."
END IF
END
```

Running this program two times produces different results. Remember that user input is shown in italic face.

```
Answer Y or N...Y
The answer is yes.
Answer Y or N...N
The answer is no.
```

Several new statements are used in this program. The combination of IF and ELSE statements allows the choice of one of two blocks of statements. If the value of Reply$ is "Y", then the condition in the IF statement is true and the first block of statements — in this case, just a single PRINT statement — is executed. If Reply$ has any other value (even a lowercase "y"), then the second block, another PRINT statement, is executed. An END IF statement is used to mark the end of the IF structure.

Any computer program can be written in terms of three structures: sequential, loop, and branch. In later sections, you will examine looping and branching in more detail.

4.3   RELATIONAL OPERATORS

You have already seen how operation of loop and branch structures depends on a condition that is either true or false. This condition is called a *logical expression*.

Simple Logical Expressions

A logical expression consists of two variables or values connected by a *relational operator*. For example, the phrase Sum = 7 is a logical expression, where Sum is a numeric variable, the equal sign is a relational operator, and 7 is a constant. This is not an assignment statement because the first word is not LET.

Note that the equal sign (=), when used as a relational operator, has a different meaning from the same character used as an assignment operator (see Chapter 3). Even if the OPTION NOLET statement is present, the context will always tell you how the equal sign is being used and there should be no confusion between a logical expression and an assignment statement.

This logical expression, Sum = 7, is true if the variable Sum has a value of 7. You can also say that the logical expression itself has a value of true. If Sum has a value other than 7, then the logical expression is false — or has a value of false.

You are already familiar with the idea of a variable having a value. Now you learn that a logical expression can also have a value. Note that this value can only be true or false; it cannot be anything else. Thus the expression itself, Sum = 7, has a value of true if Sum has a value of seven.

The six relational operators are listed here:

=	equal
<>	not equal
<	less than
<=	less than or equal
>	greater than
>=	greater than or equal

Consider some IF statement examples containing logical expressions. These statements are the simplest form of the IF structure, discussed in more detail in Section 4.6. For example, look at the following single-line IF statement:

```
IF Limit >= 0 then PRINT Limit
```

The logical expression is true if Limit has a zero or positive value and the value of Limit is displayed. On the other hand, if the logical expression (Limit >= 0) is false, the next program statement is executed.

Here is an example using a string variable:

```
IF Ans$ <> "OK" then LET Value = 0
```

Note that as before, a string constant must be enclosed in quotation marks. The logical expression is true if Ans$ has a value other than "OK."

Most string comparisons involve the equal or not equal operator. It is possible to use the other relational operators with string variables and constants, but an explanation of how these comparisons are made will be deferred until Chapter 11.

Compound Logical Expressions

So far you have seen IF statements with only simple logical expressions containing a single relational operator. It is possible to join together two or more logical expressions by using the keyword AND or OR. The result is called a *compound logical expression*. For example, consider the following statement:

```
IF (A = 5) and (B = 7) then PRINT (A + B)
```

Parentheses are not required in the logical expression but are added to make the statement a little easier to read. This statement prints the sum of A and B if variable A has a value of 5 and variable B has a value of 7. The keyword AND requires that both simple logical expressions be true for the compound logical expression to be true. If either simple expression is false, or if both are false, then the compound expression is false.

Here is another example statement:

```
IF (A < 2) or (A > 9) then PRINT "Error in A"
```

This statement will print the error message if A is less than 2 or if A is greater than 9. The keyword OR requires that either one or the other simple expression be true — or that both be true, an impossibility in this case — for the compound expression to be true. If both simple expressions are false, then the compound expression is false.

Truth Table

The properties of compound logical expressions are shown in Fig. 4.1, which is some-times called a *truth table*.

X	Y	X and Y	X or Y
T	T	T	T
T	F	F	T
F	T	F	T
F	F	F	F

Figure 4.1 *A logical truth table.*

X and Y are any two logical expressions. T means true and F means false. For example, if X is false and Y is true, then the expression (X and Y) is false, while the expression (X or Y) is true.

It is possible to combine more than two logical expressions into a compound expression. Such complicated compound expressions are seldom needed in True BASIC because of the availability of the SELECT CASE statement (see Section 4.7).

It is also possible to reverse the value of a logical expression by using the keyword NOT. For example, if the expression X = 3 is true, then the expression NOT (X = 3) is false. Note that the expression NOT (X = 3) has the same value as the expression X <> 3.

4.4   LOOPING—THE DO LOOP

The DO loop is the most general looping structure in True BASIC. Either the DO or the LOOP statement may be modified to control the duration of a loop. The modifiers are WHILE and UNTIL, and each must be followed by a logical expression containing a control variable.

The WHILE and UNTIL Tests

A DO WHILE or LOOP WHILE statement causes the loop to repeat while the logical expression is true. The following program fragments illustrate this point:

```
DO while Sum < 10
LOOP while Flag = 1
```

A DO UNTIL or LOOP UNTIL statement causes the loop to repeat until the logical expression becomes true, as shown:

```
DO until Sum >= 10
LOOP until Count = 7
```

Here is an example program using a DO loop with an UNTIL test at the end of the loop:

```
! Example Program 4-4
! Display a line, version 1.

LET Line$ = "This is a sample line of text."
DO
    PRINT Line$
    INPUT prompt "Display again (Y/N)? ": More$
LOOP until More$ = "N"
END
```

Note that the value of Line$ will be displayed at least once before the value of control variable More$ is checked at the bottom of the loop. The following results are produced:

```
This is a sample line of text.
Display again (Y/N)? Y
This is a sample line of text.
Display again (Y/N)? N
```

The DO WHILE and DO UNTIL statements check the logical expression at the top of the loop, before it is executed the first time and each subsequent time. The LOOP WHILE and LOOP UNTIL statements check the expression at the bottom of the loop, before the loop is repeated.

Good programming practice suggests that a test phrase (such as WHILE or UNTIL) be placed either at the top of the loop, after the DO statement, or at the bottom of the loop, after the LOOP statement, but not at both places. This practice follows the principle that there should be only one exit point from a loop.

Here are two more sample programs that accomplish essentially the same task as the first program but use different programming structures. The first example uses a WHILE test instead of an UNTIL test:

```
! Example Program 4-5
! Display a line, version 2.

LET Line$ = "This is a sample line of text."
DO
    PRINT Line$
    INPUT prompt "Display again (Y/N)? ": More$
LOOP while More$ = "Y"
END
```

This program produces the same results as Example Program 4-4.

Here is another version of the same program, using an UNTIL test after the DO statement:

```
! Example Program 4-6
! Display a line, version 3.

LET Line$ = "This is a sample line of text."
INPUT prompt "Display line (Y/N)? ": More$
DO until More$ = "N"
   PRINT Line$
   INPUT prompt "Display again (Y/N)? ": More$
LOOP
END
```

In this case, the first request for input is placed outside the loop and the value of More$ is checked at the beginning of the loop. If the value is "N", the string Line$ is never displayed. If the value is "Y", the line is displayed and another request for input, inside the loop, is executed. Output would look as follows if an "N" is entered at the first prompt:

```
Display line (Y/N)? N
```

The EXIT DO Statement

A final example shows how to write a direct exit from within the loop.

```
! Example Program 4-7
! Display a line, version 4.

LET Line$ = "This is a sample line of text."
DO
   PRINT Line$
   INPUT prompt "Display again (Y/N)? ": More$
   IF More$ = "N" then EXIT DO
LOOP
END
```

The IF statement tests a condition, More$ = "N", and if the condition is true, the EXIT DO statement exits the loop — transfers control to the statement following the LOOP statement. Here is the output of this program:

```
This is a sample line of text.
Display again (Y/N)? Y
This is a sample line of text.
Display again (Y/N)? N
```

In general, the EXIT DO test does not produce as readable and easily understood a program as does the WHILE or UNTIL test. The reason for this lack of clarity is that a loop exit occurs in the middle of the loop, whereas you normally look for a loop exit at the end or the beginning of the loop. I recommend that you use the EXIT DO statement only when there is no other acceptable choice.

Sometimes a programming mistake is made and a loop repeats itself over and over. The program never stops — the loop just keeps repeating. It is often caused by the programmer failing to change the value of the control variable inside the loop. This type of loop is called an *infinite loop*. **If you suspect that your program is caught in an infinite loop, you can stop it by pressing the Interrupt key** — the Ctrl-Break key on a PC or the Cmd-Period key on a Mac).

4.5 LOOPING—THE FOR LOOP

There are many occasions when you wish to repeat a loop a fixed number of times. The FOR loop is ideal for this purpose.

The FOR and NEXT Statements

Two companion statements, the FOR statement and the NEXT statement, create a FOR loop. For example, if you wish to sum the integers from 1 through 10, you might write a program containing the following loop:

```
! Example Program 4-8

    ! Sum of the first ten digits.

    LET Sum = 0
    FOR Count = 1 to 10
        LET Sum = Sum + Count
    NEXT Count
    PRINT "Sum of the first ten digits is"; Sum
    END
```

Here is the program output:

```
Sum of the first ten digits is 55
```

The variable Count is called the *control variable*. At the top of the loop, it is given the *initial limit value* of one. After this value has been added to the variable Sum, the NEXT statement returns control to the top of the loop. The control variable Count is automatically incremented by one to a value of 2 and looping continues. When Count reaches the value of 11, the FOR statement notes that this value exceeds the *final limit value* of 10 and looping stops, with control transferring to the statement following the NEXT statement.

Note that the variable Sum is initialized to a value of zero. Even though True BASIC automatically initializes every variable, it is good programming practice to initialize variables in the program. Anyone reading the program will be reminded that Sum has been initialized.

The STEP Modifier

The preceding example is a simple FOR loop and illustrates the most common use of FOR and NEXT statements. A more general FOR statement is defined as follows:

```
FOR I = A to B step C
```

The initial and final limits, A and B, must be numeric variables, constants, or expressions. The step C must also be a numeric variable, constant, or expression and may be positive or negative. As shown in Example Program 4-8, if no step is specified, a step of +1 is assumed.

After you have executed a FOR loop, the value of the control variable will often be different from the value of the final limit. You should not use this control variable value for subsequent calculations or decisions, because it may vary depending on the limit values and step value used in the FOR loop.

If the step is positive and the initial limit is greater than the final limit, the loop is never executed and the control variable retains the value of the initial limit.

Look at this variation of the previous example program:

```
! Example Program 4-9
! Loop with step greater than 1.

LET Sum = 0
LET First = 1
FOR Count = First to 10 step 4
    LET Sum = Sum + Count
NEXT Count
PRINT "Sum ="; Sum
PRINT "Final value of counter variable is"; Count
END
```

The variable Count takes on the successive values of 1, 5, and 9. The next value of Count is 13 and because this value exceeds the final limit, the loop is terminated. The value of Sum and the final value of Count are shown in the following output display:

```
Sum = 15
Final value of counter variable is 13
```

Go through the example yourself and verify these numbers.

Looping with a Negative Step

Another example of the FOR loop uses a negative step:

```
! Example Program 4-10
! Loop with negative step.

LET Total = 0
LET Jump = -2
FOR Count = 4 to -4 step Jump
    LET Total = Total + Count
NEXT Count
PRINT "Sum ="; Total
PRINT "Final value of counter variable is "; Count
END
```

This output display is produced:

```
Sum = 0
Final value of counter variable is -6
```

Note that the initial limit (4) must be greater than the final limit (-4) for the loop to work properly with a negative step (-2). Verify the final value of Total by making a hand calculation.

4.6   BRANCHING—THE IF BRANCH

The most versatile branching structure in True BASIC is the IF branch. You have already read (in Section 4.2) about the two-way branch structure using IF and ELSE statements. The syntax of this structure is as follows:

```
IF logical expression THEN
    first block of statements
ELSE
    second block of statements
END IF
```

Each block of statements consists of one or more statement lines. The "logical expression" is the type discussed in Section 4.3, either a simple expression or a compound expression. The first block is executed if the logical expression is true and control then jumps to the END IF statement.

The ELSE statement and its associated block of statements — the second block — are executed if the logical expression is false. This statement and its second block of statements are optional. The following syntax is used when the ELSE statement is omitted:

```
IF logical expression THEN
    a block of one or more statements
END IF
```

The ELSE and END IF statements must be on lines by themselves unless the IF-THEN-ELSE structure is written as a single statement. **Note that END IF must be two words; the space is significant.** An END IF statement is always required with the block IF structure.

```
! Example Program 4-11
! A normal two-way branch using the block IF structure.

INPUT prompt "Value of A? ": A
INPUT prompt "Value of B? ": B
IF (A = 0) or (B = 0) then
    PRINT "Either A or B is zero."
ELSE
    PRINT "The value of A/B is"; A/B
    PRINT "The value of B/A is"; B/A
END IF
END
```

Here are two examples of program output:

```
Value of A? 10
Value of B? 5
The value of A/B is 2
The value of B/A is .5
Value of A? 10
Value of B? 0
Either A or B is zero.
```

A simple example of the single-line IF-THEN-ELSE structure is the statement:

```
IF Ans = 17 then PRINT "Correct" else PRINT "Wrong"
```

In this case, the entire statement can, and must, be written on a single line. As before, the ELSE clause is optional and another example without that clause is the following:

```
IF Reply$ = "Y" then PRINT Value
```

Note that an END IF statement is not required — nor allowed — with the single-line IF statement.

The ELSEIF Statement

There is an extended version of the IF-THEN-ELSE structure that permits multiple branching using the additional statement ELSEIF — or ELSE IF, either form is acceptable. In the next example, a menu is displayed and the user is asked to choose one of the options. Depending on the choice, a line of different characters is displayed. If a number is entered that is not displayed on the menu, the user is told that the choice is invalid.

```
! Example Program 4-12
! Use of the ELSEIF statement.

PRINT "Command Menu"
PRINT
PRINT "1...display line of stars"
PRINT "2...display line of periods"
PRINT "3...display line of pluses"
PRINT
INPUT prompt "Your choice? ": Choice

IF Choice = 1 then
   FOR I = 1 to 50
      PRINT "*";
   NEXT I
ELSEIF Choice = 2 then
   FOR I = 1 to 50
      PRINT ".";
   NEXT I
ELSEIF Choice = 3 then
   FOR I = 1 to 50
      PRINT "+";
   NEXT I
ELSE
   PRINT "Invalid choice."
END IF
END
```

The following results are displayed:

```
Command Menu:

1...display line of stars
2...display line of periods
3...display line of pluses

Your choice? 3
++++++++++++++++++++++++++++++++++++++++++++++++++
```

Note the use of trailing semicolons in the statements that print the special characters. These semicolons keep all characters on the same line.

4.7   BRANCHING—THE SELECT CASE BRANCH

Another type of branching is the multibranch SELECT CASE structure. This structure allows one of several branches or actions to be selected. The basis of selection can be broader than the simple true or false condition of the IF-THEN-ELSE structure.

The SELECT CASE Statement

The general form of the SELECT CASE structure is as follows:

```
SELECT CASE expression
CASE test1, test2
     first block of statements
CASE test3
     second block of statements
CASE test4, test5, test6
     third block of statements
CASE ELSE
     another block of statements
END SELECT
```

The "expression" in the first line may be any expression or variable, string or numeric. If the expression is of type string, all the tests must be string tests; if numeric, all tests must be numeric. If a test is satisfied, the block of statements associated with that test is executed and control jumps to the statement after END SELECT. If no test is satisfied, the block of statements after CASE ELSE is executed.

The CASE ELSE statement and its block of statements are optional. You will get a run-time error, however, if none of the tests is satisfied and there is no CASE ELSE statement. I recommend that you always include this statement in a SELECT CASE structure.

Here is the previous example, written using the SELECT CASE structure:

```
! Example Program 4-13
! Use of the SELECT CASE statement.

PRINT "Command Menu"
PRINT
PRINT "1...display line of stars"
PRINT "2...display line of periods"
```

```
    PRINT "3...display line of pluses"
    PRINT
    INPUT prompt "Your choice? ": Choice

    SELECT CASE Choice
    CASE 1
        FOR I = 1 to 50
            PRINT "*";
        NEXT I
    CASE 2
        FOR I = 1 to 50
            PRINT ".";
        NEXT I
    CASE 3
        FOR I = 1 to 50
            PRINT "+";
        NEXT I
    CASE else
        PRINT "Invalid choice."
    END SELECT
    END
```

This program produces the same results as Example Program 4-12.

CASE Tests

Tests can be of three types. A test can be a constant value, either string or numeric, that the expression must match. If the expression is a numeric variable named Choice, a CASE statement with two tests might be

```
    CASE 7, -5
```

and would be satisfied if Choice has a value of 7 or -5, as shown in the following program fragment:

```
    SELECT CASE Choice
    CASE 7, -5
        PRINT "Choice has value of 7 or -5."
    END SELECT
```

A test can be a range of values, in the form "low value to high value", that the expression must match. Using the same expression as before, a CASE statement might be

```
    CASE 14 to 21
```

and would be satisfied if Choice has a value between 14 and 21 inclusive. The program fragment then looks as follows:

```
SELECT CASE Choice
CASE 7, -5
    PRINT "Choice has value of 7 or -5."
CASE 14 to 21
    PRINT "Choice has value from 14 through 21."
END SELECT
```

A test can be a logical comparison, in the form "is op value", which the expression must satisfy. The symbol "op" means one of the logical operators. Again using the variable Choice, a CASE statement might be

```
CASE is > 175
```

and would be satisfied if Choice has a value greater than 175. Here is the program fragment one more time:

```
SELECT CASE Choice
CASE 7, -5
    PRINT "Choice has value of 7 or -5."
CASE 14 to 21
    PRINT "Choice has value from 14 through 21."
CASE is > 175
    PRINT "Choice has value greater than 175."
END SELECT
```

Note that variables or expressions cannot be used in a CASE test, only constants can be used.

Let's look together at another, more practical example program that uses the SELECT CASE structure:

```
! Example Program 4-14
! Display the result of reading a thermometer.

INPUT prompt "Reading? ": Temperature

SELECT CASE Temperature

CASE is < 98.5
    PRINT "Temperature is subnormal."

CASE 98.5 to 98.7
    PRINT "Normal temperature."

CASE is > 98.7
    PRINT "You have a fever."

END SELECT
END
```

The following user interaction might be produced:

```
Reading? 98.6
Normal temperature.
```

Note the physical appearance of Example Program 4-14 and compare it to Example Program 4-13. Which program do you find easier to read? Blank lines can often improve the clarity and appearance of a computer program. Note also that both of these programs are easier to read than Example Program 4-12.

The following sample program uses a string expression:

```
! Example Program 4-15
! Interpret the answer to a question.

INPUT prompt "Your answer? ": Ans$

SELECT CASE Ans$

CASE "Y", "y"
    PRINT "The answer is YES."

CASE "N", "n"
    PRINT "The answer is NO."

CASE else
    PRINT "Please answer Y or N."

END SELECT
END
```

Two examples of program output are shown:

```
Your answer? n
The answer is NO.
Your answer? q
Please answer Y or N.
```

The tests in a SELECT CASE structure must be written in such a manner that the expression can choose only one block of statements to execute. If tests in two different CASE statements satisfy the expression, the program will become confused. If this situation might occur in your program, try using the IF-THEN-ELSEIF structure instead of the SELECT CASE structure.

4.8   MORE ON READING VALUES

You learned about the READ and DATA statements in Chapter 3, as well as the concept of reading information from a text file. Now you can learn how to determine if all the information in DATA statements or a text file has been read.

The END DATA and MORE DATA Tests

The two tests used with DATA statements are MORE DATA and END DATA. The logical expression MORE DATA is true as long as there are unread data values and becomes false when there are no more data to read. The expression END DATA becomes true after the program has read the last data value; otherwise, it is false.

```
! Example Program 4-16
! List names in the DATA statement.

PRINT "List of names:"
PRINT
DO until End data
   READ Name$
   PRINT Name$
LOOP

DATA John, Betty, Mary, Tom, Penelope
END
```

This program reads values until the end of the last DATA statement, reading names from the DATA statement and displaying these names on the screen. It produces the following list of names:

```
List of names:

John
Betty
Mary
Tom
Penelope
```

The END #N and MORE #N Tests

A similar pair of tests is used when reading from a file. The logical function END #1 becomes true when the end of file #1 is reached. The logical function MORE #2 becomes false when the end of file # 2 is reached. Assume that the text file NAMES.DAT contains the same names as those read by the preceding example program. The file is located in the current directory and each line contains a single name.

```
! Example Program 4-17
! List names in the file NAMES.DAT.

PRINT "List of names:"
PRINT
OPEN #1: name "NAMES.DAT"
DO until End #1
   INPUT #1: Name$
   PRINT Name$
LOOP
END
```

This program produces the same list of names as Example Program 4-16.

The data file used to test the preceding programs can be written by a True BASIC program (as you will learn in Chapter 9) or by using the True BASIC editor. I used the latter method, just writing a simple text file with one name per line and then saving it as NAMES.DAT. I want to warn you about an error that can occur during this process.

You normally press the Return key after typing each name in order to move to the next line. If you press the Return key after entering the last name, however, you add what I call an *extra null line* to the end of the file. When a True BASIC program tries to read this file using the INPUT statement, it does not know how to handle the null line and so reports a file read error. One solution is to use a LINE INPUT statement, but that does not work with numeric input. The best solution is **never press the Return key after entering the last entry into a text file of data that may be read by a True BASIC program**.

Counting and Summing Numbers

Another example program computes the average value of a sequence of numbers in DATA statements. A check is made at the beginning of the loop to see if there are any more data that have not yet been read from the DATA statements. If all data values have been read, the loop stops.

The variable Sum is used to accumulate the sum of all data values. Within the loop, a counter variable named Count is incremented each time a new data value is read and this value is added to the variable Sum.

```
! Example Program 4-18
! Calculate average value of the numbers
! in the DATA statement.

LET Count = 0
LET Sum = 0
DO while More data
   READ Number
   LET Sum = Sum + Number
   LET Count = Count + 1
LOOP
PRINT "Average value is"; Sum/Count

DATA 1,5,3,4,2,3,7,8,9,2,5,1,9
END
```

Note that both Count and Sum are initialized before the loop starts. After the loop ends, an average value is computed, dividing Sum by Count. This program displays the following answer:

```
Average value is 4.53846
```

Another program selects the smallest and largest values from a sequence of values:

```
! Example Program 4-19
! Find the largest and smallest values in a sequence
! of numbers read from the file NUMBERS.DAT.

LET Largest = -Maxnum
LET Smallest = Maxnum
INPUT prompt "File name? ": FileName$
OPEN #1: name FileName$
DO while More #1
   INPUT #1: Number
   IF Number > Largest then LET Largest = Number
   IF Number < Smallest then LET Smallest = Number
LOOP
PRINT "Largest value is"; Largest
PRINT "Smallest value is "; Smallest
END
```

Since you are comparing numbers, you can define the largest value as the most positive number and the smallest value as the most negative number. This program reads the numeric values from a file named NUMBERS.DAT, specified by the user.

Maxnum is a system variable containing the largest number recognized by the computer. The variable Largest is set initially to the smallest number (negative Maxnum).

After a number has been read in the loop body, its value is compared with the current value of Largest. If this new number is larger than Largest, it is assigned to Largest and replaces the current value. By starting off with the smallest possible number in Largest, you ensure that any larger number read from the file is assigned to the variable Largest.

Similarly, the variable Smallest is set initially to the largest number. If a number is read that is smaller than Smallest, it is assigned to Smallest and replaces the current value.

This choice of initial values for Largest and Smallest ensures that the largest and smallest values will be found. The program displays the following output when the file named NUMBERS.DAT is specified:

```
File name? NUMBERS.DAT
Largest value is 231
Smallest value is -505
```

Remember that the file specified by the user must be in the current directory of the current disk. If not, the full path name of the file must be given.

The RESTORE Statement

Sometimes you want to read a set of data values more than once. The statement RESTORE resets the system so the next item read will be the first value in the first DATA statement. You can imagine there is an imaginary *data pointer* that points to or indicates the next data value to be read. The effect of RESTORE is to reposition this pointer at the first item in the first DATA statement.

To illustrate this process, consider an example program that displays the appropriate zip code when the name of a city is entered. A table of city names and zip codes is placed into DATA statements. The user is asked to type in a city name.

The program searches through the data table for the city name. If the name is found, it is displayed. A dummy city named ZZZZZ is the last city name in the table. If the search reaches this name, a message tells the user that the search was not successful.

The processes of entering a name and searching the table are placed in a loop. At the beginning of the search, the RESTORE statement sets the data pointer to the beginning of the first DATA statement. If the user presses the Return key in response to a request for a city name, the program stops.

```
! Example Program 4-20
! Use of the RESTORE statement in a program that
! displays the zip code for a given city name.

PRINT "Capitalize the first letter of the city name."
PRINT "Press the Return key to stop."

LINE INPUT prompt "City name? ": Name$
DO until Name$ = ""
   RESTORE
   DO while More data
      READ City$, Zip$
      IF Name$ = City$ then EXIT DO
   LOOP

   IF City$ = "ZZZZZ" then
      PRINT "This name is not in the list."
   ELSE
      PRINT "Zip code for "; City$; " is "; Zip$
   END IF
   LINE INPUT prompt "City name? ": Name$
LOOP

DATA Churchville, 21028, Claiborne, 21624
DATA Clarksburg, 20734, Clayville, 23034
DATA Clear Spring, 21722, Clements, 20624
DATA Cleveland, 24225, Clinton, 20735
DATA ZZZZZ, 0
END
```

Here is an example of user interaction with the program:

```
Capitalize the first letter of the city name.
Press the Return key to stop.
City name? Clarksburg
Zip code for Clarksburg is 20734
City name? Charlottesville
This name is not in the list.
City name?
```

The Return key is pressed at the third prompt and the program is ended, but pressing this key displays no character on the screen.

Summary of Important Points

- Any computer program can be written in terms of three structures: sequential, loop, and branch.

- Avoid using the EXIT DO statement to exit a loop if a WHILE or UNTIL test can be used instead.

- When leaving a FOR loop, the value of the control variable is often different from the value of the final limit.

- Use the Interrupt key — the Ctrl-Break key on a PC or the Cmd-Period key on a Mac — to stop an infinite loop.

- The END IF statement must be two words; the space is significant.

- Only constants can be used in CASE tests.

- Do not press the Return key after entering the last entry into a text file of data that may be read by a True BASIC program — it will cause a reading problem.

Common Errors

- Using the conjunction AND in a compound logical expression when you mean OR, and vice versa.

- Using the keyword NOT incorrectly in a logical expression, as in the incorrect statement X NOT = 3 when you should write NOT(X = 3).

- Neglecting to change a DO loop control variable within the loop body, thus creating an infinite loop.

- Failing to test for both lowercase and uppercase input when a character reply is expected. This is an example of poor program design, not a syntax error.

- Using the EXIT DO statement when it is not absolutely necessary; another example of bad program design.

- Making the final limit value greater than the initial limit value in a FOR statement with a negative step.

- Assuming that the value of the control variable is equal to the final limit value after leaving a FOR loop.

- Not recognizing the difference between the block IF structure and the single-line

IF statement.

- Failing to include an END IF statement in a block IF structure. This statement is not needed — nor allowed — in a single-line IF statement.

- Forgetting to include a CASE ELSE statement in a SELECT CASE structure. This is not illegal but can cause the program to abort or crash.

- Writing a SELECT CASE structure so that it is possible to satisfy more than one CASE test, thus confusing the program.

- Setting a large initial value for the variable that is designed to hold the largest value in a sequence of values.

- Setting a small initial value for the variable that is designed to hold the smallest value in a sequence of values.

Self-Test Questions

1. Which keyword is used to mark
      (a) the beginning of a loop?
      (b) the end of a loop?

2. In a program containing an IF statement with two branches, which keyword is used to mark
      (a) the beginning of the first branch?
      (b) the beginning of the second branch?

3. What are the values (true or false) of the following logical expressions?
      (a) 1 = 1
      (b) 2 > 7
      (c) "AA" <> "AB"
      (d) 2 < 7

4. If X = 1 and Y = 2, what are the values of the following logical expressions?
      (a) X + 1 = Y
      (b) X = Y + 1
      (c) Y <> 2 * X
      (d) not (X = Y)
      (e) (X = 3) or (Y > 1)

(f) (X <> Y + 1) and (X + 1 = Y)

5.   Does the statement

```
LOOP until X = 0
```

check for further looping at

(a) the top of the loop?

(b) the bottom of the loop?

6.   If you have a choice of writing a loop using the DO WHILE statement or the EXIT DO statement as a test for exiting the loop, which statement is preferable?

7.   How do you stop a program that is executing an infinite loop?

8.   If a STEP value is not specified in a FOR statement,

(a) what step size is assumed?

(b) is it positive or negative?

9.   If the step size is positive, how many times does a FOR loop execute if the lower limit is

(a) equal to the upper limit?

(b) greater than the upper limit?

10.   Given the FOR loop

```
FOR I = 1 to 5 step 3
NEXT I
```

what is the value of I after the loop has finished executing?

11.   How many times will the following FOR loop execute?

```
FOR Count = 1 to 5 step -1
    PRINT Count
NEXT Count
```

12.   Is the ELSE keyword always required in an IF statement?

13.   Are both END IF and ENDIF valid statements?

14.   Are both ELSE IF and ELSEIF valid statements?

15.   What letter is displayed by the following program if a user just presses the Return key in response to the prompt?

```
LINE INPUT prompt "Your choice? ": Reply$
IF Reply$ = "" then PRINT "A" else PRINT "B"
```

```
END
```

16. A CASE structure starts with the statement
    ```
    SELECT CASE Result
    ```
    If Result has a value of 5, what is the logical value (true or false) of the following CASE tests?

    (a) `CASE 1, 3, 6`

    (b) `CASE 1 to 6`

    (c) `CASE is > 1`

    (d) `CASE is < 5`

17. If a program contains READ and DATA statements, what is the logical value, before the first READ statement is executed, of the expression

    (a) `MORE DATA?`

    (b) `END DATA?`

18. A program reads a sequence of numbers from a text file. What information does it have to calculate and store to compute the average value of the numbers in the sequence?

19. A variable Store is used to hold the largest number in a sequence. What initial value should be assigned to Store at the beginning of the program?

20. If variable Store is used to hold the smallest number in a sequence, what initial value should be assigned to it?

21. What does the RESTORE statement do?

Practice Programs

1. Use the FOR statement with a negative step to display the integers from 10 down to 1 on a single horizontal line.

2. Use a loop statement to display all the even integers between 1 and 20 on a single horizontal line.

3. Ask a user to enter 15 numbers and then display the largest number and the smallest number, with appropriate labels.

   Test your program using the following numbers:

2, 7, -13, 8, 19, 5, -3, 15, -6, 21, -2, 0, 13, 4, 9

4.   Ask a user to enter a sequence of positive numbers from the keyboard. Enter a negative number to stop the data entry process. Display the average value of the positive numbers.

Test your program using the following numbers:

2, 15, 6, 103, 13, 26, 78, 4, 125, -1

5.   Repeat Practice Program 4, but read the same sequence of numbers from one or more DATA statements. A negative number is not needed in this case.

6.   Ask a user to enter a number between 1 and 9. If the number is not in this range, display the message "Your number must be between 1 and 9", loop back, and let the user try again. Otherwise, display the message "Successful entry" and halt the program.

Test your program using the numbers 0, 1, 9, and -9.

7.   Display a string of 70 stars (asterisks) and then the prompt "More (Y/N)?" on a separate line. Wait for the user to enter a character. If the character is "N", halt the program. Otherwise, display the stars again on a new line and then prompt the user again.

Test your program using the characters "Y", "n", and "N".

8.   Rewrite Practice Program 7 with more careful checking of input. Allow a user to enter only one of the characters "Y", "y", "N", or "n". If any other character is entered, display an error message and ask the user to try again. Hint: Use the SELECT CASE statement.

Test your program using the characters "Y", "y", "z", "n", and "N".

9.   The Fibonacci series is a mathematical series of numbers. In this series, the next term is the sum of the previous two terms in the series. For example, if the first term is 1 and the second term is 1, then the third term is (1 + 1) or 2 and the fourth term is (1 + 2) or 3.

Ask a user to enter the number of terms (or numbers) in the series and then display the values of all the terms. Assume a value of 1 for each of the first two terms.

Test your program using a Fibonacci series of 2, 5, and 13 terms.

10.   The examination grades for a class are stored in a text file. Read all grades in the file, and calculate and display the highest grade in the class. Bonus: Calculate the two highest grades.

Test your program using the file GRADES.DAT on the example program disk.

11. A shipping department is preparing an order of transistor radios for shipment. Their large packing cases hold 100 radios, medium cases hold 20 radios, small cases hold 5 radios, and single cases hold 1 radio.

Ask a user to enter the number of radios to be shipped and display a table showing how many cases are needed of each size.

Sample output for shipping 1257 radios is shown:

```
Case              Number
....              .......
large               12
medium               2
small                3
single               2
```

Test your program using 1257, 356, and 5 items.

12. A text file contains the prices of used automobiles sold during the week by an automobile dealership. These prices include the sales tax.

Assume a sales tax of 3 percent on the first $1000 of the price and 2 percent on everything over $1000. Calculate and display the total sales tax liability for the week.

Test your program using the file CARS.DAT on the example program disk.

CHAPTER 5

Standard Functions and Program Design

5.1 INTRODUCTION

True BASIC contains many useful functions in its set of standard functions. Chapter 5 discusses specific functions of several different types; arithmetic, trigonometric, string, conversion, keyboard, and so forth. Single-line user-defined functions are also introduced.

You have now learned enough of the True BASIC language to allow you to write significant programs. I present a recommended procedure for designing computer programs. As an example, you will study the design, development, and testing of a program that averages student grades.

5.2 DEFINITION OF STANDARD FUNCTIONS

What is a *standard function*? In BASIC, it is a named identifier to which one or more values are *passed*, in the form of constants, variables, or expressions. The function performs some calculation and *returns* a new string or numeric value that is assigned to the function name. For example, the function Sqr(9) is passed a value of 9 and returns a value of 3, the square root of 9.

Every version of BASIC has standard or built-in functions but True BASIC has an especially large and comprehensive set. Many of the more useful functions are examined in detail in this chapter — you are referred to Appendix G for a complete list.

As another example, consider the function that calculates the number of characters stored in a string variable, called the length of the string. Assume that you have a string variable named Phrase$. The string value stored in Phrase$ is passed to the function Len, which performs a calculation and returns the length of the string value, as in the statement

```
LET Length = Len(Phrase$)
```

Note that the function name can be written in either uppercase or lowercase characters. I use capitalized lowercase for function names, similar to variable names.

The numeric variable Length is assigned the length of the string stored in the variable Phrase$. If variable Phrase$ has a value of "TEST FLIGHT", then Length will be assigned a value of 11. Remember that a space is a valid character and the quotation marks don't count.

The expression in parentheses is called an *argument* of the function. This particular function has only one argument, the string variable Phrase$. In general, functions may have several arguments, and they may be either string or numeric, either constants, variables, or expressions. The function also has a value, and in our example, this value is assigned to the numeric variable Length. The value of a function (that is, the value returned by a function) may be either a string value or a numeric value. If a function returns a string value, the last character in the function's name must be a dollar sign ($).

Functions may be used, like variables, in many different BASIC statements. Here are two more examples that use the Len function:

```
PRINT Len(Name$)
LET Indent = (80 - Len(Heading$)) / 2
```

5.3　ARITHMETIC FUNCTIONS

The arithmetic functions are numeric functions that perform certain fundamental arithmetic calculations.

The Abs Function

The absolute value function is Abs(X). Note that the function name does not end with a dollar sign because the function has a numeric value. It converts a negative numeric argument to a positive number. Examples are

```
Abs(-5) is 5
Abs(12) is 12
```

The Int, Round, and Truncate Functions

These three functions modify numeric variables or constants. The integer function is Int(X). It returns the greatest integer less than or equal to X. Examples are

```
Int(100) is 100
Int(125.9) is 125
Int(125.1) is 125
Int(-17.5) is -18
```

Note the last example displays the value -18 because this value is the greatest integer less than -17.5. Lesser means more negative.

The function to round a number is Round(X, N). It returns the value of X rounded to N digits after the decimal point. If N is not specified, it is assumed to be zero. This is a true rounding function, not a truncating function. Note that any digit 5 or greater in a positive number is rounded up, while any digit less than 5 is rounded down. Trailing zeroes in a number are not displayed.

Be careful with negative numbers; the result is not what you might intuitively expect. Any digit 5 or less in a negative number is rounded down, while any digit greater than 5 is rounded up. Examples are

```
Round(3.49) is 3
Round(3.49, 1) is 3.5
Round(3.94, 1) is 3.9
Round(3.95, 1) is 4            (trailing zero not printed)
Round(-3.95, 1) is -3.9
Round(-3.96) is -4
Round(-3.96, 1) is -4    (again no trailing zero)
```

A similar function is Truncate(X, N). Both arguments, X and N, are always required. This function returns a value of X, which is truncated or chopped off to N digits after the decimal point. Examples are

```
Truncate(3.95, 0) is 3
Truncate(3.95, 1) is 3.9
Truncate(-3.95, 1) is -3.9
```

The last two functions, Round and Truncate, both display unexpected results if you try to round or truncate a large number — say larger than 99999 — with one or more digits after the decimal point. For example, look at the odd results from the following statements:

```
Round(123489.05, 2) is 123489.05
Round(1234899.05, 2) is 1234899.1
Round(1235899.05, 2) is 1235899.
```

Kind of unpredictable, isn't it. The reason for this odd behavior is explained (at least partially) in Appendix E. As a practical solution, use the PRINT USING statement (introduced in Chapter 3) rather than the Round function to display large decimal numbers.

The Fp and Ip Functions

These two functions return the fractional or integer part of their argument. Function Fp(X) returns the fractional part of X — that is, the digits after the decimal point. Examples are

```
Fp(3.95) is .95
Fp(-1.01) is -.01
Fp(10) is 0
```

Function Ip(X) returns the integer part of X. Note that it sometimes produces different results from the Int function. Examples are

```
Ip(3.95) is 3
Ip(-1.01) is -1 (but Int(-1.01) is -2)
Ip(10) is 10
```

The Sqr Function

The square root function is Sqr(X) and it has a numeric value. It returns the square root of the argument X. Remember that **the square root of a negative number is not defined** and so if the argument is negative, you get an error. Examples are

```
Sqr(9) is 3
Sqr(2) is 1.41421
```

The Mod Function

The function Mod(X, Y) returns a numeric value equal to the remainder when X is divided by Y. The value of Y cannot be zero, because **division by zero is not allowed**. Examples are

```
Mod(7, 3) is 1
Mod(127, 25) is 2
Mod(5.5, 2.5) is .5
```

The Mod function is most commonly used with X and Y having integer or whole number values. One use of the Mod function is to determine whether a number is odd or even, as shown in the following example:

```
! Example Program 5-1
! Test for an even or odd number.

INPUT prompt "Enter number: ": Value
IF Mod(Value, 2) = 0 then
   PRINT "Number is even."
ELSE
   PRINT "Number is odd."
END IF
END
```

Here is an example of program output:

```
Enter number: 17
Number is odd.
```

The Max and Min Functions

The Max(X, Y) and Min(X, Y) functions compare the two numeric arguments and return a value equal to the larger or smaller argument, respectively. Examples are

```
Max(15,0) is 15
Min(-7, 5) is -7
```

Here is an example program from Chapter 4, rewritten to use the Max and Min functions:

```
! Example Program 5-2
! Find the largest and smallest values in a sequence
! of numbers read from the file NUMBERS.DAT.

LET Largest = -Maxnum
LET Smallest = Maxnum
INPUT prompt "File name? ": FileName$
OPEN #1: name FileName$
DO while More #1
   INPUT #1: Number
   LET Largest = Max(Number, Largest)
   LET Smallest = Min(Number, Smallest)
LOOP
PRINT "Largest value is"; Largest
PRINT "Smallest value is "; Smallest
END
```

This program produces the same output as Example Program 4-19, as shown:

```
File name? NUMBERS.DAT
Largest value is 231
Smallest value is -505
```

5.4   TRIGONOMETRIC FUNCTIONS

If your knowledge of trigonometry is weak, you may need to review your high school mathematics before reading this section. You will need to use trigonometric functions in only a few of the practice programs.

The Sin Function

The function Sin(X) calculates the sine of X. The argument X may be expressed in units of either radians or degrees. **The default unit is radians**, but you can change to degrees by including the statement

```
OPTION ANGLE degrees
```

in your program (see Example Program 5-3). Once this statement has been executed, all subsequent trigonometric functions will expect their arguments to be in degrees. You change back to radians by including the statement

```
OPTION ANGLE radians
```

and all subsequent functions then expect arguments in radians.

Other Trigonometric Functions

Additional trigonometric functions in all versions of True BASIC are Cos(X) for cosine of X and Tan(X) for tangent of X. The inverse trigonometric function, Atn(Y), called the arc tangent of Y, is defined and returns the value of an angle whose tangent is Y.

Other trigonometric functions were introduced in version 3 of True BASIC.

Sec(X)	secant of X	Tanh(X)	hyperbolic tangent of X
Csc(X)	cosecant of X	Cosh(X)	hyperbolic cosine of X
Cot(X)	cotangent of X	Acos(X)	arc cosine of X
Sinh(X)	hyperbolic sine of X	Asin(Y)	arc sine of Y

The Deg and Rad Functions

Two functions are useful for converting between degrees and radians. The function Deg(X) converts X radians to degrees. Rad(X) converts X degrees to radians. The constant Pi is a system constant with a value of 3.14159..., up to the maximum system precision.

Here is an example program that uses several trigonometric functions:

```
! Example Program 5-3
! Print several trigonometric function values.

OPTION ANGLE degrees
PRINT "Tangent of 45 degrees is"; Tan(45)
OPTION ANGLE radians
PRINT "Convert angle to radians and ";
PRINT "its tangent is still"; Tan(Rad(45))
PRINT "Tangent of Pi/4 radians is also"; Tan(Pi/4)
END
```

Program output is as follows:

```
Tangent of 45 degrees is 1.
Convert angle to radians and its tangent is still 1.
Tangent of Pi/4 radians is also 1.
```

Note in the next-to-last PRINT statement that the Rad function first converts 45 degrees to radians and then the Tan function finds the tangent of the angle in radians.

5.5 OTHER NUMERIC FUNCTIONS

This section discusses some of the additional numeric functions.

The Log Functions

True BASIC has three logarithmic functions. Log(X) calculates the natural logarithm of X. Log2(X) calculates the logarithm of X to the base 2. Log10(X) calculates the logarithm of X to the base 10.

```
Log(10) is 2.30259
Log2(10) is 3.32193
Log10(10) is 1
```

If you are not familiar with logarithms, you may need to review them in your high school mathematics book.

The Rnd Function

The random number function is Rnd and it returns a random number less than 1 and greater than or equal to 0. If the modifying statement RANDOMIZE is executed prior to the use of the Rnd function, the function returns a different random number or sequence of random numbers each time the program is run. When Rnd is used in a program without the RANDOMIZE statement, it always produces the same random number or sequence of random numbers.

When developing a program that uses the Rnd function to produce a sequence of random numbers, I recommend that you do not include the RANDOMIZE statement. You will find it easier to locate and correct errors when the same sequence of random numbers is produced each time the program is run. After the program is producing correct results, add a RANDOMIZE statement so that each run now produces a different sequence of random numbers.

Here is a sample program that uses the Rnd function to simulate the roll of a pair of dice:

```
! Example Program 5-4
! Simulate the roll of a pair of dice.

PRINT "Simulating the roll of a pair of dice."
RANDOMIZE
PRINT "Result:   ";
SET ZONEWIDTH 5
PRINT Int(6*Rnd + 1), Int(6*Rnd + 1)
END
```

The expression (6*Rnd + 1) produces a number between 1.0 and 6.9999.... Note that the function Int(6.9999...) has a value of 6. The RANDOMIZE statement causes the program to print a different pair of numbers each time it is run. Here is an example of program output:

```
Simulating the roll of a pair of dice.
Result:   6    3
```

You might try running this program a few times without the RANDOMIZE statement just to see what happens.

These dice are slightly "loaded" — do you know if the distribution of results is even when you roll the dice? I wrote a program to investigate that question, rolling the dice 10,000 times, and came up with the results tabulated in Fig. 5.1:

Value of roll	Number of times value came up
2	286
3	508
4	826
5	1146
6	1384
7	1700
8	1402
9	1092
10	823
11	535
12	298

Figure 5.1 Results from rolling dice 10,000 times.

I don't think I'd want to play a game of chance that used Example Program 5-4 to roll the dice — the results are obviously not evenly distributed.

5.6 STRING FUNCTIONS

A powerful set of string functions in True BASIC allows strings to be manipulated and changed.

The Len Function

You have already learned about the Len function which returns the numeric length of a string. For example, the function Len("Susan Smith") returns a value of 11.

You also remember the definition and use of substrings discussed in Chapter 3. For example, if the variable Name$ has the value "Susan Smith", then the substring Name$[1:5] has a value of "Susan." Now that you know about the Len function, you can obtain the last name by using a similar substring expression — Name$[7:Len(Name$)] — that has a value of "Smith."

The Pos and Posr Functions

True BASIC has a function named Pos that returns the location of a substring, often called a *pattern*, within a *target* string. The pattern substring can have one or more characters, and the value of the function returns the character position of the first character in the first occurrence of the substring.

The function Pos(Target$, Pattern$, Position) returns a value giving the location of the first character of the pattern string Pattern$ in the target string Target$. The optional third argument Position specifies the position in Target$ where the search starts. If Position is not specified, the search starts at the first (left-most) character of Target$. The function returns a value of zero if the pattern cannot be found. Examples are:

```
Pos("ABCDE", "C") is 3
Pos("ABCAB", "B") is 2
Pos("abcde", "A") is 0
```

Here is another example where the starting position is specified:

```
Pos("ABCAB", "B", 3) is 5
```

Note that the function returns a number representing the position of the second "B" in the string — not the first "B" — because the search starts at the third character which is after the first "B."

Remember that a blank space is a valid character in a string. If you have a person's full name (first name and last name) stored in a string variable Reply$, you can use the following program to extract the first name:

```
! Example Program 5-5
! Look for first space in the value of Reply$
! and display the first name.

LINE INPUT prompt "Enter your full name: ": Reply$
LET Space = Pos(Reply$, " ")
IF Space > 0 then
   PRINT "Hello "; Reply$[1:Space-1]
ELSE
   PRINT "You seem to have only one name!"
END IF
END
```

A LINE INPUT statement is used so that a name containing a comma, such as John P. Jones, Jr., can be entered. The variable Space is assigned the position of the first space in the string Reply$. If this value is zero, there is no space in Reply$ and you can assume that the entry was not valid. Otherwise, the first name starts at the first character in Reply$ and goes to the character at position (Space-1), the character just before the space. Here are two examples of program output:

```
Enter your full name: John
You seem to have only one name.
Enter your full name: John P. Jones, Jr.
Hello, John
```

Note that the program as written would return invalid results if a name such as "A. Douglas Tower" is entered. You might think about how to correct that problem.

Returning to the example program with the variable Name$ containing the value "Susan Smith", you can now write the first name as

```
Name$[1 : Pos(Name$, " ") - 1]
```

and the last name

```
Name$[Pos(Name$, " ") + 1 : Len(Name$)]
```

As long as the string Name$ contains only two names, separated by a space, the first substring always contains the first name and the second substring contains the last name.

The function Posr(Target$, Pattern$, Position) is similar to the Pos function but searches in a reverse direction from the right end of the string Target$. As before, Pattern$ is the pattern substring and Position is an optional numeric parameter specifying the character where the search begins. Position equal to 1 means the last character in Target$, so Position increases in value as you move to the left. Examples are

```
Posr("ABCDE", "D") is 4
Posr("ABCDE", "B") is 2
Posr("ABCAB", "B") is 5
Posr("ABCAB", "B", 3) is 2
```

This function is useful for tasks such as extracting the last name from a string containing the full name. If variable Name$ contains the value "A. Douglas Tower", you can write the last name as

```
Name$[Posr(Name$, " ") + 1 : Len(Name$)]
```

The Ucase$ and Lcase$ Functions

The string function Ucase$(Phrase$) converts any lowercase letters in Phrase$ to uppercase letters. Lcase$(Phrase$) does just the opposite, changing uppercase letters to lowercase. No other characters in Phrase$ are affected. Examples are

```
Ucase$("Bill Jones, Jr.") is BILL JONES, JR.
Lcase$("Bill Jones, Jr.") is bill jones, jr.
```

The Lcase$ or Ucase$ function is often used when you wish to compare two strings for equality without regard for whether the characters are lowercase or uppercase. Here is a program that asks a user to enter a name and compares that name with names in a list:

```
! Example Program 5-6
! Compare two names to see if they are the same.

INPUT prompt "Enter your first name: ": Name$
LET Name$ = Ucase$(Name$)
LET Found$ = "false"
DO while More data and Found$ = "false"
   READ List$
   IF Name$ = Ucase$(List$) then LET Found$ = "true"
LOOP

IF Found$ = "true" then
   PRINT "Your name is on the list."
ELSE
   PRINT "Your name is not on the list."
END IF

DATA John, Mary, Rebecca, June, Peter, Ernst, Bill
END
```

An example of program output follows:

```
Enter your first name: Bill
Your name is on the list.
```

The entered name is stored in the variable Name$ and is changed to uppercase. As each name is read from the list, it is also changed to uppercase. Both strings have all alphabetic characters converted to uppercase before a comparison is made.

The variable Found$ is used to indicate whether a comparison was successful. I call this type of variable a *logical flag*; it can have one of only two possible values, true or false. The value of Found$ is initially set to "false" and is changed to "true" if the comparison was successful. The program checks at the beginning of the loop and exits if there is no more data or if the value of Found$ is "true", meaning that the last comparison was successful.

The last part of the program is a branch structure. It prints an appropriate message depending on the value of Found$. Note that the list of names could have been stored in a text file instead of a DATA statement.

The Repeat$ and Trim$ Functions

Another string function, Repeat$(Char$, N), returns the string Char$ repeated N times. For example, the statement

```
PRINT Repeat$("*", 20)
```

displays a line of asterisks, as shown.

```
********************
```

The string function Trim$(A$) removes all leading and trailing blanks from the string argument A$. For example, strings used to store names in files are sometimes padded with blanks to make all name strings the same length. If Name$ contains the string "Jane Lively   " with 9 trailing blanks added to increase its length to 20 characters, then the statement

```
PRINT Trim$(Name$)
```

removes the trailing blanks and displays the string "Jane Lively." These two strings may look the same on the screen but they are, of course, different and not equal to each other. If you are not sure whether a string contains leading or trailing blanks, it does no harm to use the Trim$ function.

5.7 CONVERSION FUNCTIONS

These functions return values that have the effect of converting a character to its ASCII value and vice versa, and also of converting a numeric value to the corresponding string value and vice versa. Let's start with a short discussion of binary notation which is needed to explain the ASCII character set.

Binary Notation

Computers use binary arithmetic for storing numbers in memory. The smallest unit in the binary system is the bit which has a value of 0 or 1. A byte consists of eight bits and can store an integer or whole number between 0 and 255. In True BASIC, eight bytes of computer memory are used to store the value of a numeric variable in binary form.

The ASCII Character Set

Since computers can store only numbers, some sort of numeric code is needed to store characters. The usual choice is ASCII, an acronym for American Standard Code for Information Interchange. The standard ASCII character set can represent 128 characters with numeric values from 0 to 127. Each character in a string variable is stored in ASCII code in a byte of memory. Appendix C contains a table of the ASCII characters with their numeric values.

Here are some examples of ASCII values:

```
ASCII value of "A" is 65
ASCII value of "a" is 97
ASCII value of "+" is 43
ASCII value of a space is 32
```

Many computers have an additional 128 characters added to their character set with numeric code values from 128 to 255, part of the extended ASCII character set. The extended characters may consist of foreign letters, mathematical symbols, musical notes, and so forth. These additional 128 characters vary from one type of computer to another. All eight bits in a byte are used to represent the extended set of 256 characters.

The Ord and Chr$ Functions

The Ord(A$) function returns a numeric value equal to the ASCII code of the single-character string A$. A string with only one character is allowed — a longer string produces an error when the program is run.

The Chr$(X) function returns a single-character string value. This value is the ASCII character whose numeric code is X. The variable X must have a value between 0 and 255. Examples are

```
Ord("A") is 65
Chr$(66) is B
Chr$(90) is Z
```

Here is an example program that uses the Ord function to determine whether an entered character is an uppercase alphabetic character:

```
! Example Program 5-7
! Check a single character to see
! if it is uppercase alphabetic.

DO
   PRINT
   INPUT prompt "Enter a character: ": Char$
   IF Len(Char$) > 1 then
      PRINT "Only one character, please."
   END IF
LOOP until Len(Char$) = 1

IF Ord(Char$) < 65 or Ord(Char$) > 90 then
   PRINT "Not an uppercase alphabetic character."
ELSE
   PRINT "This is a valid character."
END IF
END
```

The program asks a user to enter a character and refuses to accept more than a single character. It then checks to see whether the ASCII value of the character is within the range of uppercase alphabetic characters and prints an appropriate message. User interaction with the program might look as follows in two separate runs:

```
Enter a character: QQ
Only one character, please.
Enter a character: q
Not an uppercase alphabetic character

Enter a character: Q
This is a valid character.
```

The Val and Str$ Functions

The Val(A$) function returns a numeric value equal to the number represented by the digit characters in A$. The string variable A$ may contain digits, a decimal point, plus and minus signs, and the letter E or e. If it contains any other characters or if the characters it contains do not represent a number, an error will result when the program is run.

The Str$(X) function returns a string whose characters are the same as those in the number X. Examples are

```
Val("123") is the number 123
Str$(123) is the string "123"
Val("-1.2E+5") is the number -120,000
```

Remember that numbers and strings are stored in computer memory using different coding techniques. The number 123 and the string "123" are not the same quantities and are not stored in memory in the same manner.

It is sometimes convenient to enter a number as a string and then convert it to numeric form. If a user is asked to enter a number, but enters some other characters, the program stops with an error message. A well-designed program should not stop, but rather should tell the user what error has occurred and ask for input again. Entering a number as a string makes it easier to check for errors because any sequence of characters can be entered into a string variable.

Our example is a simple version of a general numeric input program. A number is entered into a string variable named Entry$, and the program checks each character, accepting any digit, the decimal point, the plus and minus signs, and the letters "E" and "e." Any other character is rejected, and the user is asked to enter the entire string again. When a valid entry has been made, it is converted to a number using the Val function.

```
! Example Program 5-8
! Allow any sequence of characters to be entered after
! a prompt and check for the entry of a valid number.

DO
    LINE INPUT prompt "Enter number: ": Entry$
    LET Valid$ = "true" ! flag for valid number
    FOR Index = 1 to Len(Entry$)
        LET Char$ = Entry$[Index:Index]
        SELECT CASE Char$
        CASE "0" to "9", ".", "+", "-", "E", "e"
            ! no action needed
        CASE else
            PRINT "Character '"; Char$; "' not allowed"
            LET Valid$ = "false"  ! invalid number
        END SELECT
    NEXT Index
LOOP until Valid$ = "true"

LET Number = Val(Entry$)
PRINT "Entry is a valid number equal to"; Number
END
```

The CASE statement to used to check the validity of each character. If the character is not valid, the CASE ELSE branch is used to display an error message and set a flag so that another number is requested. User interaction with the program might look as follows:

```
Enter number: A23B
Character 'A' not allowed
Character 'B' not allowed
Enter number: 123E+2
Entry is a valid number equal to 12300
```

Note that this program as written will accept some strings that are not valid numbers, such as "eee" or "E-E+E", and then the Val function will fail. You might try to write a better program that will reject any invalid number. One method is to use error trapping, as discussed in Chapter 6.

5.8   PRINT AND KEYBOARD FUNCTIONS

This section introduces a function used to modify PRINT statements and a logical test or function used to detect keyboard input. Several new statements used with input or output operations are also discussed.

The Tab Function

The Tab(X) print function allows some additional format control in the PRINT statement. It is not an ordinary function because it does not return a value, but rather changes the location where the next expression in the PRINT statement is displayed. It can only be used in a PRINT statement.

Tab(X) moves the cursor to column X before the next expression is displayed. The left-hand column on the screen is column 1 and the right-hand column is usually column 80. Semicolons are used to separate this function from its neighboring expressions.

The statement

```
PRINT "A"; Tab(4); "B"; Tab(20); "XYZ"
```

displays characters spaced as shown in the following line:

```
A  B               XYZ
```

The Tab function is particularly useful when you use PRINT statements to display a table of values, as shown in the following program:

```
! Example Program 5-9
! Display a table with column headings.

PRINT "Part Number"; Tab(30); "Quantity on Hand"
PRINT
DO while More data
   READ Part, Quantity
   PRINT Tab(2); Part; Tab(36); Quantity
LOOP

DATA 131516,10,132133,25,136815,11,137442,87
END
```

This program produces the following table:

```
Part Number                Quantity on Hand

    131516                         10
    132133                         25
    136815                         11
    137442                         87
```

Note that the Tab function does not directly control the space between displayed items. Instead, it controls the location of the item immediately following the Tab function, specifying in which column that item is displayed.

The CLEAR, SOUND, and PAUSE Statements

Here are three simple statements that you will use in future programs. The statement

```
CLEAR
```

clears the screen and changes the entire screen to an output window for displaying program results. After the program has executed, the output window remains displayed until any key (or the mouse button) is pressed, at which point the normal True BASIC screen is immediately displayed again. The behavior is slightly different on a Mac when a separate output window has been opened; I suggest you try it yourself.

The statement

```
SOUND Freq, Length
```

generates a tone of frequency Freq hertz (cycles per second) and of duration Length seconds. The statement

```
PAUSE Length
```

suspends program execution for a time of Length seconds.

All three statements are useful in special situations and you should know about their existence.

The Key Input Test

The test phrase Key Input is a logical test, returning a value of true if the user has pressed a key since the last time the program read input from the keyboard. This kind of test phrase is sometimes called a *logical function* because it can have a value of only true or false.

Here is a sample program that shows how the Key Input test works. The screen is cleared, a message is displayed, and it remains displayed while the program waits in a small loop until any key is pressed. When the key is pressed, the cursor returns to the editing window, in most cases erasing the message.

```
! Example Program 5-10
! Clear the screen and display a message
! until any key is pressed.

CLEAR
PRINT
PRINT Tab(20); "Press key to return to editing window."
DO until Key Input
LOOP
END
```

You should run the program itself to see how it behaves.

Another program uses the Key Input test to turn off the computer's buzzer — actually a loudspeaker that produces a tone. These program statements could be used as part of a larger program where the computer is performing some long calculation. When the calculation is finished, the buzzer attracts the user's attention and is turned off by pressing any key.

The program generates a tone of frequency 1000 hertz and duration 0.5 seconds. After generating the tone, it waits 1 second before repeating the process. The process continues until any key is pressed.

```
! Example Program 5-11
! Sound a tone on the computer loudspeaker
! until any key is pressed.

PRINT "Press any key to turn off the sound."
DO until Key Input
```

```
    SOUND 1000, 0.5
    PAUSE 1
LOOP
END
```

When the program is run, a tone is sounded and the following sentence is displayed:

```
Press any key to turn off the sound.
```

Run the program yourself to hear how it works.

The GET KEY Statement

The keyboard input statement

```
GET KEY Variable
```

serves a similar purpose. It waits for a key to be pressed and then assigns a numeric value to Variable, corresponding to the ASCII value of the character produced by the key. If the particular key that is pressed does not produce an ASCII character (for example, one of the function keys on a PC keyboard), a number outside the ASCII range of values is assigned.

Here is a simple program that waits until a key is pressed and then prints the ASCII (or other numeric) value of that key:

```
! Example program 5-12
! Use the GET KEY statement that shows
! the numeric value assigned to any key.

PRINT "Please press any key."
GET KEY Value
PRINT "The pressed key [";
PRINT Chr$(Value);
PRINT "] has a value of"; Value
END
```

This program produces the following output when the x key is pressed:

```
Please press any key.
The pressed key [x] has a value of 122
```

You can use this example program to determine what value is returned by the GET KEY statement for any specific key on your particular keyboard.

When you run Example Program 5-11, you may notice that the character you pressed to stop the sound appears right after the next Ok prompt. The Key Input test accepts a character if a printing character key is pressed, and this character is then displayed if a PRINT statement is executed or if not, as soon as the program ends.

You can correct the problem by using the GET KEY statement to "gobble up" this unwanted character and assign it to a dummy variable. Here is a revised and better version of Example Program 5-11:

```
! Example Program 5-13
! A better Key Input test program.

PRINT "Press any key to turn off the sound."
DO until Key Input
   SOUND 1000, 0.5
   PAUSE 1
LOOP
GET KEY Dummy
END
```

The character entered to stop the program is stored in the variable Dummy (it is not displayed) and then the program ends. Program output is the same as before.

5.9 THE DEF FN STATEMENT

Both ANS BASIC and True BASIC allow the user to define a single-line function using the DEF FN statement. In most cases, a function procedure (as discussed in Chapter 7) is preferable but there are times when the DEF FN statement is useful.

Consider a financial program that often needs to calculate the future value of a principal sum where the interest is compounded annually and added to the principal. A statement like

```
DEF FNFutureValue (P, I, N) = P * ((1 + I / 100) ^ N)
```

defines a single-line function that calculates the future value of P dollars invested for N years at an interest rate of I percent. Note that the function name must start with the letters FN. This defining statement must be placed near the beginning of the program, preceding the first call to function FNFutureValue.

Here is an example program that prompts the user to enter information on principal, interest, and length of time. It displays the future value of the investment.

```
! Example Program 5-14
! Ask the user to enter the principal sum,
! interest rate, and length of investment.
! Display the future value of this sum at
! the end of the investment period.
! Future value must be less than $1,000,000.
```

```
DEF FNFutureValue (P, I, N) = P * ((1 + I / 100) ^ N)
INPUT prompt "Principal sum in dollars? ": P
INPUT prompt "Rate of interest in percent? ": I
INPUT prompt "Investment time in years": N
PRINT "The future value is ";
PRINT USING "#######.##": FNFutureValue(P, I, N);
PRINT "dollars"
END
```

This program displays the following results:

```
Principal sum in dollars? 1000
Rate of interest in percent? 11.5
Investment time in years? 7
The future value is    2142.52 dollars
```

5.10   DESIGN OF A COMPUTER PROGRAM

The recommended steps for creating a computer program start with a general, written outline of the program, refine the outline as needed to make it more specific, and only at that point start to write program statements. This is the same method used by good writers when designing a book or article. If you start from a general program outline, you are more likely to avoid logical errors and produce a program whose component parts all work together properly.

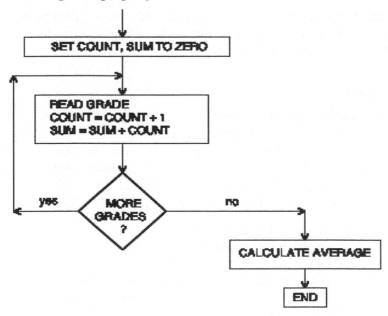

Figure 5.2 *Part of a computer program flowchart.*

I recommend that you write the outline of your program on paper, as a sequence of steps. These outline steps are often called *pseudocode* statements. If any of the steps in your outline are long or complicated, write out a secondary outline of these steps. After carefully reviewing the outline, start writing the program statements that will accomplish the steps you have written down.

It is important to write the program outline on paper, not just create it in your mind. If your program is of any size (say, over 20 statements in length), there is too much chance of forgetting some point in the outline if it is not written.

Pseudocode versus Flowcharts

Many older textbooks on computer programming advise students to draw flowcharts rather than write program outlines. A *flowchart* is a diagram that shows how a computer program works, using boxes and arrows as symbols for such actions as looping, branching, and I/O (input and output) operations (see Fig. 5.2). The symbols are joined by lines showing the flow of program control.

My experience is that flowcharts are not needed to explain small programs, and they become too complicated and difficult to draw for large programs. In both cases, it is questionable whether the benefit is worth the extra work. It is a fact that in many commercial programming operations, flowcharts are used primarily to document large programs and are drawn after the program has been completed.

On the other hand, I find that program outlines in pseudocode are easy to write — once you understand the problem — and provide invaluable guidance during program development. I strongly recommend their use.

Program Outline

Let's look at an example of program design and development. Consider a relatively simple problem, to compute the average of a student's grades. Every student in the class is identified by a number. Assume there are fewer than 100 students in the class and that a separate grade file exists for each student. The grades for the ninth student in the class are stored in a text file named GRADES09.DAT, one grade per line. Before computing a student's average grade, you want to drop his or her lowest grade.

```
ask for student number and open grade file
initialize the variables for sum and count
top of loop; exit loop if there are no more grades
              read a grade value into the grade variable
              save this grade value if it is the lowest so far
              increment the count of grades
              add the new grade value to the sum of grades
```

bottom of loop
subtract the lowest grade from the sum and reduce the count by one
calculate and print the average grade
end the program

First Version of Program

Here is the first version of your program. It calculates the average grade after dropping the lowest grade. A counting variable Count and a summing variable Sum are used. Add a variable Lowest to hold the lowest grade. This variable is initialized to 100, the highest possible grade value. As each grade is read, it is compared to the current value of Lowest and if the new grade is lower (smaller), it is stored in Lowest as the current lowest value.

```
! Example Program 5-15
! Ask user to specify the number of a student, and
! average the grades of that student while dropping
! the lowest grade.

INPUT prompt "Enter student number: ": Number$
IF Val(Number$) < 10 then LET Number$ = "0" & Number$
LET FileName$ = "GRADES" & Number$ & ".DAT"
OPEN #1: name FileName$
LET Count = 0
LET Sum = 0
LET Lowest = 100
DO until End #1
   INPUT #1: Grade
   IF Grade < Lowest then LET Lowest = Grade
   LET Count = Count + 1
   LET Sum = Sum + Grade
LOOP
LET Count = Count - 1  ! adjust for drop
LET Sum = Sum - Lowest
LET Average = Round(Sum/Count)
PRINT "Average grade is"; Average
END
```

The first three lines of the program ask the user to enter a student number, add a leading zero if the number is a single digit, and generate the name of the grade file. This file is then read, keeping track of the lowest grade. After all grades have been read, you adjust the sum by subtracting the lowest grade and reduce the number of grades to be averaged by one. It is then a simple matter to calculate the average by dividing the sum of the grades by the number of grades. Use the Round function to convert your answer to the nearest integer. This program displays the following output:

```
Enter student number: 17
Average grade is 90
```

Second Version of Program

The first version of this program always deletes a student's lowest grade. There may be times, however, when the instructor wants an average of all grades. A better version of the program would make deletion of the lowest grade an option.

You can assume that there are fewer than 100 students in the class so that the file name will not exceed eight characters in length. Whenever possible, a computer program should not have to rely on such an assumption because if the assumption is not satisfied, the program may fail. In this case, however, it is a reasonable assumption. An additional section of code is included to check the student number.

This version of the program checks the student number and makes deletion of the lowest grade an option.

```
! Example Program 5-16
! Ask user to specify the number of a student, and
! average the grades of that student.Provide an option
! for dropping the lowest grade. Check the size of the
! student number.

DO
    INPUT prompt "Enter student number: ": Number$
    IF Val(Number$) >= 100 then
        PRINT "Student number cannot exceed 99,"
        PRINT "please enter another number."
    END IF
LOOP while Val(Number$) >= 100

IF Val(Number$) < 10 then LET Number$ = "0" & Number$
LET FileName$ = "GRADES" & Number$ & ".DAT"
OPEN #1: name FileName$
LET Count = 0
LET Sum = 0
LET Lowest = 100
DO until End #1
    INPUT #1: Grade
    LET Lowest = Min(Grade, Lowest)
    LET Count = Count + 1
    LET Sum = Sum + Grade
LOOP

DO
```

```
      INPUT prompt "Drop lowest grade (Y/N)? ": Ans$
      LET Ans$ = Ucase$(Ans$[1:1])
      IF Ans$ <> "Y" and Ans$ <> "N" then
         PRINT "Answer yes or no."
      END IF
   LOOP until Ans$ = "Y" or Ans$ = "N"
   IF Ans$ = "Y" then  ! adjust for drop
      LET Count = Count - 1
      LET Sum = Sum - Lowest
   END IF

   LET Average = Round(Sum/Count)
   PRINT "Average grade is"; Average
   END
```

Here is an example of user interaction with the program:

```
Enter student number: 107
Student number cannot exceed 99,
please enter another number.
Enter student number: 17
Drop lowest grade (Y/N)? yes
Average grade is 90
```

Only two grade files are available on the Example Program disk, the files for student 9 and for student 17. Thus this program will not run if any other student number is entered. A small loop checks the entered number to be sure it does not exceed 99. If the student number is too large, an error message is printed and the user is asked to enter another number.

The lowest grade is selected using the Min function while the grades are read and this grade is stored in the variable Lowest. Another loop asks the user if the lowest grade should be dropped. The answer must be a word beginning with Y or N, in uppercase or lowercase. Any other answer is considered incorrect, and the question is asked again. This checking of an answer is good programming practice because it reduces the possibility of the program misunderstanding a user's response. If the answer is "yes", the lowest grade is dropped.

Program Testing

After a program has been designed and written, and any errors removed so that it compiles successfully, it must be tested. The first test is to see if it produces reasonable results in the expected format. Further tests are run to determine (1) if the results are accurate, (2) if the program runs without error for a wide range of input data, and (3) if the output format agrees exactly with the design specifications. **Program testing is an important and necessary part of program development.**

In this case, test for a student number of -2, 0, 1, 10, 99, or 100. Create a test file that has grades of 0, -1, 50, 100, and 105. These may not be realistic grades but it is possible that a student has done so well that her teacher has given her a 5 point bonus. How is your program going to handle that? Maybe a student has done so poorly that the teacher has given him a grade of 0 for his work and then taken off 10 points for a sloppy paper. If a grade of -10 is dropped, what affect does that have on the average grade? Use your own imagination to create and apply other tests.

As you can imagine, thoroughly testing a program is a long and sometimes tedious process. You may find errors in design that must be corrected and, more often, you will find small ways to improve the performance, clarity, or stability of the program. Don't skimp on the testing; it is one of the most important steps in program development. As I may have mentioned earlier, testing a commercial program may take more time than writing the program.

Summary of Important Points

- You cannot take the square root of a negative number.

- Division by zero is not allowed in any arithmetic expression.

- The radian is the default unit of angular measure in trigonometric functions.

- A blank space is a valid character in a string.

- If you use the Key Input function to stop a program, follow it with a statement such as GET KEY Dummy to remove the entered character.

- You should write out a program outline before starting to write program statements.

- Program testing is one of the most important and necessary parts of program development, and is often overlooked by beginning programmers.

Common Errors

- Confusing the results produced by the functions Int(X) and Round(X) when X is a negative number.

- Using the function Mod(X, Y) when Y has a value of zero, resulting in an attempt to divide by zero and a run-time error.

- Forgetting that the default unit for arguments of trigonometric functions is the radian, not the degree.

- Failing to include a RANDOMIZE statement in the final version of a program that uses the Rnd function.

- Using incorrect syntax for the Pos function by reversing the order of the Target$ and Pattern$ arguments.

- Using the Val function with a string argument containing characters that are not allowed in a number.

- Trying to use a function named Spc that does not exist in True BASIC to create a space in a PRINT statement.

- Failing to use a GET KEY statement to gobble up the entered character after executing a loop controlled by the Key Input function. See Example Program 5-13.

- Placing an END IF statement at the end of a single-line DEF FN statement.

- Starting to write program statements before writing a program outline.

- Failing to thoroughly test a newly written computer program; a common mistake made by beginning programmers.

Self-Test Questions

1.   Given the function Sqr(9), what is
   - (a)   the argument?
   - (b)   the value of the function?

2.   What is the value of Abs(-12)?

3.   What is the value of each of the following functions?
   - (a)   `Round(7.32)`
   - (b)   `Truncate(7.32, 0)`
   - (c)   `Round(12.85, 1)`
   - (d)   `Truncate(12.85, 1)`

4.   Under what conditions might you get unexpected results from the Round function?

5.   What happens when you ask the computer to calculate Sqr(-9)?

6.   What is the value of Mod(Num, 2) if the variable Num contains
   - (a)   an even number?
   - (b)   an odd number?

7.   What is the value of Max(100,101)?

8.   Which is the default unit for measuring angles?
   - (a)   the degree
   - (b)   the radian

9.   What statement is used to specify that angles will be measured in
   - (a)   radians?
   - (b)   degrees?

10.   What statement should be included in a program to prevent the Rnd function from always producing the same sequence of random numbers?

11.   What is the value of Len("Good try")?

12.   Assume that you have a string variable Line$ with a value such as "10,5,Duke", where the first number is games won, the second is games lost, and the third is the name of the team. How do you calculate the value of a variable X representing the position of the first comma?

13. Using the string whose format is given in Question 12, how do you calculate the value of a variable Y representing the position of the second comma? You can assume that the value of X has already been calculated.

14. Assuming you have calculated the value of Y in Question 13, write a substring of Line$ that contains the team name.

15. If the variable Reply$ contains the answer to a prompt, how do you construct a substring containing only the first letter, in uppercase, of the value of Reply$?

16. What logical expression can you use to compare the values of Name1$ and Name2$, where the names are considered equal if they contain the same sequence of letters, either lowercase or uppercase?

17. What logical expression can you use to compare the values of Name1$ and Name2$, disregarding leading and trailing blanks?

18. If the value of Ord("A") is 65, what is the value of Chr$(65)?

19. In computer usage, what is
    (a) a bit?
    (b) a byte?

20. A number is entered into a string variable Number$. How do you convert the value of Number$ to a numeric value and assign it to a variable Number?

21. Why might a program be designed so that numbers are entered into string variables rather than into numeric variables?

22. Can the Tab function be used in any statement other than the PRINT statement? If so, which statement?

23. What are the allowed values of the function Key Input?

24. What value is assigned to the variable KeyValue in the statement

    ```
    GET KEY KeyValue
    ```

    when the shift key is held down and the A key is pressed?

25. What is one of the important things you should do before you start writing a computer program?

Practice Programs

1. Ask a user for a positive or negative number and display it rounded to the nearest integer. If 11.5 is entered, 12 should be displayed. If -6.7 is entered, -7 should be displayed.

    Test your program using the numbers 11.5, -6.7, 3.95, 9.11, and -3.95.

2. Ask a user to enter a date in the MM-DD-YY format. The month and the day may be specified by single digits, that is, by 1-5-85 rather than by 01-05-85. Separate the numbers representing the month, day, and year, and display each number on the screen with an appropriate label. Remember that the system variables Date and Date$ are reserved words.

    Test your program using the dates 11-15-85, 12-08-86, 11-7-83, and 3-1-09.

3. Ask a user to enter a date in the MM-DD-YY format (see note in Practice Program 2). Display the date in a format with the month named, that is, May 25, 1981. Assume the date is in the twentieth century. The month names may be read from DATA statements.

    Test your program using the same dates as in Practice Program 2.

4. Ask a user to enter a time period expressed in seconds and display the same time period in hours, minutes, and seconds. Remember that the system variables Time and Time$ are reserved words. Consider using the Mod function.

    Test your program using times of 136, 9192, and 18456 seconds.

5. Ask a user to enter a number from the keyboard. If the number is zero, display the word ZERO; if it is positive, display the word POSITIVE; if it is negative, display the word NEGATIVE.

    Test your program using the numbers 12, -2, 0, and 199.

6. Ask a user to enter a number between 1 and 5 inclusive. Your program should allow the user to enter any sequence of characters. Check the input, and if it is longer than one character, is not numeric, or is not in the proper range, display an error message that describes the specific error. If the input is not correct, ask the user to try again.

Test your program using the numbers 0, 1, 4, 5, and 8, also the characters Z, #3, and A1A.

7. A palindrome is a sequence of characters that reads the same backward and forward. Punctuation marks and spaces are ignored. No distinction is made between lowercase and uppercase letters. An example palindrome is the following string: "Name no one man." Ask the user to enter a string and determine if this string is a palindrome.

    Test your program using the following string values:
    ```
    Hannah
    winchester
    Madam, I'm Adam
    ```

8. Ask a user to enter a string containing only uppercase letters. Examine the value of each key as it is pressed. Display each uppercase letter as it is entered and ignore anything else. Pressing the Return key terminates the input process. Assign the entered string of uppercase letters to a string variable named Entry$.

    Test your program using the following string values:
    ```
    SUBROUTINE
    New York
    HDK-468
    ```

9. Ask a user to enter a dollar amount that may contain a dollar sign and one or more commas. For example, the entry might be $12,575.50. Assume that the entry will not be in exponential notation. Ignore — that is, pass over — any characters that are not digits or a decimal point or a plus or minus sign. The program should ask the user to try again if the number contains more than one decimal point or more than one plus or minus sign. Store the number in a numeric variable named Amount and display it on the screen.

    Test your program using the following values:
    ```
    $12,575.50
    +125
    +-555
    $12.575.50
    ```

10. A user enters an address on one line in the format

     CITY, STATE ZIP

where STATE is a two-letter abbreviation and ZIP is a five-digit number. CITY may contain one or more words (such as Chicago or Salt Lake City). Your program should check whether the entered value for ZIP is a five-digit number and the value for STATE is a two-letter string. If an error is made in input, the program should loop and let the user try again.

Extract the zip code and assign it to a numeric variable named Zip. Display this zip code value with an appropriate label.

Test your program using the following string values:

     San Francisco, CA 94101
     Boston, MA 021095
     Worcester, 99 01601
     West Menlo Park, CAL 95691

CHAPTER
6

Finding and Correcting Errors

6.1 INTRODUCTION

A large fraction of the time spent developing a computer program is devoted to finding and eliminating errors. Several techniques for helping you find errors, including the Do Trace command, are discussed. You also learn about a program structure for trapping and handling errors.

In addition to learning how to find errors, it is important to learn how to write programs that contain few errors. I present a procedure for writing computer programs that are likely to run correctly the first time they are executed. A recommended program style is also discussed.

6.2 DEBUGGING PROGRAMS

Your goal is to write programs that contain no errors. It is probably an impossible goal to attain, but you need to learn how to reduce the number of errors to a minimum. At the same time, you must develop skill in finding errors and then removing them from your programs. This process is called *debugging*.

Playing Computer

One of the best methods for finding errors is to read through a computer program, pretending that you are the computer. You make all the calculations and decisions that would normally be made by the computer. Many simple errors will be revealed.

This method is easy to understand and to apply but it can be tedious. You will find it most useful for examining small sections of a program. In fact, it is the method we all use instinctively when a program does not run. You will make better progress if you write down intermediate results on paper, in a systematic format. If complicated arithmetic calculations are involved, progress can be slow and you should use a hand calculator.

In spite of the limitations, I recommend that you try this method first. It is a natural way to find errors if a program is not working properly.

Temporary PRINT Statements

Beginning programmers often say, "I know that the value of variable X at this point in the program is 15.2, but when I make a calculation using X and print the results, they are wrong." My response is, "How do you know that the value of X is 15.2?"

One way to answer the question is to put a temporary PRINT statement in your program and see what the value of X actually is at the point of calculation. It is surprising how often it is different from what you thought it should be.

It is not unusual to insert half a dozen temporary PRINT statements in a program before finding an error. Sometimes it is helpful to include a label in the PRINT statement to help identify its location.

For example, the statement

```
PRINT "In Report section: X ="; X
```

identifies the variable being displayed and the program section where it has this value. A single PRINT statement can also be used to print out the values of several different variables, as shown in the following statement.

```
PRINT "After first search: I, Sum = "; I; Sum
```

You must, of course, remember to delete these temporary PRINT statements after you have found the error.

A good way to help you find temporary statements is to place a comment such as ! TEMP at the end of each statement. The two example statements then look as follows:

```
PRINT "In Report section: X ="; X            ! TEMP
PRINT "After first search: I,Sum = ";I; Sum  ! TEMP
```

In many cases, these two techniques, playing computer and inserting temporary PRINT statements, are sufficient to identify programming errors.

The Do Trace Command

True BASIC now has a powerful debugging capability available in the Do Trace command. **I recommend strongly that you learn how to use this command.** It allows you to execute a program, statement by statement in slow motion, displaying the values of selected variables. The program is displayed in one window, selected variable values are displayed in another window called the *variables window*, and program output appears in a third window called the *output window*. You can select up to eight variables and monitor their current values as the program executes.

The Do Trace command must be able to read three files named TRACE.TRU, TRACE2.TRC, and TRACE3.TRC. These files are compiled True BASIC program files and should be in the current directory of your current disk. If you have sufficient memory in your computer, you can load TRACE2.TRC and TRACE3.TRC into memory and the Do Trace command executes with much less delay. The proper command for loading these files at the Ok. prompt is

```
Ok. Load TRACE2.TRC, TRACE3.TRC
```

If you need to release the memory occupied by these files at a later time, use the following Forget command:

```
Ok. Forget
```

The Command window is always visible on a PC screen, but not necessarily on a Macintosh screen. If you are using a Mac, select the Command item from the Windows menu and a command window with the Ok. prompt appears.

If the three required files are not in the current directory of the current disk, you must tell True BASIC where they can be found. The Alias command performs this function. In response to the Ok. prompt, enter the command

```
Ok. Alias do, pathname
```

where "pathname" specifies the path name of the required files. For example, if the trace files are in the directory TBDO under the directory TBASIC on the C disk of a DOS system, the proper command is

```
Ok. Alias do, C:\TBASIC\TBDO\
```

The same command is available on a Mac but the path name syntax is slightly different. See the *User's Guide* for your particular computer for further information.

I should mention one possible point of confusion. All three trace files are compiled files, but in the software shipped by True BASIC, Inc., they have different extensions as noted previously. If the names of the file extensions for TRACE2 and TRACE3 have been changed in the software you are using, the Load command must also be changed accordingly.

Returning to the Do Trace command itself, the proper syntax is

```
Ok. Do Trace, option (variables)
```

The argument *option* may be one of four choices: "step", "slow", "fast", or "break." I recommend that you use the option "step" which executes a program statement each time the space bar is pressed. This is the most convenient option for small and medium-sized programs. The other options are discussed in the *True BASIC Reference Manual*.

The argument *variables* is a list of program variables separated from one another by commas. As mentioned previously, up to eight different variables can be selected.

The technique for using the Do Trace command is simple. If you are writing a program and plan to use this command frequently, load the required trace files into memory. Enter the command from the command line, even if you are using a Mac or a PC with a mouse. Specify an option of "step." Select the variables whose values you want to watch. For example, your program might be using a FOR loop — with counter variable Index — to read information from a file into a variable named Entry$. The appropriate Do Trace command then might look as follows:

```
Ok. Do Trace, step (Index, Entry$)
```

The variable names Index and Entry$ are placed in the variables window and you can watch their displayed values change. At the same time, program output appears in the output window.

It is possible to execute the Do Trace command on a Mac or a PC with a mouse by selecting it from the Options menu. **If you select the command in this manner, however, you cannot place any variable names in the variables window.** I recommend that you always execute Do Trace from the command line.

6.3   OTHER FUNCTION KEY AND MENU COMMANDS

Before discussing the next method for finding errors, you must learn how to mark text. This is accomplished with the F4 function key on a PC keyboard. Remember that you have already used three of the function keys, the F1 key, and the F2 key, which move the cursor between the command window and the program window, and the F10 key, which is the Help key. All the remaining function keys, F3 through F9, are now discussed.

The standard keyboard for the Mac has no function keys. The Apple Extended keyboard, however, has a full set of function keys. These keys are not supported directly by True BASIC but may be supported in the future by an Apple desk accessory program. Check the *Macintosh User's Guide* for the latest information.

If you are using a Mac or a PC with a mouse, you may want to invoke these "function key commands" from one of the pull-down command menus or by using a shortcut key. The appropriate command or shortcut key is described in each case.

The Find Key

The F3 key is the Find key, used to find words or sequences of characters in your program. When you move the cursor to the editing window and press this key, the prompt

"Find:" is displayed in the command window. If you are trying to find a particular word, type in that word and press the Return key. The cursor moves to the first occurrence of the word in your program. If you want to search for the next occurrence of the word, just press the F3 key and then the Return key again. If the word you specify cannot be found, the message "Not found." is displayed.

Search always starts from the position of the cursor in the editing window when you pressed F3. If you want to start searching at the beginning of your program, move the cursor there by pressing the Home key before pressing the F3 key. This search for words is insensitive to uppercase or lowercase. If you ask the computer to find the target word *BOX*, both *BOX* and *box* are considered to match the target.

If you want to find a sequence of characters rather than a complete word, you must enclose the sequence in quotation marks. Thus if you ask to find the sequence *"box"*, the words *box* and *boxer* are both matches. The word *BOX*, however, is not a match, because when characters are enclosed in quotation marks, the search is sensitive to uppercase or lowercase.

You can search for a word or sequence of characters on a Mac by using the Find command in the Edit menu. The Find Again command allows further searches, while the Change command allows searching for test and changing the text that is found. These three commands are also available on a PC using a mouse — that is, using version 3 of True BASIC.

On a Mac, the shortcut key for the Find command is Cmd-F, for Find Again it is Cmd-G, and for Change it is Cmd-E. The equivalent keys on a PC with mouse support are Alt-F, Alt-G, and Alt-E. When entering shortcut key commands, the Cmd or Apple key on a Mac is equivalent to the Alt key on a PC.

The Mark Key

The F4 key is used to mark blocks of text that may later be moved, copied, or deleted. A marked block consists of one or more program lines. Use the arrow keys to place the cursor over the line tag of the first line to be included in the marked block and press the F4 key. Then use the down-arrow key to move the cursor to the last line to be included in the marked block and press the F4 key again. You will notice that the line tags of all lines in the marked block are now displayed in inverse mode. To mark a single line, just press the F4 key once while the cursor is over the line tag of that line.

Only one block of program lines can be marked at a time. If you have marked the wrong block or change your mind, you can erase the marking on the block by pressing the F4 key again. You can then use the same key to mark another block. Experiment with the F4 key until you are familiar with the way it works.

On a computer using a mouse, **you cannot move the cursor over a line tag by dragging.** You can, however, drag the mouse over a selection of text to mark it. You can mark part of a single program statement or several program lines. If you make a mistake in marking, just move the mouse cursor off the marked area and click the mouse — all marking will disappear. Note that there are no line tags on a Mac, but they are seldom missed because most editing is done with a mouse.

The Delete and Move Keys

A marked block of text can be deleted by pressing the Del key when the cursor is on the line tag of one of the marked lines. A marked block can be moved to a new position in your program, being inserted right after another program line. Place the cursor on the line tag of this line where the block is to be inserted and press the F6 key. The marked block will be deleted from its old location and inserted in the new location. This editing action is not intuitive — be sure to try it yourself.

The Cut and Paste commands in the Edit menu are the equivalent commands on a system using a mouse. You might want to review the discussions in Sections 2.8 and 2.9 that describe editing with a mouse and pull-down menus. Remember that you must first mark the text that you wish to move or delete, and then use the Cut command to move the marked text to the clipboard. This action deletes the marked text from its current position. If you want to insert the removed text in a new location, move the text cursor to that location and select the Paste command.

The shortcut key Cmd-X or Alt-X is equivalent to the Cut command, while Cmd-V or Alt-V is equivalent to the Paste command.

The Copy Key

The F5 key copies a marked block from its current location and inserts it in a new position. It works just like the F6 key except the marked block is not deleted from its old location.

On a computer using a mouse, the Copy command in the Edit menu is used to copy a block of marked text. This command moves a copy of the marked text to the clipboard. A subsequent Paste command inserts the block of text at another location. The shortcut key for the Copy command is Cmd-C or Alt-C.

The Undelete Key

Another useful function key is the F7 key, which serves as the "undelete" key. If you have just deleted a character or a line or a block of lines, you can recover it by pressing the F7 key. Only the last item deleted can be recovered; all previously deleted items are lost. Thus if you use the Del key to delete several characters one by one, only the last character deleted will be restored. You will find the F7 key useful for restoring program lines that you delete by mistake.

There is no direct equivalent of the Undelete command on a Mac or PC using a mouse. On the other hand, if you follow the recommendation of using only the Cut command when deleting a block of text, that block is saved on the clipboard. Prior to executing another Cut or Copy command, you can always reinsert the text in its original location with the Paste command.

The Breakpoint Key

Function key F8 is pressed to set and release a breakpoint. You learn the use of breakpoints in the next section. On a Mac, select the Breakpoint command from the Run menu. I recommend that you don't try to set breakpoints from a pull-down menu on a PC using a mouse.

The Run Key

The F9 key is used to execute or run a program, producing the same results as the Run command. If you press the F9 key when the cursor is in the editing window, it moves automatically to the command window and the program is executed. This key is a convenient alternative to the Run command.

The equivalent command on a computer using a mouse is the Run command from the Run menu. The equivalent shortcut key is Cmd-R or Alt-R.

As mentioned earlier, a list of all function keys and command menus for both PC and Mac computers is in Appendix B.

6.4 STOP AND CONTINUE PROGRAM EXECUTION

Returning now to the discussion of how to find program errors, let's examine two special True BASIC commands, Break and Continue. This pair of commands provides a way to stop an executing program, examine variables and change their values, and then continue execution from that point in the program. The command Break tells the computer program to stop execution at the first line of a marked section of the program. This marked section can be, and often is, a single program line. The command Continue tells the program to continue execution from that point.

The Break Command

On a PC, use the F4 key or the mouse to mark a program line. With a line marked, use the F8 key to set a breakpoint or go to the command window and enter the command Break. You will notice that a small triangle appears next to the line tag, indicating that a breakpoint has been set at that line.

Now press the F9 key or type the command Run and the program will start executing. It will halt with the cursor in the editing window when the breakpoint line is reached. Use the F2 key to move back to the command window.

On a Mac, click on a line where you wish to set a breakpoint and select the Breakpoint command from the Run menu. A special mark (the double right-angle bracket) now marks the breakpoint line. The shortcut key for executing the Breakpoint command is Cmd-B. If the Command window is not already open, select Command from the Windows menu to open it.

Run the program and it will halt at the special mark before executing the breakpoint line. The cursor moves to the breakpoint line.

The reason I recommend not setting a breakpoint on a PC with a mouse is that you have to specify the line number. Most True BASIC programs don't have line numbers and counting lines in a large program is tedious and leads to errors. Set your breakpoints with the F8 key or from the command line.

Examining and Changing Variable Values

With the program halted, you can examine the value of any variable by using PRINT in the immediate or *direct mode* as a command. Direct mode means that you enter the statement on the command line in response to the True BASIC prompt. Here is an example, where the prompt Ok is displayed by the computer and the following command is entered by the user:

```
Ok. PRINT X, A$
```

The values of variables X and A$ are displayed on the screen.

You can also change the value of any variable by using the assignment statement in the direct mode as a command. For example, the statement

```
Ok. LET X = -16
```

assigns the value of -16 to the variable X.

A separate command is needed to change the value of each variable. **You may not enter a new program statement or modify an existing statement while the program is stopped.**

The Continue Command

When you have finished examining your program and possibly changing the values of some variables, enter the Continue command, and the program will resume execution. If you are using a mouse and pull-down menus, select the Continue command from the Run menu.

A breakpoint is removed by entering the Break command a second time with the breakpoint line selected. If a line on a PC still has "marked" status after removing a breakpoint, it can be released from this status by pressing the F4 key.

Using a breakpoint is a little more complicated than using a temporary PRINT statement or the Do Trace command, but it is inherently the most powerful way to debug your program. You should become familiar with all debugging methods and use whichever method seems most effective under the circumstances.

General Debugging Advice

A systematic approach is needed to successfully debug a program. First, read through your program carefully and see if you can spot an obvious error. Another person will often find program errors that you have not noticed. As you read your program, you will automatically start "playing computer" and ask yourself what the values of different variables should be.

If you still have errors, then start inserting PRINT statements or use the Do Trace command, whichever method you prefer. Don't hesitate to use lots of PRINT statements. When tracing, keep track of any variable that might conceivably be of interest. Once you have narrowed down the location of an error to a section of the program, probe in depth using breakpoints.

The art of program debugging can be learned only by experience. It can be time consuming and frustrating, but if you persist, you should be able to find and eliminate most program errors. After all, a program with errors isn't very useful!

6.5   CALCULATION ERRORS

Most calculation errors are due to errors of syntax or logic, but some are due to limitations of the computer or the language. These latter errors are hard to find and require some understanding of how your computer works. Let's look at two examples.

Finite Space for Number Storage

The first type of error occurs because of a finite and limited storage space for numeric variables. Referring to earlier terminology, the mailbox or memory space allocated for storing numeric variables can hold only a given number of digits. Any additional digits are lost.

True BASIC stores its numbers in an eight-byte format, providing a precision of about 14 digits. That precision is sufficient for most applications. There are occasions, however, when you need greater precision. Here is a sample program to show the type of problem that can arise when you manipulate numbers with too many digits:

```
! Example Program 6-1
! Test how True BASIC handles large numbers.

INPUT prompt "Enter a large number X...": X
PRINT "Value of (X + 1) - X is"; (X+1)-X
PRINT "Value of (X - X) + 1 is"; (X-X)+1
END
```

As you might expect, problems start to arise when the size of the entered number approaches the numeric variable precision. When you enter the value 5e15 for the variable X, you get the correct value of one for each answer:

```
Enter a large number X...5e15
Value of (X + 1) - X is 1
Value of (X - X) + 1 is 1
```

When you enter the value 5e16, the first PRINT statement displays an incorrect value of zero. The second PRINT statement displays the correct value of one:

```
Enter a large number X...5e16
Value of (X + 1) - X is 0
Value of (X - X) + 1 is 1
```

You can also make an argument that the error is not due to a limitation of the computer, but rather to a limitation of the programmer. Subtracting two large numbers that are almost equal is never a good idea and often creates an error.

Incidentally, this program is sensitive to the type and model of computer and may produce different results on your system.

Converting Between Binary and Decimal Numbers

A second type of error occurs because computers use binary arithmetic for manipulating numbers, while people write programs that use decimal arithmetic. This means that the computer must make conversions between binary and decimal representations of numbers.

In binary arithmetic as in decimal arithmetic, certain fractions can be represented only by nonterminating sequences of digits. A familiar example in decimal arithmetic is the value of 0.333... (a nonterminating sequence of the digit 3) for the fraction 1/3. If the sequence is terminated, it is not exactly equal to the fraction. For example, the sequence 0.33333 is not exactly equal to the fraction 1/3.

The fraction 1/10000, or 0.0001, is represented in binary arithmetic by a nonterminating sequence of binary digits. If the sequence is terminated, as it must be if the number is to be stored and manipulated in a computer, it is no longer exactly equal to the fraction 1/10000.

This type of error causes problems when an equality is used to make a program decision. Here is an example:

```
! Example Program 6-2
! Failure of an equality test.

LET X = 0.999
PRINT X;
DO until X = 1
   LET X = X + 0.0001
   PRINT X;
LOOP
END
```

The problem with this program is that the value of X is never exactly equal to one, even though the PRINT statement displays a value of one. Thus the program continues indefinitely in an infinite loop, producing screen after screen of output:

```
.999  .9991  .9992  .9993  .9994  .9995  .9996
.9997  .9998  .9999  1.  1.0001  1.0002  1.0003
1.0004  1.0005...
```

The problem can be corrected, in this example, by testing whether the value of X differs by only a small amount (small compared to the increment of 0.0001) from one. Here is a program that works:

```
! Example Program 6-3
! A successful equality test.

LET X = 0.999
PRINT X;
DO until Abs(X - 1) < 1E-15
   LET X = X + 0.0001
   PRINT X;
LOOP
END
```

This modified program produces an output that terminates:

```
.999   .9991   .9992   .9993   .9994   .9995   .9996
.9997   .9998   .9999   1.
```

Note the period after the last value printed. This period indicates that the result is not exactly 1 but is equal to 1 within the accuracy limits of the computer.

The main lesson to be learned from this example is that a numeric equality cannot always be counted on to give an accurate logical value. **I recommend that you avoid using numerical equalities as logical tests in computer programs.**

These and similar types of errors can occur in computer programs written in almost any language. Try the sample programs yourself on your computer. Simple test programs, such as the ones I have listed, can be written to determine how True BASIC will behave in any particular case. With a little care, you can write computer programs that avoid these types of errors.

6.6   ERROR TRAPPING AND HANDLING

Program errors can be divided into several general classes. Compile errors (also called syntax errors) are errors in statement syntax. These errors are generated when your program is being compiled and are identified immediately. They are typically caused by mistakes in syntax. You can use the editor to correct your program and then compile the program again.

Logical errors are the result of mistakes in logic when the program was designed or written. The program may run perfectly but produce meaningless results. These errors are sometimes hard to find, and can be located and corrected only by thoroughly testing the program.

Run-time errors occur while the program is executing. These errors may be caused by logical errors or by other mistakes made when writing the program. They are usually fatal and cause the program to stop. Computer programmers say the program has "crashed." True BASIC provides a facility for *trapping* these run-time errors, allowing the user to make corrections and continue executing the program.

The syntax for trapping errors is as follows:

```
WHEN EXCEPTION IN
     protected block
USE
     exception handler block
END WHEN
```

The Protected Block of Statements

EXCEPTION is the standard ANS BASIC word for an error, but True BASIC allows the word ERROR to be used in place of the standard word and I will use ERROR in example programs. The *protected block* can be any sequence of statements in the main program unit or in a subprogram unit. It cannot include a subprogram definition statement such as SUB or FUNCTION, statements that are introduced in Chapter 7. In most applications, the protected block is a short sequence of statements.

The Error Handler Block

The *error handler block* is another sequence of statements that is executed only if there is a run-time error in the protected block. Under normal circumstances when there is no error, the program skips over the error handler block and executes the first statement after the END WHEN statement.

The Extype and Extext$ Functions

Two system functions are particularly useful in the error handler block. The numeric function Extype returns an error number when a run-time error occurs. These numbers are listed in Appendix H. The value of Extype can be used to make a decision in the error handler block.

The string function Extext$ returns the specific error message and is also listed in Appendix H. When error trapping is in operation, this message is not printed automatically. The value of Extext$ — the error message string — can be displayed or used in any other manner.

Here is a sample program using error trapping:

```
! Example Program 6-4
! Trap any errors while calculating
! the square root of a number.

LET NoError$ = "false"
DO
   LINE INPUT prompt "Enter number: ": Value$

   WHEN error in   ! protected block
        LET Number = Val(Value$)
        LET Result = Sqr(Number)
        PRINT "Square root of "; Value$; " is"; Result
        LET NoError$ = "true"
```

```
    USE  ! error handler block
        IF Extype = 3005 or Extype = 4001 then
            PRINT "Error: "; Extext$
        ELSE
            PRINT "Unexpected error: "; Extext$
        END IF
        PRINT "Please try again."
    END WHEN

    LOOP until NoError$ = "true"
    END
```

Note the use of the LINE INPUT statement to accept any sequence of characters, with checking for a proper number taking place when the Val function is invoked. Error 3005 means trying to take the square root of a negative number. Error 4001 means using the Val function on a string that is not a proper number. In either case, the appropriate error message is printed. If another, unexpected run-time error occurs, a general error message is printed.

Here is an example of program output:

```
Enter number: -9
Error: SQR of negative number
Please try again.
Enter number: 9
Square root of 9 is 3
```

Error trapping is an example of good defensive programming. You should anticipate the possibility of run-time errors and develop plans to handle them when they occur. Nothing is more discouraging to the user of an application program than to have the program suddenly stop and display an error message that seems to make no sense.

6.7   HINTS FOR WRITING CORRECT PROGRAMS

Most of the discussion in this chapter has been about methods for finding and correcting program errors. An equally important topic is how to write programs that have no errors in the first place.

When you say that a program is error-free, you mean that extensive testing has revealed no errors. There is no way of knowing absolutely that every single error has been found and corrected. Unfortunately, some errors are never found until the program has been used by many different people in many different applications. Probably some errors are never found at all!

Notice the mention of program testing. Programs written by beginning programmers are seldom tested thoroughly. **As much or more time should be spent testing a program as was spent writing it.** In practice, however, a program is often completed just before the deadline and is barely tested at all.

Throughout the book I stress logical program design, development of a program in small modules, and use of clear structures for looping and branching. Keep these points in mind as I discuss some hints for writing better programs.

Understand the Problem

You cannot write a program to solve a problem until you completely understand the problem. This is an obvious statement, but a lot of people start programming before they understand clearly what the program must do. Keep asking questions or investigate further until you do understand the problem.

Plan First, Program Later

A common mistake made by beginning programmers is to start writing their programs too soon. This doesn't mean to do nothing until just before the program is due, but it does mean to do a lot of thinking and planning before writing your first program statement. Here are two steps you can take.

First, you must decide how you will solve the problem. The method of solution is called an *algorithm*. You want an efficient algorithm that will solve the problem accurately and quickly. You learn algorithms by reading books and articles, by reading other programs, and by discussing methods of solution with experienced programmers.

Second, you must **write an outline of your program**. An outline can be written as one or more descriptive paragraphs, or in the more traditional outline form. Try to divide your problem solution into separate tasks and then outline a solution for each task. When you learn about the subprogram capabilities of True BASIC in Chapter 7, you will be able to organize your program into a collection of program units. The more detailed your outline, the easier it is to write the computer program.

Only when you have taken these two steps are you ready to start writing the program itself.

Write Simple Programs

Use all the tools you have available to write a program that is easy to read and understand. Use variable names that are as descriptive as possible. Use indentation to identify the statements in a branch or a loop. Use comments to explain the logical action of the program, not what an individual statement does.

Avoid program structures that are tricky or hard to understand. There is usually no justification for writing programs that are difficult to understand in order to make them more efficient. Remember that computer memory is becoming less expensive and computers are becoming faster. In general, programs should be written to minimize the time required for maintenance rather than to minimize the amount of memory used or the execution time.

Most important, write your program as a series of small units, as independent from one another as possible. No unit should be larger than a single page. You will learn in Chapter 7 how to write a unit as an external subroutine or function. I recommend strongly that you use this technique.

Test and Debug Carefully

Thoroughly test each program unit before adding it to your program. Small units tend to be easier than large programs to write and debug. If each unit is free of errors, the resulting program should also be error-free.

If you are careful in writing your program, it should contain few errors. Test your program for as many conditions as possible that might cause an error. Look carefully at extreme conditions, such as the largest and smallest values of key variables. Ask someone else to run your program and see if they can make it fail. As mentioned previously, you should budget as much time for testing your program as for writing it. **Most program failures are due to inadequate testing.**

A common type of error is called the "off by one bug." This is the error that occurs, for example, when you are counting and the sum turns out to be one less or one greater than it should be. Look carefully at your logic and you should be able to find the mistake. If you start counting at one and the computer starts counting at zero, you may produce this type of error.

Your ability to write error-free programs will improve quickly if you follow these suggestions. There will be times, however, when in spite of your best efforts, you cannot get a program to work. You should then go back and examine your program outline. If you are not satisfied with it, you may save time by starting over again. It is difficult to write a good program from a bad outline.

6.8 PROGRAM STYLE

I have included a discussion of program style in this chapter because good style reduces programming errors. Some of these styles are my personal preference. There is no reason you have to follow every one of them. But whatever you do, be consistent.

Indentation

You should always indent the statements in the body of a loop. Indentation makes it easier to see where the loop starts and stops. The usual indentation is two to six spaces. An indentation of one space may not be noticed, while an indentation of more than six spaces tends to make program statements too long. Long statements may not display on one line of the screen or print on paper of normal width.

Indentation becomes especially important when you have nested loops — that is, when one loop is part of the body of another loop. In fact, it is extremely difficult to read a computer program that has multiple-nested loops and no indentation. Compare the following two example programs:

```
! Example Program 6-5
! Nested loops without proper indentation.

OPEN #1: name "READINGS.DAT"
FOR I = 1 to 2
FOR J = 1 to 3
FOR K = 1 to 3
INPUT #1: Reading
PRINT Reading;
NEXT K
PRINT
NEXT J
PRINT
PRINT
NEXT I
END


! Example Program 6-6
! Nested loops with proper indentation.

OPEN #1: name "READINGS.DAT"
FOR I = 1 to 2
    FOR J = 1 to 3
        FOR K = 1 to 3
            INPUT #1: Reading
            PRINT Reading;
        NEXT K
        PRINT
    NEXT J
    PRINT
    PRINT
NEXT I
END
```

I think most readers would agree that Example Program 6-6 is easier to understand.

The statements that make up each branch of a branching structure should also be indented. Your program is more readable and you can see more clearly what the computer program does when a particular branch is selected.

Use of Comments

Comments are another feature that make a program more readable. A block of comments at the beginning of the program should explain what the program does. This comment block may contain additional information such as the name of the programmer, the date the program was last revised, the number of the revision, and so forth. Other comments can be placed between blocks of program statements or after individual statements. These comments should be used to explain program logic, not program syntax. You can assume that the reader already knows True BASIC syntax.

It is possible, but not common, to overuse comments. Certainly there should seldom be a need to place a comment after every statement in a program. On the other hand, if you are using a complex algorithm that is difficult to understand, lots of comments may make the program easier to read.

Variable Names

Descriptive variable names should be chosen. True BASIC is a compiled version of BASIC, not an interpreted version, so there is no penalty attached to using long variable names. The traditional one-letter names of interpreted BASIC should only be used in special circumstances.

In many cases, the most descriptive variable name consists of two or more words. As you know, you cannot include space characters in variable names. You can, however, make up a variable name of two or more words and use capital letters to mark the beginning of each word. For example, the name format

```
MyBigChance
```

might be chosen. It is certainly more readable than the name format

```
mybigchance
```

although both variable names refer to the same memory location.

The Do Format Command

After you have finished writing a program, you can run a special formatting program with the Do Format command. It has the following syntax.:

```
Ok. Do Format
```

The Do Format command is also available in the pull-down Custom menu of a Mac or a PC using a mouse.

This command converts all program statements in the current program to a standard format. Keywords in statements are capitalized but variable names are not changed. Program structures are indented an appropriate amount. Comments following program statements are aligned vertically.

The current program is altered by the Do Format command and remains in memory. After you have executed the command, you can save or replace the program on disk.

Summary of Important Points

- Learn to use the Do Trace command to help locate program errors.

- Always execute the Do Trace command from the command line so that watch variables can be specified.

- Never modify a program statement or add a new statement when a breakpoint is executed.

- I recommend that you avoid using numerical equalities as logical tests in computer programs.

- As much or more time should be spent testing a program as was spent writing it.

- You must understand the problem before writing a program to solve the problem.

- Always write down a program outline before starting to write program statements.

- Develop your program as a series of small, simple units that have been thoroughly tested.

- Avoid using tricky or complicated logic in order to make a program shorter or more efficient.

- Always indent statements in the body of a loop.

Common Errors

- Assuming that you know the value of a variable when you can easily check that value with a PRINT statement.

- Failing to put labels in temporary PRINT statements and then not knowing which value belongs to which variable.

- Changing a statement or adding a new statement when the program has paused at a breakpoint.

- Not using the Do Trace command immediately when your program compiles (has no syntax errors), but is not producing the correct results or is stopping with a run-time error. A good debugger is the most effective tool for finding and correcting program errors.

- Using noninteger numeric values in an equality statement that controls a decision branch or a loop.

- Failing to trap an invalid character used in a Val function argument, and thus causing the program to crash.

- Writing your program outline after you have finished the program, when it can provide no help in writing the code.

- Starting to design and write a program so late that there is not enough time to test it thoroughly before it is due.

- Assuming that the user of a program will always enter proper and accurate data, and thus failing to check for data entry errors.

- Allowing a program to crash when incorrect data is entered by the user rather than trapping the error and giving the user another chance.

Self-Test Questions

1. What is meant by the term "debugging"?

2. What is the method of "playing computer"?

3. What statement can you insert into a program to display the value of a variable?

4. Which function key is used on a PC to
    (a) start marking part of your program?
    (b) stop marking?

5. Which function key on a PC can be used to remove the marking from a block of marked text?

6. What is the easiest way on your computer to delete a block of several program lines?

7. On a PC running True BASIC, what is the function of
    (a) the F5 key?
    (b) the F6 key?

8. How do you recover a line that has been deleted by mistake?

9. When program execution has been stopped by entering the Break command, can you
    (a) change the value of a program variable?
    (b) insert a new program statement?
    (c) delete an existing statement?

10. After a program has been stopped with the Break command, what command do you enter to restart execution?

11. (a) What problem may occur when you use an equality like X = 5 in a program to test whether a process (such as a loop) should be stopped?

    (b) How can you avoid the problem?

12. When an error occurs in a protected block of program statements, control transfers to the error handler block. Which statements are used to denote
    (a) the beginning of the error handler block?
    (b) the end of the error handler block?

13. If an error occurs, what general type of expression is assigned to

    (a)   Extext\$?

    (b)   Extype?

14. (a)   What is an algorithm?

    (b)   Can you develop an algorithm for a problem if you do not understand the problem?

15. Why is a written program outline preferable to a mental outline?

16. Why is it important to write programs that are clear and easy to understand?

17. How much time should be budgeted for testing a program?

18. (a)   What is the purpose of the Do Format command?

    (b)   Name two changes that this command might make in program appearance.

Practice Programs

1. You are asked to calculate the roots of the equation

```
A*X^2 + B*X + C = 0
```
Recall that the roots are given by the expressions

```
X1 = (-B + Sqr(B*B - 4*A*C)) / (2*A)
X2 = (-B - Sqr(B*B - 4*A*C)) / (2*A)
```

You write the following program:

```
! Program with a logical error.

INPUT prompt "Value of A? ": A
INPUT prompt "Value of B? ": B
INPUT prompt "Value of C? ": C
LET X1 = (-B + Sqr(B*B - 4*A*C)) / (2*A)
LET X2 = (-B - Sqr(B*B - 4*A*C)) / (2*A)
PRINT "The roots are"; X1; "and"; X2
END
```

A user enters a value of 3 for A, 2 for B, and 2 for C. The program responds with a run-time error. What is wrong? Use the Do Trace command to step through the program statement by statement. Write a corrected program that will handle this set of values.

2. Practice Programs 2 and 3 in Chapter 5 ask a user to enter a date in MM-DD-YY format. The month and the day may be specified by single digits — that is, 1-5-85 rather than 01-05-85.

    Write a program that requests such a date and then checks the validity of the entry. If a user enters an invalid date, the program should loop back and allow the date to be entered again. Assume 29 days in February.

    Test your program using the following date values:

    ```
    13-20-85
    2-30-81
    11-31-88
    1-17-77
    ```

3. If you have not already done so, write Practice Program 1 with a protected block for the root calculations and an error handler block. Use the numeric entries specified in that problem to test your program.

4. A user is asked to enter two numbers, A and B, and the quotient A/B is displayed. Place the calculation of A/B in a protected block and use an error handler block to report if division by zero is attempted. If an error occurs, display the text of an appropriate error message. All error-trapping and error-handling statements should be within a loop so that the user can enter new values if an error is detected.

    Test your program using the following number pairs:

    ```
    13.5, 7.7
    0, 33.2
    125, 0
    25, 5
    ```

5. Write a program similar in function to Example Program 5-8 that uses a protected block and an error handler block to warn a user if an entry is not a valid number.

Test your program using the following values:

```
125.99
11,234.50
13.2E-3
13.2E+-3
+e+e+e
-55
```

6.   This exercise is designed to give you practice with the function keys on a PC. Using Example Program 5-15, perform the following operations.

(a)   Move the cursor to the top of the program in the program window and use the F3 key to find all occurrences of the word Ans$. Change each occurrence of Ans$ to the word Reply$.

(b)   Look up the command Change and use it to change all occurrences of Reply$ back to Ans$.

(c)   Delete the line "LET Count = Count - 1". Use the F5 key to make a copy of the line "LET Count = Count + 1" and insert it where you deleted the first line. Change the plus sign to a minus sign.

(d)   Move the program fragment

```
LET Average = Round(Sum/Count)
PRINT "Average grade is"; Average
```

and insert it after the first DO loop. Mark and delete the second DO loop and the following IF block.

(e)   Mark and delete the three comment lines at the beginning of the program. Use the F7 key to restore this deletion.

PART 2

Advanced Programming Techniques

CHAPTER
7

Writing Programs Using Procedures

7.1 INTRODUCTION

Modern computer languages allow a program to be designed as a series of independent program units or procedures. Two types of procedures are used frequently in True BASIC — the external function and the external subroutine.

Arguments and parameters allow information to be passed to external procedure and, in the case of external subroutines, to return information to the original program. Local variables provide isolation between the main program and procedures, and between individual procedures. Libraries of procedures can be constructed, saved on disk, and subsequently incorporated into new True BASIC programs. Libraries with special properties, called modules, are useful in larger programs.

7.2 PROGRAM UNITS

As a program becomes larger, it is advantageous to divide it into smaller units. These units are called *program units* and are further identified as the *main program* and additional *procedures*. The main program (or one of the procedures) can make use of one or more other procedures as it carries out its task, and it is then identified as the *calling* program unit. Any procedure can be called from any other procedure or from the main program.

There are several benefits to be derived from writing programs in this fashion.

Well-designed programs. Programs designed as collections of smaller units are easier to write and debug, easier to read and understand, and easier to maintain and modify. This type of design is called *modular program design*; dividing a large program into smaller modules or program units. The term "modular" refers to dividing a large program into smaller units, it does not refer exclusively to True BASIC modules, introduced in Section 7.5.

For example, suppose that you want to write a program to develop a classroom schedule. That is not an easy problem to solve and you have not yet learned all the techniques required to write such a program. You can, however, analyze the problem and see how it can be divided into subtasks.

> *Task:* Develop a classroom schedule.

> *Subtask A:* Enter list of classes with time and size of each class. Enter list of classrooms with size of each room.

> *Subtask B:* Sort classes by hour of the day. For each hour, sort classes by descending size. Sort classrooms by descending size.

> *Subtask C:* For each hour, assign class to room, starting with the largest size class. Note any class that cannot be assigned.

> *Subtask D:* Print list of classes not assigned to rooms. Print list of rooms showing hours not assigned.

Whereas the task is complex and stated in general terms, each subtask is more specific and thus easier to understand. There may be a further division of one of the listed subtasks; for example, a general sorting routine might be a separate subtask within subtask B. After more experience, you will be able to write a program based on such a modular design.

Isolation. Isolation implies that each program unit is separate and distinct from the other units. Complete isolation means that a variable in one program unit is completely different from a variable with the same name in another program unit. Changes in the value of a variable are confined to a single program unit.

The importance of isolation is that a change in a variable value in one program unit can never cause an unexpected change in another program unit. Lack of program unit isolation can be a major and hard-to-find source of errors in large programs.

In practice, complete isolation is not possible when you need to return or pass back information from a called program unit to the calling program unit. The goal of isolation is still desirable, however, and to the extent that this goal can be achieved, the chance of errors is reduced.

Procedure libraries. Libraries of well-designed and error-free procedures can be created and used in many different programs. A procedure that does a particular job and does it well should not be written over and over again from scratch. It should be placed in a library and used when appropriate in any new programs. These library functions and subroutines serve as language extensions to True BASIC and are discussed at the end of this chapter.

In view of all the preceding benefits, you will see modular program design used in many of the large example programs in this and subsequent chapters.

Here is a list of program units:

> main program
> external functions
> external subroutines
> external pictures
> internal functions
> internal subroutines

The main program is the type of True BASIC program that you have written in previous chapters. Its last statement is always an END statement. Other statements in the main program must name and identify all external procedures.

External functions and subroutines are discussed in the next two sections. They must be located after the main program's END statement or in a separate library file (see Section 7.5).

External pictures are mentioned here for completeness but are not discussed until Chapter 12.

Internal functions and subroutines are introduced at the end of this chapter. They are not used in any of the example programs in this book.

7.3 EXTERNAL FUNCTIONS

You are already familiar with built-in functions and single-line user-defined functions, defined in Chapter 5. A similar definition describes an *external function unit*. It is a procedure consisting of a separate block of program statements identified by name. It can have values passed to it from the calling program unit. The external function unit performs some calculation and returns a string or numeric value that is assigned to the function name.

An example might be a function to calculate the volume of a rectangular box, given the length, width, and height. That specific function is developed in this section and used in Example Programs 7-1 and 7-2.

The external function is invoked or *called* when its name is used in an expression. **A value must be assigned to the function name before control returns to the calling program unit.** When I refer to a function in this section, I mean an external function.

For example, a function named Volume can be designed to calculate the volume of a box. When you call or invoke this function, you have to pass to it — make it aware of — the length, width, and height values of a specific box. To display the volume of a box that is 10 inches long, 5 inches wide, and 3 inches high, you might use the statement

```
PRINT Volume (10, 5, 3)
```

The numeric values in parentheses are called *arguments* of the function Volume.

The external function unit itself consists of the following statements:

```
EXTERNAL FUNCTION Volume (L, W, H)
    LET Volume = L * W * H
END FUNCTION
```

The function named Volume is assigned a value equal to the volume of the box. The variables L, W, and H are called *parameters* of the function Volume.

Function Unit Heading

The first statement in a function unit is

```
EXTERNAL FUNCTION Name (Parameters)
```

where Name is the function name and Parameters is a list of variable names, separated by commas. The function name must follow the same rules that apply to variable names (see Chapter 3). The function value may be either numeric or string and if the function has a string value, the function name must end with a dollar sign.

The word EXTERNAL is optional. This word is required in ANS BASIC but may be omitted in True BASIC. If the word EXTERNAL is omitted, any procedure listed after the main program END statement or in a library file is considered an external procedure.

In the preceding example, the heading statement is

```
EXTERNAL FUNCTION Volume (L, W, H)
```

and the parameters are the variables L, W, and H. The syntax

```
FUNCTION Volume (L, W, H)
```

without the word EXTERNAL is equally valid in True BASIC.

Function Parameters

The parameters in a function heading statement are variables, separated from one another by commas, and are of type string or numeric. These variables are called *local variables*, meaning that they are known and can be used only within the function unit itself. Variables with the same name in any other part of the program are considered different from these local variables.

Values are assigned or *passed* to parameter variables when the function is called. This method of passing information through parameters is called *pass by value* and the parameters are called *value parameters* or sometimes, *one-way parameters*.

The concept of local variables is important because they provides isolation between an external function and other program units. In addition to the parameter variables, any other variable introduced and used in the function unit is a local variable.

Consider the case of a main program with a variable named Reply$ and an external function with a variable named Reply$. These two variables have the same name but they refer to different mailboxes or memory locations. Thus a value assigned to Reply$ in the function is placed in one mailbox, while the value of Reply$ in the main program is contained in another mailbox. The two variables may have the same name but they are really completely different variables.

As an analogy, post office box 572 in the main post office contains entirely different letters than post office box 572 in a branch post office, although they both have the same identifying number or name and are in the same town.

Other FUNCTION Statements

The last statement in a function unit must be

```
END FUNCTION
```

The unit which calls the function — often the main program — must have a declaration statement containing the function name. One declaration statement may contain several function names and there may be more than one declaration statement. The syntax is

```
DECLARE FUNCTION Name1, Name2,...
```

Finally, there must be a specific assignment statement — a LET statement — in the function unit that assigns a value to the function name. This value may be either a number or a string, depending on the function type. The value must be assigned before the END FUNCTION statement is executed.

The complete example program looks as follows:

```
! Example Program 7-1
! Short program that uses an external function.

! Main program
DECLARE FUNCTION Volume
PRINT "Volume of box is"; Volume(10, 5, 3)
END

! Function procedure
EXTERNAL FUNCTION Volume (L, W, H)
    LET Volume = L * W * H
END FUNCTION
```

The following output is displayed:

```
Volume of box is 150
```

It is possible to exit a function at points other than the END FUNCTION by using the phrase

```
EXIT FUNCTION
```

An error occurs if the function has not been assigned a value before exiting. I recommend that you use this phrase sparingly and normally exit through the END FUNCTION statement.

When a function is called, the values passed to it can be the values of variables or constants or expressions, as demonstrated in the next example program:

```
! Example Program 7-2
! Using different types of arguments
! in an external function.

DECLARE FUNCTION Volume
LET L = 10
PRINT "Volume of box is"; Volume(L, L/2, 3)
END

FUNCTION Volume (Length, Width, Height)
    LET Volume = Length * Width * Height
END FUNCTION
```

The function call in the PRINT statement obtains its first argument value from the variable L, its second value from the expression L/2, and its third value from the constant 3. The output is the same as that of Example Program 7-1.

Writing and Using Functions

Here are some other example programs that use functions. The first program uses a function to calculate the factorial value of a non-negative integer entered from the keyboard. For example, the factorial value of 5, denoted 5! by mathematicians, is equal to 1×2×3×4×5 or 120. By definition, zero factorial equals 1. This program prompts the user to enter a number from the keyboard. If the number is negative or not an integer, the program displays an error message and stops. Otherwise, the factorial value of the number is calculated and displayed:

```
! Example Program 7-3
! Calculate the value of a factorial number.

DECLARE FUNCTION Factorial
INPUT prompt "Enter number: ": Number
IF Number < 0 then
   PRINT "The number must be positive or zero."
ELSEIF Number <> Int(Number) then
   PRINT "The number must be an integer."
ELSE
   PRINT "The factorial value of"; Number;
   PRINT "is"; Factorial(Number)
END IF
END

FUNCTION Factorial (X)
    ! Calculate the factorial value of parameter X.
    LET Result = 1  ! initialize the variable Result
    FOR I = 1 to X
        LET Result = Result * I
    NEXT I
    LET Factorial = Result
END FUNCTION
```

If the number is positive or zero and an integer, the function Factorial is called by the PRINT statement. The factorial value is calculated in the function procedure and the result is returned to the main program. If X has a value of zero, the FOR loop never executes and a value of one is assigned to Factorial.

In the main program, the value of the entered number is stored in the variable Number and this value is passed to the variable X in the function. Variable X is a local variable defined only in the function.

Here are three examples of typical program runs:

```
Enter number: -5.2
The number must be positive or zero.

Enter number: 5.2
The number must be an integer.

Enter number: 5
The factorial value of 5 is 120
```

Another example program uses string functions to find palindromes. A palindrome is a sentence or sequence of letters that reads the same backward and forward. To test a palindrome, all letters must be converted to the same case (say, uppercase) and all non-alphabetic characters (including spaces or blanks) must be removed from the sentence.

The main program asks the user to enter a string of characters from the keyboard. The standard function Ucase$ is called to convert all letters to uppercase. The user-defined function Remove$ is called to remove all nonalphabetic characters. Finally, the user-defined function Reverse$ is called to write a new string that is the reverse of the original string:

```
! Example Program 7-4
! Find a palindrome.

DECLARE FUNCTION Remove$, Reverse$
LINE INPUT prompt "Enter string: ": String$
LET String$ = Ucase$(String$)
LET String$ = Remove$(String$)
LET Compare$ = Reverse$(String$)
IF String$ = Compare$ then
   PRINT "String is a palindrome."
ELSE
   PRINT "String is not a palindrome."
END IF
END

FUNCTION Remove$ (Item$)
   ! Remove nonalphabetic characters from string A$.
   LET Copy$ = ""   ! a null string
   FOR I = 1 to Len(Item$)
      IF Item$[I:I] >= "A" and Items$[I:I] <= "Z" then
         LET Copy$ = Copy$ & Item$[I:I]
      END IF
   NEXT I
   LET Remove$ = Copy$
END FUNCTION
```

```
FUNCTION Reverse$ (Item$)
    ! Reverse the order of characters in a string.
    LET Copy$=""
    FOR I = Len(Item$) to 1 step -1
        LET Copy$ = Copy$ & Item$[I:I]
    NEXT I
    LET Reverse$ = Copy$
END FUNCTION
```

If you try this program yourself with the well-known palindrome "Madam, I'm Adam," you should get the following results:

```
Enter string: Madam, I'm Adam
String is a palindrome.
```

Note that the string Copy$ is initially assigned a null value in each function. The selected characters are then added to Copy$, one by one. The resulting string, Compare$, is then compared with the original string, String$, and if they are the same, the original string is a palindrome.

True BASIC allows you to use the word DEF in place of the standard word FUNCTION in a function heading. The word FUNCTION is more descriptive but the word DEF is shorter. You may use either word in your programs. Remember that the word EXTERNAL is optional in the function unit heading.

Functions may be nested, meaning that one function may call another function. The calling function must have a DECLARE statement naming the called function.

Each time a function is called, all local parameter variables have values passed to them. Other local variables are reinitialized, numeric variables to zero and string variables to the null string.

The next example program illustrates the error created by expecting a local variable to hold its value between function calls:

```
! Example Program 7-5
! *** THIS IS NOT A VALID PROGRAM ***
! Display the sum of a sequence of numbers
! entered from keyboard.

DECLARE FUNCTION Add
PRINT "Display the sum of a sequence of numbers."
PRINT "Enter zero to stop input."
INPUT prompt "Number? ": Number
DO until Number = 0
    LET Result = Add(Number)
    INPUT prompt "Number? ": Number
```

```
    LOOP
    PRINT "The sum is"; Result
    END

    FUNCTION Add (N)
        ! Add the number N to a sum.
        LET Sum = Sum + N
        LET Add = Sum
    END FUNCTION
```

The following results are obtained:

```
    Display the sum of a sequence of numbers.
    Enter zero to stop input.
    Number? 5
    Number? 3
    Number? 0
    The sum is 3
```

The local variable Sum is reset to zero each time Add is called and so contains only the value of the last parameter N that was added to it. No sum is accumulated and the program displays the last value entered (3) rather than the correct sum (8).

7.4   EXTERNAL SUBROUTINES

In contrast to a function, the general purpose of a subroutine is to perform some task or carry out some action, such as printing a standard business form.

Subroutine Unit Heading

Like functions, external subroutines are separate blocks of program statements. They are identified by name, and the first statement in a subroutine program unit must be

```
    EXTERNAL SUB Name (Parameters)
```

In True BASIC, the word EXTERNAL may be omitted and thus the syntax

```
    SUB Name (Parameters)
```

is also allowed.

Unlike a function, **no value is associated with a subroutine name**. A subroutine name cannot represent a string value and the dollar sign character is not allowed. The name is used only to identify the subroutine and never has any value assigned to it.

The parameters in a subroutine heading statement are local variable names, separated from one another by commas. These parameters are different from the value parameters of a function. Their behavior is discussed in detail in the next section. Any other variables used in the subroutine are also local variables.

The last statement in a subroutine block must be

```
END SUB
```

and it is the normal exit point. Any other exit point must be identified by the phrase

```
EXIT SUB
```

The same caution applies here about use of the EXIT SUB statement when it is not absolutely necessary.

The following subroutine displays a string parameter named Value$ on the screen, centered between the left and right margins. The parameter Width is the width of the screen in columns.

```
EXTERNAL SUB Center (Value$, Width)
    PRINT Tab((Width - Len(Value$))/2); Value$
END SUB
```

Calling a Subroutine

A subroutine is called from another program unit by the statement

```
CALL Name (Arguments)
```

Arguments in the CALL statement may be variables, constants, or expressions. They must agree in number and type (numeric or string) with the parameter list in the subroutine heading statement. The calling program unit may be the main program, a function, or another subroutine.

Using the preceding example subroutine, the call statement might be

```
CALL Center ("Analysis of 1983 Earnings", 80)
```

It creates the following centered display:

```
                    Analysis of 1983 Earnings
```

Subroutine Parameters

A major difference between functions and subroutines is the way that information is passed through parameters. In the CALL statement, names of argument **variables** refer to specific mailboxes or memory locations. In the SUB heading statement, names of parameter variables are **local names for these same mailboxes**. Thus if a change is made in the value of one of the local parameter variables in a subroutine, the value of the corresponding variable in the calling program is also changed.

Using the previous analogy, your post office box may be known officially as box 572, but when you forget the key and ask the postmaster for your mail, you usually refer to it as John Blair's box. The public knows this box as 572, but the postmaster knows it as John Blair's box. These are just two names for the same box. Obviously, the contents of box 572 and John Blair's box are the same.

Passing information in this manner does not provide complete isolation between the subroutine and the calling program unit, because both argument and parameter variable names refer to the same mailbox and the value it contains. In fact, the information that is passed is the *address* of the memory location or mailbox. On the other hand, this type of parameter does allow information to be passed back to the calling unit because the value in the mailbox is accessible to the calling unit — the address of the mailbox is known. This method of passing information through parameters is called *pass by reference* and the parameters are called *variable parameters* or sometimes, *two-way parameters*.

Remember that a subroutine passes information back to the calling program through variable arguments and parameters. On the other hand, a function passes information back to the calling program through the function name.

Here is a simple program that uses a subroutine to halve a numeric parameter. The program contains lots of PRINT statements that show a user what is going on at various points in the program. I suggest that you run this program if you are uncertain about just how variable parameters behave in subroutines.

```
! Example Program 7-6
! A demonstration of how variable parameters work.

INPUT prompt "Assign a value to variable In...": In
PRINT "Before calling subroutine, In ="; In
CALL Halved (In)
PRINT "After returning from subroutine, In ="; In
END

SUB Halved (New)
    ! Divide the value of New in half.
    PRINT "Start of subroutine named Halved"
    PRINT "Entering the subroutine, New ="; New
    LET New = New / 2
    PRINT "After division, New ="; New
END SUB
```

The preceding example is a good illustration of how you can use PRINT statements to see what is happening inside a program. These results are displayed:

```
Assign a value to variable In...10
Before calling subroutine, In = 10
Start of subroutine named Halved
Entering the subroutine, New = 10
After division, New = 5
After returning from subroutine, In = 5
```

The variable In had an original value of 10. It was passed to the variable New in the subroutine, divided by two, and thus its value was changed to 5. Back in the main program, the value of In also changed to 5. Why? Because In and New are just two different names for the same memory location and the value stored in that location is now 5.

Those arguments in the CALL statement that are are constants or expressions have their values assigned to temporary variables when the CALL statement is executed. These variables can then be referenced by the corresponding parameter variables in the subroutine and the values used in the subroutine. The temporary variables are deleted, however, when control returns to the calling program and the information in them is lost. **Values cannot be passed back to the calling program through temporary variables.** In effect, constant and expression arguments in subroutines behave just like function arguments.

For example, the statement

```
CALL Blank (Num, Sum - 1, List$)
```

can result in the subroutine changing the values of Num and List$ in the calling program (both are variables) but not the value of Sum. Sum is part of an expression, Sum - 1, and the value of the expression is assigned to a temporary variable that is deleted when control returns to the calling unit.

If you want a variable used as an argument to behave like an expression, surround it with parentheses. In the statement

```
CALL Blank ((Num), Sum -1, (List$))
```

all arguments behave like one-way or value parameters and values are not passed back to the calling program. Just the simple act of enclosing a variable in parentheses makes it an expression. This technique does provide complete isolation between the subroutine and the calling program.

Look at the next two example programs to get a better idea of how parameters pass information. In the first program, the argument in the CALL statement behaves as a value parameter because of the extra set of parentheses.

```
! Example Program 7-7
! Subroutine with value parameter.

PRINT "Subroutine with a value parameter."
LET Number = 5
PRINT "Before calling subroutine, Number is"; Number
CALL New ((Number))  ! note double parentheses
PRINT "After calling subroutine, Number is"; Number
END

SUB New (X)
    LET X = 10
END SUB
```

The following output is produced:

```
Subroutine with a value parameter.
Before calling subroutine, Number is 5
After calling subroutine, Number is 5
```

This program displays a final value of 5 because the new parameter value 10 is not passed back to the main program.

On the other hand, the second program demonstrates the use of a variable parameter:

```
! Example Program 7-8
! Subroutine with variable parameter.

PRINT "Subroutine with a variable parameter."
LET Number = 5
PRINT "Before calling subroutine, Number is"; Number
CALL New (Number)
PRINT "After calling subroutine, Number is"; Number
END

SUB New (X)
    LET X = 10
END SUB
```

In this case, a different output is produced:

```
Subroutine with a variable parameter.
Before calling subroutine, Number is 5
After calling subroutine, Number is 10
```

A final value of 10 is displayed by the program because this value is passed back to the main program from the subroutine. The variables Number and X both refer to the same memory location. Study these two examples carefully until you understand thoroughly the different behavior of value and variable parameters.

Substrings used as arguments are considered expressions and thus cannot be changed. For example, the statement

```
CALL Blank (12, Sum, List$[2:5])
```

allows only the value of Sum in the calling program to be changed because 12 is a value and List$[2:5] is an expression.

All variables in a subroutine are local variables and except for parameter variables, are reinitialized each time the subroutine is called.

The next example program asks the user to enter a report title from the keyboard. The program clears the screen and then calls a subroutine named Box that displays the centered title inside a box of asterisks. A previous subroutine example, named Center, is used to center each line of the boxed title on the screen. The variable X is a return variable that is set to a value greater than zero if the title in its box of asterisks will not fit between the margins.

Subroutine Box uses the ASK MARGIN statement to assign the value of the right margin to the variable Width. The width of the screen, reduced by 4 to account for the asterisk and space at each end of the title, is compared with the length of the title string. If the string is too long, the return variable is set to the number of characters by which the name exceeds the available space, an error message is displayed, and the subroutine is exited. If the length is acceptable, subroutine Center is called to print a row of asterisks, the specified name with an asterisk and space at each end, and finally another row of asterisks.

The CLEAR statement is used to clear the screen, and the Repeat$ function to create a row of asterisks. Note that after the title has been written, a GET KEY statement with a dummy variable is executed. This statement requires a user to press any key in order to execute the END statement and return to the normal True BASIC screen. If the program did not have this statement, the title would appear only briefly on the screen and then disappear as the END statement was executed.

```
! Example Program 7-9
! Get title and display it in a box of asterisks.

PRINT "Press any key to clear screen after display."
LINE INPUT prompt "Enter title: ": Title$
LET X = 0  ! initialize the return variable
CALL Box (Title$, X)
IF X > 0 then
    PRINT "Title is"; X; "characters too long."
END IF
END
```

```
SUB Box (String$, Ret)
    ! Display the title in a box of asterisks.
    ASK margin Width
    IF Len(String$) > (Width - 4) then  ! too long
       LET Ret = Len(String$) - (Width - 4)
    ELSE
       CLEAR  ! clear the screen
       LET Stars$ = Repeat$("*", Len(String$) + 4)
       LET TitleLine$ = "* " & String$ & " *"
       CALL Center (Stars$, Width)
       CALL Center (TitleLine$, Width)
       CALL Center (Stars$, Width)
       GET KEY Dummy  ! pause until a key is pressed
    END IF
END SUB


SUB Center (Value$, Width)
    ! Print a centered string.
    PRINT Tab((Width - Len(Value$))/2); Value$
END SUB
```

This example program produces the following centered output when the title "Analysis of 1983 Earnings" is entered:

```
*****************************
* Analysis of 1983 Earnings *
*****************************
```

Remember that **each type of program unit (main program, function, and subroutine) can declare its own local variables**. Even if the same variable name (not a parameter variable name) is used in two different program units, that name represents two different variables.

Summary of Argument and Parameter Behavior

I think the hardest part of learning procedures is understanding how arguments and parameters work. Remember these five points:

- Arguments are part of the calling statement, parameters are part of the procedure heading.
- Parameters are always variables.
- Function arguments always provide only one-way communication through arguments and parameters — a value can be passed back through the function name.
- Subroutine arguments that are variables provide two-way communication — the address of the argument variable is passed to the subroutine parameter.

- Subroutine arguments that are expressions or values provide one-way communication — only the value of the expression argument or value argument is passed to the subroutine parameter.

7.5 OTHER PROGRAM STRUCTURES

Now let's move on to examine two other program structures: libraries and modules. The use of internal functions and subroutines is also explained.

Libraries

External functions and subroutines can be kept in special files called *libraries*. A library file is not a program that can be run, but rather a collection of functions and subroutines that can be included in and made available to any program.

A library file must start with the statement

```
EXTERNAL
```

on a line by itself as the first statement. This statement identifies the file as a library file, not a True BASIC program. The remainder of the file is a sequence of external procedures. An END statement is neither required nor allowed.

Here is an example of a library file containing some useful functions and subroutines for handling strings:

```
! Example Library 7-10
! Procedure units to manipulate strings.

EXTERNAL  !to identify this file as a library file

DEF Ans$(Question$)
   ! Check Y/N answer to a question.
   DO
      PRINT Question$;
      LINE INPUT prompt "": Reply$
      LET Reply$ = Ucase$(Reply$[1:1])
      SELECT CASE Reply$
      CASE "Y", "N"
           LET Ans$ = Reply$
           LET Finished$ = "true"
      CASE else
           PRINT "Answer YES or NO."
           PRINT
```

```
            LET Finished$ = "false"
        END SELECT
    LOOP until Finished$ = "true"
END DEF


DEF Reverse$ (String$)
    ! Reverse the characters in a string.
    LET Temp$ = "" ! null string
    FOR Index = Len(String$) to 1 step -1
        LET Temp$ = Temp$ & String$[Index:Index]
    NEXT Index
    LET Reverse$ = Temp$
END DEF


DEF More$(Question$)
    ! Check Y/N/Q answer to a question.
    DO
        PRINT Question$;
        LINE INPUT prompt "": Reply$
        LET Reply$ = Ucase$(Reply$[1:1])
        SELECT CASE Reply$
        CASE "Y", "N", "Q"
            LET More$ = Reply$
            LET Finished$ = "true"
        CASE else
            PRINT "Answer YES, NO or QUIT."
            PRINT
            LET Finished$ = "false"
        END SELECT
    LOOP until Finished$ = "true"
END DEF


SUB Center (String$)
    ! Print a centered string.
    ASK margin Width
    LET Space = (Width - len(String$))/2
    PRINT Tab(Space); String$
END SUB


SUB Outline (String$)
    ! Print string in box.
    ASK margin Width
    LET Space = (Width - len(String$))/2
    PRINT Tab(Space - 2); "+";
    PRINT Repeat$("-", Len(String$) + 2);
```

```
        PRINT "+"
        PRINT Tab (Space - 2); "| "; String$; " |"
        PRINT Tab(Space - 2); "+";
        PRINT Repeat$("-", Len(String$) + 2);
        PRINT "+"
    END SUB

    SUB Vertical (String$, Column)
        ! Print a vertical string in a specified column.
        FOR I = 1 to Len(String$)
            PRINT Tab(Column); String$[I:I]
        NEXT I
    END SUB
```

Note that the word DEF is used to identify a function rather than the word FUNC-TION. The main advantage is that it produces a slightly shorter statement line.

After a library file is written, it must be saved as a disk file. The library file may be given any legal file name. I recommend that whenever possible, you use a name containing the letters LIB to identify the file as a library file and to distinguish it from a True BASIC program.

Let's assume that you have saved your example library file under the name STR-GLIB.TRU. If this file is in the current directory, you can use it in a program by including the statement

```
    LIBRARY "STRGLIB.TRU"
```

as one of the first statements in your program. If the library file is in another directory or on another disk, the name in quotation marks must be its complete path name.

A library function must be declared before it can be used. If you want to access the function Reverse$, for example, you must include the statement

```
    DECLARE DEF Reverse$
```

or the equivalent statement

```
    DECLARE FUNCTION Reverse$
```

in your program.

The library statement must be placed ahead of any reference to a procedure in that library. A program may contain more than one library statement and each library statement may refer to one or more library files with their individual file names in quotation marks and separated by commas.

A library subroutine is called by a CALL statement in the program that wants to use that subroutine. Two procedures in a program cannot have the same name, whether they are located in a library attached to the program or written as part of the program itself.

Here is an example of a short program using the library of string procedures. It is designed to test single names and determine if they are palindromes.

```
! Example Program 7-11
! A simplified palindrome program
! for use with names.
! It assumes that the library file.
! is in the current directory.

LIBRARY "STRGLIB.TRU"
DECLARE DEF Reverse$
LINE INPUT prompt "Enter a name: ": Name$
LET Palindrome$ = Reverse$ (Name$)
IF Ucase$(Palindrome$) = Ucase$(Name$) then
   PRINT Name$; " is a palindrome."
ELSE
   PRINT Name$; " is not a palindrome."
END IF
END
```

This program recognizes palindromes only if they contain no spaces or punctuation marks. The following output is produced in two program runs:

```
Enter a name: Hannah
Hannah is a palindrome.

Enter a name: Jasmine
Jasmine is not a palindrome.
```

Several library files are currently distributed with the True BASIC system and other library files will undoubtedly become available in the future. As an example, the file FNMLIB.TRU contains many mathematical and statistical functions while the file MENULIB.TRU contains subroutines useful for writing a program menu system.

Modules

A *module* is a library of external functions and subroutines with some special properties. Like any other library file, it is included in a program by naming it in a LIBRARY statement. The format of a module is as follows:

```
MODULE Name
     module header
     module initialization
     module functions and subroutines
END MODULE
```

The module Name is an identifier, used primarily by True BASIC to identify error messages that apply to a specific module. The module itself is a separate file, similar to a library file, with its own file name. We recommend that you use a file name containing the letters MOD to remind you that the file contains a True BASIC module. Note that an EXTERNAL statement is not needed in the file, it is identified as a library file by the MODULE statement.

The module header specifies which module variables are *shared* by all module procedures. The SHARE statement identifies variables (including array variables; see Chapter 8) and channel (file) numbers whose values and file associations are known everywhere within the module **but not outside the module**. These variables are sometimes called *static variables*. As you move from one procedure to another within the module, these shared variables keep their values and the files remain open. Note that this behavior is quite different from that of local variables and channel numbers in ordinary library procedures.

The module header also specifies which of the module's variables or procedures are *public* and which ones are *private*. The PUBLIC statement lists those variables that can be accessed from outside the module. These variables are often called *global variables*. Their values are known everywhere throughout the program. Any program unit that wishes to use one of these variables must include its name in a DECLARE PUBLIC statement.

The PRIVATE statement lists certain procedures in the module that may not be accessed from outside the module. These are usually procedures that the module's author wishes to keep hidden in the module because they can cause damage if used indiscriminately in the program. Only a few, if any, procedures in a module are normally declared private.

The code for module initialization — if any such code is needed — appears after the module header and before the first module procedure. OPTION statements, if any, in the initialization section apply to all procedures of the module.

The module procedures, both functions and subroutines, are just like those in an ordinary library file. Any procedure that is not private can be used like any other external procedure. Functions must first be declared by a DECLARE statement in your program. If you want to use a public variable in your program, it must first be identified in a DECLARE PUBLIC statement.

Here is an example module that contains three procedures. The subroutine GetFileName asks the user to specify a student number and then generates the grade file name for that student. The file name is declared a global variable by the PUBLIC statement, making its value known in any program that uses this module.

The subroutine ProcessGrade processes an individual grade, while the function Average calculates the average grade. The lowest grade is excluded automatically from the average. Note that three variables are specified as shared variables so that they can retain their values between procedure calls. This module is stored in a file named GRADEMOD.TRU.

```
MODULE Grades
    ! Example Module 7-12
    ! Three procedures that generate a grade file name,
    ! drop the lowest grade in that file, and calculate
    ! the average grade.

    ! The variable FileName$ is a global variable.
    PUBLIC FileName$

    ! The following variables retain their values
    ! between procedure calls.
    SHARE Count, Sum, Lowest
    LET Count = 0
    LET Sum = 0
    LET Lowest = 100

    ! The subroutines start here.
    SUB GetFileName
        ! Generate an appropriate grade file
        ! name as a global variable.
        INPUT prompt "Enter student number: ": Number$
        IF Val(Number$) < 10 then
           LET Number$ = "0" & Number$
        END IF
        LET FileName$ = "GRADES" & Number$ & ".DAT"
    END SUB

    SUB ProcessGrade (Grade)
        ! Process an individual grade.
```

```
        LET Count = Count + 1
        LET Sum = Sum + Grade
        LET Lowest = Min(Grade, Lowest)
   END SUB

   DEF Average
        ! Calculate the average grade.
        LET Count = Count - 1
        LET Sum = Sum - Lowest
        LET Average = Round(Sum / Count)
   END DEF


   END MODULE
```

A variation of Example Program 5-15 demonstrates how the preceding module can be used. As you may recall, this example program asks for a student's number, generates the name of that student's grade file name, reads grades from the file, drops the lowest grade, and displays the average grade. Remember that the class must have less than 100 students.

```
! Example Program 7-13
! Ask user to specify the number of a student, and
! average the grades of that student, dropping the
! lowest grade. This program uses the GRADEMOD module.

LIBRARY "GRADEMOD.TRU"
DECLARE DEF Average
DECLARE PUBLIC FileName$  ! global variable
CALL GetFileName
OPEN #1: name FileName$
DO until End #1
   INPUT #1: Grade
   CALL ProcessGrade (Grade)
LOOP
PRINT "File name is "; FileName$
PRINT "Average grade is"; Average
END
```

Once again, grade files are available on the Example Program disk only for student 9 and student 17. Here is an example of the displayed output:

```
Enter student number: 17
File name is GRADES17.DAT
Average grade is 90
```

The module GRADEMOD.TRU is accessed through a LIBRARY statement. The variable FileName$, whose value is generated in the module, is declared public and thus becomes a global variable. All three procedures in the module are used by the main program.

Internal Functions and Subroutines

Procedures may be written within the main program unit — before the END statement — and then they are called internal functions or internal subroutines. They share one of the advantages of external procedures, the ability to create a modular program that is easier to understand. As you might expect, the word EXTERNAL is never used with internal procedures.

The most serious disadvantage of internal procedures is that they do not maintain the desired isolation between procedure variables and main program variables. **Values of variables declared in an internal procedure are known throughout the main program unit, including all its internal procedures.** Thus the change of a variable value in one procedure will affect all variables with the same name in any other internal procedure and in the main program. To avoid unwanted interaction between variables, I recommend that you use only external functions and subroutines in your programs.

Summary of Important Points

- Each program unit in True BASIC (main program, external function, external subroutine, or external picture) may have its own local variables.

- All external functions used in a program unit must be declared in one or more DECLARE statements.

- A value must be assigned to the function name before control returns to the calling program unit.

- Function parameters are one-way or value parameters.

- No value is associated with a subroutine name.

- Subroutine parameters are two-way or variable parameters.

- A subroutine passes information back to the calling program through its parameters. A function passes information back to the calling program through its function name.

- Values cannot be passed back through temporary variables from an external subroutine to the calling program.

- A library file (not a module) must start with the statement EXTERNAL on a line by itself.

- Variables declared in internal functions and subroutines are known throughout the main program.

Common Errors

- Writing a long main program without any procedures.

- Leaving a function procedure before assigning a value to the function name.

- Using an EXIT statement to exit a procedure that could just as easily have been exited through the END statement.

- Passing an address to a subroutine parameter rather than passing a value when maximum isolation is desired between the calling unit and the subroutine.

- Passing a value to a subroutine parameter rather than passing an address when information must be passed back through the parameter to the calling unit.

- Forgetting to place an additional set of parentheses around a simple variable argument in a subroutine when you wish to pass information by value.

- Trying to calculate the factorial value of a negative number.

- Testing a string to determine if it is a palindrome without converting all letter characters to the same case.

- Forgetting to place an EXTERNAL statement or a MODULE statement at the beginning of a library file.

Self-Test Questions

1. What is an advantage of writing a program as a collection of small program units?

2. What is meant by the concept of isolation between program units?

3. Can the dollar sign character be included as part of

    (a)   a subroutine name?

    (b)   a function name?

4. Does an external function require an assignment statement to assign a value to the function name?

5. What is meant by a local variable in a program unit?

6. If a local variable named Number in an external subroutine is assigned a value of 5, what will be the value of the same variable, Number, when the subroutine is called again?

7. (a) Is a value assigned to a subroutine name when the subroutine is called

    (b) Is a value assigned when control returns from a subroutine to the calling program?

8. If an external function named First$ is to call another external function named Second$, what declaration statement (if any) must be included in the first function?

9. Are the following words palindromes?

    (a)   WILLIAM

    (b)   HANNAH

    (c)   BABY

10. What is the factorial

value of 4 (in mathematical notation, what is the value of 4!)?

11. If a main program unit has a variable named One and an external function declares a variable named One, do these two variables refer to the same or different memory locations?

12. What is meant by the term "pass by value"?

13. What statement must be the last statement in

    (a)   an external function?

    (b)   an external subroutine?

14. What word does True BASIC allow you to use as a substitute for the word FUNCTION?

15. Is the word EXTERNAL optional or required in the heading statement of a subroutine unit that follows the main program END statement?

16. If a main program CALL statement has an argument variable named Two and the called external subroutine has a corresponding parameter variable named Two, do these two variables refer to the same or different memory locations?

17. What is meant by the term "pass by reference"?

18. Can values be passed to an external subroutine through
    - (a) variable parameters?
    - (b) constant parameters?
    - (c) expression parameters?

19. Can values be returned to a calling program unit from an external subroutine through
    - (a) variable parameters?
    - (b) constant parameters?
    - (c) expression parameters?

20. What statement must be the first statement in a True BASIC library file?

21. If a program contains an internal function, are variables declared in the function
    - (a) local to the function?
    - (b) known throughout the main program?

22. (a) Is a PUBLIC variable automatically shared?
    (b) Is a SHARED variable automatically public?

Practice Programs

These problems ask you to write procedures. To show how each procedure works, you must also write a short main program unit for each problem that tests the procedure. For example, you might write a subroutine called Swap in Practice Program 1, and test this subroutine using a short program such as the following test program:

```
! Test Practice Program 1
LET A = 5
LET B = 10
PRINT "Before swap, A ="; A; "and B ="; B
CALL Swap (A, B)
PRINT "After swap, A ="; A; "and B ="; B
END
```

1. Write a subroutine to exchange or swap two numbers that are passed as parameters. Test your subroutine using the numbers 0 and 1.

2. Write a subroutine to swap two strings that are passed as parameters. Test your subroutine using the strings "TRUE" and "FALSE".

3. Write a function Pred$ that returns the predecessor (in the ASCII table) of a character parameter. If the parameter string is longer than one character, the function returns the predecessor of the first character.

    Test your function using the string values "C", "A", "@", and "qed".

4. Write a function Succ$ that returns the successor (in the ASCII table) of a character parameter. If the parameter string is longer than one character, the function returns the successor of the first character.

    Test your function using the string values "C", "z", "*", and "ABC".

5. Write a subroutine to display N characters of type C$ on the screen. Both N and C$ are parameters.

    Test your subroutine using the following pairs of values:
          20, "*"
          50, "-"
          10, "x"

6. Write a function Cube that returns the cube of its numeric parameter. Test your function using the numbers 2, 5, and 132.

7. Write a function Decimal that returns the decimal part of its numeric parameter. Don't use the Fp standard function. Test your function using the numbers 12.75, 35, 3.3333333, and -1.001.

8. Write a subroutine to clear the entire screen and fill it with an 80-by-24 grid of dots. Such a subroutine might be used in a computer graphics program.

9. Write a function that returns the volume of a sphere whose radius is passed as a parameter. Test your function using radii of 5, 10, and 2.32 units.

10. Write a function that returns the English word corresponding to its single-digit numeric parameter; that is, TWO for parameter 2, SEVEN for 7, and so forth.

    Test your function using the digits 0, 9, and 5.

11. Write a function Today$ that returns the current date in MM-DD-YY format. This problem assumes that your computer has a built-in clock or that you entered the correct date when you turned on the system. Review the date and time functions in Appendix G.

12. Write a function that compares two string parameters, returning one if they are equal and zero if not equal.

    Test your function using the following pairs of string values:

    > "abc", "xyz"
    > "aaa", "aaa"
    > "abc", "abcdef"
    > "abc", "ABC"

13. Write a function that returns the number of words in a string. Assume there is a word (no initial blank) at the beginning of the string and a word (no final blank) at the end of the string. Any other sequence of one or more characters surrounded by blanks is defined as a word. Assume only one blank between words.

    Test your function using the following phrases:

    > This is a test string.
    > Will you dance? Will you dance? Will you dance?

14. Write a function that returns the number of times that a character appears in a string. Uppercase and lowercase characters are considered the same. For example, the function should show that the character "T" appears four times in the string "THIS IS THE STRAIGHT WAY". Both the string and the character are parameters.

    > "T" in "THIS IS THE STRAIGHT WAY"
    > "X" in "Use the Xerox machine"
    > "*" in "!***********"

15. Write a function that analyzes a sentence and returns the average word length in a string parameter. Use the function developed in Practice Program 13.

Test your function using the following sentences:

Dependents must furnish evidence of eligibility.

Now is the time for all good men to fight or flee.

16. Write your own version of a Val function that includes error trapping and returns a value of Maxnum if you try to convert a nonnumeric string. This specification means that your function cannot be used to convert the string equivalent of Maxnum, not a serious limitation.

Test your function using the following entered values:

25.2

A1A

-133

210-55-8787

$12,033.75

#9

CHAPTER

8

Arrays for Lists and Tables

8.1   INTRODUCTION

Lists and tables are examples of arrays; a new type of variable that is introduced in this chapter. You learn how to determine the size of an array and how to use an index number to identify a specific item in an array.

Several application programs using arrays are presented. The first program develops and maintains a room occupancy list for a motel. The second program uses a mileage table to calculate the distance between two cities.

8.2   ARRAYS WITH ONE DIMENSION

You understand now that a variable can be thought of as a mailbox in which a value may be placed. As you know, the mailbox is just a symbol for a memory location. There are times when it is convenient to be able to refer to a group of mailboxes rather than to a single mailbox, such as when a group of mailboxes contains a collection of similar quantities. The group is designated by a single name and each mailbox within the group is identified by a number or *index*. This group of mailboxes or memory locations is called an *array variable*.

Let's look at some examples of array variables. The index is a number and is enclosed in parentheses. The variable Day$ represents the days of the week and each mailbox in the array can be assigned the name of a day.

Day$(1) is the first mailbox and is assigned a value of "Sunday".

Day$(4) is the fourth mailbox and is assigned a value of "Wednesday".

The variable Room represents the rooms in a motel and each mailbox can be assigned a value representing the number of occupants in that room. In this case, the index number is the same as the room number.

Room(10) contains the number of occupants in room 10.

Room(35) contains the number of occupants in room 35.

The individual mailboxes are called *elements* of the array, and the number of elements in the array is called the *size* of the array. Each element is identified by a numeric index that usually starts at one for the first element and goes up to the size of the array. In this section, you use only arrays with a single index and call these arrays *one-dimensional arrays*.

The rules for naming an array variable are the same as those for naming a simple variable — the kind of variable discussed in preceding chapters. An individual element is identified by the array name followed by an index number enclosed in parentheses. Arrays whose elements can be assigned string values are called string arrays and the last character in the array name must be a dollar sign. Numeric arrays have elements that can be assigned numeric values.

Referring to the preceding examples, Day$(1) is the first element of the array Day$. When Day$ is used in a program, element Day$(1) is assigned a value of Sunday. Room(35) is the thirty-fifth element of the array Room. In a later example program, this element is assigned a numeric value equal to the number of occupants in room 35.

Declaring an Array

Before using an array in a BASIC program, you must tell the computer its size. This is done with the DIM statement. **An array can be declared only once in a DIM statement. The same DIM statement cannot be executed more than once.** This means, for example, that a DIM statement cannot be placed in a loop where it would be executed on each pass through the loop.

DIM statements are usually placed together near the beginning of a program. An example DIM statement is

```
DIM Day$(1 to 7)
```

indicating that the array Day$ has 7 elements that can each hold a string value. Day$(1) is the first element and Day$(7) is the last element. When this array is used in a program, element Day$(1) might be assigned a value of "Sunday" and Day$(7) might be assigned a value of "Saturday".

Another example is

```
DIM Room(70)
```

which indicates that there are 70 elements — corresponding to the number of rooms in the motel. By default, the first element is Room(1). Note that the size of the array (the value in parentheses) must be an integer value and a constant. **It cannot be a variable or an expression.**

This restriction on the DIM statement is an important point and should be carefully noted. Variables **cannot** be used in a DIM statement to dimension an array. The DIM statement also initializes an array, assigning the value zero to each element of a numeric array and the null string to each element of a string array.

Array Bounds

The smallest or most negative value of the index is called the *lower bound* of the array. The default value of the lower bound is one. The largest or most positive value of the index is called the *upper bound* and has a default value equal to the size of the array. Thus the array Room, as dimensioned, has a lower bound of one and an upper bound of 70.

True BASIC allows both the lower bound and the upper bound to be specified in the DIM statement. The Room array can be dimensioned as

```
DIM Room(1 to 70)
```

or as

```
DIM Room(1:70)
```

The two statements are equivalent but I think the form of the first statement is the best. It is more descriptive than the original DIM statement that showed only the upper bound and it is less apt to cause mistakes. I recommend its use.

The lower bound of an array does not necessarily have to be one, as illustrated by the following examples:

```
DIM Census(1950 to 1999)
DIM Strain(-32 to 212)
```

Remember that the lower and upper bounds must be integer values in the range of -1E9 to +1E9. If you want to change the default lower bound of all arrays in a program from one to zero, place the statement

```
OPTION BASE 0
```

in your program before you write the first DIM statement.

The bounds of an array may be changed while the program is running, as explained in Section 8.6. The system functions Lbound(N) and Ubound(N) return the current values of the lower and upper bounds of the array named N. The system function Size(N) returns the number of elements in the array named N. Referring to the preceding DIM statements, Lbound(Census) has a value of 1950, Ubound(Strain) has a value of 212, and Size(Strain) has a value of 245. How is that last number (245) calculated? There are 212 elements above zero, 32 elements below zero, and 1 element for zero, making a total of 245 elements.

Array Indexing

The elements of an array variable can be used in a True BASIC program in most of the same ways that simple variables are used. Elements can be assigned values, used in expressions, and displayed on the screen. An array element cannot be used as the control variable in a FOR statement; that is, the statement

```
FOR A(2) = 1 to 5  ! not allowed
```

is not a valid statement.

Here is an example that does not do much but illustrates how array elements can be manipulated:

```
! Example Program 8-1
! Manipulating an element in an array.

DIM Strength(1 to 20)
LET Strength(5) = 134.72
LET WorkingStrength = Strength(5) / 2
PRINT "Working strength is"; WorkingStrength
END
```

The array named Strength is declared large enough to hold 20 numeric values. A value of 134.72 is assigned to the fifth element of the array, element Strength(5). Note that the numbers in parentheses in the DIM statement show the size of the array, while in the LET statement the number is an index referring to a particular element of the array. The element Strength(5) can be manipulated in expressions just like a simple variable. This program displays the following output:

```
Working strength is 67.36
```

The index can be a numeric constant, as in the previous example, or it can be a numeric variable. Because individual array elements can be designated by index and the size of the array is known, arrays are often manipulated with FOR loops.

In the next example program, you read values from a DATA statement and assign these values to elements of an array. You display the array elements, change one of the element values, and display the array elements again.

```
! Example Program 8-2
! Use a variable index to load an array and
! then display the array element values.

! Load values into the array from a DATA statement.
DIM Structure(1 to 5)
FOR Index = 1 to 5
    READ Structure(Index)
NEXT Index

! Display the contents of the array.
PRINT "Old values: ";
FOR Index = 1 to 5
    PRINT Structure(Index);
NEXT Index
PRINT  ! move to next line
PRINT  ! put in a blank line

! Change value of one element and display again.
LET Index = 2
LET Structure(Index) = 133.55
PRINT "New values: ";
FOR Index = 1 to 5
    PRINT Structure(Index);
NEXT Index
PRINT

DATA 128.21, 167.33, 135.01, 142.84, 134.72
END
```

A FOR loop is used to display the sequence of array values that are read from the
DATA statement. A new value is then assigned to the element whose index is 2 and
the sequence of array elements is displayed again. Note that the value of only one element is changed. Here is the program output:

```
Old values:  128.21  167.33  135.01  142.84  134.72

New values:  128.21  133.55  135.01  142.84  134.72
```

Another example program assigns values to the array Day$ and then displays the day of the week corresponding to a number entered by a user:

```
! Example Program 8-3
! Use an array to display the day name
! corresponding to a number.

DIM Day$(1 to 7)
FOR I = 1 to 7
    READ Day$(I)
NEXT I
DATA Sunday, Monday, Tuesday, Wednesday
DATA Thursday, Friday, Saturday

PRINT "Enter a number between 1 and 7"
PRINT "and the corresponding day of the week"
PRINT "is displayed. Enter zero to stop."
PRINT
INPUT prompt "Day number? ": Number
DO until Number = 0
    PRINT "Day number"; Number; "is "; Day$(Number)
    INPUT prompt "Day number? ": Number
LOOP
END
```

This program designates Sunday as the first day of the week, It continues to request input and display names until a zero is entered. Program interaction might look as follows:

```
Enter a number between 1 and 7
and the corresponding day of the week
will be displayed. Enter zero to stop.

Day number? 2
Day number 2 is Monday
Day number? 6
Day number 6 is Friday
Day number? 0
```

An Array as a List

You might think of a one-dimensional array as an indexed list. A list can have either string elements or numeric elements. The maximum size or length of the list is declared in a DIM statement. You can refer directly to any element of the list by using its index number, which is usually its position in the list.

Using Part of an Array

There are times when you want to use an array for storing information but do not know how many items will need to be stored. As already noted, **the size of an array in a DIM statement cannot be a variable**. If the maximum number of items to be stored can be determined, however, you can set the size of the array to this value. The array can then be used for storing any number of items up to this maximum, using a counter to keep track of the actual number of items stored.

Here is an example of this technique, creating a list of names in a partially filled array. After all names have been entered, the number of names is displayed and the names are listed on the screen for verification.

```
! Example Program 8-4
! Store up to 100 names in an array.
! Enter a single period to stop.

DIM Names$(1 to 100)
PRINT "Enter up to 100 names, one name per line."
PRINT "Enter a single period to stop the process."
LET Count = 0

LINE INPUT prompt "Name? ": Reply$
DO until Reply$ = "." or Count >= 100
   LET Count = Count + 1
   LET Names$(Count) = Reply$
   IF Count < 100 then
      LINE INPUT prompt "Name? ": Reply$
   END IF
LOOP

PRINT
PRINT Count; "names entered"
PRINT "Here is the list:"
PRINT
FOR I = 1 to Count
   PRINT Names$(I)
NEXT I
END
```

The array Names$ is dimensioned to hold up to 100 names. Each name is typed in and assigned to a variable named Reply$. If the name is a single period, the entry process stops. If not, the counter Count is incremented and the name is placed in the array Names$. After all names have been entered, a simple loop uses the final value of Count to display the stored names. Here is an example of program output:

```
Enter up to 100 names, one name per line.
Enter a single period to stop the process.
Name? Lawrence Simpson
Name? Ruth Lopez
Name? .

 2 names entered
Here is the list:

Lawrence Simpson
Ruth Lopez
```

If a period is entered in response to the prompt, the DO loop is terminated and a list of the names already entered is displayed. Note the care used to stop the program at the correct point.

When the 100th name is entered, variable Count is incremented to 100 and the entered name is stored in the array. The IF statement in the DO loop prevents another name from being requested. The UNTIL test in the DO statement terminates the loop because Count has a value of 100. Note that a "greater than or equal" test is used to avoid testing a numerical equality (see Chapter 6, Section 6.5). As before, a list of the entered names is displayed.

Study this loop carefully and be sure you understand the logic. The loop must terminate properly if either a period is entered or the number of entered names reaches 100 (and thus no period is entered).

Arrays as Procedure Parameters

Arrays containing either number or string values may be used as parameter variables in functions and subroutines. Passing an array to a subroutine as a variable parameter means that the array is given two names; the name used in the calling program and the name used in the subroutine. Only one copy of the array exists in memory, and the values of all array elements can be accessed by either program unit.

Passing an array to a function means that the values of all the array elements are copied into the corresponding elements of a local array. If the array is large, many memory locations are needed to store this second copy of the array. Limited memory may become a problem on some small computers.

In the procedure parameter list, an array parameter must be identified by empty parentheses so it can be distinguished from a simple variable parameter. Here is an example program that uses a list of names as an array parameter. The array is passed to a subroutine that converts each name to uppercase.

```
! Example Program 8-5
! Use a subroutine to convert all names
! in a list to uppercase.

DIM Name$(1 to 5)
FOR Index = 1 to 5
    READ Name$(Index)
NEXT Index
CALL Capital (Name$)  ! empty parentheses not needed
FOR Index = 1 to 5
    PRINT Name$(Index)
NEXT Index

DATA John, Rob, Ginny, Peter, Sally
END

SUB Capital (List$())  ! empty parentheses required
    ! Change characters in string to uppercase.
    FOR I = Lbound(List$) to Ubound(List$)
        LET List$(I) = Ucase$(List$(I))
    NEXT I
END SUB
```

The names Name$ and List$ are two different names for the same array and thus the converted uppercase values can be printed by the main program. The array is dimensioned in the calling program and so does not have to be dimensioned again — in fact, cannot be dimensioned again — in the subroutine.

The argument Name$ is recognized as an array in the main program where it is dimensioned and so empty parentheses are not needed (nor allowed). The parameter List$() needs empty parentheses to tell the subroutine that this variable is a one-dimensional array.

The following program output is produced:

```
JOHN
ROB
GINNY
PETER
SALLY
```

The functions Lbound and Ubound are used to calculate the lower and upper bounds of the array List$ in the subroutine. This practice makes the subroutine more general, and it can now be used to convert the elements of any one-dimensional string array to uppercase.

8.3   EXAMPLE PROGRAM USING A LIST

In this section you design and write a somewhat larger program that uses a one-dimensional array.

Designing the Program

Your task is to design a computer program that stores information about motel room occupancy. The motel has 70 rooms and the desk clerk needs to know whether or not each room is occupied. If the room is occupied, she would like to know the number of occupants. This program will be run by the desk clerk during afternoon and evening hours as travelers come in off the highway. You decide to store the room occupancy information in an array and choose an array named Room.

Your program must be able to store information on room occupancy, to find the next vacant room, to ask for the number of new occupants in this room, and to display the total number of guests staying in the motel.

Note that your program is not as versatile as you might wish because you store information in an array in memory and when the computer is turned off, the information is lost. In the next chapter, you will learn how to store this type of information on a disk file in a more permanent fashion. The program as written, however, provides useful occupancy information to a desk clerk if used as designed. Here is an outline of the program:

> initialize the room array
>
> top of main loop, continue until no vacant rooms remain
>
>> find next vacant room and assign occupants
>>
>> display new occupancy total
>>
>> check whether to continue or quit
>
> bottom of main loop
>
> end program

Writing the Program

One section of the program declares the size of the array and initializes its elements:

```
DIM Room(1 to 70)
FOR Index = Lbound(Room) to Ubound(Room)
    LET Room(Index) = 0
NEXT Index
```

The room number serves as the array index. The following program section finds the next vacant room and asks for the number of occupants. Note that the array Room is just a list of room occupancy: the first number in the list is the number of occupants of room 1, the second number is the occupants in room 2, and so forth. The section is written as a subroutine and the array Room and the room number Number are passed to it as parameters.

```
SUB Assign (Room(), Number)
    ! Find and assign the next vacant room.
    DO
       IF Room(Number) <> 0 then
          LET Number = Number + 1
       END IF
    LOOP until Room(Number) = 0
    PRINT "Room"; Number; "is vacant."
    INPUT prompt "How many occupants? ": Room(Number)
END SUB
```

The next section gives the total number of occupants in the motel. It uses the familiar summing technique with the sum stored in variable Sum. This variable does not need to be included as a parameter — for passing information back to the main program — because displaying the results is done in the subroutine.

```
SUB Occupancy (Room())
    ! Calculate total room occupancy.
    LET Sum = 0
    FOR Index = Lbound(Room) to Ubound(Room)
        LET Sum = Sum + Room(Index)
    NEXT Index
    PRINT "Total occupancy is"; Sum
END SUB
```

You must also provide a way for the user — the desk clerk — to stop the program. Another subroutine asks if the user wishes to continue and the reply is converted to a single uppercase character. If the user enters "QUIT" or "quit" or just "q", the program interprets it as a signal to stop. This signal is passed back to the calling program through the variable More$. A null prompt in the LINE INPUT statement suppresses the usual question mark.

Checking input in this way is an example of careful programming to protect and help the user, a program characteristic sometimes called *user-friendly*. I urge you to design your programs in this manner. Here is the subroutine that checks user input:

```
    SUB Check (More$)
        ! See if user wants to stop the program.
        PRINT "Type Q to stop the program."
        PRINT "Press the Return key to continue."
        LINE INPUT prompt "": More$
        LET More$ = Ucase$(More$[1:1])
    END SUB
```

Now let's put everything together in a working program. Remember that this program and the computer must run continuously, so most of the program consists of one big loop.

```
    ! Example Program 8-6
    ! Motel occupancy record program.
    ! Initialize the occupancy list and two variables.

    DIM Room(1 to 70)
    FOR Index = Lbound(Room) to Ubound(Room)
        LET Room(Index) = 0
    NEXT Index
    LET Count = Lbound(Room)              ! room number counter
    LET More$ = ""                        ! flag to continue

    !Now call the appropriate subroutines.
    CALL Check (More$)
    DO until Count >= Ubound(Room) or More$ = "Q"
       CALL Assign (Room, Count)
       CALL Occupancy (Room)
       CALL Check (More$)
    LOOP
    IF Count = Ubound(Room) then
       PRINT "There are no vacant rooms."
    END IF
    END  ! of main program

    SUB Assign (Room(), Number)
        ! Find and assign the next vacant room.
        DO
           IF Room(Number) <> 0 then
              LET Number = Number + 1
           END IF
        LOOP until Room(Number) = 0
        PRINT "Room"; Number; "is vacant."
        INPUT prompt "How many occupants? ": Room(Number)
    END SUB  ! Assign
```

```
SUB Occupancy (Room())
    ! Calculate total room occupancy.
    LET Sum = 0
    FOR Index = Lbound(Room) to Ubound(Room)
        LET Sum = Sum + Room(Index)
    NEXT Index
    PRINT "Total occupancy is"; Sum
    PRINT
END SUB  ! Occupancy

SUB Check (More$)
    ! See if user wants to stop the program.
    PRINT "Type Q to stop the program."
    PRINT "Press the Return key to continue."
    LINE INPUT prompt"": More$
    LET More$ = Ucase$(More$[1:1])
END SUB  ! Check
```

The main structure of this program is a loop, The program is assembled from several small sections or units. Just as an article is more readable if separated into paragraphs, a computer program is more easily understood if separated into program units. Three of the units are subroutines and have a descriptive comment at their beginning. Within each program unit, indentation is used to set off the body of each loop and branch. It is important that you use these techniques as you design new programs; it is a way to develop good programming style.

Here is the information displayed while three transactions are processed:

```
Type Q to stop the program.
Press the Return key to continue

Room 1 is vacant.
How many occupants? 2
Total occupancy is 2

Type Q to stop the program.
Press the Return key to continue

Room 2 is vacant.
How many occupants? 1
Total occupancy is 3

Type Q to stop the program.
Press the Return key to continue.
```

```
Room 3 is vacant.
How many occupants? 2
Total occupancy is 5

Type Q to stop the program.
Press the Return key to continue.
Q
```

8.4   ARRAYS WITH TWO DIMENSIONS

The arrays discussed in previous sections have a single index and are called one-dimensional arrays. An example is the familiar list. You can also have arrays with two or more indices and these are called *multidimensional* arrays.

An example of a two-dimensional array is a table that has several rows and columns. The location of an element in the table is specified by two indices, one index specifying the row number and the other specifying the column number. Our discussion is restricted to two-dimensional arrays, although True BASIC supports arrays with more than two dimensions. **Note that a one-dimensional array and a two-dimensional array in the same program cannot have the same name.**

Two-Dimensional Array Notation

Assume that a two-dimensional array containing string values is named Salesman$. Fig. 8.1 shows how the array might look when displayed as a table with labels and numbers added to identify rows and columns.

Column Row	1	2	3
1	John Adams	Chicago	312-202-5674
2	Bill Cullins	New York	212-405-1298
3	Gary Despio	Atlanta	404-813-8824
4	Bill Morris	Miami	305-222-5141
5	Jack Williams	Boston	617-267-0351

Figure 8.1 *Table of sales information.*

The element in the third row and first column is designated as Salesman$(3,1) and has a value of "Gary Despio". If you visualize the array as a table, the horizontal lines of element values are called *rows* and the vertical lines are called *columns*. It is common convention for the first index to refer to the row number and the second index to refer to the column number.

Tables are often organized in this manner, with each column referring to a different type of information and each row referring to a different person or item. In row 3, for example, element Salesman$(3,1) in column 1 contains a salesman's name, element Salesman$(3,2) in column 2 contains that salesman's city, and Salesman$(3,3) in column 3 contains that salesman's telephone number.

Declaring Two-Dimensional Arrays

Arrays with two dimensions are declared with the DIM statement, in a manner similar to one-dimensional arrays. For example, the statement

```
DIM Salesman$(1 to 100, 1 to 3)
```

declares an array with 100 rows and 3 columns. This array can hold 300 string values. There is now a size associated with each dimension. The size of the first dimension, given by Size(Salesman$, 1), is 100, and the size of the second dimension, given by Size(Salesman$, 2), is 3.

Remember that a string array is initialized just like any other string variable, with a null string assigned to each element. As with one-dimensional arrays, it is not necessary that every element be assigned a value different from the initial value. In this example, new values — that is, information on salesmen — have been assigned to only the first five rows.

Two-Dimensional Arrays as Tables

An example of a two-dimensional numeric array is the table, often found on road maps, showing distances between cities. The array variable Distance represents this table. If you want to find the distance between Boston and New York, you go down the left margin until you find the row labeled Boston and then across that row until you find the column labeled New York. Where this row and column intersect, you find the distance in miles. If Boston is the label for row 2 and New York the label for column 6, then the distance between these two cities is given by the value of element Distance(2,6). In the next section, a program to create and use such a table is presented.

Nested FOR Loops

Two-dimensional arrays can be initialized with nested FOR loops. Here is an example that uses this structure to assign a value of zero to each element of an array:

```
! Example Program 8-7
! Initialize a two-dimensional array.

DIM Grid(1 to 12, 1 to 30)
FOR Row = 1 to 12
    FOR Column = 1 to 30
        LET Grid(Row, Column) = 0
    NEXT Column
NEXT Row
PRINT "The array Grid has been initialized to zero."
END
```

Note that for each value of Row in the outer loop, the variable Column runs through its set of values from 1 to 30 in the inner loop This process is repeated for each row (or value of Row) from 1 to 12. The program assigns values to the array elements by row.

Note also that the outer Row loop must completely surround and contain the inner Column loop. If the two NEXT statements are reversed, the loops overlap and the program will not work. **Nested FOR loops cannot overlap.** Indentation helps to show how the inner Column loop nests within the outer Row loop.

This program displays the following statement:

```
The array Grid has been initialized to zero.
```

Another example program reads numbers from a file into a two-dimensional array and then displays the array. A small array with three rows and five columns is used so it will fit easily on the screen. This program demonstrates the use of FOR loops for reading two-dimensional arrays and for printing these arrays in a formatted display. Here is the program:

```
! Example Program 8-8
! Fill an array from a text file and
! print the array in a formatted display.

! Fill an array from a text file.
DIM Table(1 to 3, 1 to 5)
INPUT prompt "File name? ": FileName$
OPEN #1: name FileName$
FOR Row = 1 to 3
    FOR Column = 1 to 5
        INPUT #1: Table(Row, Column)
    NEXT Column
```

```
    NEXT Row

    ! Display the filled array.
    PRINT
    FOR Row = 1 to 3
        FOR Column = 1 to 5
            PRINT Table(Row, Column);
        NEXT Column
        PRINT
    NEXT Row
    END
```

In the display module, the semicolon at the end of the second PRINT statement causes all values in a row to be displayed on the same line, although this won't work properly if there are too many columns to fit on the screen. The third PRINT statement moves the cursor to the next line on the screen after a row of values has been displayed. This program produces the following output display when a test file named ARRAY.DAT, located in the same directory or folder as the program, is used. If the data file is located in another directory or folder, the user must enter a full path name rather than just a simple file name.

```
    File name? ARRAY.DAT

    3  5  7  3  8
    4  1  0  3  4
    5  2  7  5  3
```

The program assumes that the file contains at least 15 numeric values. If that is not the case, the program will crash. Another few lines of code are added to the program, checking to see that the file contains 15 values or more. If it does not, the user is given a chance to specify another file or stop the program.

```
    ! Example Program 8-9
    ! Fill an array from a text file and
    ! print the array in a formatted display.
    ! Check that the file contains 15 values.

    DIM Table(1 to 3, 1 to 5)

    ! Open a file and check its contents.
    INPUT prompt "File name? ": FileName$
    DO until Count >= 15 or Ucase$(FileName$[1:1]) = "Q"
       LET Count = 0
       OPEN #1: name FileName$
       DO until End #1
          INPUT #1: Value
```

```
         LET Count = Count + 1
     LOOP
     IF Count < 15 then
        PRINT "This file does not contain enough data."
        PRINT "Enter a new file name or type Q to stop."
        CLOSE #1
        INPUT prompt "File name? ": FileName$
     END IF
LOOP

! Fill an array from a text file.
RESET #1: begin
FOR Row = 1 to 3
    FOR Column = 1 to 5
        INPUT #1: Table(Row, Column)
    NEXT Column
NEXT Row

! Display the filled array.
PRINT
FOR Row = 1 to 3
    FOR Column = 1 to 5
        PRINT Table(Row, Column);
    NEXT Column
    PRINT
NEXT Row
END
```

As is often the case, checking for possible errors makes the program longer and more complicated. Program output is essentially the same as that of Example Program 8-8 if the file is valid. Here is an example of output for a file named BAD.DAT that does not contain enough data values:

```
File name? BAD.DAT
This file does not contain enough data.
Enter a new file name or type Q to stop.
File name? Q
```

Two-Dimensional Arrays as Parameters

Two-dimensional arrays can also be used as parameters in subroutines and functions. The procedure heading must show that the parameter is a two-dimensional array by having a comma between the dummy parentheses. Here are two examples of procedure heading statements:

```
DEF Trace (X(,))
SUB Rotate (One(), Two(), Three(,))
```

In the second example, arrays One and Two are one-dimensional while array Three is two-dimensional.

The functions Ubound and Lbound can still be used, but they now require two parameters. The first parameter is the name of the array; the second parameter is the number of the dimension. For example, function Ubound(Table, 1) returns the upper bound of the first dimension of the array Table while Ubound(Table, 2) returns that of the second dimension.

The function Size also requires two parameters, the first parameter being the array name, and returns the size of the dimension specified by the second parameter. For example, function Size(Table, 1) returns the size of the first dimension of the array Table.

The next example program passes the values of a two-dimensional array to a function that calculates the trace of an array. The trace is a mathematical value that can be calculated for an array of numeric values when the number of rows equals the number of columns. Such an array is called a *square array*. Its trace is equal to the sum of all elements that have the same index for row and column.

As an example, in the array

1	3	6
2	7	8
9	2	4

the trace is 1 + 7 + 4 and equals 12.

Here is the program itself:

```
! Example Program 8-10
! Read an array from DATA statements
! and calculate its trace.

DIM Array(1 to 3, 1 to 3)
DECLARE FUNCTION Trace
PRINT "The array is"
PRINT
FOR I = 1 to 3
    FOR J = 1 to 3
```

```
        READ Array(I, J)
        PRINT Array(I, J);
    NEXT J
    PRINT
NEXT I
PRINT
PRINT "Its trace is"; Trace (Array)

DATA 1,3,6,2,7,8,9,2,4
END

FUNCTION Trace (X(,))
    ! Calculate the trace.
    LET Sum = 0
    FOR K = Lbound(X,1) to Ubound(X,1)
        LET Sum = Sum + X(K, K)
    NEXT K
    LET Trace = Sum
END FUNCTION  ! Trace
```

In this case, the trace equals the sum of the numeric elements X(1,1), X(2,2), and X(3,3). Note the notation X(,) in the heading statement of the function, telling the function that X is a two-dimensional array. The array X in the function unit is a local copy of the array Array in the main program unit. As before, the array is dimensioned in the calling program. Note the upper limit of the FOR statement in the function Trace. In this case, we can use either Ubound(X,1) or Ubound(X,2) because the two dimensions of X are the same size.

8.5 EXAMPLE PROGRAM USING A TABLE

Let's now return to an example mentioned earlier, the mileage table showing the distance between cities. The example program contains the following sections:

> read a list of cities
>
> read a mileage table of distances between cities
>
> ask the user to enter the names of two cities
>
> look up and display the distance between cities
>
> end the program

This program reads the list of cities and table of distances from data files. Separate subroutines are used for reading the list of cities (a one-dimensional string array) and the table of distances (a two-dimensional numeric array).

Here is a straightforward subroutine to read the list of cities. The list array is passed to the subroutine as a parameter. This subroutine assumes that the file is in the same directory as the program and contains the correct number of cities for Example Program 8-11.

```
SUB ReadList (List$())
    ! Read the list of cities from a file.
    INPUT prompt "Name of the cities file? ": FileName$
    OPEN #1: name FileName$
    FOR Line = 1 to Ubound(List$)
        LINE INPUT #1: List$(Line)
    NEXT Line
END SUB
```

A list of the seven cities in the file is shown in Fig. 8.2. Each city is identified by a number.

1	ATLANTA
2	BOSTON
3	CHICAGO
4	DETROIT
5	MIAMI
6	NEW YORK
7	WASHINGTON

Figure 8.2 *List of cities.*

Another subroutine reads the mileage table (shown in Fig. 8.3) and assigns the values to a two-dimensional array named Distance. The same assumption is made as before on the location of the file and the number of entries. In this example, the information is placed in an array with seven rows and seven columns.

Column Row	1	2	3	4	5	6	7
1	0	1065	675	715	665	850	605
2	1065	0	965	710	1515	215	445
3	675	965	0	270	1335	790	695
4	715	710	270	0	1370	620	520
5	665	1515	1335	1370	0	1300	1080
6	850	215	790	620	1300	0	230
7	605	445	695	520	1080	230	0

Figure 8.3 *Table of distances between cities.*

The table or array must have the same number of rows and columns because each row represents one of the cities in the list and each column represents one of the cities in the same list. The same order of city names is used for both rows and columns.

Note that the distance between two cities with the same name is zero; that is, the distance from BOSTON to BOSTON is zero. All these zeroes lie along what is called the *principal diagonal* of the Distance array, running from the upper left corner of the table to the lower right corner. The elements lying below the principal diagonal contain the same information as those lying above this diagonal. For example, the distance from BOSTON to ATLANTA is the same as the distance from ATLANTA to BOSTON.

Looking carefully at the values in the Distance array, you see that of the total 49 values (7 rows and 7 columns), the 7 values along the principal diagonal are zeroes. Among the remaining 42 values, the corresponding values above and below the principal diagonal are the same, so there are only 21 unique distance values. These values are contained in the file DISTANCE.DAT.

All elements along the principal diagonal, of the type Distance(I, I), have a value of zero. Corresponding values above and below the principal diagonal are equal, so that element Distance(I, J) has the same value as element Distance(J, I).

This discussion helps to explain the subroutine used to read the table of distances. The program first sets all elements along the principal diagonal equal to zero. Then it reads in the 21 elements lying above the principal diagonal and as each value is read, assigns that value also to the corresponding element lying below the principal diagonal.

The following subroutine reads the table of distances:

```
SUB ReadTable (Table(,))
   ! Read the table of distances.

   INPUT prompt "Name of distance file? ": FileName$
   OPEN #2: name FileName$
   FOR Index = 1 to Ubound(Table, 1)
      LET Table(Index, Index) = 0
   NEXT I

   FOR Row = 1 to (Ubound(Table, 1) - 1)
      FOR Column = (I + 1) to Ubound(Table, 2)
         INPUT #2: Table(Row, Column)
         LET Table(Column, Row) = Table(Row, Column)
      NEXT Column
   NEXT Row
END SUB
```

Figure 8.4 lists the numbers in file DISTANCE.DAT with a note next to each number explaining what it represents.

1065	(distance, city 1 to 2)
675	(distance, city 1 to 3)
715	(distance, city 1 to 4)
665	(distance, city 1 to 5)
850	(distance, city 1 to 6)
605	(distance, city 1 to 7)
965	(distance, city 2 to 3)
710	(distance, city 2 to 4)
1515	(distance, city 2 to 5)
215	(distance, city 2 to 6)
445	(distance, city 2 to 7)
270	(distance, city 3 to 4)
1335	(distance, city 3 to 5)
790	(distance, city 3 to 6)
695	(distance, city 3 to 7)
1370	(distance, city 4 to 5)
620	(distance, city 4 to 6)
520	(distance, city 4 to 7)
1300	(distance, city 5 to 6)
1080	(distance, city 5 to 7)
230	(distance, city 6 to 7)

Figure 8.4 *Numbers in file DISTANCE.DAT.*

In the preceding subroutine, note particularly the FOR loops used to read information from the data file. Only rows 1 through 6 are read because these rows include all elements lying above the principal diagonal. Thus Row ranges from 1 to 6 or in more general notation, from 1 to (Ubound(Table, 1) - 1).

In row 1, the program starts reading at column 2, in row 2 at column 3, and so forth. That is, it starts reading values in row Row at column (Row + 1). Thus the variable Column ranges from (Row + 1) to 7 or in more general notation, from (Row + 1) to Ubound(Table, 2).

One disadvantage of using an array to hold the distance values is that over half the storage space in the array is wasted. This might become a problem with very large tables, but this example program uses comparatively little memory space. A compensating advantage is that a two-dimensional array is probably the simplest and easiest structure to use for the table of distances and produces a simple and easy-to-understand program.

A function is used to calculate the numerical position of any city in the list of cities. This information is needed to calculate the indices of the appropriate distance table element. The name of the city is passed to the function as parameter Name$, along with the array List$ containing the list of cities. The position of this city in the list is assigned to the function Location.

```
DEF Location (Name$, List$())
    ! Find location of a city in the city list.
    LET CityNum = 0
    LET Count = 1
    DO
       IF Name$ = List$(Count) then
          LET CityNum = Count
       END IF
       LET Count = Count + 1
    LOOP until CityNum > 0 or Count > Ubound(List$)
    LET Location = CityNum
END DEF
```

Note that if a city name cannot be found in the list, a value of zero is returned by the function. I used the shorter name DEF in this problem rather than the name FUNCTION.

Finally, all the modules are put together in a complete program. The name of the first city is First$ and its location in the city list is First. The second city is Second$ and its location is Second. The distance between these two cities is simply the array element Distance(First, Second).

```
! Example Program 8-11
! Calculate the distance between two cities.

DECLARE FUNCTION Location
DIM City$(1 to 7), Distance(1 to 7, 1 to 7)
CALL ReadList (City$)
CALL ReadTable (Distance)
INPUT prompt "Name of first city? ": First$
LET First = Location (Ucase$(First$), City$)
INPUT prompt "Name of second city? ": Second$
LET Second = Location (Ucase$(Second$), City$)
IF First = 0 or Second = 0 then
   PRINT "One of the city names is not in the list."
ELSE
```

```
            PRINT "Distance between "; First$; " and "; Second$;
            PRINT "is"; Distance (First, Second); "miles."
        END IF
        END  !  of main program

SUB ReadList (List$())
        ! Read the list of cities from a file.
        INPUT prompt "Name of the cities file? ": FileName$
        OPEN #1: name FileName$
        FOR Line = 1 to Ubound(List$)
            LINE INPUT #1: List$(Line)
        NEXT Line
END SUB  ! ReadList

SUB ReadTable (Table(,))
        ! Read the table of distances.
        INPUT prompt "Name of distance file? ": FileName$
        OPEN #2: name FileName$
        FOR Index = 1 to Ubound(Table, 1)
            LET Table(Index, Index) = 0
        NEXT Index

        FOR Row = 1 to (Ubound(Table, 1) - 1)
            FOR Column = (Row + 1) to Ubound(Table, 2)
                INPUT #2: Table(Row, Column)
                LET Table(Column, Row) = Table(Row, Column)
            NEXT Column
        NEXT Row
END SUB  ! ReadTable

DEF Location (Name$, List$())
        ! Find location of a city in the city list.
        LET CityNum = 0
        LET Count = 1
        DO
            IF Name$ = List$(Count) then
                LET CityNum = Count
            END IF
            LET Count = Count + 1
        LOOP until CityNum > 0 or Count > Ubound(List$)
        LET Location = CityNum
END DEF  ! Location
```

A user is asked to enter the names of two cities. If both cities are in the city list, the distance between them is displayed. If not, an error message appears on the screen.

Here is an example of user interaction with the program. It assumes that the two data files are in the same directory or folder as the program.

```
Name of the cities file? CITIES.DAT
Name of distance file? DISTANCE.DAT
Name of first city? New York
Name of second city? Washington
Distance between New York and Washington is 230 miles.
```

8.6   REDIMENSIONING ARRAYS

The DIM statement establishes the size of an array, either by specifying both bounds or only the upper bound of each dimension. If the array is larger than needed, you can use just part of the array (see Example Program 8-4). If the array is too small, you cannot write a second DIM statement with larger upper bounds or smaller lower bounds. A further restriction on the DIM statement is that the array bounds can only be numeric constants, not variables or expressions.

There are at least two ways, however, that the size of an array can be changed. Both of these methods use MAT statements that are discussed in greater detail in Chapter 13. The word MAT is an abbreviation of *matrix*, a mathematician's name for an array of numbers.

The MAT REDIM Statement

This statement allows you to change the size of an existing array by changing the values of one or more bounds. If all elements in the array contain information and the array is made smaller, some information is obviously lost. If the array is made larger, all the original information is preserved and new elements are initialized to zero for numbers and to a null string for strings. **Redimensioning cannot be used to change the number of dimensions**; that is, a one-dimensional array cannot be changed to a two-dimensional array.

The following example program shows what happens when a one-dimensional array is redimensioned:

```
! Example Program 8-12
! Examine how the MAT REDIM statement changes
! the element values of a one-dimensional array.

DIM Array1(1 to 4)
FOR I = 1 to 4
    READ Array1(I)
NEXT I
!
```

```
    PRINT "Original array: 4 elements"
    PRINT "Element", "Value"
    FOR I = Lbound(Array1) to Ubound(Array1)
        PRINT I, Array1(I)
    NEXT I
    !
    MAT redim Array1(2 to 3)
    PRINT
    PRINT "Redimensioned to a smaller array: 2 elements"
    PRINT "Element", "Value"
    FOR I = Lbound(Array1) to Ubound(Array1)
        PRINT I, Array1(I)
    NEXT I
    !
    MAT redim Array1(1 to 5)
    PRINT
    PRINT "Redimensioned to a larger array: 5 elements"
    PRINT "Element", "Value"
    FOR I = Lbound(Array1) to Ubound(Array1)
        PRINT I, Array1(I)
    NEXT I
    !
    DATA 10, 20, 30, 40
    END
```

Program output appears as shown:

```
Original array: 4 elements
Element       Value
 1               10
 2               20
 3               30
 4               40

Redimensioned to a smaller array: 2 elements
Element       Value
 2               10
 3               20

Redimensioned to a larger array: 5 elements
Element       Value
 1               10
 2               20
 3                0
 4                0
 5                0
```

The original array contains four elements. It is redimensioned to a smaller array with only two elements having indices of 2 and 3. Note that the first two values in the original array are preserved, not the contents of the original elements with indices of 2 and 3. This redimensioning changes the values of elements 2 and 3.

This new two-element array is redimensioned again to create a larger, five-element array. Three new elements are added and initialized to values of zero. Elements 1 and 2 now have their original values.

Arrays with two dimensions follow the same principle of trying to preserve as much information as possible when redimensioned. Another example program shows what happens:

```
! Example Program 8-13
! Examine how the MAT REDIM statement changes
! the element values of a two-dimensional array.

DIM Array2(2, 3)
FOR I = 1 to 2
    FOR J = 1 to 3
        READ Array2(I, J)
    NEXT J
NEXT I
!
PRINT "Original array: 2 by 3"
PRINT
FOR I = 1 to 2
    FOR J = 1 to 3
        PRINT Array2(I, J);
    NEXT J
    PRINT
NEXT I
!
PRINT
PRINT "Redimensioned array: 3 by 5"
MAT redim Array2(3, 5)
PRINT
FOR I = 1 to 3
    FOR J = 1 to 5
        IF Array2(I, J) = 0 then PRINT " ";
        PRINT Array2(I, J);
    NEXT J
    PRINT
NEXT I
!
DATA 10, 20, 30, 40, 50, 60
END
```

Note the IF statement in the latter part of the program. This statement puts an extra space before displayed zeroes so that they line up properly.

The example program produces the following output:

```
Original array: 2 by 3

  10  20  30
  40  50  60


Redimensioned array: 3 by 5

  10  20  30  40  50
  60   0   0   0   0
   0   0   0   0   0
```

The original array has been significantly modified by redimensioning. For example, element Array2(2, 1) has been changed from 40 to 60, while element Array2(2, 2) has been changed from 50 to 0.

I expect by now you are thoroughly confused! In view of all the changes that can take place, it is usually safer and less confusing to reinitialize an array after it is redimensioned.

The Zer and Nul$ Values

The MAT assignment statement, used with the standard array Zer or the standard array Nul$, reinitializes and redimensions an existing array. All the elements of the Zer array have a value of zero, while the Nul$ array has elements that are null strings.

The syntax of this redimensioning statement is

```
MAT Array = Zer(LowerBound to UpperBound)
```
or
```
MAT Array$ = Nul$(LowerBound to UpperBound)
```

Remember that a lower bound of one is assumed if this bound is not specified. Note that the word LET is not used in the MAT assignment statement.

The variable names Array and Array$ denote arrays that have already been dimensioned with a DIM statement. The identifiers LowerBound and UpperBound denote constants, variables, or expressions that specify the new lower and upper bounds of the array. As before, redimensioning cannot change the number of dimensions. The new lower- and upper-bound values may be larger or smaller than the original values.

For example, assume that an array has been dimensioned with the statement

```
DIM Ratio(1 to 5, 1 to 4)
```

Here are some example statements that change the size of the array Ratio and reinitalize its elements to zero:

```
MAT Ratio = Zer(2, 2)
MAT Ratio = Zer(1 to N, 2)
MAT Ratio = Zer(3 + Abs(Y), X)
```

In the first example, Ratio is redimensioned to an array with two rows and two columns. This array is called a square array because it has the same number of rows and columns. In the second example, Ratio is redimensioned to an array with N rows and two columns. Note that the lower bound of both dimensions remains at 1. Variable N must have already been assigned a value.

The third example is more complex. An arithmetic expression, 3 + Abs(Y), is evaluated and its rounded integer value is the new number of rows. The integer value X is the new number of columns.

It is often convenient to dimension an array originally to a nominal size, say, a value of 1 for each dimension and then redimension it when the size of each dimension is known. Either redimensioning technique can be used.

Another example program allows a user to specify the maximum number of items that can be stored in an array and then redimensions that array. Here is Example Program 8-4 rewritten to allow the size of array Names$ to be changed:

```
! Example Program 8-14
! Store up to N names in an array where
! the value of N is specified by the user.
! Enter a single period to stop.

DIM Names$(1)                      ! an arbitrary size
PRINT "What is the maximum number of names"
PRINT "that you plan to enter in the array";
INPUT N
MAT redim Names$(1 to N)

PRINT
PRINT "Enter up to"; N; "names, one name per line."
PRINT "Enter a single period to stop the process."
LET Count = 0

LINE INPUT prompt "Name? ": Reply$
DO until Count >= N or Reply$ = "."
   LET Count = Count + 1
   LET Names$(Count) = Reply$
   IF Count < N then LINE INPUT prompt "Name? ": Reply$
```

```
LOOP
PRINT
PRINT Count; "names entered."
PRINT "Here is the list:"
PRINT
FOR I = 1 to Count
    PRINT Names$(I)
NEXT I
END
```

The following output is produced:

```
What is the maximum number of names
that you plan to enter in the array? 10

Enter up to 10 names, one name per line.
Enter a single period to stop the process.
Name? Tony
Name? Roberto
Name? .

 2 names entered
Here is the list:

Tony
Roberto
```

Note that the MAT REDIM statement was used to redimension the array but a MAT assignment to the standard array Nul$ could also have been used. My own preference is the MAT REDIM statement.

Summary of Important Points

- An array can be declared only once in a DIM statement.

- The same DIM statement cannot be executed more than once.

- The size of an array cannot be specified by a variable or an expression when using a DIM statement.

- Nested FOR loops cannot overlap.

- In the parameter list of a procedure, an array parameter must be identified by dummy parentheses

- Use the Lbound and Ubound functions instead of constants to specify array bounds in a procedure.

- A one-dimensional array and a two-dimensional array in the same program cannot have the same name.

- Redimensioning cannot change the number of dimensions of an array.

Common Errors

- Placing a DIM statement in a loop and thus trying to execute the statement more than once.

- Using a variable in a DIM statement to declare an array.

- Trying to read the value of an array element whose index is greater than the upper bound or less than the lower bound.

- Failing to identify properly an array parameter in a procedure parameter list.

- Using an array element as the control variable in a FOR statement.

- Failing to record the number of items stored in a partially filled array, and subsequently reading information from an element that contains old data or "garbage."

- Writing overlapping FOR loops when you mean to write nested FOR loops.

- Reversing the positions of the row and column indices in the DIM statement of a two-dimensional array.

- Writing only one argument in the Ubound function of a two-dimensional array.

- Using the MAT REDIM statement to try to change the number of dimensions of an array.

Self-Test Questions

1. Define the following terms:
   (a) array
   (b) array element
   (c) dimension of an array
   (d) size of an array dimension

2. If an array is dimensioned with the statement DIM Name$(50), can a value be assigned to the element
   (a) Name$(0)?
   (b) Name$(50)?

3. If a variable N has an integer value of 7, is the statement DIM Bound(N) a legal statement? If not, why not?

4. If an array is dimensioned with DIM Value(-5:5), how many elements are contained in the array?

5. If an array is dimensioned with DIM Structure(5) and all its elements are assigned positive values, is the statement FOR I = 0 TO Structure(3) a legal statement? If not, why not?

6. Which of the following dimension statements are allowed?
   (a) DIM Array(15)
   (b) DIM Array(1,15)
   (c) DIM Array(1;15)
   (d) DIM Array(1-15)
   (e) DIM Array(1 to 15)
   (f) DIM Array(1 through 15)

7. If an array is dimensioned with DIM List$(100), what is the value of
   (a) Ubound(List$)?
   (b) Lbound(List$)?

8. If a one-dimensional array named Structure is passed as a parameter to an external subroutine named Analyze, what is the proper form of
   (a) the subroutine call statement?
   (b) the subroutine unit heading statement?

9. If an array is dimensioned in the main program unit and passed as a parameter to an external function, should it be dimensioned again in the function unit?

10. What, if anything, is wrong with the following program?

```
FOR I = 1 to 5
    DIM Num(1 to 5)
    LET Num(I) = 0
NEXT I
END
```

11. A subroutine heading statement is written as EXTERNAL SUB Capital(List$(,)).

    (a)   Is the statement syntax correct?

    (b)   The array List$ has how many dimensions?

12. (a)   What function returns the upper-bound value of the second dimension of the two-dimensional array Result?

    (b)   What function returns the lower-bound value of the same dimension?

13. What is meant by the principal diagonal of a square array?

14. What, if anything, is special about the values of the two indices of elements along the principal diagonal of a square array?

15. An array representing a table is dimensioned DIM Table(5,3). This table contains

    (a)   how many columns?

    (b)   how many rows?

16. What, if anything, is wrong with the following program?

```
DIM Table(1 to 5, 1 to 3)
FOR I = 1 to 5
    FOR J = 1 to 3
        LET Table(I, J) = 0
    NEXT I
NEXT J
END
```

17. The following program is supposed to display the array Mileage as a table with rows and columns:

```
DIM Mileage(1 to 2, 1 to 2)
FOR I = 1 to 2
    FOR J = 1 to 2
        PRINT Mileage(I, J);
    NEXT J
NEXT I
END
```

Will it display the table with 2 rows and 2 columns? If not, how would you correct the program to make it work properly?

18. If a program contains the statement

```
        DIM Mileage(5,5), List$(1 to 50)
```

what, if anything, is wrong with the following statements?

```
        (a)    MAT Mileage = Nul$(7,7)
        (b)    MAT redim Mileage(5)
        (c)    MAT redim List$(1:100)
        (d)    MAT List$ = Zer(1 to 10)
```

Practice Programs

1.   A matrix is a one-dimensional or two-dimensional array of numbers. A square matrix has the same number of rows and columns. The principal diagonal of a square matrix goes from the upper left corner to the lower right corner. The identity matrix is a square matrix with elements along the principal diagonal having a value of 1, and the other elements having a value of 0. Here is an identity matrix displayed by a True BASIC program:

```
1  0  0  0
0  1  0  0
0  0  1  0
0  0  0  1
```

Using FOR statements, create and display an identity matrix with 10 rows and columns (a 10-by-10 matrix).

2.   A transposed matrix is a square matrix (see Practice Program 1) whose rows and columns have been interchanged. Thus old row 1 becomes new column 1, old row 2 becomes new column 2, and so forth. Read the elements of a 6-by-6 matrix from DATA statements, transpose the matrix, and display the transposed matrix. Do not use the MAT statements discussed in Chapter 13.

Test your program using the following DATA statements:

```
DATA 1,5,3,6,7,2
DATA 7,1,4,9,2,3
DATA 9,0,2,1,6,3
DATA 0,1,3,2,7,5
DATA 6,4,7,3,8,9
DATA 4,6,2,2,3,1
```

3.   Enter 10 names from the keyboard, using an indexed variable to store the names as they are entered. After the tenth name has been entered, display the list of names in reverse order.

Test your program using the following names:

    Simpson
    Johnson
    Clemons
    Thornton
    Newcomb
    Tuttle
    Maury
    Cocke
    Jefferson
    Washington

4. Enter a sentence from the keyboard. Place the alphabetic characters in the sentence into an array, converting any uppercase characters to lowercase characters. Pass over any nonalphabetic characters, including spaces and punctuation marks. Display the array in reverse order.

   Test your program using the following sentence:

   He said "Hello! How are you?", and I smiled.

5. Read part names and associated prices from a data file and place these values in a two-dimensional array with 100 rows and 2 columns. Names are placed in column 1 and prices in column 2. The data file has one item per line, either a name or a price. Use your True BASIC editor to look at the file structure.

   Write a program that searches the array for the name of the highest-priced part and the lowest-priced part. Display these two part names and prices with appropriate labels.

   Test your program using the file named TOOLS.DAT.

6. A primitive way to encode a short message is to substitute a number for each word. Write a function to do the encoding. The value of the function will be the code number when a word is passed to it as a string parameter. Return a value of zero if a word is not found. For example, if the function is passed the code word MONEY, it might return the code number 4.

   The function is passed an array parameter containing values that have been read from a data file named CODE.DAT. The data file has one word per line and the position of the word in the file is the code number. Use your True BASIC editor to look at the file structure. You may assume there are no more than 100 words in the file.

   Use this function in a program designed to display a sequence of code numbers that encode a sentence entered from the keyboard. Your message is limited to one sentence and to the words contained in the data file. Do not include any punctuation marks in the sentence and use only uppercase letters.

   Test your program by encoding the following message:
   SEND MONEY STOP FAMILY SENT HOME STOP DANGER TO EAST END

7. Using the same data file as in Practice Program 6, write another function that returns a word when a code number parameter is passed to it. The function should return a null string value if the parameter is not a valid number.

   Use this function in a program to display an English sentence for a sequence of code numbers entered from the keyboard. Enter the code numbers one by one.

A value of zero tells the program that all code numbers have been entered and thus zero cannot be one of your code numbers.

Test your program by decoding the following message:

4 22 17 3 6 18

8. Information on common stocks is contained in several DATA statements. The stock symbol, highest price for the year, lowest price for the year, and current price are listed for each stock, in that order.

Read the DATA statements into a two-dimensional array and display the information in a table with column headings of SYMBOL, HIGH, LOW, CURRENT. Here are the DATA statements as they should appear in your program:

```
DATA RCA,44,34.75,43.12
DATA RIHL,4,1.5,3.75
DATA RY,32,27.5,27.75
DATA SHRM,10.5,6,10
DATA SWS,33,29.5,30.5
DATA SOCR,10.75,6.75,8.75
DATA SMLS,10.25,5.5,6
DATA SEEQ,7.5,2.5,2.75
DATA SLON,9,4,7.25
DATA SY,56.75,39.25,51
```

Calculate the relative position of the current price of each stock within the range between its lowest and highest price for the year. The term "relative position" is best explained by an example. Consider two stocks A and B. Stock A has a high of 100, a low of 10, and a current price of 15. Stock B has a high of 20, a low of 10, and a current price of 15. These values are shown in Fig. 8.5

SYMBOL	HIGH	LOW	CURRENT
A	100	10	15
B	20	10	15

Figure 8.5 *Stock price information.*

Each stock has a current price that is $5.00 higher than its low price. For stock A, this represents a relative position of (5/(100-10)) or 0.055. Expressed in percentage, stock A has risen 5.5% from its low. For stock B, the relative position is (5/(20-10)) or 0.5, representing a 50% rise from its low.

Display, with appropriate labels, the symbol of the stock with the highest relative position and that with the lowest relative position.

CHAPTER
9

Storing Information In Text Files

9.1   INTRODUCTION

Disk files provide a relatively permanent way to store information in a computer system. You must learn how to name and open text files from True BASIC programs, how to write information on files, and how to read information from files. You should also examine some of the limitations of text files.

Files of data are used widely in business for storing company records such as payrolls, inventories, mailing lists, and so forth. You will design and develop a simple database program that creates and uses a telephone directory file containing customer names and telephone numbers.

9.2   SEQUENTIAL TEXT FILES

Disk files were introduced briefly in Chapter 2, along with a discussion of file names and path names. Sequential text files were discussed in Chapter 3 and you learned how to read information from those files and use that information in True BASIC programs. Let's now look at text files in more detail, learn how to write information on these files, and design a program that makes extensive use of files.

Let me remind you again that simple, sequential text files have lines or items of information consisting of ASCII characters, these lines are stored sequentially and they are separated from one another by line delimiters. A line may contain numeric characters and represent a numeric value, or it may contain any characters and represent a string value. There is no other structure inherent in the file itself; it is only a sequence of lines of text (ASCII) characters.

A True BASIC program can write information on a sequential file or read information from the file. Writing on a newly created file starts at the beginning of the file. Writing can also start at the end of an existing file, adding new information to that which already exists. Reading from a file always starts at the beginning and continues as long as requested by the program or until the end of the file is reached.

These descriptions of writing and reading may seem obvious but they are crucial to understanding the nature of sequential files. **You cannot start reading some-where in the middle of a sequential file, only at the beginning. You cannot go to the beginning or the middle of an existing sequential file and write new information.** If you try to do either of these things, you receive an error message.

Let's examine the writing process in more detail. It is useful to imagine an *imaginary file pointer* that indicates or "points to" the position in the file where the next charac-ter will be written. If you have opened the file for writing but have not yet written any-thing on it, the pointer indicates the beginning of the file. When you write one charac-ter on the file, the pointer moves to a position immediately after that character, indi-cating where the next character will be written. At the same time, this position is denoted as the current end of file. When you write the next character, the pointer moves ahead again and its new position becomes the end of file.

Files are identified by their names. Both DOS and Mac file names and path names were discussed in Chapter 2. You might want to review that information at this time. Optional file name suffixes are allowed in either operating system and most frquently seen in DOS. The computer does not care whether the information stored in a file is a program or data or a document. The user, however, does need to distinguish files con-taining one type of information from files containing another type and especially in the DOS system, descriptive suffixes can be helpful for that purpose.

You have already learned the process of opening a text file in True BASIC using the OPEN statement. You remember that this statement must always contain a NAME phrase that specifies the file name. Let's now discuss optional phrases that can be added to the OPEN statement. These phrases are separated from one another and the NAME phrase by commas.

The ACCESS Phrase—Default Value Is OUTIN

The syntax of this phrase is

```
access Mode$
```

The identifier Mode$ must have a value of INPUT, OUTPUT, or OUTIN. It can also be a string variable or expression containing one of these words as its value. INPUT mode means that the file is opened for reading only and information cannot be written on it. OUTPUT means that the file is opened for writing only — a seldom-used option. OUTIN means that the file is opened for both writing and reading. If the ACCESS phrase is not present, the file is opened by default for both writing and reading. You generally use this default access mode when writing on a file. The possible phrases are

```
access input
access output
access outin
```

The CREATE Phrase—Default Value Is OLD

The syntax of this phrase is

```
create Action$
```

The identifier Action$ must have a value of NEW, OLD, or NEWOLD. The value NEW means that you are creating a new file. If a file already exists with the same name, you receive an error message. OLD means that you are using an existing file. If a file with that name does not exist, you receive an error message. NEWOLD means that you are using an old file if it exists or creating a new file if it does not exist. If the CREATE phrase is not present, the OLD action is assumed by default. Note that the NEWOLD action must be specified explicitly if you are uncertain whether or not a file exists. The possible phrases are

```
create new
create old
create newold
```

The ORGANIZATION Phrase—Default Value Is TEXT

The syntax of this phrase is

```
organization Type$
```

For a text file, the identifier Type$ must have a value of TEXT. If this phrase is omitted, True BASIC checks the organization of an existing file or assumes an organization type of TEXT for a new file as soon as a line of text is written on it. The word ORGANIZATION in an OPEN statement is usually abbreviated to ORG.

To sum up our discussion of the OPEN statement, here is the complete statement for opening an existing text file named NEWS, as the file in channel #N, for reading only:

```
OPEN #N: name "NEWS", access input, create old, org text
```

It is possible at any time to determine the organization of the file using channel #N by executing the following program fragment:

```
ASK #N: ORG OrgType$
PRINT OrgType$
```

9.3   WRITING TEXT FILES

You can now examine the different ways of writing information on a text file.

Opening a File for Writing

Assuming the normal defaults, the usual statement to open a new text file for writing is as follows:

```
OPEN #1: name PathName$, create new
```

The file name or path name must have been assigned to the variable PathName$.

Here are is another example of a statement to open a text file for writing, assuming N = 2, Reply$ = "A:\HW1.DAT", and Use$ = "new":

```
OPEN #N: name Reply$, create Use$
```

Variables are used to set the OPEN statement options rather than values.

When using the DOS operating system, True BASIC handles file names without a suffix in a special way. If you open a new file for writing with the statement

```
OPEN #1: name "LETTER", create new
```

this file is given the file name of LETTER.TRU. If you don't want the file name to have the TRU suffix, you must use the statement

```
OPEN #1: name "LETTER.", create new
```

where a trailing period after LETTER suppresses any suffix in the file name. Note that this behavior applies only to the DOS operating system — on a Mac, a file is given the name that appears in the OPEN statement.

If you open an old file for further writing (or for reading; see Section 9.4) in the DOS operating system, the statement

```
OPEN #1: name "LETTER", create old
```

produces a run-time error if the file named LETTER.TRU does not exist. The statement

```
OPEN #1: name "LETTER.", create old
```

allows you to open a file that has no suffix, like a file named LETTER. Note the trailing period after the file name in the OPEN statement. Again, a Mac computer does not have these complications, the file name is whatever name is written.

Setting the File Pointer

When a text file containing text is opened for writing, **you can start to write only at the end of the file if you want to keep the existing text.** You cannot start writing at any other point in the file. The place where you start to write is designated by the imaginary file pointer. An appropriate statement to position the file pointer at the end of file #1 is the statement

```
SET #1: POINTER end
```

You should always use this or the following statement when adding text to an existing file. In True BASIC, an abbreviated version of the statement to set the pointer is often used, as shown:

```
RESET #1: end
```

If you try to overwrite part of an existing file, you will get an error message.

If you have just created a new, empty file, the file pointer is already located at the end of the file — or the beginning, they are the same for an empty file.

A similar statement moves the file pointer to the beginning of file #1:

```
RESET #1: begin
```

Remember that when you first open a file, the file pointer is set to the beginning of the file.

If you want to write new information on an existing file, use the statement

```
ERASE #1
```

The contents of file #1, not the file itself, are erased and the file pointer is set to the beginning of the file, ready for writing.

Writing on a File

A modified form of the PRINT statement is used to write information on a file, as shown on the following line:

```
PRINT #N: Item
```

The identifier Item represents a variable, expression, or constant, either string or numeric. If Item is numeric, however, the digits and other characters in the number are still stored on the file as individual ASCII characters.

You may choose to have more than one variable in your PRINT statement and if so, the variables should be separated by commas or semicolons. The syntax is as follows:

```
PRINT #N: Item1, Item2, Item3...
```

Values represented by the identifiers will be formatted on the file in the same way they would be formatted on the display screen. This means that several blanks may be stored on the disk between item values, especially if commas are used as separators.

I recommend that you use the PRINT statement with only a single variable, expression, or constant. Using a single item in the PRINT statement produces a simpler file structure with each item value on a separate line and thus makes the file easier to read. There may be special occasions when you need to write two or more items on a line, but in most cases reading a file is easier if it contains only one item per line.

The main advantage of using a single item is that its value will be separated from the next value on the file by a carriage return and line feed. You know this pair of control characters as the delimiter that serves to separate adjacent line values. A program fragment like

```
LET First$ = "First Line"
PRINT #1: First$
PRINT #1: "Second Line"
PRINT #1: "Third Line"
```

writes a file whose schematic diagram is shown in Fig. 9.1.

```
First line(CRLF)Second line(CRLF)Third line(CRLF)(EOF)
```

Figure 9.1 Schematic diagram of a partial disk track.

You can think of the schematic diagram as depicting part of a magnetic disk track, showing the characters and delimiters that have been written on that section of the track. The symbol (CRLF) means the pair of characters, carriage return and line feed, used as a line delimiter.

When only one item is written on a line, you can read all the information on that line with a file version of the LINE INPUT statement, as discussed in the next section. This method of reading a file ensures that all information on the line has been read, nothing has been missed.

Closing a File

After you have finished writing on a file, you can release the specific file name from the channel number by closing the file. The statement to close file #1 is as follows:

```
CLOSE #1
```

While it is not strictly necessary to close a file unless you plan to use the channel number again with a different file name, it is good programming practice to do so. Closing a file makes certain that all information you have written on the file has actually been transferred from a section of memory called a *file buffer* to the disk.

It does no harm and produces no error message to close a file that is already closed. **I recommend that you close every file when you are through writing on it.**

Programs to Write Files

Let's look first at a simple and fundamental program to accept information from the keyboard and write it on a text file. This type of program is part of every application program that manipulates text, such as a text editor or word processor. The program creates and uses a file named TEST.DAT which is located in folder Chapter 09 on the disk Example Programs. As you can tell from the disk and folder names, the computer is a Macintosh. Remember that the MacOS operating system uses colons as path name separators. A character that would not normally appear as the first and only character on a line of text — in this case, a period — is used to signal the end of text entry.

```
! Example Program 9-1
! Write a new sequential text file.

! You may change the path name as necessary.
LET PathName$ = "Example Programs:Chapter 09:TEST.DAT"
OPEN #1: name PathName$, create new
PRINT "Type a line of text after each ? prompt."
PRINT "Enter a single period to stop the program."
LINE INPUT Reply$
DO until Reply$ = "."
   PRINT #1: Reply$
   LINE INPUT Reply$
LOOP
PRINT "File "; PathName$; " is written."
CLOSE #1
END
```

A new file named TEST.DAT is created and opened with read and write access (the default choice). If you want to write the file on a different disk or in a different directory or folder, just change the path name. The DO loop prints string values to the file until entering a single period causes the program to exit the loop. You will get an error if the file already exists, so be sure you delete or "unsave" any old file named TEST.DAT before running this program. After exiting the loop, the file is closed and the program ends.

Note that the program displays a message telling the user that the file has been written. This kind of feedback is important to a user who has no other way of knowing that the program has actually done something. Typical program interaction might look as follows:

```
Type a line of text after each ? prompt.
Enter a single period to stop the program.
? This is the first line of text
? and this is the second line.
? .
File Example Programs:Chapter 09:TEST.DAT is written.
```

When developing a program that writes on a file, I often write output first on the screen so I can see if everything is working properly. Once I see that the proper lines are being written on the screen, I modify the program to write on a file.

The method used is simple. Put an exclamation point (!) before every specific file statement, such as OPEN, CLOSE, ERASE, RESET, and so forth, changing these statements to remarks. Change all PRINT #N statements to PRINT #0 statements, directing output to channel 0 which is the display screen. Here is the previous program with these changes:

```
! Example Program 9-2
! Write a new sequential text file.
! This is a test version of the program.

! You may change the path name as necessary.
LET PathName$ = "B:\CH09\TEST.DAT"
! Modify the next line for testing.
! OPEN #1: name PathName$, create new
PRINT "Type a line of text after each ? prompt."
PRINT "Enter a single period to stop the program."
LINE INPUT Reply$
DO until Reply$ = "."
   ! Modify the next line for testing.
   PRINT #0: Reply$
   LINE INPUT Reply$
LOOP
! Modify the next two lines for testing.
! CLOSE #1
! PRINT "File "; PathName$; " is written."
END
```

Note that four statement lines have been modified for testing. You can run the modified program to check your logic and to see if the proper results are displayed. Then remove the changes and your program will usually work properly. If it has any errors, they are probably in one of the statements that you changed. This program produces the following output on the screen, but does not write any information on a file:

```
Type a line of text after each ? prompt.
Enter a single period to stop the program.
? This is the first line of text
This is the first line of text
? and this is the second line.
and this is the second line.
? .
```

When the changes are removed and the file is written, the program will create a file named TEST.DAT in directory CH09 on the disk in drive B. You should be able to tell from the path name that the computer is an IBM PC-compatible machine using the DOS operating system.

Remember that you can use the True BASIC editor to view any text file. The command

```
Ok.  Old B:\CH09\TEST.DAT
```

displays the file TEST.DAT, located in directory CH09 on the disk in drive B, in the program window.

A slight modification of the first program allows additional information to be written or appended onto an existing text file. In this example, the user is asked to specify the file name or path name:

```
! Example Program 9-3
! Append information to an existing text file.

INPUT prompt "Name of existing file? ": PathName$
PRINT
OPEN #1: name PathName$, create old
RESET #1: end
PRINT "Type a line of text after each ? prompt."
PRINT "Enter a single period to stop the program."
LINE INPUT Reply$
DO until Reply$ = "."
   PRINT #1: Reply$
   LINE INPUT Reply$
LOOP
CLOSE #1
PRINT "Text added to file "; PathName$
END
```

The user is prompted to enter a file name that is assigned to the variable PathName$. This file is assumed to exist — the program will stop with an error message if the file does not exist. The RESET statement is essential, it moves the file pointer to the end of the file so that newly entered text is appended to the existing test. Here is how the output might appear:

```
Name of existing file? TEST.DAT

Type a line of text after each ? prompt.
Enter a single period to end the program.
? Third line of text.
? .
Text added to file TEST.DAT
```

One further variation of this file writing program allows an existing file to be rewritten:

```
! Example Program 9-4
! Rewrite an existing text file.

INPUT prompt "Name of existing file? ": PathName$
PRINT
OPEN #1: name PathName$
ERASE #1  ! erase existing contents
PRINT "Type a line of text after each ? prompt."
PRINT "Enter a single period to stop the program."
LINE INPUT Reply$
DO until Reply$ = "."
   PRINT #1: Reply$
   LINE INPUT Reply$
LOOP
CLOSE #1
PRINT "File "; PathName$; " is rewritten."
END
```

The ERASE statement has the effect of deleting all information from a file, making it an empty file. The file pointer is set to the beginning of the file. An error message is displayed if the file has not been opened or if the access mode is INPUT or read only. After the following user interaction with the program, file TEST.DAT contains only the two new lines:

```
Name of existing file? TEST.DAT

Type a line of text after each ? prompt.
Enter a single period to end the program.
? First new line.
? Last new line.
? .
File TEST.DAT is rewritten.
```

Text lines can be formatted on a file in the same way they are formatted on the screen.

For example, the statement

```
PRINT #1, using "####": 12
```

writes the digits 1 and 2 right-justified in a field of four spaces.

Print zone width and right margin (screen width) can be determined and changed using the following statements:

```
ASK #N: ZONEWIDTH Var
ASK #N: MARGIN Var
SET #N: ZONEWIDTH Expr
SET #N: MARGIN Expr
```

where variable N is the file or channel number, Var is a numeric variable, and Expr is any valid numeric expression. Right margin or screen width of a file refers to a *virtual* screen width. A large right margin or screen width is sometimes required when a long string must be written on a text file, as discussed in Section 9.5.

9.4 READING TEXT FILES

Statements similar to those for writing are used when reading information from sequential text files, as discussed in Chapter 3. The same optional phrases that were introduced in Section 9.3 may be used with the OPEN statement.

If a file is to be used for reading only, the OPEN statement might be

```
OPEN #1: name PathName$, access input
```

A file opened in this manner may not be used for writing, only for reading. It must already exist and have information stored in it. If both reading and writing capability are desired and the file may not exist, use the statement

```
OPEN #1: name PathName$, create newold
```

Remember that the default access mode is OUTIN, so both reading and writing are allowed. Of course, you can't read anything from a newly created file if nothing has been written on that file.

If you want to avoid creating a new file when the named file does not exist, you can use the statement

```
OPEN #1: name PathName$, create old
```

This format has the same meaning as the format

```
OPEN #1: name PathName$
```

introduced in Chapter 3 because the default create action is OLD. Both of these statements produce an error message if the named file does not exist.

When a file is opened with any of the foregoing statements, the file pointer is placed at the beginning of the file. This is the only place where you can start reading a sequential text file.

Programs to Read Files

You have already learned in Chapter 3 how to use the LINE INPUT and INPUT statements to read data from a text file. Another fundamental program reads text information from a file specified by the user and displays it on the screen. This type of program is also part of every application program that manipulates text. It must start reading at the beginning of the file and continue until it reaches the end of the file.

```
! Example Program 9-5
! Read a sequential text file and
! use the End # function to detect end-of-file.

INPUT prompt "Name of file? ": PathName$
PRINT
OPEN #1: name PathName$, create old
DO until End #1
   LINE INPUT #1: Line$
   PRINT Line$
LOOP
CLOSE #1
END
```

Remember that you must enter the complete path name if the file you wish to read is not in the current directory or folder.

The user is asked to name an existing file and it is opened. If the file does not exist, an error message is displayed. The logical function, End #1, is used to check for the end of file #1. It has a value of true if the file pointer has reached the end of the file; otherwise, it has a value of false. It is used as part of a DO UNTIL statement to control the DO loop. The file is closed and the program ends after all information has been read. Note that phrase "create old" is not really needed because that is the default value.

Closing a file is not necessary when you have finished reading it unless you want to assign the same file number to another file. It does no harm, however, to close a file that is either open or already closed and I usually close every file that I am through using.

Assume that the file NAMES.DAT is stored in directory CH09 of the example program disk and this disk has been inserted in drive B of an IBM PC-compatible computer. The following output is produced when Example Program 9-5 is executed:

```
Name of file? B:\CHO9\NAMES.DAT

Tom
Dick
Harry
```

Another logical function is More #1, which has a value of true if there is more information in file #1. It can be used in place of the End #1 function to control the DO loop.

```
! Example Program 9-6
! Read a sequential text file and
! use the More function to detect end-of-file.

INPUT prompt "Name of file? ": PathName$
PRINT
OPEN #1: name PathName$, create newold
DO while More #1
   LINE INPUT #1: Line$
   PRINT Line$
LOOP
CLOSE #1
END
```

This program uses the NEWOLD option to avoid an error message if the file does not exist, although no information will be read in that case because the newly created file is empty. Assume this time that the file Names is stored in folder Chapter 09 of a floppy disk named Example Programs and this disk has been inserted in the floppy disk drive of a Mac. The following output is produced when Example Program 9-6 is executed:

```
Name of file? Example Programs:Chapter 09:Names

Tom
Dick
Harry
```

After writing a program to read a file, you can test it by reading any text file, including a True BASIC program file. Remember that this type of program file is just a sequential text file.

9.5　FILES AS PROCEDURE PARAMETERS

File names may be passed as string values to both functions and subroutines. **File or channel numbers may be passed as parameters to subroutines, but not to functions.** If a file is opened by name in a function, it is closed automatically when control returns to the calling unit. If a file is opened by name in a subroutine and the file number is not listed as a parameter, the file is closed automatically when control returns to the calling unit.

When channel numbers are passed to subroutines, a special notation is used. The channel number must be a numeric constant, not a numeric variable, and it must be preceded by the symbol "#". For example, the statement

```
CALL Sort (List$, #1)
```

in the calling program unit makes the file designated #1 available to the subroutine Sort. Parameter List$ is the name of a one-dimensional array. The heading statement of subroutine Sort might be as follows:

```
EXTERNAL SUB Sort (A$(), #9)
```

This heading makes the file identified as channel #9 in the subroutine the same as the file identified as channel #1 in the calling program unit. The channel number used in the subroutine is completely arbitrary — it can be the same as the channel number in the calling unit but it doesn't have to be the same. If the file is opened in the calling program unit, it will remain open in the subroutine and continues to remain open when control returns to the calling unit:

Here is a sample program that writes a line of text to a file, calls a subroutine that reads that line from the file and displays it, and then returns to the calling program unit:

```
! Example Program 9-7
! Use the same file in two different program units.

OPEN #1: name "TEST.DAT", create newold
ERASE #1
PRINT #1: "This is a test line."
PRINT "A line has been written on file TEST.DAT"
PRINT " in the main program."
CALL View (#1)
CLOSE #1
END
```

```
SUB View (#9)
    ! Read a line from the file.
    RESET #9: begin
    INPUT #9: Entry$
    PRINT
    PRINT "The same line has been read";
    PRINT " from file TEST.DAT"
    PRINT "in the subroutine and is displayed here."
    PRINT
    PRINT """"; Entry$; """"
END SUB
```

A new file named TEST.DAT is opened by the main program unit in channel #1 and a string is written on it. The modifier "newold" is used so that the program does not stop with an error message if a file with this name already exists. The ERASE statement erases the contents of an existing file.

File TEST.DAT is designated as channel #9 in the subroutine. The file pointer is moved to the beginning of the file and the string is read, stored in the variable Entry$, and displayed. Note the special syntax used in True BASIC to print double quotation marks. Control then returns to the main program unit where the file, again known as #1, is closed.

Here is an example of program output:

```
A line has been written on file TEST.DAT
in the main program.

The same line has been read from file TEST.DAT
in the subroutine and is displayed here.

"This is a test line."
```

The SET MARGIN statement (introduced in Section 9.3) has an important use when writing string values on files. Remember that the default value of MARGIN is 80 columns. Sometimes when writing on files, you need to write strings that are longer than 80 characters. If you leave the margin set at the default value, a long string (over 80 characters) will be written on the file as a series of substrings, each substring shorter than 80 characters.

A solution to this problem is to set a wider margin with the SET MARGIN statement. Many word processors produce files with each text paragraph stored as a single long string. Here is an example program that copies text from a word processor (XyWrite) file to a True BASIC text file. The system constant Maxnum is the largest number available in your particular implementation of True BASIC.

This program uses a subroutine named OpenFile to open files. One parameter of the subroutine is the desired prompt for a file name and another is information on whether the file is old or new. The file number is passed as the third parameter. In this particular example, the output file is opened with the modifier "newold" and its contents are erased if the file already exists.

```
! Example Program 9-8
! Read a text file with long strings
! and copy to another file.

CALL OpenFile ("Input file", "old", #1)
CALL OpenFile ("Output file", "newold", #2)
ERASE #2
SET #2: MARGIN Maxnum              ! for long strings
DO until End #1
   LINE INPUT #1: Line$
   PRINT #2: Line$
LOOP
CLOSE #1
CLOSE #2
PRINT "The input file has been copied."
END

SUB OpenFile (Prompt$, Mode$, #9)
   ! Prompt for path name and open file.
   LET FileOpened$ = "false"
   DO
      WHEN error in
           PRINT Prompt$;
           LINE INPUT PathName$
           OPEN #9: name PathName$, create Mode$
           LET FileOpened$ = "true"
      USE
           PRINT "Error: "; Extext$
           PRINT "Check path name and try again."
           PRINT
      END WHEN
   LOOP until FileOpened$ = "true"
END SUB
```

The subroutine sets the flag FileOpened$ to false, prints the prompt, and tries to open the file using a path name supplied by the user. If the file is successfully opened, the flag is set to true. If not, the error message is displayed, and the user is asked to enter the path name again. The loop continues until a file is opened. A subroutine of this type is useful in any program where a file is opened and you will see it in subsequent example programs.

Here is the program output:

```
Input file? TEXT.DAT
Output file? NEW.DAT
The input file has been copied.
```

9.6   THE PRINTER AS A FILE

True BASIC allows you to treat an attached printer as a sequential text file. You can write information on a printer, but you cannot, of course, read information from a printer. A printer is identified by the keyword PRINTER and is assigned a channel number using the statement

```
OPEN #N: printer
```

If you are using a computer connected to a network that supports printers, the preceding statement may not work. You may need first to write the desired information on a disk file and then use network software to transfer that information from the disk file to a shared network printer. On a computer where output is spooled to the printer, printing may not start until the program terminates.

True BASIC tries to send an error message to the screen if an attached printer is not turned on or properly connected, but on some computer systems the message is not displayed. The computer may wait for a while and then continue executing the program. All information sent to the printer is lost. If this happens to you, all you can do is interrupt the program by pressing the Interrupt key (see Chapter 2). A warning message is included in the example program to remind the user to turn on an attached printer.

Here is a simple program that prints a text file specified by the user. It uses a subroutine to check whether the text file exists and if it does not exist, asks the user to try again.

```
! Example Program 9-9
! Print a text file on an attached printer.

CALL OpenFile ("Name of file", "old", #1)
PRINT "Be sure printer is attached and turned on."
PRINT "Press any key to continue."
GET KEY Dummy
OPEN #2: printer
DO until End #1
   LINE INPUT #1: Line$
```

```
    PRINT #2: Line$
LOOP
CLOSE #1
CLOSE #2
END

SUB OpenFile (Prompt$, Mode$, #9)
    ! Prompt for path name and open file.
    LET FileOpened$ = "false"
    DO
       WHEN error in
            PRINT Prompt$;
            LINE INPUT PathName$
            OPEN #9: name PathName$, create Mode$
            LET FileOpened$ = "true"
       USE
            PRINT "Error: "; Extext$
            PRINT "Check path name and try again."
            PRINT
       END WHEN
    LOOP until FileOpened$ = "true"
END SUB
```

Note the GET KEY statement after the two PRINT statements that display a message to the user. You have seen this statement before — it freezes the screen display so a message can be read. Pressing any key allows program execution to continue. You cannot see an example of program output because all output is redirected to the printer.

9.7   A SAMPLE DATABASE PROGRAM

As an example of the use of files, let's develop a telephone directory program. This program maintains a file of telephone subscriber names and numbers. Such a file is commonly called a *database*, although that term more properly denotes a collection of several related data files.

The telephone directory program is a simple example of one of the most important uses of computers, maintaining information in files and allowing that information to be searched. It is a substantial program, longer and more complex than anything you have written so far.

The directory file is a text file and each line contains one item of information. For each directory entry, there are two items or lines of information, a name and a telephone number. The entry is called a *logical record* and each item is called a *field* of the record. Thus the directory file consists of an indeterminate number of logical records, each record containing two lines.

A menu, which allows the user to select one of several commands, controls the program. Your first step is to decide which commands should be included in the menu. Let's design a program with the following five commands:

C	Create a new directory file
A	Add information to the file
L	List the directory file
S	Search for a name
Q	Quit the program

The menu section of the program should display the foregoing information on the screen and ask the user to make a selection. This selection must be one of the characters C, A, L, S, or Q. If any other character is entered, the program should reject it and ask the user to make another selection.

A menu-driven program lends itself to *modular design*. Note that the term "module" is used in the sense of a small program unit, not a True BASIC module. Each command module is written in the form of an external subroutine and uses the SELECT CASE statement to select the appropriate module for a specified command. Comments are used to label each module and blank lines to separate modules. This extra effort in program design and formatting produces a program that is easy to read and understand. It is good programming practice.

Program Outline

As usual, start your program design by writing an outline of the main program:

> initialize constants (for example, screen length)
> ask for file name and open file
> begin loop
>> display the command menu
>> ask for command choice
>> check validity of command
>> branch to selected command subroutine
> end loop if command is the letter Q

Main Program Unit

The main program unit first takes care of such preliminary matters as clearing the screen, setting the screen length constant, and opening the telephone directory file. Then within a loop structure, the menu is displayed, the user is asked to make a selection, the user entry is checked for errors, and a SELECT CASE statement calls the appropriate command subroutine.

```
! Example Program 9-10
! Telephone Directory Program

CLEAR                        ! Clear the screen
LET Page = 21                ! Number of lines on screen
LET Ins = 20                 ! Tab insert for menu
CALL OpenFile ("Directory file name", "old", #1)

DO                           ! top of main loop
   CLEAR
   PRINT Tab(Ins); "COMMAND MENU"
   PRINT
   PRINT Tab(Ins); "C.....Create a new directory file"
   PRINT Tab(Ins); "A.....Add data to the directory"
   PRINT Tab(Ins); "L.....List the directory file"
   PRINT Tab(Ins); "S.....Search for a name"
   PRINT Tab(Ins); "Q.....Quit the program"
   PRINT
   PRINT Tab(20); "Your selection";
   LINE INPUT Command$
   LET Command$ = Ucase$(Command$[1:1])
   SELECT CASE Command$
   CASE "C"                  ! Create new directory file
        CALL Create (#1)
   CASE "A"                  ! Add data to the file
        CALL Add (#1)
   CASE "L"                  ! List the directory file
        CALL List (#1, Page)
   CASE "S"                  ! Search for a name
        CALL Search (#1)
   CASE "Q"                  ! Quit the program
   CASE else
        PRINT Tab(Ins); "Enter C, A, L, S, or Q."
        PRINT Tab(Ins); "Press any key to continue."
        GET KEY Dummy
   END SELECT
LOOP until Command$ = "Q"   ! bottom of main loop
CLOSE #1
END  ! of main program
```

As noted in the comments, the first statement clears the screen and changes it to an output window. A variable named Page is assigned a value representing the maximum number of lines that will be displayed on the screen. The previously developed OpenFile subroutine is used to open the file.

At the beginning of the main loop, the screen is cleared again and the menu is displayed. The user is asked to enter a command character that is assigned to the variable Command$. The value of Command$ is used to make a CASE statement selection and an appropriate subroutine is called. If this character is not C, A, L, S, or Q, an error message is displayed and the loop is repeated until a valid command is entered. If command Q is chosen, the program exits the main loop, the directory file is closed, and the program ends.

The Create Subroutine

The first subroutine executes the Create command. This command creates a new directory file after closing the current file. Creating a new directory just establishes a new file, it does not place any information in that file. The Add command must be run after a new directory has been created to write information on the file.

```
SUB Create (#9)
    ! Create a new directory file.
    CLEAR
    CLOSE #9
    CALL OpenFile ("New directory path name", "new", #9)
END SUB
```

After the screen is cleared, the old directory file is closed, and a new file is opened with the same file number. To open the new file, use the same OpenFile subroutine that was used in the main program.

The Add Subroutine

The next subroutine executes the Add command. There are two items or lines of information for each directory entry, the name of a person and the corresponding telephone number. Here is an outline of this subroutine:

> set directory file to end of file
> top of loop
>> exit loop if name is a null string
>> request name and telephone number
>> print name and number on directory file
> bottom of loop
> end subroutine

The following subroutine is written from this outline:

```
SUB Add (#9)
   ! Add data to the directory.
   CLEAR
   RESET #9: end
   PRINT "Press Return key after Name prompt to stop."
   PRINT
   LINE INPUT prompt "Name: ": Name$
   DO until Name$ = ""
      LINE INPUT prompt "Phone number: ": Phone$
      PRINT #9: Name$
      PRINT #9: Phone$
      PRINT
      LINE INPUT prompt "Name: ": Name$
   LOOP
END SUB
```

Before writing any information on the directory, the file pointer is set to the end of the file so that new information is added to existing information. A loop is established for entering new values into the variables Name$ and Phone$. The values of Name$ and Phone$ are written on the directory file with two separate PRINT statements, ensuring that each value is written as a separate line.

The user is told to press the Return key in response to the Name prompt to stop adding new information. This action assigns a null string to Name$ and if the program finds that value, it exits the loop.

The List Subroutine

The List subroutine is next and again you should start by writing down an outline:

set directory file to beginning of file

initialize a screen line counter

      top of loop

           exit loop if end of file is reached

           input name and telephone number from file

           display name and number on the screen

           if screen is full, pause and reset counter

      bottom of loop

      pause again to view the last screen

end subroutine

The directory file pointer is set to the beginning of the file for reading. Information is read from the file and displayed on the screen. A counter variable Count keeps track of the number of lines currently displayed on the screen. After the column headings and a blank line are printed, the counter is set to 2 because two lines are already displayed.

When 21 lines are displayed on the screen, the program pauses until the user presses any key. This technique prevents information from scrolling off the screen faster than it can be read. A similar pause is located at the end of the module, where the user must press a key before the program will return to the command menu.

```
SUB List (#9, Page)
   ! List the directory file.
   CLEAR
   PRINT "NAME"; Tab(30); "PHONE"
   PRINT
   LET Count = 2
   RESET #9: begin
   DO until End #9
      LINE INPUT #9: Name$, Phone$
      PRINT Name$; Tab(30); Phone$
      LET Count = Count + 1
      IF Count >= Page then
         LET Count = 0
         PRINT "Press any key to continue."
         GET KEY Dummy
         CLEAR
         PRINT "NAME"; Tab(30); "PHONE"
         PRINT
         LET Count = 2
      END IF
   LOOP
   PRINT
   PRINT "Press any key to return to menu."
   GET KEY Dummy
END SUB
```

The first pause is created by the GET KEY statement. Program execution stops until any key is pressed. The code value of the pressed key is assigned to the variable Dummy but is not used in the program. A second, similar pause is used at the end of the subroutine.

The Search Subroutine

The next subroutine executes the Search command. Here is an outline for that command:

> set directory file to beginning of file
>
> request target name
>
> top of loop
>
>> exit loop if end of file is reached
>>
>> input name and telephone number from file
>>
>> compare name from file and target name
>>
>> if equal, display number and stop the search
>
> bottom of loop
>
> if name is not found, display an error message
>
> pause to view the screen
>
> end subroutine

The user is asked to specify a name and then the directory file is searched sequentially from the beginning until the desired name is found. If the name is found, the corresponding telephone number is displayed. If it is not found, the user is informed that the name is not in the directory. Sequential searching is a simple search technique, adequate for small files but too slow for large files. A large file might be defined as one with 1000 records or more. Faster search methods are discussed in Chapter 11.

When making comparisons, True BASIC tests for an exact match between the entered name and the directory name. For example, the name "Peter Toms" does not match the name "PETER TOMS". To avoid this kind of mismatch, both names are converted to uppercase characters before a comparison is made.

```
SUB Search (#9)
   ! Search for a name.
   CLEAR
   LET Found$ = "false"
   LINE INPUT prompt "What name? ": Target$
   LET Target$ = Ucase$(Target$)
   RESET #9: begin
   DO until End #9 or Found$ = "true"
      LINE INPUT #9: Name$, Phone$
      IF Ucase$(Name$) = Target$ then
         PRINT "Phone number: "; Phone$
         LET Found$ = "true"
      END IF
   LOOP
```

```
        IF End #9 and Found$ = "false" then
            PRINT "This name is not in the directory."
        END IF
        PRINT
        PRINT "Press any key to return to menu."
        GET KEY Dummy
    END SUB
```

This command module asks the user to specify a target name that is assigned to the variable Target$. A flag variable named Found$ is set to "false." Each record in the directory file is read, one by one, and the value of Target$ is compared with the value of Name$. Flag variable Found$ is set to "true" if a match is found. The search is continued until a match is found or the end of file is reached..

If the end of file is reached and Found$ has a value of "false", the user is told that the target name is not in the directory. Both the end of file and variable Found$ are checked at this point to suppress a false "not in directory" message if the desired name happens to be the last name in the file. As before, a pause is placed at the end of the module so the screen can be read before the menu is displayed.

The complete program consists of the main program unit and the four external subroutines, plus the subroutine OpenFile. This is a substantial program but easy to understand if you examine it unit by unit. Additional subroutines might be written to delete a name from the directory (see Practice Program 10) or to search for a telephone number and display the associated name.

```
! Example Program 9-10
! Telephone Directory Program

CLEAR                       ! Clear the screen
LET Page = 21               ! Number of lines on screen
LET Ins = 20                ! Tab insert for menu
CALL OpenFile ("Directory path name", "old", #1)

DO                          ! top of main loop
    CLEAR
    PRINT Tab(Ins); "COMMAND MENU"
    PRINT
    PRINT Tab(Ins); "C.....Create a new directory file"
    PRINT Tab(Ins); "A.....Add data to the directory"
    PRINT Tab(Ins); "L.....List the directory file"
    PRINT Tab(Ins); "S.....Search for a name"
    PRINT Tab(Ins); "Q.....Quit the program"
    PRINT
    PRINT Tab(20); "Your selection";
```

```
        LINE INPUT Command$
        LET Command$ = Ucase$(Command$[1:1])
        SELECT CASE Command$
        CASE "C"                 ! Create new directory file
            CALL Create (#1)
        CASE "A"                 ! Add data to the file
            CALL Add (#1)
        CASE "L"                 ! List the directory file
            CALL List (#1, Page)
        CASE "S"                 ! Search for a name
            CALL Search (#1)
        CASE "Q"                 ! Quit the program
        CASE else
            PRINT Tab(Ins); "Enter C, A, L, S, or Q."
            PRINT Tab(Ins); "Press any key to continue."
            GET KEY Dummy
        END SELECT
    LOOP until Command$ = "Q"  ! bottom of main loop
    CLOSE #1
    END  ! of main program


    SUB Create (#9)
        ! Create a new directory file.
        CLEAR
        CLOSE #9
        CALL OpenFile ("New directory path name", "new", #9)
    END SUB


    SUB Add (#9)
        ! Add data to the directory.
        CLEAR
        RESET #9: end
        PRINT "Press Return key after Name prompt to stop."
        PRINT
        LINE INPUT prompt "Name: ": Name$
        DO until Name$ = ""
            LINE INPUT prompt "Phone number: ": Phone$
            PRINT #9: Name$
            PRINT #9: Phone$
            PRINT
            LINE INPUT prompt "Name: ": Name$
        LOOP
    END SUB
```

```
SUB List (#9, Page)
    ! List the directory file.
    CLEAR
    PRINT "NAME"; Tab(30); "PHONE"
    PRINT
    LET Count = 2
    RESET #9: begin
    DO until End #9
       LINE INPUT #9: Name$, Phone$
       PRINT Name$; Tab(30); Phone$
       LET Count = Count + 1
       IF Count >= Page then
          LET Count = 0
          PRINT "Press any key to continue."
          GET KEY Dummy
          CLEAR
          PRINT "NAME"; Tab(30); "PHONE"
          PRINT
          LET Count = 2
       END IF
    LOOP
    PRINT
    PRINT "Press any key to return to the menu."
    GET KEY Dummy
END SUB

SUB Search (#9)
    ! Search for a name.
    CLEAR
    LET Found$ = "false"
    LINE INPUT prompt "What name? ": Target$
    LET Target$ = Ucase$(Target$)
    RESET #9: begin
    DO until End #9 or Found$ = "true"
       LINE INPUT #9: Name$, Phone$
       IF Ucase$(Name$) = Target$ then
          PRINT "Phone number: "; Phone$
          LET Found$ = "true"
       END IF
    LOOP
    IF End #9 and Found$ = "false" then
       PRINT "This name is not in the directory."
    END IF
    PRINT
    PRINT "Press any key to return to the menu."
```

```
        GET KEY Dummy
    END SUB

    SUB OpenFile (Prompt$, Mode$, #9)
        ! Prompt for path name and open file.
        LET FileOpened$ = "false"
        DO
           WHEN error in
                PRINT Prompt$;
                LINE INPUT PathName$
                OPEN #9: name PathName$, create Mode$
                LET FileOpened$ = "true"
           USE
                PRINT "Error: "; Extext$
                PRINT "Check path name and try again."
                PRINT
           END WHEN
        LOOP until FileOpened$ = "true"
    END SUB
```

Here is one display from the program but you should run the program yourself to see
how it works and check out all the displays. When the program starts, the name of the
directory file is requested, as shown:

```
Directory file name? PHONES.DAT
```

This screen is cleared and the command menu is displayed:

```
COMMAND MENU

C.....Create a new directory file
A.....Add data to the directory
L.....List the directory file
S.....Search for a name
Q.....Quit the program


Your selection? L
```

Note that the user has selected the List command. The screen is cleared again and the
following information is displayed:

```
NAME                    PHONE

Bill Peters             3415
John Williams           4452
Mary O'Hara             5343
Jane Carey              6424
```

```
Phillip Johnson          7605
Peter Martin             1024
Susan White              4113
Charles Rebel            3090

Press any key to return to the menu.
```

When a key is pressed, the screen is cleared once more and the menu displayed again. Any one of the listed commands can be selected, and selecting the Q command eventually stops the program.

9.8   OTHER TYPES OF FILES

True BASIC supports other types of files in addition to sequential text files. *Record files* store information in fixed-length records that can be accessed directly. Direct access means that you can move directly to any record in the file and write information on or read information from that record. Record files are often used to store information that is to be searched.

Byte files store information as a sequence of bytes with no concern about what data types these bytes represent. These files provide the most efficient method for storing information on a disk, but they are difficult to read and write and are not often used in simple application programs.

Version 3 of True BASIC adds two additional file types. *Random files* are similar to record files but allow several fields to be stored in each record. *Stream files* are sequential files that store information in an internal format rather than as ASCII characters.

Record files and random files are discussed in Chapter 11; you are referred to the *True BASIC Reference Manual* for further information about other file types.

Summary of Important Points

- Spaces or blank characters are not allowed in DOS file names, but are allowed in Mac file names.

- When a text file containing text is opened for writing, you can start to write only at the end of the file.

- It is good practice to erase a temporary file before writing on it.

- It is good practice to close a file after you are through using it, especially if you have written new information on it.

- I recommend that you use the PRINT # statement with only a single variable, expression, or constant when writing on a file.

- You cannot start reading somewhere in the middle of a sequential text file, only at the beginning.

- Channel numbers can be passed as parameters to subroutines, but *not* to functions.

- True BASIC tries to send an error message to the screen if an attached printer is not turned on or properly connected, but on some computer systems the message never gets through and is not displayed.

Common Errors

- Forgetting that the default create value is OLD when trying to open a new file without specifying a create value.

- Trying to write new information in the middle of an existing text file.

- Opening a text file for INPUT access and then trying to write information on it.

- Failing to close a file after writing on it. This may not hurt but you never know.

- Opening a file for OUTPUT access and then trying to read information from it. There is seldom any good reason to open a file for output only.

- Forgetting to erase an existing file before writing new information on it.

- Writing more than one item per line on a text file, and then failing to tell every user of the file what you have done.

- Using the LINE INPUT statement to read digits from a text file and assign them to a numeric variable. Use the INPUT statement instead, or use the Val function to convert a string of digits to a numeric value.

- Trying to pass a file number as a parameter to a function.

- Failing to set a wide margin when writing long strings on a text file, thus breaking up each string into multiple substrings.

Self-Test Questions

Unless specified otherwise, the word "file" in these questions means a sequential text file.

1. Is a True BASIC program file (for example, the file MYPROG.TRU) a sequential text file?

2. What delimiter is used to separate lines of text in a file?

3. Can you start to read a file
   - (a) at the beginning of the file?
   - (b) in the middle of the file?

4. Can you start to write new information on an existing file
   - (a) at the beginning of the file?
   - (b) in the middle of the file?
   - (c) at the end of the file?

5. When you have opened a new file for writing but have not yet written anything on it, where is the file pointer?

6. What is the default value of the access mode in an OPEN statement when a file is opened?

7. How many files can be open in a program at one time?

8. If the first file opened in a program is assigned a channel number of 1, does the next file opened have to be assigned a channel number of 2?

9. Can the first file opened in a program be assigned a channel number of
   - (a) 9?
   - (b) -9?
   - (c) 990?
   - (d) 1900?

10. Is it possible to write information on a file that has not been assigned a channel number?

11. What is the default value of the create mode in an OPEN statement when a file is opened?

12. What organization type is assumed when a new file is opened and a line of characters is written on the file?

13. What statement is used to set the file pointer to the
    - (a) end of file #3?
    - (b) beginning of file #4?

14. What is a disadvantage of having more than one variable in a PRINT statement used to write information on a file?

15. If a file has been opened as file #1, what statement must you execute before you can open another file as file #1?

16. Can you read a file that has been opened with an access mode of OUTPUT?

17. What is an advantage of the LINE INPUT statement over the INPUT statement when reading lines of text from a file?

18. If each line in file #1 represents a single number, what statement or statements can you use to read a line and assign it to a variable named Number?

19. What is the value of the logical function End #1 if file #1 contains several lines of text and the file pointer is at the

    (a)   beginning of the file?

    (b)   end of the file?

20. Can channel numbers be passed as parameters to

    (a)   external subroutines?

    (b)   external functions?

21. If a file is opened in an external function, is that file open or closed when control returns to the calling unit?

22. If a file is specified as file #1 in the CALL statement of an external subroutine, does it have to be specified as file #1 in the heading statement of the subroutine?

23. What is the value of the logical function More #1 if the logical function End #1 has a value of true?

24. Assume a DOS file is opened for writing with the statement

```
OPEN #1: name "PROB07", create new
```

What file name is used by the operating system to identify this file?

25. A DOS file is opened for reading with the statement

```
OPEN #1: name PathName$
```

What value must be assigned to PathName$ if the desired file is named HOMEWORK and is located in the directory named LECTURE7 on the disk in drive B?

Practice Programs

1. Write a text file consisting of lines of characters. A user specifies the file name

and then enters text from the keyboard. Signify the end of text by entering a period as the first and only character in a line. Do not write this period on the file.

Test your program by writing the preceding lines to a file named FIRST.TXT.

2. Ask a user to specify the name of a text file. Read the file and display the text on the screen. Notify the user when the last line has been displayed.

    Test your program using the file FIRST.TXT written in Practice Program 1, or any other text file if you have not done Practice Program 1.

3. A text file named GRADES.DAT contains student grades, stored as ASCII characters, one grade per line. Read the file and calculate the average grade, the minimum grade, and the maximum grade. Display these three values on the screen with appropriate labels.

4. A text file named NAMES.DAT contains customer names, stored one name per line in the format of first name, optional middle initial, last name. Examples are

    John H. Williams

    Judith Spencer

    Enter a last name from the keyboard. Search through the file and display the names of all customers who have that last name. Your search should be insensitive to case; that is, both SMITH and smith should match Smith.

    Test your program using the names WILLIAMS, smith, and SMITH.

5. Rewrite Practice Program 2 to display only 20 lines on the screen and then display the prompt "More?". A reply of Y (or YES or yes) displays 20 more lines. A reply of Q or N in either uppercase or lowercase stops the program.

    Test your program using the file PREFACE.TXT.

6. A file named PARTS.DAT is a text file, containing four lines of inventory information on each part:

    part number

    part name

    quantity in stock unit

    cost

    A file named ORDER.DAT is a text file containing three lines of ordering information on each part:

    part number

minimum quantity before reordering

quantity to reorder

Read the information for each item from file PARTS.DAT and check the quantity in stock against the minimum quantity before reordering in file ORDER.DAT. If an order is indicated, display the following information on the screen, using one line for each item:

quantity to order

part name

total cost for this item

At the end, display the grand total cost for the entire order. This screen display could be used to generate an order for replacing inventory.

7. Write an external subroutine that copies information from one text file onto a second text file. The names of both files should be passed as parameters. If the first file does not exist, notify the user and allow the file name to be entered again. If the second file exists, it should be erased after checking with the user. Your program should be able to handle strings in the input file that are up to 10,000 characters long. Lines of text in the output file should be no wider than your screen width.

Use this subroutine in a program for copying text files where the user specifies both file names. Test your program by copying the contents of file TEXT.DAT into a file named COPY.TXT.

8. Add a command to Example Program 9-10 that deletes a specified name and its associated telephone number. Use statements similar to those used in the Search command to find the name.

Deleting items from a sequential file requires that you open another temporary file (possibly named TEMP.DAT) with OUTIN access. Assume that you have found the specified name and it is the fourth name in the directory file. To delete this name, read the first three names and telephone numbers from the directory file, one by one, and write them on the temporary file. Next read the fourth name and number from the directory file, but do *not* write it on the temporary file. Then read all the remaining names and numbers, one by one, from the directory file and write them on the temporary file.

The temporary file now contains all the information in the directory file except the specified name and telephone number. Erase the directory file and copy everything in the temporary file onto the directory file. Note that the directory file must also have OUTIN access. The temporary file can then be deleted using the program statement

```
UNSAVE "TEMP.DAT"
```

Test your command by deleting the names John Williams and Jane Carey from the directory file named PHONES.DAT and then list the modified file.

9. Write a file-copying subroutine similar to the one in Practice Program 7. In this case, however, lines of text in the output file can end only at spaces between words. Each line must still be shorter than or equal to the screen width.

Test this subroutine in the same way you tested Practice Program 7.

PART 3

Specialized Features

CHAPTER 10

Formatted Reports and Displays

10.1 INTRODUCTION

In many computer applications, the final product of a computer program is a printed report. The quality of that report is judged, in part, by its appearance. To produce an attractive and high-quality report, you must be able to control its format.

In this chapter, further variations of the PRINT USING statement are investigated. These variations provide you with better format control of information printed on paper or displayed on the screen. You learn how to divide the screen into two or more independent windows so that more than one display can be observed simultaneously. You also learn how to determine the current position of the cursor on the screen and how to change this position.

10.2 THE PRINT USING STATEMENT WITH NUMBERS

Commas and semicolons used as variable separators in PRINT statements provide limited format control of printed reports and screen displays. The Tab function provides some additional format control. It is difficult, however, to format a complicated report with just these capabilities.

The solution is to use the PRINT USING statement whose general syntax is shown in the following statement:

```
PRINT USING Format$: Item1, Item2...
```

The expression Format$ is either a string variable or string constant containing special characters called *format characters*. You will remember that you used a simple version of this statement in Chapter 3. All the format characters are listed here and most of them are discussed in subsequent paragraphs.

Here is a list of the numeric format characters:

#	any digit, print leading zeroes as spaces
%	any digit, print leading zeroes as zeroes
*	any digit, print leading zeroes as stars
+	print number with leading plus or minus sign
-	print number with leading space or minus sign
$	print number with leading dollar sign
^	print the exponent field of a number

String format characters are as follows:

#	any character
<	any character, left-justify string
>	any character, right-justify string

These format characters are used to control the appearance of the items appearing in the PRINT USING statement As with the regular PRINT statement, the items can be constants, variables, or expressions. Note that the items in the PRINT USING statement are separated by commas. These commas are used only as separators; they do not cause the item values to be displayed in different print zones. Semicolons cannot be used as separators.

In general, commas and semicolons cannot be used to format the output of PRINT USING statements. An exception is the trailing semicolon which still suppresses the normal carriage return and line feed after a statement is executed.

Displaying Simple Numbers

Let's look first at those special format characters used to control the display of numbers. The most common format character, a sharp sign (#), represents any digit. Here again is the example program from Chapter 3:

```
! Example Program 10-1 (same as 3-16)
! Display several numbers with PRINT USING statements.

PRINT using "####": 125
PRINT using "####": 1285.9
PRINT using "####": 34562
PRINT
PRINT using "###.##": 12.5
PRINT using "###.##": -12.521
PRINT using "###.##": -133.33
END
```

This program produces the following display:

```
 125
1286
****

 12.50
-12.52
******
```

The format string in a PRINT USING statement may be a string variable instead of a string constant, as illustrated by the following program fragment:

```
LET Format$ = "####"
PRINT using Format$: 125
```

The quantity to be printed may be a variable instead of a constant, as in the following example:

```
LET Number = 125
LET Format$ = "####"
PRINT using Format$: Number
```

Any characters included in the format string, other than format characters, are displayed as entered. For example, the statement

```
PRINT using "The total is ###,###.": 56752
```

displays the sentence

```
The total is  56,752.
```

The letters, spaces, and period are not format characters and are displayed as entered. The comma behaves a little differently — it is only displayed if there are four or more digits in the number.

Displaying Dollar Amounts

A common use of the PRINT USING statement is to display numbers representing dollars and cents with the decimal point properly aligned. For this purpose, the dollar sign ($) is used as a format character. A period is included in the format string to mark the column where the decimal point is located. **Commas or other characters cannot be inserted between the dollar signs.**

If you wish to display an amount with a leading dollar sign, use a statement like the following:

```
PRINT using "$$$$$$.##": N
```

with dollars signs acting as format characters to the left of the decimal point and sharp signs to the right of the point.

The dollar sign preceding the displayed number "floats," remaining always just to the left of the first digit. All the dollar signs except the first one are place holders for digits, so the largest number that can be printed using this format string is 99999.99. **This type of format string can only be used with numeric constants, variables, or expressions**, it cannot be used to format strings.

If N has a value of 10, the statement displays the following output:

```
$10.00
```

with three spaces are printed to the left of the dollar sign.

If you want the dollar sign to appear always in the same column, use a statement such as this:

```
PRINT using "$#####.##: N
```

If N still has a value of 10, the output is displayed as

```
$   10.00
```

Here is a program to display a column of dollar amounts, with a floating dollar sign in front of each number and the decimal points aligned:

```
! Example Program 10-2
! Display a column of formatted dollar amounts.

DO while More data
   READ Cost
   PRINT using "$$$$$$.##": Cost
LOOP

DATA 23.75, 1244.82, .237, 31112.5
END
```

Program output looks as follows:

```
   $23.75
 $1244.82
     $.24
$31112.50
```

Neither of the preceding techniques meets a common need, the ability to print a left-justified number with a leading dollar sign and embedded commas. The next example program shows how this task can be accomplished. It uses the function Using$(F$, N), which produces a string from the number N based on the format string F$. This function is similar to the PRINT USING statement, but assigns a formatted string to the function rather than displaying that string on the screen.

```
! Example Program 10-3
! Display a left-justified number
! with a leading dollar sign.

INPUT prompt "Value? ": Value
LET F$ = "###,###,###.##"
LET Value$ = "$" & Trim$(Using$(F$, Value))
PRINT Value$
END
```

The user is prompted to enter a number. The function Using$ converts the number Value to a formatted string and the function Trim$ removes any leading or trailing spaces. A dollar sign is appended to the beginning of the new string and it is assigned to the variable Value$. Here are two examples of output:

```
Value? 123.45
$123.45


Value? 123456.789
$123,456.79
```

Displaying Leading Algebraic Signs

The regular PRINT statement places a blank space in front of a number if it is positive and a minus sign in front of the number if it is negative. To achieve the same format with the PRINT USING statement, place a minus sign (-) as a format character at the beginning of the format string. A plus sign (+) as a leading format character will display a plus sign if the number is positive and a minus sign if the number is negative. Multiple plus or minus signs in the format string cause a single "floating" plus or minus sign to be displayed. These characters behave like the dollar sign format character, all the plus and minus signs except the first one are place holders for digits.

```
! Example Program 10-4
! Control the display of numeric signs.

LET N = 12
LET X = -35
PRINT using "-###": N
PRINT using "-###": X
PRINT
PRINT using "+++#": N
PRINT using "+++#": X
PRINT
PRINT using "--#": N
PRINT using "--#": X
```

```
PRINT
PRINT using "##": N
PRINT using "##": X
END
```

Here is the output produced by this program:

```
  12
- 35

 +12
 -35

  12
 -35

12
**
```

Note that the last PRINT USING statement displays error symbols (*) because the number -35 requires a format string of at least three characters.

If a PRINT USING statement has more variables than there are format character groups in the format string, the format string is used over and over again until all the variable values have been printed. Any remaining characters in the format string are ignored after the last variable is displayed.

I use vertical bars (|) in this and several following examples to help you see the exact space occupied by the displayed values. A vertical bar is not a format character and thus is just displayed at the point where it occurs in the format string.

Examine the next example program:

```
! Example Program 10-5
! Repeated use of a format string.

LET First = 77.5
LET Second = 925
LET Third = 1.75
LET Form$ = "|##.##  ####|"
PRINT using Form$: First, Second, Third
END
```

which produces the following display:

```
|77.50   925|| 1.75
```

In this example, note that the first two numbers are formatted by one use of the format string Form$. This accounts for the first two vertical bars. The same format string is then used again to format the third number but only the first part of Form$ is required, thus the final vertical bar is never displayed.

Displaying Leading Zeroes

The usual format character (#) displays numbers with leading blank spaces. An alternate format character, the percent sign (%), displays numbers with leading zeroes. This format is sometimes used when displaying such items as part numbers or zip codes. These two format characters cannot be mixed in a single format character string.

For example, the statement

```
PRINT using "%%%%": 32
```

displays

```
0032
```

but the statement

```
PRINT using "%%##": 32
```

is not allowed and displays an error message.

Displaying Numbers with Exponents

The exponential notation for numbers is seldom used in business applications, but often appears in scientific or technical documents. The PRINT USING statement can display numbers in this form and a few examples are shown. The caret (^) is used as a format character to indicate the size of the exponent field, including the letter "e" and the numeric sign. The exponent field must be a least three characters long.

Another example program displays this format:

```
! Example Program 10-6
! Display numbers in exponential form.

PRINT using "###^^^": 2.5e+7
PRINT using "#.##^^^": 2.5e7
PRINT using "#.##^^^^^^": 2.5E7
PRINT using "##^^^": 87654321
END
```

It produces the following display:

```
250e+5
2.50e+7
2.50e+007
88e+6
```

Let's Program It . . . in True BASIC

Note in the last value displayed how the original value is rounded and six significant figures are lost. This format accepts a number containing either an "e" or an "E" but displays all results with the lowercase "e."

10.3 THE PRINT USING STATEMENT WITH STRINGS

String variables may also be formatted with PRINT USING statements. The same format character (#) is used to indicate the field in which the string value is displayed. If the field is longer than the string value, the value is centered in the field. If the field is shorter, a string of asterisks (*) is printed.

If the leftmost format character (#) is replaced by another format character, the left angle bracket (<), then the string value is left-justified in the field. A right angle bracket (>) in the same position right-justifies the string value. Angle brackets cannot be used to justify numeric values.

Consider the following example program:

```
! Example Program 10-7
! Display a string variable.

LET Title$ = "abc"
PRINT using "|#######|": Title$
PRINT using "|<######|": Title$
PRINT using "|>######|": Title$
PRINT using "|##|": Title$
END
```

Here is the output:

```
|  abc  |
|abc    |
|    abc|
|**|
```

Again I have used vertical bars to show the limit of format strings. Observe that the first display of "abc" is centered, the second is left-justified, and the third is right-justified. The fourth display is an error display because the format string is too short.

Displaying Both Strings and Numbers

A format string can be used to control the display of a combination of strings and numbers. Here is an example that displays lines from a typical price list, showing the number, description, and price of certain items:

```
! Example Program 10-8
! Display both strings and numbers.

LET Format$ = "%%%%  <#############  $$$.##"
DO while More data
   READ PartNum, Item$, Price
   PRINT using Format$: PartNum, Item$, Price
LOOP

DATA 245, "Cleat, 4 inch", 12.50
DATA 1705, Bow Light, 34.50
DATA 12, Boat Cushion, 3.95
DATA 717, Shackle, 5.50
DATA 718, Pin, 2.25
END
```

This program displays the following price list:

```
0245  Cleat, 4 inch    $12.50
1705  Bow Light        $34.50
0012  Boat Cushion      $3.95
0717  Shackle           $5.50
0718  Pin               $2.25
```

The format string contains several numeric format characters, then a group of string format characters, and finally more numeric format characters. In between are blank spaces which are not format characters and thus display as blank spaces.

Printing on Files and on a Printer

Printing on files can be formatted with a modified PRINT USING statement. The statement syntax is as follows:

```
PRINT #1, using Format$: Title$
```

This statement prints the value of the variable Title$ on file #1, using the format string contained in Format$.

Remember that an attached printer can be thought of as a file and assigned to a channel number with the statement

```
OPEN #N: printer
```

Here is the previous program rewritten to print the price list on an attached printer. Be sure that a printer is connected to your computer and is turned on before running this program.

```
! Example Program 10-9
! Print both strings and numbers on an attached printer.

OPEN #1: printer
LET Format$ = "%%%%   <#############   $$$.##"

DO while More data
   READ PartNum, Item$, Price
   PRINT #1, using Format$: PartNum, Item$, Price
LOOP

DATA 245, "Cleat, 4 inch", 12.50
DATA 1705, Bow Light, 34.50
DATA 12, Boat Cushion, 3.95
DATA 717, Shackle, 5.50
DATA 718, Pin, 2.25
END
```

Printer output is identical to the display produced by Example Program 10-8.

10.4   EXAMPLE OF A PROPOSAL REPORT

You should now be able to understand a larger example program that prepares a proposal report for a school microcomputer laboratory. This report is shown in Fig. 10.1 and is a good example of how output formatting is used in True BASIC.

Information for the report is read from a text file named PROPOSAL.DAT whose contents are shown in Fig. 10.2. This file contains several different types of information. The first number (3) specifies the number of lines in the title and is followed by the title lines themselves. The next number (also 3) specifies the number of sections or categories in the report. It is followed by name of the first category. The next eight lines contain information on the items in the first category, two lines per item. A negative number (-1) is used as a *sentinel* to mark the end of the first category. Information on items in the other categories is shown using the same format.

Let's look more carefully at the specification for printer cables which is contained in the two following lines:

```
5
Printer cable, 31.75
```

The first line specifies the number of cables, 5. The second line specifies the item name, `Printer cable`, and the unit price, $31.75. This same specification format is used for all items in the proposal.

```
                    Computer Laboratory Proposal
                              for
                      Newtown High School

================================================================
NO.     ITEM                          PRICE       COST
================================================================

Hardware:

20     ABC microcomputers            2295.00     45900.00
20     Model 15 monitor               175.50      3510.00
 5     Model XX-50 printer            520.00      2600.00
 5     Printer cable                   31.75       158.75

                              Subtotal:   $52168.75


Software:

20     DOS 7.0 operating system        60.00       800.00
20     True BASIC language system      19.95       399.00
10     Borland C++ compiler           149.95      1499.50

                              Subtotal:    $2698.50


Furniture:

10     Table, 3 ft. x 7 ft.          180.00      1800.00
20     Chair                          37.50       750.00

                              Subtotal:    $2550.00

                                 Total:   $57417.25
```

Figure 10.1 Proposal report from Example Program 10-10.

Figure 10.2 shows the structure of the input data file.

```
3
Computer Laboratory Proposal
for
Newtown High School
3
Hardware
```

```
20
ABC microcomputer, 2295
20
Model 15 monitor, 175.5
5
Model XX-50 printer, 520
5
Printer cable, 31.75
-1
Software
20
DOS 7.0 operating system, 40
20
True BASIC language system, 19.95
20
Borland C++ compiler, 149.95
-1
Furniture
10
"Table, 3 ft. x 7 ft.", 180
20 Chair, 37.5
-1
```

Figure 10.2 Contents of data file PROPOSAL.DAT.

Program Outline

The first step is to examine an outline of the program:

> display the proposal report title
>
> create format strings
>
> display column headings
>
> for each category of items
>
>> display quantity, item, unit price, cost
>>
>> display subtotal cost for the category
>
> display the grand total cost
>
> end the program

The main program unit opens the data file PROPOSAL.DAT as file #1 for reading only — assume that this file is in the current directory. If not, the complete path name should be entered into the program. Note that the data file uses channel #1 in the main program and channel #9 in the procedures.

The program is written so that it can be modified easily to write the report on any output device. As written, it will display on the screen which is designated channel #0. If you want to write the report on an attached printer or on a file, add an appropriate file opening statement to the program and assign a different numeric value to the channel number variable N.

The PUBLIC Statement and Global Variables

Four *global variables* are defined — that is, variables that are known in both the main program and all external procedures. These global variables are defined in a PUBLIC statement that must be located before any other reference to the variables. Each of the procedures that uses one or more of the global variables must include a DECLARE PUBLIC statement. Remember that without such as process to create global variables, all variables in the main program or any procedure are local to that program unit. Using global variables is an alternative to passing variables as parameters. In most cases the use of parameters is preferred, but when the variable values are constant, as they are in this program, it is just as acceptable and probably simpler to make them global by defining them as PUBLIC.

The proposal report is designed to fit on a page that is 60 columns wide and that value is assigned to the variable Width. The SET statement makes sure that the screen is set to the same width as the page.

The format strings for column headings and values are created next. By placing these strings close together and using format string names of the same length, it is easy to see how the values line up under the individual column headings. The heading format string H$ and the value format string F$ are written in two parts that are then concatenated together. This procedure avoids a program statement that is too long to be displayed as a single line on the screen.

Here is the main program, containing statements to accomplish the preceding tasks and calls to three subroutines that do the actual printing of the report:

```
! Example Program 10-10
! Program to produce a formatted proposal report.

! Open the data file and initialize variables.

OPEN #1: name "PROPOSAL.DAT", access input
PUBLIC N, Width, H$, F$     ! global variables
LET N = 0                   ! N is the output channel number
LET Width = 60              ! width of the page in columns
SET #N: margin Width
```

```
! Create format strings for headings and values.
LET H1$ = "###        ####                          "
LET F1$ = "##    <############################"
LET H2$ = "      #####        ####   "
LET F2$ = "      ####.##    #####.##"
LET H$ = H1$ & H2$
LET F$ = F1$ & F2$

CALL DisplayTitle (#1)
CALL DisplayHeadings (#1)
CALL DisplayValues (#1)
END
```

The DisplayTitle Subroutine

The first subroutine displays the report title, using a technique discussed earlier for centering lines of text with the Tab function. The program is designed to handle a multiline title, the number of lines being specified by a variable TitleLines that is the first item read from the data file. In this example, the value of TitleLines is 3, indicating that the next three items read from the data file are lines of the title. A Tab function in the PRINT statement centers the string Line$ in the designated page width. Note that N and Width are declared public in this subroutine.

```
SUB DisplayTitle (#9)
    ! Display the title of the proposal.
    DECLARE PUBLIC N, Width
    INPUT #9: TitleLines  ! number of lines in title
    FOR Count = 1 to TitleLines
        INPUT #9: Line$
        PRINT #N: Tab((Width - Len(Line$))/2); Line$
    NEXT Count
    PRINT #N
END SUB  ! DisplayTitle
```

The DisplayHeadings Subroutine

The next subroutine creates column headings. The Repeat$ function displays two horizontal lines that separate the column headings from the rest of the table. In this subroutine, variables N, Width, and H$ are declared public.

```
SUB DisplayHeadings (#9)
    ! Display the column headings.
    DECLARE PUBLIC N, Width, H$
    PRINT #N: Repeat$("=", Width)
```

```
        PRINT #N, using H$: "NO.", "ITEM", "PRICE", "COST"
        PRINT #N: Repeat$("=", Width)
        PRINT #N
    END SUB  ! DisplayHeadings
```

The DisplayValues Subroutine

The last subroutine displays the proposal table itself. The F$ format string is used to format each line. The table is divided into NumCat categories where the variable NumCat is the next item read from the data file. In this example, there are three separate categories in the report. The program calculates a cost subtotal within each category and a total cost for the complete project.

Two summing variables, SubTotal and GrandTotal, are used. SubTotal calculates the total cost for a category, while GrandTotal calculates the total cost for the project. Note that SubTotal must be reset to zero at the beginning of each category. The number -1 — read from the data file — indicates that there are no more data items for that particular category. This number is called a sentinel. Note again which variables are declared public.

```
    SUB DisplayValues (#9)
        ! Display the individual values and totals.
        DECLARE PUBLIC N, Width, F$
        LET GrandTotal = 0
        INPUT #9: NumCat
        FOR Count = 1 to NumCat
            INPUT #9: SubHeading$
            PRINT #N: SubHeading$; ":"
            PRINT #N
            LET SubTotal = 0      ! reset for each category
            INPUT #9: Num
            DO until Num < 0      ! stop at negative trailer
               INPUT #9: Item$, UnitPrc
               LET Cost = Num * UnitPrc
               LET SubTotal = SubTotal + Cost
               PRINT #N, using F$: Num, Item$, UnitPrc, Cost
               INPUT #9: Num
            LOOP
            PRINT #N
            PRINT #N: Tab(Width - 20); "Subtotal:   ";
            PRINT #N, using "$$$$$$$.##": SubTotal
            PRINT #N
            LET GrandTotal = GrandTotal + SubTotal
        NEXT I
        PRINT #N: Tab(Width - 17); "Total:   ";
```

```
    PRINT #N, using "$$$$$$$.##": GrandTotal
END SUB  ! DisplayValues
```

Let's look at this subroutine in more detail. First, the variable GrandTotal is set to zero. The number of categories is read from the data file and a FOR loop with this number is used to print all the categories. In this example, there are three categories of items.

For each category, a subheading is read and printed and the variable SubTotal is set to zero. A small loop reads the quantity and then the description and price of each item from the data file, calculates the cost for this quantity of the item, and prints a line of the proposal. The value of SubTotal is updated.

As mentioned earlier, a quantity value of -1 serves as a sentinel to signify the end of a category of items. At this point, the value of SubTotal is printed with an appropriate label and is added to the grand total cost. The FOR loop then goes to the next category of items. After all categories have been printed (as determined by the value of NumCat), the value of GrandTotal is printed with an appropriate label.

Looking again at the data file, note that one of the item descriptions is enclosed in quotation marks. If this is not done, the comma after "Table" will be interpreted as a data separator and the wrong description will be printed. Moreover, the program will halt with an error message when a nonnumeric string is read for the item price.

The Final Program

Here is the complete program consisting of a main program and three subroutines:

```
! Example Program 10-10
! Program to produce a formatted proposal report.

! Open the data file and initialize variables.
PUBLIC N, Width, H$, F$      ! global variables
OPEN #1: name "PROPOSAL.DAT", access input
LET N = 0                ! N is the output file number
LET Width = 60           ! width of the page in columns
SET #N: margin Width

! Create format strings for headings and values.
LET H1$ = "###      ####                          "
LET F1$ = "##    <############################"
LET H2$ = "       #####        ####  "
LET F2$ = "      ####.##     #####.##"
LET H$ = H1$ & H2$
LET F$ = F1$ & F2$
```

```
    CALL DisplayTitle (#1)
    CALL DisplayHeadings (#1)
    CALL DisplayValues (#1)

END  ! of main program

SUB DisplayTitle (#9)
    ! Display the title of the proposal.
    DECLARE PUBLIC N, Width
    INPUT #9: TitleLines  ! number of lines in title
    FOR Count = 1 to TitleLines
        INPUT #9: Line$
        PRINT #N: Tab((Width - Len(Line$))/2); Line$
    NEXT Count
    PRINT #N
END SUB  ! DisplayTitle

SUB DisplayHeadings (#9)
    ! Display the column headings.
    DECLARE PUBLIC N, Width, H$
    PRINT #N: Repeat$("=", Width)
    PRINT #N, using H$: "NO.", "ITEM", "PRICE", "COST"
    PRINT #N: Repeat$("=", Width)
    PRINT #N
END SUB  ! DisplayHeadings

SUB DisplayValues (#9)
    ! Display the individual values and totals.
    DECLARE PUBLIC N, Width, F$
    LET GrandTotal = 0
    INPUT #9: NumCat
    FOR Count = 1 to NumCat
        INPUT #9: SubHeading$
        PRINT #N: SubHeading$; ":"
        PRINT #N
        LET SubTotal = 0     ! reset for each category
        INPUT #9: Num
        DO until Num < 0     ! stop at negative trailer
            INPUT #9: Item$, UnitPrc
            LET Cost = Num * UnitPrc
            LET SubTotal = SubTotal + Cost
            PRINT #N, using F$: Num, Item$, UnitPrc, Cost
            INPUT #9: Num
        LOOP
```

```
        PRINT #N
        PRINT #N: Tab(Width - 20); "Subtotal:   ";
        PRINT #N, using "$$$$$$$.##": SubTotal
        PRINT #N
        LET GrandTotal = GrandTotal + SubTotal
    NEXT Count
    PRINT #N: Tab(Width - 17); "Total:   ";
    PRINT #N, using "$$$$$$$.##": GrandTotal
END SUB  ! DisplayValues
```

This program produces the proposal report shown in Fig. 10.1.

10.5   CONTROLLING THE SCREEN DISPLAY

You have learned to control the format of the display screen using a format string in a PRINT USING statement. Another method of format control is to specify the position of the cursor on the screen, thus designating the position where a display will start.

Setting the Cursor Position

The statement

```
SET CURSOR Row, Column
```

moves the cursor to the location specified by the values of Row and Column. For example,

```
SET CURSOR 1,1
```

moves the cursor to the upper left corner of the screen window. The values of Row and Column cannot, of course, exceed the maximum number of rows or columns available on the current display window.

On a PC, the SET CURSOR statement does two things. First, it clears the normal two-window display and changes the entire screen to an output window. Any characters displayed in the command window are erased and lost. Second, it moves the cursor to the specified window location. When the program ends, you must press any key (or the left mouse button) to return to the normal split screen showing both editing and command windows.

On a Mac, True BASIC can have three separate windows — editing, output, and command — although the command window is seldom used. The SET CURSOR statement does not clear the output window but does move the cursor to the specified location on the output window, making that window the active window. If the editing window is not currently displayed, pressing any key or the mouse button returns the editing window to the screen and makes it the active window. If both the editing and output windows are displayed, the editing window automatically becomes the active window when the program ends.

The preceding discussion is complicated and behavior does vary with different monitors. Try using the SET CURSOR statement in some small programs on your particular combination of computer and monitor. It is important to note that **a program containing SET CURSOR statements cannot be used to control the format of printed output**, only the format of a screen display.

You may have as many SET CURSOR statements as you wish in a program. You may move the cursor up or down, right or left on the screen. You cannot, however, move the cursor off the screen. On a typical PC monitor, the column value is between 1 and 80 while the row value is between 1 and 25.

If you don't know the size of your screen, run the following program that introduces the ASK MAX CURSOR statement:

```
! Example Program 10-11
! Calculate output window size.

CLEAR
ASK MAX CURSOR Height, Width
PRINT "Height of output window ="; Height; "rows"
PRINT "Width of output window ="; Width; "columns"
END
```

This program gives the screen size if the output window is made large enough to fill the entire screen.

If you run this program on a PC with the normal monitor, you should get the following output:

```
Height of output window = 25 rows
Width of output window = 80 columns
```

On the other hand, if you run the program on a Mac with a built-in monitor, you see a different output, as follows:

```
Height of output window = 19 rows
Width of output window = 72 columns
```

On a 17-inch Mac monitor, you might see this output:

```
Height of output window = 46 rows
Width of output window = 145 columns
```

The SET CURSOR statement is used in an example program to draw a box around a menu on the screen, using the familiar menu from the telephone directory program in Chapter 9. Figure 10.3 shows how the screen display will appear.

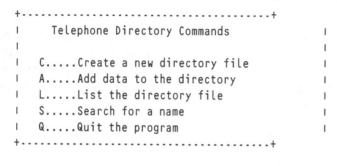

```
+-----------------------------------+
|      Telephone Directory Commands          |
|                                            |
|    C.....Create a new directory file       |
|    A.....Add data to the directory         |
|    L.....List the directory file           |
|    S.....Search for a name                 |
|    Q.....Quit the program                  |
+-----------------------------------+


        Your selection..........
```

Figure 10.3 Screen display from Example Program 10-12.

A major part of this program is a subroutine that draws a box of width W columns and height H rows on the screen, centered at location column X and row Y. Here is an outline for the subroutine:

> assign characters for box outline
>
> assign box boundaries
>
> check if box will fit on screen
>
> draw the box

The characters used to draw the boundaries of the box are assigned to variables in the section labeled "Box components." The dimensions of the box are calculated and used to assign values to variables Xminus, Xplus, Yminus, and Yplus. The next section of the subroutine checks to make sure that the box is not too big to fit on the screen. This is another example of good defensive programming.

The box is drawn by using plus signs (+) for the corners, minus signs (-) for the horizontal lines, and vertical bars (|) for the vertical lines. It is possible to draw a much better looking box by using the graphical capabilities of True BASIC, as you will learn in Chapter 12. On a PC, it is also possible to use the special line characters in the extended ASCII set.

Returning to the main program, another subroutine is called to display the text. A SET CURSOR statement is used to place the cursor inside the box and the menu is displayed. A SET CURSOR statement must be used before each PRINT statement. Another SET CURSOR statement moves the cursor outside the box so that the command prompt can be displayed.

This is not a complete program in the sense that it does nothing — it just stops — no matter what character you type in. The purpose of the program is to demonstrate how you can control the placement of characters on the screen. If you want to, you can add this menu system to Example Program 9-10.

```
! Example Program 10-12
! Use cursor control to display menu in box.

LET BoxOK$ = "true"
CALL DisplayBox (40, 8, 40, 12, BoxOK$)
IF BoxOK$ = "false" then
   PRINT "Press any key to stop."
   GET KEY Dummy
   STOP
END IF
CALL DisplayText (Command$)
END   ! of main program

SUB DisplayBox (W, H, X, Y, BoxOK$)
   ! Display box is centered at column X, row Y.
   ! Box has width W and height H.

   ! Box components
   LET Corner$ = "+"
   LET VertLine$ = "|"
   LET HorLine$ ="-"

   ! Box boundaries
   LET Xminus = X - W/2
   LET Xplus = X + W/2
   LET Yminus = Y - H/2
   LET Yplus = Y + H/2

   ! Error exits from the subroutine
   CLEAR
   ASK MAX CURSOR Height, Width
   IF Xplus > Width or Xminus < 0 then
      PRINT "Screen is not wide enough for this box."
      LET BoxOK$ = "false"
      EXIT SUB
   END IF
   IF Yplus > Height or Yminus < 0 then
      PRINT "Screen is not high enough for this box."
      LET BoxOK$ = "false"
      EXIT SUB
   END IF
```

```
            ! Display the box
            SET CURSOR Yminus, Xminus
            PRINT Corner$;
            FOR I = (Xminus + 1) to (Xplus - 1)
                PRINT HorLine$;
            NEXT I
            PRINT Corner$
            FOR Row = (Yminus + 1) to (Yplus - 1)
                SET CURSOR Row, Xminus
                PRINT VertLine$;
                SET CURSOR Row, Xplus
                PRINT VertLine$
            NEXT Row
            SET CURSOR Yplus, Xminus
            PRINT Corner$;
            FOR I = (Xminus + 1) to (Xplus - 1)
                PRINT HorLine$;
            NEXT I
            PRINT Corner$
        END SUB  ! DisplayBox

        SUB DisplayText (Command$)
            ! Display the list of commands.
            SET CURSOR 9,26
            PRINT "Telephone Directory Commands"
            SET CURSOR 11,24
            PRINT "C.....Create a new directory file"
            SET CURSOR 12,24
            PRINT "A.....Add data to the directory"
            SET CURSOR 13,24
            PRINT "L.....List the directory file"
            SET CURSOR 14,24
             PRINT "S.....Search for a name"
            SET CURSOR 15,24
            PRINT "Q.....Quit the program"
            SET CURSOR 18,28
            PRINT "Your selection..........";
            LINE INPUT prompt "": Command$
        END SUB  ! DisplayText
```

A CLEAR statement at the beginning of the subroutine clears the entire screen for use by the program. An ASK MAX CURSOR statement determines the width and height of the screen. You will notice that the flag BoxOK$ is set to false if the subroutine is exited because the box is too big. If this flag is set, there is a pause in the main program so that the error message can be read and when a key is pressed, the program stops.

Here is how the output looks when the command Q is entered:

```
+........................................+
|      Telephone Directory Commands      |
|                                        |
|   C.....Create a new directory file    |
|   A.....Add data to the directory      |
|   L.....List the directory file        |
|   S.....Search for a name              |
|   Q.....Quit the program               |
+........................................+


        Your selection..........Q
```

Try running this program again after changing the "CALL Box" statement to specify a box that is wider than the normal screen width of 80 columns. The following statement specifies a box width of 90 columns.

```
CALL DisplayBox (90, 8, 40, 12, BoxOK$)
```

You should receive an error message because the box is too wide for the screen.

Finding the Cursor Position

The statement

```
ASK CURSOR Row, Column
```

determines the current position of the cursor, assigning the current cursor row value to the variable Row and the column value to the variable Column.

You can also turn the cursor on and off by using the statement

```
SET CURSOR Condition$
```

where the string variable Condition$ may have only the values of "off" or "on" (in either uppercase or lowercase letters). A companion statement

```
ASK CURSOR Value$
```

assigns the value of ON or OFF to the variable Value$, indicating whether the cursor is on or off.

Other variable names may be used in any of these cursor statements. The only restriction is that the variables must be of the correct type, string or numeric, for each case.

10.6   SCREEN WINDOWS

Application programs are often easier to use if the screen can be divided into two or more separate and independent windows. You already know how convenient it is in True BASIC to have both the editing window and command window open at the same time. Several modern screen editors allow two files to be displayed on the screen at one time, each file in its own window. Information can be read from one file while the other file is being edited.

True BASIC allows you to write programs that divide the screen into several independent windows and to move as you wish from one window to another. Each window is denoted by a window number. There is no boundary or box around a window unless you explicitly draw one. Techniques for drawing graphic boxes are introduced in Chapter 12.

Window numbers are just channel numbers, similar to file numbers. **The same channel number cannot be used as both a file number and a window number in the same program.**

Creating Windows

The default window is designated as window #0 and includes the entire screen. Remember that you used this notation in Example Program 9-2 when you directed output to the display screen before writing it on a file.

Another window, smaller than the whole screen, can be opened with the statement

```
OPEN #N: SCREEN Left, Right, Bottom, Top
```

where N is the window number. The numeric expressions Left, Right, Bottom, and Top define the position where this window appears on the screen.

True BASIC uses screen coordinates with a range from 0 to 1 in both the horizontal and vertical directions for these numeric expressions. The coordinates of the lower left corner of the screen are (0,0), while those of the upper right corner are (1,1). Thus the values of Left, Right, Bottom, and Top must be between 0 and 1, inclusive.

Figure 10.4 is a picture of window #0, the full screen, showing the coordinates of each corner.

Figure 10.4 A full-screen window.

As an example, the statement

```
OPEN #1: screen 0, 0.5, 0, 1
```

designates the left half of the display screen as window #1. When this window is opened, it becomes the *current window*. All further display operations take place in the current window. If another window is opened, it then becomes the current window.

The statement

```
OPEN #2: screen 0.5, 1, 0, 1
```

opens a second window on the right half of the screen. Overlapping windows should be avoided because, on some computers, information written on one window can erase information on another overlapping or underlying window. These two windows are shown in Fig. 10.5. Note that a vertical line does **not** appear on the screen separating the two windows.

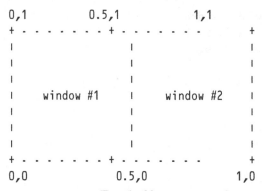

Figure 10.5 Two half-screen windows.

The statement

```
CLOSE #N
```

is used to close window #N when it is no longer being used. When any window is closed, the default window (window #0) is automatically reopened.

Moving Between Windows

You can move from one window to another by using the statement

```
WINDOW #N
```

which switches to window #N as the active or current window. True BASIC remembers the current cursor location, color, window coordinates, and so forth, and it automatically restores these values when you switch back to a window.

You can control the cursor location in a window by using the SET CURSOR statement that was introduced in the last section. **Note that the row and column values specifying cursor location are relative to the current window, not the entire screen.** Use the ASK MAX CURSOR statement to determine the maximum row and column values for the current window. An error message is displayed if you try to move the cursor outside the window.

Remember that you must be aware of two different sets of coordinates. Window size is specified in screen coordinates, discussed in the preceding paragraphs. Cursor position is specified in row and column coordinates, discussed in Section 10.5.

Here is an example program that divides the screen into two windows. A table of the months is displayed in the left window. The user is asked to enter a month number in the right window and the name of the corresponding month is displayed in the same window. At the same time, an arrow moves to mark that particular month in the left window table.

```
! Example Program 10-13
! Demonstrate use of two screen windows.

ASK MAX CURSOR Height, Width
OPEN #1: screen 0, 0.5, 0, 1
OPEN #2: screen 0.5, 1, 0, 1

! Display table of months in first window.
DIM Month$(1 to 12)
WINDOW #1
PRINT Tab(7); "MONTHS"
! Read month names into an array.
PRINT
FOR Index = 1 to 12
    READ Month$(Index)
    PRINT Tab(7); Month$(Index)
NEXT Index

! Draw dividing line between windows.
WINDOW #2
```

```
FOR Row = 1 to Height
    SET CURSOR Row,  1
    PRINT "|"
NEXT Row


! Run program in second window.
SET CURSOR 1, 3
PRINT Tab(3); "Type 0 to stop."
CALL GetMonth (Number)
DO until Number = 0
    PRINT Tab(3); "You have selected "; Month$(Number)
    PRINT
    ! Mark month in first window.
    WINDOW #1
    ! Erase the old arrows and print a new arrow.
    ! Month names are displayed in rows 3 thru 15.
    FOR Row = 3 to 15
        SET CURSOR Row, 3  ! arrow starts at column 3
        PRINT "  "          ! erase old arrow
    NEXT Row
    ! Mark the specified month.
    SET CURSOR Number + 2, 3
    PRINT "->"              ! mark month with arrow
    ! Return to second window.
    WINDOW #2
    CALL GetMonth (Number) ! get next month number
LOOP

DATA January, February, March, April
DATA May, June, July, August
DATA September, October, November, December
END  ! of main program


SUB GetMonth (Number)
    ! Get zero or valid month number.
    DO
        PRINT Tab(3); "Number of month";
        INPUT Number
        IF Number > 12 or Number < 0 then
            PRINT Tab(3); "Enter number between 0 and 12."
            PRINT
        END IF
    LOOP until Number >= 0 and Number <= 12
END SUB  ! GetMonth
```

Window #1 is opened first and a table of the months is displayed. Then window #2 is opened and the subroutine GetMonth is called, which asks the user to enter a number. Number 0 stops the program. Any number less than 0 or greater than 12 is considered an error, and the user is asked to enter the number again.

When a valid number is entered, the name of the corresponding month is displayed in window #2. Display is switched to window #1, any existing arrows are erased, and a new arrow is printed next to the current month. Display is switched back to window #2, and the name of another month is requested.

Figure 10.6 shows how the display screen looks after a user runs the program and enters a month number of 5.

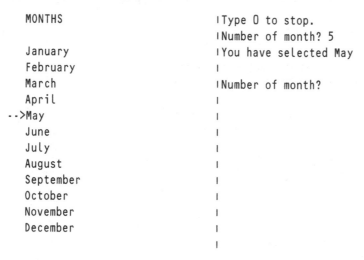

```
    MONTHS                    I Type 0 to stop.
                              I Number of month? 5
    January                   I You have selected May
    February                  I
    March                     I Number of month?
    April                     I
 -->May                       I
    June                      I
    July                      I
    August                    I
    September                 I
    October                   I
    November                  I
    December                  I
                              I
```

Figure 10.6   Screen display from Example Program 10-13.

Summary of Important Points

- Commas and semicolons (except a trailing semicolon) cannot be used to format the output of a PRINT USING statement.

- A format string containing dollar signs and a period cannot be used to format a string variable.

- Commas cannot be inserted between the dollar signs in a format string.

- Angle brackets in a format string cannot be used to justify numeric values.

- When changing windows or clearing the screen, you may need to insert pauses so the display is not erased before the user is able to read it.

- A program containing SET CURSOR statements cannot be used to control the format of output from a printer.

- The same channel number cannot be used for both a file number and a window number in the same program.

- Row and column values specifying the cursor location are relative to the current window, not the entire screen.

- Window size is specified by screen coordinates, cursor position is specified by row and column coordinates.

Common Errors

- Designing a format string that is too short for the variable that will use it, resulting in an error display.

- Inserting commas in a format string containing dollar signs.

- Forgetting to turn on the printer before executing a program that uses that printer.

- When using global variables, failing to declare them in a DECLARE PUBLIC statement.

- Trying to use SET CURSOR statements to control the appearance of a printed report.

- Dividing the screen into two or more windows without creating some type of line or marker to denote the boundaries between windows. Not so much an error as confusing to the user.

Self-Test Questions

1. Which of the following characters can be used as format characters in a format string?

   (a) #   (f) ;
   (b) %   (g) *
   (c) $ (h) +
   (d) ?   (I) =
   (e) <   (j) -

2. Can semicolons be used to separate items in a PRINT USING statement?

3. Is a trailing semicolon allowed in a PRINT USING statement? If so, what does it do?

4. What is displayed when the number 12345 is printed with a format string of "####"?

5. (a) Is "$$###" a valid format string? If not, why not?

   (b) Is "%%###" a valid format string? If not, why not?

6. What is displayed when the number 12.5 is printed with a format string of

   (a) "-##.##"?
   (b) "+##.##"?

7. Is the string "$$,$$$.##" a valid format string? If not, why?

8. Can the format string ">###" be used to print a numeric variable Num containing the value 256?

9. Can the number -999 be printed with a format string of "###"?

10. (a) If the string "THE" is printed using a format string of "#####", will it be located in the five-character field?

    (b) Can the string "THE END" be displayed using the same format string?

11. Can a single format string be used to print both a numeric variable value and a string value? Explain.

12. What statement is used to assign an attached printer to a file number of 9?

13. Can the PRINT USING statement be used to write numeric variable values on a disk file?

14. (a) What is the purpose of the CLEAR statement?

(b) What is the location of the cursor after this statement is executed?

15. What channel number is used to designate the display unit?

16. What is the purpose of a sentinel value in a data file?

17. In the statement

    `SET CURSOR A, B`

    what is the meaning of
    - (a) variable A?
    - (b) variable B?

18. Which True BASIC statement
    - (a) moves the cursor to the upper left corner of the screen?
    - (b) turns off the cursor?

19. If the statement

    `ASK MAX CURSOR A, B`

    is executed on your computer, what is the value of
    - (a) variable A?
    - (b) variable B?

20. What happens when the statement

    `GET KEY Dummy`

    is executed?

21. If a window is opened as window #1, can you also open a file as
    - (a) file #2?
    - (b) file #1?

22. (a) What coordinate system is used to specify the size of a window?

    (b) Is this system different from the coordinate system used to specify the position of the cursor? Explain.

23. What statement is used to
    - (a) open window #3?
    - (b) move the cursor to window #3?
    - (c) close window #3?

24. Can you use the SET CURSOR statement to move the cursor from window #1 to #2?

Practice Programs

1. Read accounts payable information, the name of the payee and the amount owed, from a text file named ACCOUNTS.DAT. Print a check (on paper) for each payee in the format shown in Fig. 10.7, separating one check from another with three blank lines. Use the characters discussed in Example Program 10-12 to create the outline of the check. Enter the desired date and the number of the first check from the keyboard. Number the following checks sequentially. Identifiers in angle brackets will be replaced by actual values read from the data file. Remember that SET CURSOR statements cannot be used for printing information, only for displaying information on the screen.

```
+ - - - - - - - - - - - - - - - - - - - - - - - - - - +
I  ACME SALES CORPORATION                 <check date>        I
I     Detroit, Michigan                                       I
I                                                             I
I  Pay to: <payee>                         <amount>           I
I                                                             I
I                                                             I
I                                                             I
I                                                             I
I  No: <check number>      _____        I
I                                               Treas.        I
+ - - - - - - - - - - - - - - - - - - - - - - - - - - +
```

Figure 10.7 Sample bank check.

Test your program using the file ACCOUNTS.DAT.

2. Read names and addresses from a text file named MAILING.DAT. The following information is available for each person:

> name
> street address
> city
> state
> zip code

Each item of information (field) is stored on a separate line in the file. Print or display mailing labels in the format of two labels across the page, as shown.

```
John H. Smith                 Mary Z. Wheeler
25 Oak Drive                  1350 Main Street
Richmond, VA 23219            Willowdale, VA 23230
```

Each label has a maximum width of 36 columns. In order to print or display any line in a label that exceeds 36 characters, you must develop and use an algorithm to reduce its length. The two-character state abbreviation and the five-character zip code cannot be shortened.

Test your program using the file MAILING.DAT.

3.   Modify the Box subroutine of Example Program 10-12 to draw a double box as shown in Fig. 10.8.

Figure 10.8 Modified box for Example Program 10-12.

The height of the upper part of the box is denoted by the variable H1 and of the lower part by H2.

Rewrite the program to place the menu in the upper part of the box and the command prompt in the lower part. Test your program by showing how the menu of Example Program 10-12 will look in the new box.

4.   It is often useful to be able to display and compare two text files at the same time. Divide the output window horizontally into two equal windows. Ask the user for the names of two text files, file A and file B. Display the first 10 lines of file A in the top window and the first 10 lines of file B in the bottom window.

If a user presses the Alt-1 key (hold down the Alt key and press the 1 key), 8 more lines of file A are displayed in the top window. If a user presses the Alt-2 key, 8 more lines of file B are displayed in the bottom window. If a user presses any other key, the program stops. When using the GET KEY statement on a standard PC keyboard, the Alt-1 key returns a numeric code of 376 and the Alt-2 key returns a numeric code of 377.

You will have to use different key combinations on a Mac, possibly Option-1 and Option-2. Remember that Example Program 5-12 can always be used to determine the numeric code created by any key combination and you should check your own keyboard.

Test your program using the file UPPER.TXT for file A and LOWER.TXT for file B. Show the screen displaying the first 10 lines of file A and the lines of file B after it has scrolled up 16 lines.

CHAPTER
11

Applications and Record Files

11.1 INTRODUCTION

In this chapter, you learn about several interesting computer applications. Two algorithms that are used frequently in business applications are introduced: a sorting algorithm that arranges the contents of files into ascending or descending order, and a binary search algorithm that quickly finds a specified item in a sorted file.

To search a file record by record, you must be able to read any particular record. The concept of a record file is introduced which allows you to access any record directly.

Another useful application is the conversion of data files from one format to another and an example of this technique is presented.

11.2 A SIMPLE SORTING TECHNIQUE

The need to sort lists into numeric or alphabetic order occurs frequently in computer programs. Sorting time can be a significant part of a program's execution time, and so considerable research effort has been devoted to developing fast and efficient sorting algorithms. Unfortunately, many of these fast sorting methods are complicated and difficult to understand.

As a simple example of sorting, the *bubble sort* algorithm is introduced. It is not a fast sorting method but it is easy to understand. The example program sorts a list of names that has been placed in a string array.

Comparing Two Strings

You need to understand how the computer determines if one string is larger than another string. If you compare two string variables named A$ and B$, you want to know if the logical expression (A$ > B$) is true or false.

Comparison of two strings is done character by character and is based on the ASCII values of the characters. The computer compares the ASCII value of the first character of A$ with that of the first character of B$. If the character in A$ has the greater value, then the expression (A$ > B$) is true. Remember that an uppercase letter and the corresponding lowercase letter are different characters and have different ASCII values.

"C" is greater than "B", and "a" is greater than "A".

If the character in A$ has the lesser value, then the expression (A$ > B$) is false. If the first characters in A$ and B$ are identical, then a comparison is made between the ASCII values of the second character in each string.

This process continues until (1) the value of a character in one string is greater or less than the value of the corresponding character in the other string, or (2) the end of one string is reached while the other string still contains more characters, or (3) the ends of both strings are reached because they are equal in length and have the same sequence of characters.

If the ASCII value of a character in string A$ is greater or less than the ASCII value of the corresponding character in string B$, then the last comparison determines whether the expression is true or false.

"ABC" is greater than "ABB" because "C" is greater than "B".

If A$ is longer than B$ and the two strings have an identical sequence of characters up to the end of string B$, then string A$ is considered the greater and the expression is true.

"QED" is greater than "QE" because "QED" is longer than "QE".

If both strings, A$ and B$, are of equal length and have the same sequence of characters, then the two strings are equal and the expression (A$ > B$) is false.

"xyz" is equal to "xyz".

The Bubble Sort Algorithm

Now examine the bubble sort algorithm and see how it works. You go through a list of names, from one end of the list to the other end, comparing names in pairs. The first pair consists of the first name and the second name in the list, the second pair consists of the second name and the third name, and so forth. This process is called *scanning the list*.

If a pair is in the wrong alphabetic order, you swap or interchange the two names. If a pair is in the correct alphabetic order, you move on to the next pair.

This process repeats until you can scan the list without having to swap any names. Then you know that the list is in sorted order.

Swapping Two Values

You have to use a third temporary value when swapping two names. To swap the values of A$ and B$, put the value of A$ into the variable Temp$, assign the value of B$ to A$, and then assign the value of Temp$ to B$. The following program statements can be used:

```
LET Temp$ = A$  ! put value of A$ in Temp$
LET A$ = B$     ! put value of B$ in A$
LET B$ = Temp$  ! put value of Temp$ in B$
```

Using a Logical Flag

You have already used string variables as logical flags in several example programs. In this case, **a logical flag tells the program when the list has been scanned without any interchanges**. Each time you start a new scan of the list, set the flag to true — assign the flag variable a value of "true." If you make an interchange during this scan of the list, the flag is changed to "false." Examine the flag at the end of each scan and if it is true, you know that no interchanges were made during the last scan through the list and that the list is in sorted order.

11.3   SORTING A LIST OF NAMES

Your program must contain statements to perform the three following tasks:

> read names from an input file and assign them to an array
>
> sort the array of names in memory
>
> write the sorted array back to another file

This program assumes that you have enough memory so that the entire file can be placed in a memory array. It is much easier and quicker to sort a list in memory than it is to sort a list on a disk file. A subroutine is used for the actual sorting.

Here is an outline of the sorting subroutine.

> begin a loop
>> set the sorted flag to true
>> for each pair of strings
>>> compare the two string values
>>> swap the two values if not in proper order
>>> set the sorted flag to false
> loop until the sorted flag is true

The sorting subroutine uses an array Array$ containing N string values. A flag variable named Sorted$ is used to determine when to stop scanning the array.

```
! Example Subprogram 11-1
! Subroutine for bubble sort algorithm.
! Sort array in ascending alphabetic order.
! Parameters: Array$()   array of strings
!             N          no. of strings in array

SUB Sort (Array$(), N)
    ! Bubble sort a string array
    ! in ascending alphabetic order.
    DO
       LET Sorted$ = "true"
       FOR Index = 1 to (N - 1)
          IF Array$(Index) > Array$(Index + 1) then
             LET Temp$ = Array$(Index)
             LET Array$(Index) = Array$(Index + 1)
             LET Array$(Index + 1) = Temp$
             LET Sorted$ = "false"
          END IF
       NEXT Index
    LOOP until Sorted$ = "true"
END SUB
```

The flag Sorted$ is set to true at the beginning of the scan loop. Pairs of names denoted by Array$(Index) and Array$(Index + 1) are compared and are swapped if not in sorted order. If swapping occurs, the flag is set to false. The scan loop is repeated until the flag remains true.

Note that the FOR loop only goes up to Index = N - 1 because one index in the comparison is Index + 1 and the last name in the list is Array$(N). If the index Index were assigned a value of N, the program would try to compare the string elements Array$(N) and Array$(N + 1) and would produce unpredictable results because no name has been assigned to Array$(N + 1).

This subroutine will sort a list of strings in ascending alphabetic order. To sort in descending order, reverse the logical sense of the comparison, changing the IF statement as follows:

```
IF Array$(Index) < Array$(Index + 1) then
```

The program assumes that the names are stored in a text file, one name per line. The array that will hold the names is dimensioned by the user. Here is the complete program:

```
! Example Program 11-2
! Sort a text file containing names.

DIM List$ (1)
PRINT "Maximum number of names that you plan to sort";
INPUT Capacity
MAT redim List$(1 to Capacity)
LET ArrayFull$ = "false"
LET Count = 0
CALL OpenFile ("Input file name", "old", #1)
CALL OpenFile ("Output file name", "newold", #2)

DO while more #1 and ArrayFull$ = "false"
   LET Count = Count + 1
   IF Count <= Capacity then
      LINE INPUT #1: List$(Count)
   ELSE  ! Count > Capacity
      LET ArrayFull$ = "true"
      ! The next statement avoids array overflow
      ! during sorting in the Sort subroutine.
      LET Count = Capacity
   END IF
LOOP
IF ArrayFull$ = "true" then
   PRINT "Only part of the file could";
   PRINT " be read because the"
   PRINT "maximum number of names";
   PRINT " specified was too small."
END IF
CALL Sort (List$, Count)
ERASE #2
FOR Index = 1 to Count
    PRINT #2: List$(Index)
NEXT Index
CLOSE #1
CLOSE #2
PRINT "A list of"; Count; "names has been sorted."
END  ! of main program

SUB OpenFile (Prompt$, Mode$, #9)
    ! Prompt for file name and open file.
    LET FileOpened$ = "false"
    DO
       WHEN error in
            PRINT Prompt$;
```

```
            LINE INPUT FileName$
            OPEN #9: name FileName$, create Mode$
            LET FileOpened$ = "true"
        USE
            PRINT "Error: "; extext$
            PRINT "Check path name and try again."
            PRINT
        END WHEN
    LOOP until FileOpened$ = "true"
END SUB  ! OpenFile

SUB Sort (Array$(), N)
    ! Bubble sort a string array
    ! in ascending alphabetic order.
    DO
        LET Sorted$ = "true"
        FOR Index = 1 to (N - 1)
            IF Array$(Index) > Array$(Index + 1) then
                LET Temp$ = Array$(Index)
                LET Array$(Index) = Array$(Index + 1)
                LET Array$(Index + 1) = Temp$
                LET Sorted$ = "false"
            END IF
        NEXT Index
    LOOP until Sorted$ = "true"
END SUB  ! Sort
```

The user is asked to specify the maximum number of names to be sorted and the array is redimensioned to that size, storing the size value in the variable Capacity. Using the same OpenFile subroutine that you used in Chapter 9, two text files are opened. The input file contains an unsorted list of names, one name per line. The sorted list of names will be written on the output file. An input loop reads the names into an array named List$, counting the number of names that are read.

If the number of names reaches the size of the array before the end of the file, the loop stops and the user is told that only part of the file could be read. Otherwise, the input loop continues until all names in the file have been read.

The flag ArrayFull$ is changed to true only if all elements in the array have been filled and one or more names still remain unread in the file. At the same time, the value of Count must be adjusted (made equal to Capacity) to avoid array overflow during sorting. The subroutine Sort is then called, the array is sorted, and another small loop writes the sorted list on the output file. Only those names that are read into the array are sorted.

Note that it would have been possible to erase the input file after the names were read and then write the sorted list back on the same file. There is always a danger in this procedure, however, of having the computer stop unexpectedly after the original file has been erased and before the sorted file has been completely written. It is better programming practice to read the data from one file and write it on another file.

To test the sorting program, you need a short text file containing several names. The following program creates such a file, named TEST.DAT:

```
! Example Program 11-3
! Create a test file.

OPEN #1: name "TEST.DAT", create newold
ERASE #1  ! if the file already exists
DO while More data
   READ Name$
   PRINT #1: Name$
LOOP
CLOSE #1
PRINT "File TEST.DAT now contains ten names."

DATA John, Mary, Elizabeth, William, Spencer
DATA Jules, Johnson, Bruce, Aaron, Ruth
END
```

This program displays the output statement

```
File TEST.DAT contains ten names.
```

If you examine file TEST.DAT with the True BASIC editor, you should see the following list of names:

> John
> Mary
> Elizabeth
> William
> Spencer
> Jules
> Johnson
> Bruce
> Aaron
> Ruth

You can now use this file of names as an input file for Example Program 11-2 and write the sorted list on a file named TEST.SRT. Here are the results:

```
Maximum number of names that you plan to sort? 100
Name of input file? TEST.DAT
Name of output file? TEST.SRT
A list of 10 names has been sorted.
```

The file TEST.SRT should contain the following list of names:

> Aaron
>
> Bruce
>
> Elizabeth
>
> John
>
> Johnson
>
> Jules
>
> Mary
>
> Ruth
>
> Spencer
>
> William

Here are the results of another program run where the maximum number of names specified is less that the number of names in the file.

```
Maximum number of names that you plan to sort? 5
Name of input file? TEST.DAT
Name of output file? TEST.SRT
Only part of the file could be read because the
maximum number of names specified was too small.
A list of 5 names has been sorted.
```

Note that only the first five names are read from the file and then sorted. The file TEST.SRT should contain the following list of names:

> Elizabeth
>
> John
>
> Mary
>
> Spencer
>
> William

As the size of the array is made larger, you soon reach a practical limit because small computers cannot hold very large arrays in memory. More sophisticated sorting algorithms have been developed that allow large disk files to be sorted on disk, quickly and efficiently.

11.4 SEARCHING TECHNIQUES

When you developed the database program in Chapter 9, you included a command to search the file for a specified string. I now discuss searching techniques in more detail, introducing another method for searching a file or list.

Searching an Unsorted List

If a list or file has been created by adding items to it from time to time, it is usually not in sorted order. The searching method used in Chapter 9 to search an unsorted text file is called a *sequential search*. As you remember, it asked the user to specify a target name. Starting at the beginning of the file, each name from the file is read, in sequence, and compared to the target name. If the two names are equal, the program reports success. If the target name is not equal to any name in the file, the program reports failure.

A sequential search can take a long time with a large list or file. However, **if the names in a list are not sorted but arranged in random order, a sequential search is the simplest method to use**, and probably is preferable to more sophisticated methods for short to medium-length lists.

What do I mean by a "short to medium-length list?" If you have a reasonably fast computer, you should not hesitate to use the sequential search method on a file of 100 or so names. Maybe as large as 500 names. For any list longer than that, I recommend that you first sort the file and then search it.

Searching a Sorted List

When the items in a list or file are in sorted order, you can use another, faster searching method called a *binary search*. This method works by repeatedly dividing or halving the list, resulting in successively shorter lists to search.

Assume that a list is sorted in ascending order with the highest-valued item on the right, and a target name has been specified. Compare the target name with the name at the middle of the list. If the target name is greater than the middle name, you can confine further searching to the right half of the list. If the target name is less than the middle name, you search only the left half of the list. One comparison has effectively cut the length of the list in half, and the process is repeated until the desired name is found or the search fails.

Consider using the binary search method to search a sorted file of names. This method requires that you be able to access any name in the file. You cannot use a text file because that file structure will not allow you to read directly an individual name in the middle of the file. You can only start reading at the beginning and read through to the end of the file. Thus a discussion of searching is interrupted in order to introduce a new kind of file structure, the *record file*.

11.5   USING RECORD FILES

A *record* in a record file is definded as a fixed amount of space on the disk containing a single data item. The data item may be a numeric expression or a string expression. The contents of a record are stored in an internal format, not in the ASCII character format used in text files. This means that the stored information cannot be viewed directly on the screen, but can be read only through a True BASIC program. Reading and writing information on record files is faster than on text files.

The fixed size of each record allows the computer to know exactly where each record begins and ends. This knowledge is not available for a sequential text file where each line may be of a different length. **Thus any record in a record file can be accessed directly for either reading or writing.** True BASIC allows you to write new information on an existing record without fear of overflowing that record and causing damage to an adjoining record. If the information item that you are writing is larger than the record size, a run-time error message is displayed and the program stops.

Opening a Record File

The phrase ORG RECORD should be added to the OPEN statement, specifying that the file will be created as a record file. The record size must be specified before a record file can be used. You can do this in the OPEN statement by including the RECSIZE phrase, as shown in the following statement:

```
OPEN #1: name Fname$, create new, org record, recsize 64
```

A new record file is opened in channel #1 with its record size set to 64 bytes.

A program written in a version of True BASIC prior to version 3 knows that it is reading from a record file because (1) the OPEN statement contains an ORG RECORD phrase, or (2) the OPEN statement contains a RECSIZE phrase, or (3) the first item read is in record file format, not text file format.

Version 3 introduces random files that are similar to record files. They contain a RECSIZE phrase and the first item read is not in text file format. If you are using version 3, include an ORG RECORD phrase in the OPEN statement to identify a record file; an ORG RANDOM phrase to identify a random file.

You need a record size of eight bytes for a record that contains a numeric value. A record that contains a string value must have a size equal to or greater than the number of characters in the string. If a file is opened without the RECSIZE phrase, you can specify the record size with a separate SET statement, as shown in the following statement:

```
SET #1: RECSIZE 128
```

You should use one of these two methods to specify the record size before writing information on a record file. If you are reading an existing record file, you can determine the record size with the statement

```
ASK #2: RECSIZE Length
```

where Length contains the length of the record in bytes.

The only way to change the record size of an existing record file is to erase the file, using the ERASE #N statement, and then set a new record size.

Setting the File Pointer

There are several SET statements for moving the file pointer in a record file. One of the most useful is the statement

```
SET #N: RECORD R
```

which sets the file pointer to the beginning of record R. For example, the statement

```
SET #1: RECORD 5
```

moves the file pointer to the start of record 5 in file #1.

You can also use the statement

```
ASK #N: RECORD RecNum
```

to find out the present location of the file pointer, where the variable RecNum returns a record number — the pointer points at the beginning of that record.

The following SET statements are also available:

```
SET #N: POINTER begin  ! set pointer to start of file
SET #N: POINTER end    ! set pointer to end of file
SET #N: POINTER next   ! set pointer to the next record
SET #N: POINTER same   ! set pointer to previous record
```

The last statement may be a bit ambiguous. As you will see later, reading a file record advances the file pointer automatically to the beginning of the next record. Thus the "POINTER same" phrase backs the pointer up one record and allows the same record to be read again.

I usually use the following abbreviated forms of these statements that are available in True BASIC:

```
RESET #N: begin
RESET #N: end
RESET #N: next
RESET #N: same
```

Record numbering starts with record 1. You cannot use these statements to move the pointer before the beginning of the file or beyond the end of the file.

Writing on a Record File

Writing on a record file is done with the WRITE statement. The format is as follows:

```
WRITE #N: Item1, Item2,...
```

The items can be constants, expressions, or variables, either string or numeric. Each item is written on a separate record. The first item is written on the record at the current pointer position, and the pointer then advances to the next record. If you try to write past the end of the file, the file is extended by creating a new record.

The fixed-length item written on a record is often a string variable, possibly containing several pieces of information in substrings. Each substring is called a *field* and a record may contain one or more fields. If you try to write an item (usually a string) that is longer than the record length, you receive a run-time error.

Each piece of information can be written to a different file record rather than being placed in a substring, and these several file records then constitute a *logical record*. I find this method of file organization cumbersome and usually prefer the first method, using a substring for each field. As discussed in the next section (Section 11.6), the random file organization of version 3 now provides a more direct method for handling multiple-field records.

Reading from a Record File

Reading from a record file is done with the READ statement. The format is as follows:

```
READ #N: Item1, Item2,...
```

The items can be either numeric or string variables. An item written on the file as a string value must be read as a string value and assigned to a string variable. An item written as a numeric value must be assigned to a numeric variable. **Unlike text files, you cannot read a string of numeric characters and assign them to a numeric variable.**

The first item is read from the record at the current pointer position, and the pointer then advances to the next record. If you try to read past the end of the file, you receive an error message. Each item is read from a different record.

Here is a simple demonstration program using a record file for both reading and writing. The file is opened with a record size of 30 bytes or characters. Five expense ledger titles are read from a DATA statement and written on the file, one title in each record. Then the user is asked to specify a record number and the title in that record is displayed. If the number specified is greater than 5, an error message is displayed.

```
! Example Program 11-4
    ! Demonstration of using a record file.
```

```
OPEN #1: name "NAME.REC", create newold, org record
ERASE #1  ! if the file already exists
SET #1: RECSIZE 30  ! record size in bytes

! Add information to the file.
RESET #1: begin  ! just a precaution
FOR I = 1 to 5
    READ Title$
    WRITE #1: Title$
NEXT I
PRINT "A record file of ledger titles has been created."
PRINT

! Specify a record number.
PRINT "Enter zero to stop."
INPUT prompt "Display which record? ": RecNum
DO until RecNum = 0
   IF RecNum > 0 AND RecNum <= 5 then
      SET #1: RECORD RecNum
      READ #1: Title$
      PRINT "Title: "; Title$
   ELSE
      PRINT "There are only 5 records."
   END IF
   PRINT
   INPUT prompt "Display which record? ": RecNum
LOOP

DATA Labor, Equipment, Supplies, Travel, Utilities
END
```

Interaction with the program might produce the following results:

```
A record file of ledger titles has been created.

Enter zero to stop.
Display which record? 4
Title: Travel

Display which record? 1
Title: Labor

Display which record? 0
```

There are times when you would like to know how many records are being used in a record file. This information is available from the ASK FILESIZE statement whose syntax is as follows:

```
ASK #N: FILESIZE Size
```

After this statement is executed, the variable Size contains a value representing the number of records in file #N.

Dividing a Record into Fields

If a record file is used to store general information, each record usually consists of a single string. Remember that a string can be over 65,000 characters long. The record is often subdivided into several fields, each field containing a different piece of information.

One way to create fields is to divide the record string into fixed-length substrings. Each substring field must be long enough to hold the longest piece that will be stored in that field. If the piece is shorter than this maximum length, it must be padded with blanks to increase its length to the fixed value.

Fixed-length fields are introduced in Chapter 14. This method requires some effort to add and remove the padding blanks, and the space they occupy on the disk does not hold useful information. Fixed-length fields work best when most items to be stored in a field are about the same length.

Another and simpler way to create fields is to use variable-length substrings for each field. It is then necessary to place a special character as a separator between adjacent fields. The separator character must be one that is never used in a field value.

The following record string consists of the concatenation of variable-length field strings and separators. It is also of variable length, but must be no longer than the fixed length of the record. For example, a typical name-and-address record, using a vertical bar (|) character as the separator, might look as follows:

John Butler | 13 South St. | Worcester | MA | 03120

Here is another example program with two fields of information placed in each record. The variable Entry$ contains both a name field and a telephone number field, separated by a vertical bar (|), and is written on the file record.

The file is subsequently sorted and a value is read from a record and assigned to a string variable. Then the value assigned to the variable is separated into the two field values, name and telephone number, using substrings. A new statement

```
ASK #1: FILESIZE Size
```

assigns a value to the variable Size equal to the number of records in file #1. Here is the program:

```
! Example Program 11-5
! Another demonstration of a record file
! with two items of information in each record.

OPEN #1: name "PHONES.REC", create newold, org record
ERASE #1              ! if the file already exists
SET #1: RECSIZE 60
CALL Add (#1)         ! add information to the file
CALL SortFile (#1)    ! sort the file by name
ASK #1: FILESIZE Size
PRINT "A telephone directory file";
PRINT " was created and sorted."
PRINT

! Specify a record number.
PRINT "Enter zero to stop."
INPUT prompt "What record? ": RecNum
DO until RecNum = 0
   IF RecNum > 0 AND RecNum <= Size then
      SET #1: RECORD RecNum
      READ #1: Item$
      LET X = Pos (Item$, "|")
      LET Name$ = Item$[1:X-1]
      LET Phone$ = Item$[X+1:Len(Item$)]
      PRINT "Name: "; Name$; Tab(40); "Phone: "; Phone$
   ELSE
      PRINT "There are only"; Size; "records."
   END IF
   PRINT
   INPUT prompt "What record? ": RecNum
LOOP
END  ! of main program

SUB Add (#9)
   ! Add information to the file.
   RESET #1: begin
   DO while more data
      READ Name$, Phone$
      LET Entry$ = Name$ & "|" & Phone$
      WRITE #9: Entry$
   LOOP
```

```
        DATA Jane Ulan, 9788, Bill Miller, 3103
        DATA Susan Moody, 1882, Joe Stove, 1586
        DATA Robert Heilman, 9017
    END SUB  ! Add


    SUB SortFile (#9)
        ! Sort a record file.
        ASK #9: FILESIZE N
        DO
           LET Sorted$ = "true"
           FOR I = 1 to (N - 1)
               SET #9: RECORD I
               READ #9: First$, Second$
               LET F = Posr(First$, " ")
               LET S = Posr(Second$, " ")
               IF First$[F+1:60] > Second$[S+1:60] then
                   SET #9: RECORD I
                   WRITE #9: Second$, First$
                   LET Sorted$ = "false"
               END IF
           NEXT I
        LOOP until Sorted$ = "true"
    END SUB  ! Sort
```

Here is an example of program interaction with the user:

```
A telephone directory file was created and sorted.

Enter zero to stop.
What record? 6
There are only 5 records.

What record? 1
Name: Robert Heilman              Phone: 9017

What record? 0
```

The subroutine Add is called first to add names and telephone numbers to the file. These items are read from DATA statements in the subroutine but could just as well be entered from the keyboard. The subroutine Sort is called next to sort the file in ascending order. The bubble sort algorithm is still used but sorts the file directly rather than copying the file to an array and sorting the array. Note particularly how two record values are interchanged; they are read from the file in one order (First\$, then Second\$) and written back to the file in reverse order (Second\$, then First\$).

The file is sorted in ascending alphabetic order by last name. The beginning of each last name is found by looking for the space before the last name —assuming that there is no space in the telephone number field. You may also assume that there is no suffix (such as Jr. or III) following the last name and separated from it by a space. When comparing records in the sorting routine, substrings that begin with the last name are compared, resulting in a list alphabetized by last name.

Do you understand my comment about "no space in the telephone number field?" What happens if there is a space? How could you change the program to extract last names if the telephone number field contained one or more spaces? Hint: How about searching for the vertical bar?

After the file is written and sorted, the user is asked to specify a record number. The string value in this record is assigned to the variable Item$. The Pos function is used to find the location of the vertical bar and string Item$ is then separated into two substrings, one consisting of the characters before the vertical bar and the other consisting of the characters after the bar. These substrings are assigned to the variables Name$ and Phone$ which are then displayed. Note that an error message is returned if the specified record number is greater than the number of records in the file.

11.6   USING RANDOM FILES (PC Version 3)

A new type of file organization is introduced in version 3 of True BASIC. It is called *random organization* and is similar to the record organization you have just learned. A random file allows multiple string and numeric fields to be written in a single record, something you can't do with a record file. That capability eliminates the need to place separators between the fields of a record, as was done in the preceding examples. It also allows numbers to be stored as numeric values, not as strings of digits.

In a random file, each record is written by a single WRITE statement. The WRITE statement may contain several items (variables, constants, or expressions) and each item is considered a separate field of the record. For example, the statement

```
WRITE #1: Name$, Salary, Occupation$
```

writes a record that contains three fields on file #1. Two fields, Name$ and Occupation$, have string values. Note that Salary is written as a numeric value and thus no precision is lost in converting between an internal numeric representation and an ASCII representation.

This record can be read by a single READ statement that also has three field variables, as shown:

```
READ #1: Name$, Salary, Occupation$
```

As you know, the variable names in the READ statement can be different from the names in the WRITE statement — they just happen to be the same in this case. Remember that a separate read or write statement is needed to access each record. Furthermore, each field item in the record must be specified in the read and write statements.

About the only disadvantage I can see in random files is that a user reading a file must know the record structure — that is, the order and type of fields in a record. If you are given a file with no description of record structure, I don't know any way to determine it.

As with record files, the pointer can be set to point at any record or at the end of the file. To estimate the record size of a random file, add four bytes to the length of each string field, allow nine bytes for each numeric field, and then add six bytes for the record header and ending. You might want to add a few more bytes just to be safe.

Here is the preceding example program rewritten using a random file. Remember that this program will not run on any version of True BASIC prior to version 3.

```
! Example Program 11-6
! Create and access a file with random organization
! containing two fields of information in each record.

OPEN #1: name "PHONES.RND", create newold, org random
ERASE #1              ! if the file already exists
SET #1: RECSIZE 60
CALL Add (#1)         ! add information to the file
CALL SortFile (#1)    ! sort the file by name
ASK #1: FILESIZE Size
PRINT "A telephone directory file";
PRINT " was created and sorted."
PRINT


! Specify a record number.
PRINT "Enter zero to stop."
INPUT prompt "What record? ": RecNum
DO until RecNum = 0
   IF RecNum > 0 AND RecNum <= Size then
      SET #1: RECORD RecNum
      READ #1: Name$, Phone
      PRINT "Name: "; Name$; Tab(40); "Phone:"; Phone
   ELSE
      PRINT "There are only"; Size; "records."
   END IF
   PRINT
   INPUT prompt "What record? ": RecNum
```

```
LOOP
END   ! of main program

SUB Add (#9)
    ! Add information to the file.
    RESET #9: begin
    DO while More data
       READ Name$, Phone
       WRITE #9: Name$, Phone
    LOOP

    DATA Jane Ulan, 9788, Bill Miller, 3103
    DATA Susan Moody, 1882, Joe Stove, 1586
    DATA Robert Heilman, 9017
END SUB

SUB SortFile (#9)
    ! Sort a random file.
    ASK #9: FILESIZE N
    DO
       LET Sorted$ = "true"
       FOR I = 1 to (N - 1)
           SET #9: RECORD I
           READ #9: Name1$, Phone1
           READ #9: Name2$, Phone2
           LET F = Posr(Name1$, " ")
           LET S = Posr(Name2$, " ")
           IF Name1$[F+1:60] > Name2$[S+1:60] then
               SET #9: RECORD I
               WRITE #9: Name2$, Phone2
               WRITE #9: Name1$, Phone1
               LET Sorted$ = "false"
           END IF
       NEXT I
    LOOP until Sorted$ = "true"
END SUB
```

This program produces the same output as Example Program 11-5. Note that only name fields are used in sorting the file. The beginning of each last name is detected by looking for the space before the last name in the Name$ field, using the Posr function. As before, you may assume that there is no suffix (such as Jr. or III) following the last name and separated from it by a space. When comparing names in the sorting routine, you compare substrings that contain the last name, resulting in a list alphabetized by last name.

After the file is written and sorted, the user is asked to specify a record number. The variables Name$ and Phone are read from the record and displayed. Again, an error message is displayed if the specified record number is too large.

11.7   THE BINARY SEARCH METHOD

Returning to the problem of searching a sorted list, you can now develop a program that uses the binary search method.

Searching an Array

The program asks a user to enter a name to be found, called the target name. Assume the list of names is an indexed list (an array) and is sorted in ascending order from top to bottom.

A *top point*, a *bottom point*, and a *midpoint* must be defined. At the start, the top point is the index of the first name in the list. This index is usually one. The bottom point is the index of the last name in the list. The midpoint is approximately halfway between the top and bottom points.

Use the midpoint (rounded to an integer value) as an index and designate the name with that index the *midpoint name*. Then compare the target name to the midpoint name. If the target name equals the midpoint name, you have completed your search. If the target name is less than the midpoint name, you know that further searching can be confined to the top half of the list. Leave the top point unchanged but designate a new bottom point equal to the midpoint minus one. In effect, the length of list to be searched has been cut in half, as shown in Fig. 11.1.

Figure 11.1 Target name is in top half of list.

Conversely, if the target name is greater than the midpoint name, you know that your search can be confined to the bottom half of the list. Leave the bottom point unchanged and designate a new top point equal to the midpoint plus one. Figure 11.2 shows this result.

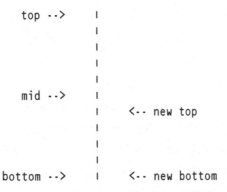

Figure 11.2 Target name is in bottom half of list.

Here is the list of names that was used in the last section, sorted in ascending alphabetic order from top to bottom, and a list of indices:

1 Aaron
2 Bruce
3 Elizabeth
4 John
5 Johnson
6 Jules
7 Mary
8 Ruth
9 Spencer
10 William

An outline of the search process reads as follows:

target name is Ruth
top point is 1
bottom point is 10
calculate midpoint, its rounded value is 6
midpoint name for index of 6 is Jules
note that Ruth is greater than Jules
set new top point at 7
bottom point remains at 10

After the first search, you have created have a list of reduced length:

7	Mary	top point
8	Ruth	
9	Spencer	
10	Williams	bottom point

The search process continues, as described in the following outline:

> calculate new midpoint of 9
>
> midpoint name for index of 9 is Spencer
>
> note that Ruth is less than Spencer
>
> top point remains at 7
>
> set new bottom point at 8
>
> calculate new midpoint of 8

You observe that the midpoint name for an index of 8 is your target name, Ruth, and the search has ended with success.

Searching a Record File

As an example of a searching program, let's look for a specified name in a sorted record file. This file contains the same list of names used in the preceding paragraphs and contained in the sorted text file produced by Example Program 11-2. You remember that this program produced a sequential text file, a type of file structure that cannot be searched with the binary search algorithm. We must first convert the text file to a record file and then search the latter file.

The first example program converts the sorted text file named TEST.SRT to a sorted record file named TEST.REC. A record length of ten bytes or characters is used.

```
! Example Program 11-7
! Convert a sequential text file TEST.SRT
! to a record file TEST.REC

OPEN #1: name "TEST.SRT", org text
OPEN #2: name "TEST.REC", create newold, org record
ERASE #2  ! if the file already exists
SET #2: RECSIZE 10
DO while More #1
   LINE INPUT #1: Item$
   WRITE #2: Item$
LOOP
```

```
CLOSE #1
CLOSE #2
PRINT "Record file TEST.REC has been created."
END
```

This program produces the output line

```
Record file TEST.REC has been created.
```

which informs the user that the program has completed its task.

It is often convenient to be able to inspect the contents of a record file. Remember that this type of file cannot be displayed with a text editor. Here is an example program that lists the contents of a record file containing string values. It will not work with a record file containing numeric values.

```
! Example Program 11-8
! Display a record file of strings.

INPUT prompt "Name of file? ": FileName$
OPEN #1: name FileName$
LET Count = 0
DO until End #1
   LET Count = Count + 1
   READ #1: Item$
   PRINT Count; ": "; Item$
LOOP
CLOSE #1
END
```

Here are the results when the file TEST.REC is displayed:

```
Name of file? TEST.REC
 1 : Aaron
 2 : Bruce
 3 : Elizabeth
 4 : John
 5 : Johnson
 6 : Jules
 7 : Mary
 8 : Ruth
 9 : Spencer
10 : William
```

The next example program searches a sorted record file for a given name. If the name is found, its record number is displayed. The user is told if the name cannot be found. This version of the program allows the user to enter several names, one at a time. Entering the letter "Q" tells the program to stop.

The main program is straightforward, asking for the file name and the target name.

The results of the search are displayed. Two parameters, the file name and the target name, are passed to the function named Search. Note that the file must be opened in the function because channel numbers cannot be passed to functions.

In the function Search, the local variable Top is the index number of the record at the top of the search range, initially record 1. The number of records in the file is determined by the ASK FILESIZE statement and is assigned to variable N. Local variable Bottom is the index number of the record at the bottom of the search range, initially record N.

Variable Mid is the index number of the record in the middle of the search range. This record is read and its value compared to the target string value. If they are equal, function Search is assigned the value of Mid (the number of the desired record), and control returns to the main program. If they are not equal, either the top or bottom of the search range is changed, a new value of Mid is calculated, and the comparison process repeated.

A search is considered unsuccessful when the top and bottom points cross, and this result is denoted by assigning a value of zero to the function Search. Remember that the technique of binary searching depends on having a file in sorted order. If the file is not in sorted order, the program will usually fail to find the requested record.

```
! Example Program 11-9
! Search a record file for a given name.

DECLARE FUNCTION Search
LINE INPUT prompt "File name? ": File$
PRINT "Enter the letter Q to stop the program."
PRINT
LINE INPUT prompt "Name to find? ": Name$
DO until Ucase$(Name$) = "Q"
   LET Result = Search(File$, Name$)
   IF Result = 0 then
      PRINT Name$; " cannot be found."
   ELSE
      PRINT Name$; " is in record"; Result
   END IF
   PRINT
   LINE INPUT prompt "Name to find? ": Name$
LOOP
END  ! of main program

FUNCTION Search (FileName$, Look$)
    ! Search a record file using
    ! the binary search algorithm.
    ! Look$ contains the target name.
```

```
     OPEN #9: name FileName$, org record
     ASK #9: FILESIZE N
     LET Top = 1
     LET Bottom = N
     LET Found$ = "false"
     LET Look$ = Ucase$(Look$)
     DO
        LET Mid = Round((Top + Bottom)/2)
        SET #9: RECORD Mid
        READ #9: Rec$
        IF Look$ = Ucase$(Rec$) then
           LET Found$ = "true"
        ELSEIF Look$ > Ucase$(Rec$) then
           LET Top = Mid + 1
        ELSE
           LET Bottom = Mid - 1
        END IF
     LOOP until Bottom < Top or Found$ = "true"
     IF Found$ = "true" then
        LET Search = Mid
     ELSE
        LET Search = 0
     END IF
     CLOSE #9
  END FUNCTION  ! Search
```

Here is an example of program output:

```
File name? TEST.REC
Enter the letter Q to stop the program.

Name to find? William
William is in record 10

Name to find? Tony
Tony cannot be found.

Name to find? q
```

Note that all strings are converted to uppercase before comparisons are made. If the function returns a value of zero, a search failure message is displayed. Otherwise, the record number and the value of the desired record are displayed.

11.8   STRING AND FILE CONVERSIONS

A common requirement when writing programs is the ability to convert dates or times from one format to another. True BASIC has two system variables, Date$ and Time$, that contain the current date and time. These values may not be in the desired format and must converted before being displayed.

The system variable Date$ has the current date value stored in YYYYMMDD format. For example, the value might be

19930307

and you would like to change it to the more readable format

March 7, 1993

Table Lookup

In the next example, the idea is introduced of using a table of values from which a certain value can be selected. Let's say that you have the names of the months stored in DATA statements in alphabetic order. You can read the DATA statements and assign each name to an array element. This procedure gives you a table in memory containing the names of all the months. If you want to find the name of the third month, look at the third element in the array and note that it contains the value "March."

The same technique can be used to create a much larger table by reading the array element values from a text file. The only limit on the size of the table is the amount of free memory available to hold the array.

The example program is designed to change the format of the current date, stored in the system variable Date$, into a format with the name of the month spelled out. A subroutine contains the DATA statements holding the month names and assigns these names to an array. A function is used to convert the date to the new format.

```
! Example Program 11-10
! Display the current date in expanded format.
! Table of month names is read from a file.

DECLARE DEF LongDate$
DIM Month$(1 to 12)
CALL MonthTable (Month$)
PRINT "The current date is "; LongDate$(Month$)
END  ! of main program

SUB MonthTable (Month$())
    ! Read DATA statements and
    ! create table of month names.
```

```
        FOR I = 1 to 12
            READ Month$(I)
        NEXT I

        DATA January, February, March, April
        DATA May, June, July, August
        DATA September, October, November, December
    END SUB  ! MonthTable

DEF LongDate$(M$())
    ! Convert current date to an expanded format.
    LET Year$ = Date$[1:4]
    LET Num = Val(Date$[5:6]) ! month number
    LET Day$ = Date$[7:8]
    IF Day$[1:1] = "0" then LET Day$ = Day$[2:2]
    LET LongDate$ = M$(Num) & " " & Day$ & ", " & Year$
END DEF  ! LongDate$
```

The current date in Date$ is broken up into substrings for the year, month, and day. If the day substring has a leading zero, it is stripped off. The month number Num is used as an index for the month name array M$. A new string is created by concatenating the month name, the day and the year, and the result is assigned to the function LongDate$. Here is an example of program output.:

```
The current date is October 10, 1995
```

Conversion of File Formats

Many professionals who know the BASIC language do not write large programs. They use their computers for running application programs such as word processors, electronic spreadsheets, and database managers. They sometimes find that the file produced by one application cannot be read by another application.

One solution to that problem is to write your own True BASIC program to convert the format of a file. If the file is a text file containing only ASCII characters, such a conversion is relatively easy to accomplish.

The next example demonstrates the conversion of a file of information, commonly called a data file. This file consists of names (data items) separated from each other by blank spaces. The names themselves do not contain any spaces. Thus the only role of spaces is to serve as data item delimiters or separators. The data items are contained in text lines that end with the usual carriage return and line feed characters.

This data file will be read by an application program that requires that every data item be enclosed in quotes and that the items be separated from each other by commas. Spaces are not allowed. A pair of characters, carriage return and line feed, is expected at the end of each line.

Here is a line from the original data file:

```
JOHN WILLIAM MARY PETER SUSAN JENNIFER
```

Here is how the line must look if is to be read by the application program:

```
"JOHN","WILLIAM","MARY","PETER","SUSAN","JENNIFER"
```

As you can imagine, it would be a time consuming job to convert this data file by hand. You can write a True BASIC program to make the conversion.

Both an input file and an output file are opened. A line of text is read from the input file, its format is changed, and it is written on the output file. The process continues until the end of the input file is reached.

The conversion is accomplished by scanning a line of text, using the Pos function to find the location of the first space. The characters to the left of the space are enclosed in quotes. Note the odd-looking string """" that represents a quotation mark as a string constant. The characters to the right of the space are the remainder of the old line of text, and this line is analyzed again as the program searches for the next space. A new line of text is gradually constructed and, when finished, is written on the output file. The process continues until the entire input file has been read.

Here is the conversion program:

```
! Example Program 11-11
! Convert the format of a text data file.
! Input file strings are separated by spaces.
! Output strings are in quotes and separated by commas.

LINE INPUT prompt "Input file: ": InName$
OPEN #1: name InName$
LINE INPUT prompt "Output file: ": OutName$
OPEN #2: name OutName$, create newold
ERASE #2                         ! if it already exists

DO while More #1                 ! read a line
   LINE INPUT #1: Old$
   LET New$ = ""
   DO                            ! scan old line
      LET X = Pos(Old$, " ")  ! look for a space
      IF X = 0 then
         LET New$ = New$ & """" & Old$ & """"
      ELSE
         LET Temp$ = Old$[1:X-1]
```

```
            LET Old$ = Old$[X+1:Maxnum]
            LET New$ = New$ & """" & Temp$ & ""","
        END IF
    LOOP until X = 0
    PRINT #2: New$                    ! write modified line
  LOOP
  CLOSE #1
  CLOSE #2
  PRINT
  PRINT "The format of "; InName$; " has been converted."
  PRINT "and the data written on file "; OutName$; "."
  END
```

Try running this program using as input the file NAMES.DAT. You should get the following output with file NAMES.CVT containing the lines in the new format:

```
Input file: NAMES.DAT
Output file: NAMES.CVT


The format of NAMES.DAT has been converted
and the data written on file NAMES.CVT.
```

Summary of Important Points

- When strings are compared in logical expressions, they are compared character by character using the ASCII values of the characters.

- A third temporary variable is needed when interchanging the values of two variables.

- A logical flag can be used to indicate whether or not a certain task has been accomplished.

- A sequential search is the simplest technique for searching an unsorted list.

- The binary search technique works only for a list in sorted order.

- A record file contains fixed-length records. A string record can be divided into two or more fields.

- A random file contains fixed-length records with one or more string or numeric fields.

- Any record in a record or random file can be accessed directly and information can be either read from or written on the record.

- Unlike text files, you cannot read a string of numeric characters from a record file and assign them to a numeric variable.

- A True BASIC program can often be written to convert one text file format to another format.

Common Errors

- Modifying the wrong statement when changing the bubble sort algorithm from an ascending sort to a descending sort.

- Attempting to sort a text file directly on the disk.

- Writing a long text file to an array for sorting when there is insufficient memory for the array. One solution is to convert the text file to a record file and then sort the file directly on disk.

- Comparing two strings representing numeric values rather than comparing the numeric values themselves. Note that "+12.7" is less then "12.3" — because "+" is less than "1" — but the number +12.7 is greater than 12.3.

- Searching an unsorted list with the binary search algorithm.

- Trying to display a record file with a text editor.

- Failing to consider the differences between lowercase and uppercase characters during a search.

- Opening a file with random organization in a program designed to run on any versions of True BASIC. This type of file organization is supported only in version 3.

Self-Test Questions

1. What is the name of the sorting algorithm used in the example programs in this chapter?

2. Which string in each of the following pairs of strings is larger?
    - (a) ZY or XY
    - (b) JOHN or John
    - (c) qe35 or QE37
    - (d) ABC or CBA
    - (e) simplification or simplifications

3. Write a three-statement program fragment that will swap the values of variables Num1 and Num2.

4. Does a list need to be in sorted order for a
    - (a) sequential search?
    - (b) binary search?

5. When making a binary search of a list sorted in ascending order, if the target name is greater than the midpoint name, what is the new index value of the
    - (a) top point?
    - (b) bottom point?

6. Will your answers in the previous question be different if the list is sorted in descending order? If yes, what are the index values (in symbols, like top, bottom, mid) of the new points?

7. What statement moves the file pointer to record 7 of a record file denoted as file #2?

8. If record 10 of a record file contains information, can you overwrite the old information with new information?

9. What happens if you write a string containing 45 characters on a record file whose record size is 44 bytes?

10. What statement establishes the record length of a record file?

11. What statement moves the file pointer to the
    - (a) beginning of the next record?
    - (b) beginning of the same record?

12. Given the statement

    ```
    READ #1: Name1$, Name2$
    ```

    for a record file, the value of what record is assigned to Name1$ if Name2$ is assigned the value of record 5?

13. What statement tells you the number of records in a record file?

14. What appears on the screen if you use the TYPE command of DOS to display the contents of a record file?

15. What format is used to display the current date stored in the system variable Date$?

16. If you are copying all the information from record file #1 to record file #2, what test can you use to stop the program when everything has been copied?

Practice Programs

1. The bubble sort algorithm in Example Program 11-2 scans through the entire list, each time comparing every contiguous pair of elements in the list. Note that the first scan positions the largest element at the right end of the list. This means that the second scan needs to cover only the first N - 2 pairs of elements, not N - 1 pairs.

    Rewrite Example Program 11-2 to take advantage of this fact. Your FOR statement might be

    ```
    FOR I = 1 TO ScanLimit
    ```

    where ScanLimit starts at N - 1 and is decreased by one after each scan.

    Test your program by reading the file of names, TEST.DAT, created in Example Program 11-3, and writing the sorted list of names to a new file named TEST1.DAT.

2. Rewrite the sorting algorithm of Example Program 11-2 so that it will sort an array in either ascending or descending order. You need to pass a third parameter to the sub-routine, a string variable containing the letter "A" for ascending sort or the letter "D" for descending sort.

    Test your program by reading the file of names, TEST.DAT, created in Example Program 11-3, and writing the sorted list of names to a new file named TEST2.DAT.

3. True BASIC has two system time variables. The string variable Time$ contains the current 24-hour clock time in HH:MM:SS format. The numeric variable Time contains a value representing the current time expressed in seconds since midnight.

    Assuming that your system has a built-in clock, modify Example Program 11-2 to measure the elapsed time taken by the sorting algorithm in that program. Be sure to include only the time used for sorting, not the time taken to read the file.

    Test your program using the file RANDOM.DAT, which contains 80 ten-character strings of random characters.

4. It is difficult to compare different sorting methods when using short lists because the time differences may be very small. It is also difficult to think of a large number of different names, say, 100 names, to create a longer test list.

    Write a program to create a text file with the number of lines specified by the user. Each line is a 10-character string, consisting of a random group of letters selected using the RND function discussed in Chapter 5. Create a test file named LONG.DAT containing 200 strings.

Use this file to measure the performance of the sorting routine in Example Program 11-2 (with timing statements added) and one other sorting routine (we recommend the routine in Practice Problem 1). Measure sorting times only and do not write output files. If the sorting times are equal, create and use a longer test file.

5. Assume that you want to sort a file containing two or more items per logical record, such as the database file used in Chapter 9. There are at least two ways to store this information in an array.

    One method, as illustrated in Example Program 11-5, is to combine the two items, name and telephone number, in a single string with a special character separator. The strings are then stored in a one-dimensional array and sorted using the subroutine already developed. Sorting order is usually determined by the first few characters of the string.

    Another method is to store the information in a two-dimensional array, with names stored in column 1 and telephone numbers stored in column 2. An example of this structure follows:

John H. Smith	217-202-3132
Mary White	617-627-0030
Clarence Goode	804-213-3137

    Develop a sorting subroutine to sort a two-dimensional string array with two columns, where sorting orders the elements in the first column in ascending order. Pass as parameters the array and the number of rows.

    Write a test program to show how your subroutine works, using the file PHONES.DAT in the directory or folder named CH11 on the example program disk. This file contains the same information as the file with the same name in directory or folder CH09, but has the first and last names in reverse order.

6. Extend the concepts of Practice Program 5 to write a more general sorting subroutine. This subroutine sorts an array containing a variable number of columns, where sorting orders the elements in a specified column. Pass as parameters the array, the number of rows, the number of columns, the column number designated for sorting, and the letter "A" or "D" for an ascending or descending sort.

    Demonstrate how your subroutine works by sorting a price list array with four columns containing part number, item name, quantity, and unit price. Sort the price list in ascending order by unit price (column 4). Remember that all values in the array are string values, so you will have to be careful when comparing prices. Use the file PARTS.DAT in directory or folder CH11.

7. Using the file PHONES.REC in directory or folder CH11, write a program that allows a user to specify the desired telephone number. The file is now sorted by name and you must sort it again by telephone number. A binary file search is used to find the number and the corresponding user name is then displayed. You might find it helpful to review Example Program 11-7.

   Test your program with the numbers 9788, 3103, and 1885.

8. If several string items are to be concatenated together and written on a file as a single string, you must use some method that allows you to separate the individual items when the file is read. One method is to use a special character as a separator, a character that will not be used within any of the items. Another method is to convert variable-length strings to fixed-length strings before concatenation.

   Write a subroutine that converts a variable-length string to a fixed-length string by adding blanks to the end of the string. Pass the string variable name and the new fixed length as parameters. Be sure to check that the current string length is not longer than the new fixed length.

   Test your subroutine in a program, using a string value of "Oars" and a length of 20, also a string value of "Inflatable row boats" and the same length.

9. A record file has records with fixed-length strings, each string containing three items of information. The fixed-length string is 30 characters long and is divided as follows:

item description	20 characters
reorder point	4 characters
reorder quantity	6 characters

   The first item is padded with trailing blanks. The other two items are padded with leading zeroes. The file is ordered in ascending order, sorted alphabetically by item description.

   Write a program containing a binary search subprogram (function or subroutine) to search for a specified record by item description. Ignore uppercase and lowercase differences when searching. Display the record items with appropriate labels after stripping off trailing blanks and leading zeroes.

   Test your program using the record file REORDER.REC and the item names "Oars", "Paddle", and "Turnbuckle".

10. A text file contains information stored as one string per line. A logical record consists of six lines containing the following information:

    last name

    first name

    department

    current salary

    date when last hired

    date of last pay increase

    Create a new text file with a different format. Each line of the new file will contain the six strings of a logical record, each string enclosed in quotation marks and separated from one another by commas.

    Test your program using the input file PAYROLL.DAT and the output file NEWPAY.DAT.

11. This program is designed for PCs although a similar problem could be developed for Macs. An XyWrite word processor is used to write an article containing True BASIC programs. It is easy to isolate a program listing from the surrounding text and write it on a separate file, but the program source code still contains special formatting characters that keep it from executing.

    Ask the user to specify the name of an input file containing True BASIC program statements, and the name of an output file. Read and examine each line of the input file. Delete any block of characters that starts with the double left angle bracket (ASCII value 174) and ends with the double right angle bracket (ASCII value 175). The characters within these double angle brackets are formatting instructions to the word processor. Write the corrected line to the output file.

    Test your program using the input file XYWRITE.TXT and an output file named ASCII.TXT.

CHAPTER 12

Computer Graphics

12.1 INTRODUCTION

True BASIC provides extensive capabilities for creating graphic images on the display screen. In this chapter, you learn about the graphics mode and how window coordinates can be established. You can then examine the graphics primitives; statements for drawing points, lines, areas, and text.

Advanced graphics statements allow you to draw simple figures such as rectangles and circles, to save and retrieve graphics figures, and to change their color or intensity. The external picture unit provides a graphics procedure capability similar to the external subroutine. Graphics figures can be transformed using either user-designed or built-in transformation routines.

A final section shows how to use the graphics capabilities of True BASIC in two application programs. One example program draws the front elevation of a simple house. The other program demonstrates how interactive graphics can be used to draw diagrams on the screen.

12.2 SETTING THE GRAPHICS ENVIRONMENT

The monitor screen on PCs is normally used to display characters, most often in a format of 24 or 25 lines containing up to 80 characters per line. Each character on the screen is composed of a number of illuminated dots or *pixels*. A set of alphanumeric and special characters is stored in memory and when text mode is in use, only these characters are available to create displays on the screen.

This same screen can also be used in graphics mode to display other images by selecting and illuminating patterns of pixels. Maximum flexibility can be achieved when each pixel is controlled by one or more bits of computer memory. This type of display is called *bit-mapped computer graphics* and is the standard display mode for both lines of text and graphics figures on Macs.

All the standard IBM PC color display units support graphics. The VGA black-and-white display unit also supports graphics. Almost all modern PCs (including both desk top and lap top models) support graphics on their standard display units, either in color or gray-scale or black-and-white.

Computer graphics is a complicated subject, dependent on both the type of computer and the specific display unit being used. This discussion of computer graphics in True BASIC will not be comprehensive, but rather will focus on PCs with VGA graphics display units and on Macs with built-in monitors. If you need information on other graphics displays, especially color displays, consult the reference material for your particular computer system.

The statement that establishes the type of graphics or screen mode is

```
SET MODE Type$
```

where Type$ must contain one of the predefined values listed in the *True BASIC Reference Manual* for the computer in use. The corresponding statement

```
ASK MODE Value$
```

returns a string value denoting the current screen mode.

Text Mode on PCs

If you are using a color display unit, the default value of Type$ is usually "80". This mode has the following attributes:

> the screen displays 80 columns and 25 rows of text
> all 256 extended ASCII characters are available
> text characters are "white"
> the background is black
> graphics is not supported
> a blinking text cursor is displayed

This mode is called the *text mode*, displaying the *text screen*. It is the normal mode of operation of a PC running DOS. The default color of text characters is white but another color can be selected with the SET COLOR statement. How to change colors is discussed later in this chapter.

Graphics Mode on PCs

A different mode is used to display graphics on the screen. Many color display units support several graphics modes. The amount of video memory available is often a limiting factor. For a given type of display and amount of memory, a low-resolution mode — meaning that the illuminated pixels are larger and thus fewer in number — permits a wide range of colors to be displayed. A high-resolution mode creates smaller pixels and shows greater detail but restricts the display to a more limited selection of colors.

The statement

```
SET MODE "GRAPHICS"
```

changes the screen mode so that graphics can be displayed in addition to text. This statement makes an appropriate choice of a specific graphics mode based on the graphics card or graphics hardware that is installed in your computer. Both color, gray-scale, and black-and-white monitors are supported.

The mode chosen by the preceding statement provides a broad range of colors but is not necessarily the mode of highest resolution. You may need to specify a different mode if you want high resolution — consult your *True BASIC Reference Manual* for details. Most modern computers have a VGA card that provides a resolution of at least 640 by 480 pixels without a special mode command.

As mentioned previously, assume for discussion purposes that you have a VGA color monitor. The graphics mode is called "VGA" and has the following attributes:

> the screen displays 307,200 (640 by 480) pixels
> both text and graphics can be displayed
> all 256 extended ASCII characters are available
> the default foreground color is usually white
> the default background color is usually black
> **the blinking text cursor is not displayed**

This mode is called the *graphics mode*, displaying the *graphics screen*. VGA mode is the PC graphics mode used in the example programs.

When the computer executes the mode statement for graphics, the current screen clears and a screen capable of supporting graphics, with no blinking cursor, is displayed. After the program ends, you must press the Return key to return to the text mode and the familiar split screen with command and editing windows.

Windows on PCs

You may wonder why no mention has been made of Windows. The latest version of True BASIC is a DOS program, not a Windows program. It will, however, run under Windows as a DOS program and has many windows-like attributes such as mouse support, a pull-down menu bar, a scroll bar, and so forth. A full Windows version is in the final stages of development, but had not been released when this edition of the book went to press.

Text and Graphics Modes on Macs

There is little need to distinguish between text and graphics on a Mac because the screen display is always capable of displaying graphics. The original Macs with 9-inch built-in monitors have black-and-white screens. The Mac II computers and most of the later Macintosh models, on the other hand, have separate monitors and support color or gray-scale graphics.

If you execute the program fragment

```
ASK MODE Value$
PRINT Value$
END
```

the mode value of "B/W" or "COLOR" is displayed. This mode is comparable to the text mode on PCs, but remember that a Mac can display both text and graphics in this default mode. Mode "B/W" shows black characters and figures on a white background.

The statement

```
SET MODE "GRAPHICS"
```

has a special meaning on a Mac. It switches to a new full-screen output even if you have opened a small output window. Press the mouse button to clear the output window and return to the editing window.

 If you do not want to display your output in a full-screen output window, remove the SET MODE "GRAPHICS" statements from the example programs in this chapter. Then before running programs, pull down the Windows menu and select the Output command. A separate output window opens and you can adjust it to the size you want. You cannot clear this window by pressing the mouse button but you can delete the window by selecting the Close Output command from the Windows menu.

The Graphics Screen

Here is a simple program that demonstrates the graphics screen:

```
! Example Program 12-1
! Accessing the graphics mode.

SET MODE "graphics"
LINE INPUT prompt "Enter a sentence: ": Phrase$
PRINT Phrase$
PRINT "Press the Return key to leave graphics mode."
END
```

It displays the following output:

```
Enter a sentence: This is graphics mode.
This is graphics mode.
Press the Return key to leave graphics mode.
```

Each character in the displayed sentences after the input statement is drawn individually by the program.

Another version of this program uses the ASK MODE statement to determine the screen mode when the program starts, and then returns to that same mode after the graphics screen has been displayed. Two PAUSE statements are used to halt the computer for three seconds so screen displays can be observed.

```
! Example Program 12-2
! Change to the graphics mode and
! then return to the original mode.

ASK MODE Type$
PRINT "Original screen mode is "; Type$
PAUSE 3
SET MODE "GRAPHICS"
PRINT "Screen is now in GRAPHICS mode"
PAUSE 3
SET MODE Type$
PRINT "Press the Return key to exit."
END
```

This program displays a sentence in the command window, pauses for three seconds, and then displays another sentence in the graphics screen. After another three second pause, instructions to "Press the Return key" appear in text mode and full-screen output. You should run the program yourself to observe the difference between TEXT mode (called "80") and GRAPHICS mode.

The program really only makes sense on a PC because there is no difference in the appearance of text and graphics modes on a Mac. You may notice on PCs that text characters on the graphics screen look somewhat different from the corresponding characters on the text screen.

The Graphics Window

Having established the graphics mode, the next step is to create a graphics window on the screen. This window may include the entire screen or only part of the screen (see Chapter 10). Most of the example programs use full-screen windows. To refer to a point in the window, a system of *window coordinates* must be defined.

The SET WINDOW statement is used to create a window coordinate system. Only full-screen windows are created and discussed. The general syntax is as follows:

```
SET WINDOW Xmin, Xmax, Ymin, Ymax
```

The vertical or Y coordinate is used to locate the vertical position of a point between the bottom and top of the window. A minimum value of Y (Ymin) is assigned to the bottom of the window and a maximum value of Y (Ymax) to the top. The vertical position of any point in the window can then be described by specifying a Y value between Ymin and Ymax.

In the same manner, a horizontal or X coordinate can be defined by assigning values for Xmin and Xmax. The position of any point can now be specified by giving its X and Y coordinate values, usually in the format (X, Y) where X and Y are numeric values.

Figure 12.1 shows how the screen and window appear. The corner coordinates (for example, Xmax, Ymax) are not displayed on the computer screen.

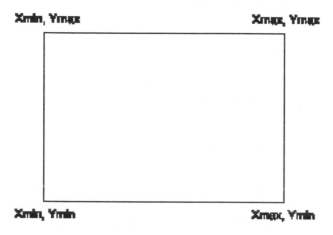

Figure 12.1   *Graphics window and coordinate system.*

{These pictures of full-screen windows should have rounded corners}

If a graphics window has already been established, you can determine its boundaries with the statement

```
ASK WINDOW Xmin, Xmax, Ymin, Ymax
```

As an example, suppose that you want the horizontal coordinate value to go from 0 to 100 and the vertical coordinate value to go from -10 to +10. The following statement produces a window coordinate system meeting these specifications:

```
SET WINDOW 0, 100, -10, 10
```

Note that the lower left corner of the window is the point (0, -10), while the upper right corner is the point (100, 10). The result of executing the preceding statement is shown in Fig. 12.2. As before, corner coordinates are not displayed.

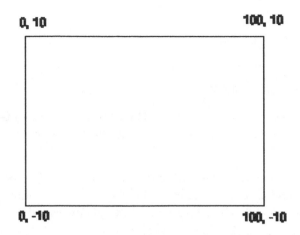

Figure 12.2 *A specific graphics coordinate system.*

When using the graphics window, you do not need to be concerned about the screen resolution or number of pixels. True BASIC makes an automatic translation from window coordinates to pixel position on the screen.

If you do not include a SET WINDOW statement in your program, the window coordinates are the default full-screen set of 0, 1, 0, 1. Note that the graphics coordinate system — that is, the window coordinate system — is not the same as the row-and-column coordinate system used in text-oriented statements like the PRINT statement.

Selecting an Aspect Ratio

Almost any appropriate coordinate system can be chosen for the graphics window if you are plotting a graph. If you are drawing a geometric figure, however, you must consider the *aspect ratio* of your particular screen.

The aspect ratio is the ratio of the width (horizontal dimension) of the screen to the height (vertical dimension). Most display screens are not square but rectangular, with the wide dimension horizontal. Thus if a unit length is to be the same in both horizontal and vertical directions, the number of unit lengths in the horizontal or X direction must be greater than the number in the vertical or Y direction.

On the several computers that I used when writing this book, satisfactory screen aspect ratios are between 1.2 and 1.7. The IBM PC VGA screen has an aspect ratio of about 1.4, while the built-in monitor screen of one of the small Macs with built-in monitor has a ratio of about 1.6. My PowerMac with a 17-inch monitor also has an aspect ratio of 1.4.

To produce squares that look square and circles that are round on an IBM display unit, you should use the statement

```
SET WINDOW 0, 140, 0, 100
```

or

```
SET WINDOW -70, 70, -50, 50
```

to establish the screen coordinate system. The first statement puts the origin at the lower left corner of the screen, while the second statement centers the origin on the screen.

Similar statements can be used with other display units once the aspect ratio has been determined. Later in this chapter in Example Program 12-8, I show you how to adjust your coordinate system to produce figures that are geometrically correct.

It is important to note that the aspect ratio of your printer may be different from the aspect ratio of your screen. This means that a square that looks correct on the screen will appear rectangular when printed on paper. The only solutions to this problem are to use different versions of the program with different aspect ratios for displaying and printing, or to modify your program so it requests the desired aspect ratio before displaying or printing output. The latter technique is used in Example Program 12-6.

12.3 FUNDAMENTALS OF DRAWING

Every computer graphics system has a set of primitive operations that produce simple, fundamental figures. Let's look next at a group of statements for drawing points, lines, areas, and text.

Drawing Points

The True BASIC statement to draw or plot a point at the position X,Y on the graphics screen is

```
PLOT POINTS: X,Y
```

In many applications, you want to plot several points and then the statement becomes

```
PLOT POINTS: X1,Y1; X2,Y2;...
```

The position identifiers X1, X2, Y1, and Y2 can be numeric variables, constants, or expressions. Each position pair, X and Y, represents the coordinates of a point to be plotted. The pairs are separated by semicolons. There is no trailing semicolon when you plot a single point. As usual in almost all graphics statements, these positions are expressed in terms of the window coordinate system.

You can, of course, use the PLOT POINTS statement in a loop to plot a sequence of points. Here is a program that demonstrates that procedure:

```
! Example Program 12-3
! Plot a sequence of points.

SET MODE "GRAPHICS"
SET WINDOW 0, 10, 0, 100
FOR X = 0 to 10 step 0.1
    LET Y = X*X
    PLOT POINTS: X, Y
NEXT X
PRINT "Press Return key to clear screen."
END
```

Program output is shown in Fig. 12.3.

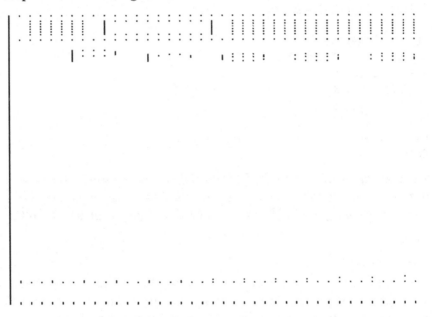

Figure 12.3 *Graph produced by plotting points.*

This program plots the equation Y = X*X, a parabolic curve. After you run the program and the curve is displayed, press the Return key to return to the normal text screen. I tried this program first without the "step 0.1" phrase, but like it better the way it is now written with the points plotted closer together. If you are plotting on a large display screen, change the STEP value from 0.1 to 0.01. Try running this program yourself with different STEP sizes.

The screen displays that are shown in this chapter were produced on a PowerMac with a 17-inch monitor, but essentially the same displays can be produced on a PC.

Drawing Lines

The statement

```
PLOT LINES: X1,Y1; X2,Y2
```

is used to draw a line between points (X1, Y1) and (X2, Y2). You can connect several points together with lines by using a modified PLOT LINES statement, as shown here:

```
PLOT LINES: X1,Y1; X2,Y2; X3,Y3...
```

If the coordinates of the first point are the same as those of the last point, you will produce a closed figure — that is, the line will close on itself.

Here is the previous example, rewritten to display a line plot rather than a point plot:

```
! Example Program 12-4
! Plot a line between points.

SET MODE "GRAPHICS"
SET WINDOW 0, 10, 0, 100
FOR X = 0 to 10
    LET Y = X*X
    PLOT LINES: X, Y;
NEXT X
PRINT "Press Return key to clear screen."
END
```

Note the trailing semicolon in the PLOT LINES statement which causes a line to be drawn from one point to the next point. In this case, a step of one is used so that the curve is drawn more quickly. The program produces the graph shown in Fig. 12.4.

Drawing Areas

Having learned to draw lines, you can now connect lines to produce a shape, still using the PLOT LINES statement. This technique produces an outline figure. The PLOT AREA statement can be used to fill in the area enclosed by the outline. Here is an example program that uses both statements. Example Program 12-5 first draws an outline of a square and then, after a short pause, fills in the square.

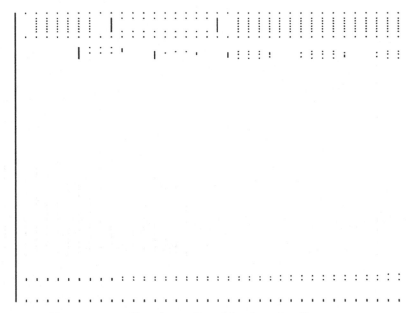

Figure 12.4 *Graph produced by drawing lines.*

```
! Example Program 12-5
! Display outline and filled figures.

SET MODE "GRAPHICS"
LET Ratio = 1.4
SET WINDOW 0, (100*Ratio), 0, 100

! Display an outline square.
PLOT LINES: 10,10; 10,50; 50,50; 50,10; 10,10
PAUSE 2

! Display a filled square.
PLOT AREA: 10,10; 10,50; 50,50; 50,10; 10,10
PRINT "Press Return key to clear screen."
END
```

Figure 12.5 shows the filled square. Note that I chose a coordinate system to match a screen aspect ratio of 1.4, the ratio of my PowerMac monitor. By assigning the aspect ratio to a variable named Ratio, it is easy to change this variable when you run the program on a computer whose display unit has a different aspect ratio.

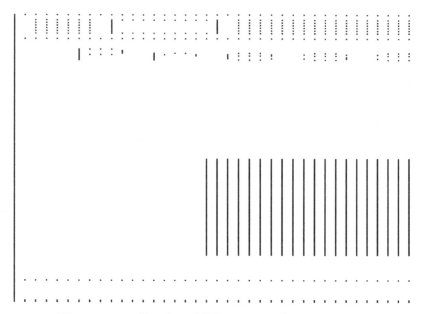

Figure 12.5 *Results of filling an outline square.*

Using Colors

The possibility of displaying text and figures in color has not yet been discussed. Of course, if you have only a black-and-white or gray-scale monitor, your graphics figures cannot be displayed in color. If you have a color monitor, you can choose one of several colors for your text and figures, depending on the computer and monitor that you are using. The statement to establish a new foreground color is

    SET COLOR Name$

where Name$ contains the name of the desired color. In general, True BASIC will support at least the following colors:

RED	CYAN
MAGENTA	BROWN
YELLOW	WHITE
GREEN	BLACK
BLUE	BACKGROUND

A similar statement

    SET COLOR BACKGROUND Name$

is used to establish a new background color. This last statement can be abbreviated to

    SET BACK Name$

Note that the color BACKGROUND means the figure will be displayed in the same color as the background, thus effectively erasing an existing figure. Here is an example of this technique:

```
! Example Program 12-6
! Show method for erasing a figure.

PRINT "Typical aspect ratios are between 1.2 and 1.8."
INPUT prompt "Aspect ratio of your screen? ": Ratio
ASK COLOR Original$
SET MODE "GRAPHICS"
SET WINDOW 0, (100*Ratio), 0, 100

! Display an outline square.
PLOT LINES: 10,10; 10,50; 50,50; 50,10; 10,10
PAUSE 2

! Now erase the figure.
SET COLOR "BACKGROUND"
PLOT LINES: 10,10; 10,50; 50,50; 50,10; 10,10
SET COLOR Original$
PRINT "Press Return key to clear screen."
END
```

It is difficult to show the results of this program but you should run it yourself. The INPUT statement asks the user to enter an aspect ratio.

If you have a color monitor, you can draw a square with red lines by inserting the statement

```
SET COLOR "RED"
```

after the statement

```
SET MODE "GRAPHICS"
```

Displaying Text

It is often desirable to display text in a graphics window. Displayed text is needed for such purposes as labeling figures or displaying instructions for a user.

The familiar PRINT statement can be used but it may not place the text just where you want it. A more useful statement is

```
PLOT TEXT, AT X,Y: Label$
```

where Label\$ is a string variable containing the desired text. This text will be located in the window so that the lower left corner of the first character is at coordinate position (X, Y). This statement is used in the next program which plots a bar graph — also called a histogram — of data values:

```
! Example Program 12-7
! Display a bar graph with labels.

SET MODE "GRAPHICS"
SET WINDOW 0, 120, 0, 100
FOR X = 20 to 100 step 20
    READ Y
    PLOT AREA: X-5,0; X-5,Y; X+5,Y; X+5,0
    LET Label$ = Str$(Y)
    PLOT TEXT, at X-5,Y+5: Label$
NEXT X

DATA 52.3, 21.7, 72.8, 30.1, 66.7
END
```

The label must be a string value and thus the numeric variable Y is converted to a string. Each individual label starts with a different character having a different lower left point. This fact causes each label to be located in a slightly different position with respect to its histogram bar.

The text characters were too small on my first run of this program. I changed character size by using the Set Output Font command in the Windows drop-down menu. A font choice of Monaco face in 36 point size creates the graph shown in Fig. 12.6. Note that the program no longer reminds the user to press the Return key.

Figure 12.6 *Bar graph with labels.*

Determining the Aspect Ratio

Here is a program that you can use to determine the aspect ratio of your own screen. Run the program and measure carefully the width and height of the square displayed on the screen. If these two dimensions are not the same, try again when prompted and enter a new aspect ratio. If the square as displayed is too wide, increase the aspect ratio; if too narrow, decrease the ratio.

Both Ymin and Xmin are set to zero. Ymax is set to 100 and Xmax is set to 100 times the aspect ratio. When a new aspect ratio is entered, the value of Xmax is recalculated and the test square is displayed again in the modified coordinate system.

```
! Example Program 12-8
! Determine the aspect ratio of your screen.

! Display instructions.
CLEAR
PRINT "Program to Determine Screen Aspect Ratio"
PRINT
PRINT "Carefully measure the width and height of"
PRINT "the displayed square. If it is too wide,"
PRINT "increase the aspect ratio; if too narrow,"
PRINT "decrease the aspect ratio."
PRINT
PRINT "Press any key to display the square.";
GET KEY Dummy

! Set mode and initial aspect ratio.
ASK MODE Type$
SET MODE "GRAPHICS"
LET Ratio = 1.5
DO
   CLEAR
   LET Xmax = 100*Ratio
   SET WINDOW 0, Xmax, 0, 100
   ! Display a filled square.
   PLOT AREA: 30,20; 30,80; 90,80; 90,20; 30,20
   LET Label$ = "Aspect ratio is " & Str$(Ratio)
   PLOT TEXT, at 40,90: Label$
   ! Check for another display.
   LINE INPUT prompt "Try again? ":Reply$
   LET Reply$ = Ucase$(Reply$[1:1])
   ! Ask for new aspect ratio and display square again.
   IF Reply$ <> "N" then
      INPUT prompt "Aspect ratio? ": Ratio
   END IF
```

```
LOOP until Reply$ = "N"
SET MODE Type$
END
```

Note that this example program preserves the original display mode in the variable Type$ and resets the screen to this mode before exiting.

12.4 DRAWING SIMPLE SHAPES

The PLOT statements described in the previous section can be used to draw any figure consisting of straight lines. Another set of statements, the BOX statements, allows simple figures to be drawn more easily and quickly. The additional drawing speed makes BOX statements a good choice for animation programs where drawings must change rapidly.

Drawing with BOX Statements

Rectangles can be drawn and erased using one of the following statements:

```
BOX LINES Xmin, Xmax, Ymin, Ymax
BOX AREA Xmin, Xmax, Ymin, Ymax
BOX CLEAR Xmin, Xmax, Ymin, Ymax
```

The BOX LINES statement draws a rectangle that extends horizontally from Xmin to Xmax and vertically from Ymin to Ymax. This is a line drawing, similar to that produced by the PLOT LINES statement. The BOX AREA statement draws a solid rectangle in the selected color, with dimensions again determined by the values of Xmin, Xmax, Ymin, and Ymax. The BOX CLEAR statement erases a rectangle drawn previously by either the BOX LINES or BOX AREA statement. Here is an example program:

```
! Example Program 12-9
! Use the BOX statements to draw rectangles.

SET MODE "GRAPHICS"
LET Ratio = 1.4
SET WINDOW 0, (100*Ratio), 0, 100

! Draw a rectangle.
BOX LINES 10, 60, 10, 60
PAUSE 2

! Erase the rectangle.
BOX CLEAR 10, 60, 10, 60
PAUSE 2
```

```
! Draw a solid rectangle.
BOX AREA 70, 120, 40, 90
PAUSE 2

! Erase again.
BOX CLEAR 70, 120, 40, 90

END
```

PAUSE statements have been inserted to separate the different BOX statements. Note particularly the speed with which the BOX AREA statement fills a rectangle compared to the speed of the PLOT AREA statement. You should run all the example programs in this chapter on you own computer to see exactly what output they produce.

Another BOX statement draws an ellipse or circle within a rectangular area. Remember that a circle is just the special case of an ellipse drawn within a square. This statement has two forms, as shown:

```
BOX ELLIPSE Xmin, Xmax, Ymin, Ymax
BOX CIRCLE Xmin, Xmax, Ymin, Ymax
```

Here is an example program that uses these statements:

```
! Example Program 12-10
! Use a BOX statement to draw a circle.

SET MODE "GRAPHICS"
LET Ratio = 1.4
SET WINDOW 0, (100*Ratio), 0, 100

! Draw a square.
BOX LINES 10, 60, 10, 60
PAUSE 2

! Erase the square.
BOX CLEAR 10, 60, 10, 60
PAUSE 2

! Draw a circle.
BOX CIRCLE 10, 60, 10, 60

END
```

It is difficult to show you output in the book because the drawing changes as the program is executed. Run the program yourself. If you prefer, you can use the statement BOX ELLIPSE instead of BOX CIRCLE — the results will be identical.

Coloring an Area

The FLOOD statement lets a user "fill in" an outline figure with solid color. The coordinates in the FLOOD statement can be any point within the outline figure. Here is an example program similar to the preceding one, but the ellipse is now drawn within a rectangle, not a square, and is filled in with the default color:

```
! Example Program 12-11
! Use the BOX statement to draw an ellipse
! and flood the figure with the default color.

SET MODE "GRAPHICS"
LET Ratio = 1.4
SET WINDOW 0, (100*Ratio), 0, 100

! Draw a rectangle.
BOX LINES 10, 120, 30, 80
PAUSE 2

! Erase the rectangle.
BOX CLEAR 10, 120, 30, 80
PAUSE 2

! Draw an ellipse.
BOX ELLIPSE 10, 120, 30, 80
PAUSE 2

! Flood the ellipse with red.
SET COLOR "red"
FLOOD 50, 50
END
```

Note that the coordinates of the FLOOD statement must refer to a point inside the ellipse. Try running this program with different FLOOD statement coordinates and see what happens.

Saving Graphics Figures

Two additional BOX statements are used to save and redisplay a portion of the graphics screen. This process is much faster than erasing and redrawing the figure.

```
BOX KEEP Xmin, Xmax, Ymin, Ymax IN Var$
BOX SHOW Var$ AT Xmin, Ymin
```

The BOX KEEP statement saves all or a portion of the graphics window (actually a portion of the computer's display memory) in the string variable Var$. The BOX SHOW statement allows the contents of Var$ to be displayed at any selected location on the graphics screen, with the lower left corner of the saved figure placed at the point Xmin, Ymin.

Some display units with high resolution and many colors require a lot of memory to store a large image. The BOX KEEP statement is limited by the amount of storage space available in a string and in memory. On a PC with a VGA display unit, you can usually store an area slightly less than half the size of the screen. On a Mac, you are not limited by lack of string space but may not have enough memory to store some images. For detailed information, consult the *Reference Manual* for your particular computer system.

Here is an example that first draws a circle, then saves the circle figure and erases the screen, and finally displays the saved figure again at four new locations:

```
! Example Program 12-12
! Save and redisplay a graphics image.

SET MODE "GRAPHICS"
LET Ratio = 1.4
SET WINDOW 0, (100*Ratio), 0, 100

! Draw and flood a circle.
BOX CIRCLE 60, 70, 45, 55
SET COLOR "blue"
FLOOD 65, 50
PAUSE 2

! Save and erase this figure.
BOX KEEP 60, 70, 45, 55 in Figure$
BOX CLEAR 60, 70, 45, 55
PAUSE 2

! Display the figure in four new locations.
BOX SHOW Figure$ at 10, 10
BOX SHOW Figure$ at 10, 80
BOX SHOW Figure$ at 110, 80
BOX SHOW Figure$ at 110, 10

END
```

Selecting Different Colors

A color monitor can display a range of colors. Sometimes this range is limited, maybe only eight different colors. Other monitor and graphic card combinations can display many millions of different colors, but True BASIC supports no more than 256 colors.

The typical modern PC or Mac color monitor displays 256 different colors or more. Older monitors and notebook color screens may display only 16 different colors. These colors are designated by color number, starting with zero. On most monitors, number 0 represents the background color and thus a figure drawn in color 0 is not visible.

Here is a program that allows you to investigate the colors available on your computer and display unit. For each color number, a small filled box is drawn and the color number is displayed. The complete display has room for 256 colors — if your monitor supports only 16 colors, each column of color samples looks the same.

```
! Example Program 12-13
! Examine different colors or intensities.

SET MODE "GRAPHICS"
LET Ratio = 1.4
SET WINDOW 0, (160*Ratio), 0, 160

! Display individual colors by number.
FOR Col = 0 to 15
  FOR Row = 0 to 15
    LET ColorNum = Row + 16*Col
    SET COLOR ColorNum
    BOX AREA 1+12*Col, 6+12*Col, 155-10*Row, 158-10*Row
    LET Label$ = Str$(ColorNum)
    PLOT TEXT, at 7 + 12*Col, 155 - 10*Row: Label$
  NEXT Row
NEXT Col
END
```

Another version of the program displays colors identified by color name rather than by color number. It uses the eight color names that are generally available on color display units.

```
! Example Program 12-14
! Examine different color names.

SET MODE "GRAPHICS"
LET Ratio = 1.4
SET WINDOW 0, (100*Ratio), 0, 100

DO while more data
  READ ColorName$
  SET COLOR ColorName$
  BOX AREA 30, 70, 30, 70
  PRINT "Color name is "; ColorName$
  PAUSE 2
```

```
    CLEAR
LOOP

DATA BLUE, GREEN, CYAN, RED
DATA MAGENTA, BROWN, WHITE, YELLOW
END
```

All these color names may not be available on your system or conversely, additional color names may be available. Furthermore, the color name does not always correspond to the color displayed.

If you plan to do serious color work with a Mac, be sure to read the discussion on this subject in the *True BASIC Reference Manual*. To quote from my copy of that manual: "BOX SHOW USING works poorly on the Macintosh because the image string contains internal color numbers....Other BOX SHOW options have similar problems. We can't give you any advice on how to use these options on the Macintosh other than trial and error."

12.5 PICTURE PROCEDURES

A graphics program unit is called a *picture*. It is the graphics equivalent of a True BASIC subroutine. While both internal and external pictures are allowed, only external pictures are discussed.

External Picture Units

An external picture unit must start with the statement

```
EXTERNAL PICTURE Name (Parameters)
```

where Name is the picture name and Parameters is a list of variable names. The picture name must follow the same rules that apply to variable names (see Chapter 3). In True BASIC, the word EXTERNAL may be omitted but the picture unit must be placed after the main program END statement. The parameters are local variable names, separated from one another by commas. Information is passed to these parameters by reference, just as with subroutines. In fact, the use of temporary variables, passing of file or channel numbers and so forth, all behave with pictures as they do with subroutines.

The last statement in a picture unit must be END PICTURE and other exit points are identified by the EXIT PICTURE phrase. A picture unit is invoked from another program unit by the statement

```
DRAW Name (Arguments)
```

where the arguments may be variables, constants, or expressions.

Here is an example program that uses a picture unit to draw a circle at a specified location. The user is asked to enter the radius of a circle to be drawn on the screen. If the radius is zero, the program stops. The user is then asked to enter the center coordinates of the circle and an external picture is called to draw the figure.

```
! Example Program 12-15
! Use picture unit to draw a circle.

ASK MODE Type$
DO
   CLEAR
   PRINT "Enter zero to stop the program."
   INPUT prompt "Radius of circle? ": Radius
   IF Radius > 0 then
      INPUT prompt "Center coordinates (X,Y)? ": X, Y
      SET MODE "GRAPHICS"
      LET Ratio = 1.7
      SET WINDOW -50*Ratio, 50*Ratio, -50, 50
      DRAW Circle (Radius, X, Y)
      PAUSE 3
      ! Set original mode.
      SET MODE Type$
   ELSE IF Radius < 0 then
      PRINT
      PRINT "You cannot have a negative radius."
      PAUSE 2
   END IF
LOOP until Radius = 0
END

PICTURE Circle (R, X, Y)
   ! Draw a circle of radius R at point X, Y
   BOX CIRCLE X-R, X+R, Y-R, Y+R
END PICTURE
```

The initial screen mode is saved in a variable named Type$. A user is asked to specify the radius and center coordinates of the circle, and the display mode is changed from text to graphics. An external picture named Circle draws the figure, with the radius and center coordinates passed as parameters. Upon returning to the main program unit, the screen is restored to its original text mode so that text prompts with a cursor can again be displayed.

Once again, it is difficult to show program output because there are so many window changes. You should run the example program yourself.

Transforming a Graphics Figure

One advantage of using picture units for computer graphics is that the figures specified in the picture unit can be transformed when the picture is drawn. Transforming a picture means changing its appearance in some geometric fashion, using the statement

```
DRAW Pic WITH Trans
```

where Pic is the name of a picture unit and Trans is the name of a transformation. If you wish to apply more than one transformation, use the statement

```
DRAW Pic WITH Trans1*Trans2...
```

where Trans1, Trans2, and so forth are the names of the same or different transformations.

True BASIC has five standard or built-in transformations, as follows.

Shift (A, B) Move the figure A units in the X direction and B units in the Y direction. Every point plotted at (X, Y) is moved to (X + A, Y + B).

Scale (A) Change the size of the figure by A units. Every point plotted at (X, Y) is moved to (X * A, Y * A).

Scale (A, B) Change the size of the figure by A unitd in the X direction and by B units in the Y direction. Every point plotted at (X, Y) is moved to (X * A, Y * B).

Rotate (A) Rotate the figure A radians or degrees counterclockwise about the origin of the window coordinate system. **Note that the figure is not rotated about its own center.** Radians are used unless your program contains an OPTION ANGLE DEGREES statement.

Shear (A) Tilt all vertical lines in the figure to the right (clockwise) by A radians or degrees. Every point plotted at (X, Y) is moved to (X + (Y * TAN(A)), Y). Radians are used unless your program specifies the use of degrees.

If you are going to transform a picture unit, it must contain PLOT statements, not BOX statements. Figures drawn with BOX statements cannot be transformed. In addition to the built-in transformations just listed, you can develop and apply your own custom transformations. That process is not discussed here but it is covered in many advanced books on computer graphics. See the *True BASIC Reference Manual* for further information.

Here is an example program using a picture unit with transformations. It first draws a simple square and then redraws the same figure with several different transformations applied. Figure 12.7 shows the drawing produced by this program.

```
! Example Program 12-16
! Using transformations with a picture.

SET MODE "GRAPHICS"
LET Ratio = 1.4
SET WINDOW -(50*Ratio),(50*Ratio),-50,50
OPTION ANGLE degrees

DRAW Square(10,-35,25)
PLOT TEXT, at -60,5: "Original square"

DRAW Square(10,35,25) with shear(10)
PLOT TEXT, at 5,5: "Sheared 10 degrees clockwise"

DRAW Square(10,0,0) with rotate(45)*shift(35,-25)
PLOT TEXT, at 5,-45: "Rotated 45 degrees"

DRAW Square(10,-25,-25) with scale(1.5,1)
PLOT TEXT, at -60,-45: "Widened 50 percent"
END

PICTURE Square (Size, X, Y)
    ! Draw a square centered at the point X, Y.
    LET P = Size/2
    PLOT LINES: -P+X,P+Y; P+X,P+Y;
    PLOT LINES: P+X,-P+Y; -P+X,-P+Y; -P+X,P+Y
END PICTURE
```

The window coordinate system is centered on the screen. To rotate a square, draw it so its center coincides with the center of coordinates. When you rotate the square, it rotates about its own center and after rotation, you can move it to the desired position (see Figure 12.7).

Picture Libraries

Library files of pictures can be created in the same manner as library files of functions or subroutines. A file named GRAPHLIB.TRU is distributed with True BASIC and contains picture units for drawing polygons, arcs of circles, window axes, line graphs, and bar graphs. On a Mac, this file is named "Graphlib" and is in a folder named "TB Library".

To use any of the pictures in this library, add the statement

```
LIBRARY "graphlib"
```

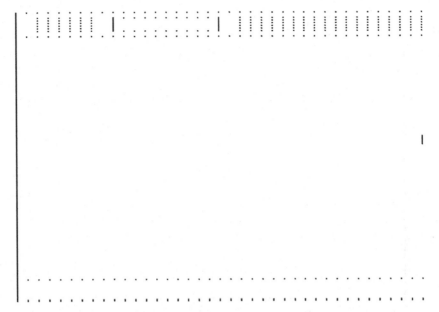

Figure 12.7 *Transformations of a simple square.*

to the beginning of your program. You can find out how to use these library pictures by examining the graphics library file.

12.6 EXAMPLES OF COMPUTER GRAPHICS APPLICATIONS

In this final section of Chapter 12, two example programs are presented that illustrate computer graphics applications.

Computer-Aided Design

The process of using computer graphics to assist architects and engineers who create drawings is called *computer-aided design (CAD)*. Most CAD systems produce drawings that are much more sophisticated and detailed than this example, the front view of a simple house.

This house is 30 feet wide and the peak of the roof is 27 feet off the ground. It has an exterior chimney on the left side that is 3 feet wide. The front door is 3.5 feet by 7 feet. Most of the windows are 2.5 feet by 4 feet, but one small attic window is only 1.5 feet by 1.5 feet. There is a 4-foot-wide step at the front door. Two horizontal lines on the chimney show where its depth is reduced at 5 feet off the ground. The design is shown in Fig. 12.8.

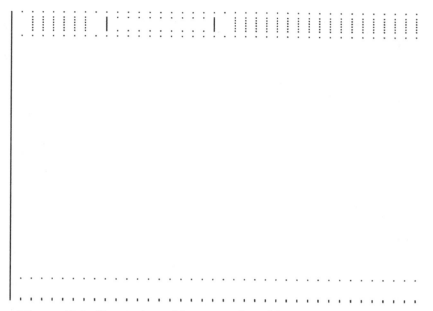

Figure 12.8 *Front view of house produced by a CAD program.*

A coordinate system was chosen so that the screen width represents 70 feet and the screen height represents 50 feet. This gives an aspect ratio of 1.4, the correct ratio for my display unit. You can easily change the aspect ratio to match your particular computer. Here is an outline of the program:

> draw front outline of house
> draw chimney
> draw roof overhang
> draw front step
> use picture to draw front door
> use pictures to draw windows

CAD systems for architects usually have libraries or collections of drawings for such items as doors and windows. An architect may be able to choose from several dozen door and window designs and place these items where needed on the drawing. In this program, one picture unit is used to draw a 3.5-foot by 7-foot door. The coordinates of the center of the door are passed to the picture unit when it is called.

There are two different types of windows and thus two different picture units for windows. The first draws a standard 2.5-foot by 4-foot window. The second draws a small 1.5-foot by 1.5-foot window. The center coordinates of a window are passed to a picture unit when it is called. In an actual CAD program, the door and window drawings would show a lot more detail than in this example.

```
! Example Program 12-17
```

```
! Draw the front view of a house.

SET MODE "GRAPHICS"
LET Ratio = 1.4
SET WINDOW -(25*Ratio), (25*Ratio), 0, 50
! Draw house outline.
PLOT LINES: -15,0; -15,18; 0,27; 15,18; 15,0; -15,0
! Draw chimney.
PLOT LINES: -18,0; -18,24; -15,24; -15,0; -18,0
PLOT LINES: -18,5; -15,5
PLOT LINES: -18,6; -15,6
! Draw roof overhang.
PLOT LINES: 15,18; 16,17.4; 15,17.4
PLOT LINES: -15,18; -16,17.4; -15,17.4
ASK COLOR Hue$
SET COLOR background
PLOT LINES: 15,18; 15,17.4
PLOT LINES: -15,18; -15,17.4
SET COLOR Hue$
! Draw front step.
PLOT LINES: -2,0; -2,1; 2,1; 2,0
! Draw front door.
DRAW Door1 (0,4.5)
! Draw windows.
DRAW Window1 (-8,5)
DRAW Window1 (8,5)
DRAW Window1 (-8,14)
DRAW Window1 (0,14)
DRAW Window1 (8,14)
DRAW Window2 (0,22)
END  ! of main program


PICTURE Door1 (X,Y)
    ! Draw 3.5 foot by 7 foot door,
    ! centered at X, Y.
    LET Xmin = X - 1.75
    LET Xmax = X + 1.75
    LET Ymin = Y - 3.5
    LET Ymax = Y + 3.5
    BOX LINES Xmin, Xmax, Ymin, Ymax
    ! Draw door knob.
    DRAW Circle (0.1, X - 1.2, Y - 0.4)
END PICTURE  ! Door1

PICTURE Window1 (X,Y)
```

```
    ! Draw a 2.5 foot by 4 foot window,
    ! centered at X, Y.
    LET Xmin = X - 1.25
    LET Xmax = X + 1.25
    LET Ymin = Y - 2
    LET Ymax = Y + 2
    BOX LINES Xmin, Xmax, Ymin, Ymax
    ! Draw individual window panes.
    PLOT LINES: X, Y - 2; X, Y + 2
    PLOT LINES: X - 1.25, Y; X + 1.25, Y
END PICTURE  ! Window1

PICTURE Window2 (X,Y)
    ! Draw a 1.5 foot by 1.5 foot window,
    ! centered at X, Y.
    LET Xmin = X - .75
    LET Xmax = X + .75
    LET Ymin = Y - .75
    LET Ymax = Y + .75
    BOX LINES Xmin, Xmax, Ymin, Ymax
END PICTURE  ! Window2

PICTURE Circle (R, X, Y)
    ! Draw a circle of radius R,
    ! centered at X, Y.
    BOX CIRCLE X - R, X + R, Y - R, Y + R
END PICTURE  ! Circle
```

The main program draws the house outline, chimney, roof overhang, and front step. It calls external picture units to draw the front door and the six windows. While the resulting drawing is not very sophisticated, the method used is similar to that used by commercial CAD programs.

Interactive Computer Graphics

All the preceding example programs have drawn screen figures based on coordinate values in graphics statements. If you wanted to draw another figure, you would have to change these values or even the statements themselves. An interactive graphics program allows you to draw a figure by moving an indicator on the screen, and thus a large number of different figures can be drawn using the same program.

The indicator used in the example program is a set of cross-hairs and it is moved with the cursor arrow keys or a mouse. As you might expect, the Left Arrow key moves the cross-hairs left, the Up Arrow key moves the cross-hairs up, and so forth. The movement is fairly slow, but if the arrow key is held down, the cross-hairs will move continuously in the specified direction. If the Control key (Ctrl) is held down when the arrow key is pressed, the cross-hairs move to the edge of the screen in the specified direction.

A mouse is a much better device for controlling the position of the cross-hairs and can be used to advantage if available. Just move the mouse and observe the movement of the cross-hairs.

The statement that produces the cross-hairs is

```
GET POINT: X,Y
```

This statement is the graphics input statement. When it is executed, cross-hairs are displayed at the center of the active window or at the last point specified on the graphics screen. The cross-hairs can be moved as described previously and when they are at the desired point, the user presses the Return key or mouse button — left button if there are two or three buttons. This action assigns the coordinates of that point to the variables X and Y.

A pixel is now illuminated at the point that was chosen and appears as a small bright spot on the screen — look carefully, it may be hard to see. As many points as desired can be chosen and the coordinates of each point will be assigned to the GET POINT statement variables.

For example, to draw a line between two points, use the following program fragment:

```
GET POINT: X1, Y1
GET POINT: X2, Y2
PLOT LINES: X1,Y1; X2,Y2
```

The first GET POINT statement assigns the coordinate values of the first point to X1 and Y1, while the second statement assigns values to X2 and Y2. The PLOT LINES statement then draws a line between the two designated points.

This example program creates a split screen, with the upper window a graphics window and the lower window a command window. A border is drawn around the graphics window. The prompt "Command?" appears in the command window. No cursor is visible, because the entire screen has been placed in graphics mode.

The eight commands available in this program are shown in Fig. 12.9.

h	help, display the available commands
l	draw a single line between two points
b	draw a rectangular box
t	write a single line of text
-l	erase a line
-b	erase a box
-t	erase text and its enclosing box
q	quit the program

Figure 12.9 Command table for Example Program 12-18.

The Help (h) and Quit (q) commands are self-explanatory. The Draw Line (l) command draws a line after you mark two points. Move the cross-hairs to the first point (using mouse or arrow keys) and press the mouse button or Return key. Repeat this process for the second point and a line appears immediately, joining the two points.

The Draw Box (b) command draws a box after you mark the locations of its lower left and its upper right corners. Follow the same procedure of moving the cross-hairs and pressing the Return key as you did with the Line command. The Write Text (t) command first asks you to enter a line of text in the command window. It writes that text in the graphics window after you move the cross-hairs to the position where the first character — specifically, its lower left corner — should be placed, and then press the mouse button or Return key.

Remember that you must press the mouse button or Return key after entering each command, the normal procedure that you have followed in most other programs.

The Delete Line (-l) command erases a line after you mark both ends with the cross-hairs. The Delete Box (-b) command erases a box in the same way, but in this case you must mark the lower left and the upper right corners of the box. Be careful to mark these points accurately because if you don't, some pieces of the line or box may be left on the screen.

The Delete Text (-t) command erases a line of text **only if the line is enclosed in a box**. Place the cross-hairs anywhere inside the box and press the mouse button — or the Return key if you have no mouse — and both the text and the box will disappear. Incidentally, you can use the Delete Text command to delete any box and its contents, even an empty box. If no box exists, this command erases the whole window. Another tip: If you have pieces of a line or box left on the screen, draw a box around them and use the Delete Text command to erase the box and its contents.

Here is the complete interactive graphics program:

```
! Example Program 12-18
! Draws lines, boxes and text on the screen,
! and allows these figures to be erased.

! Open windows and establish coordinates.
SET MODE "GRAPHICS"
OPEN #1: screen 0, 1, 0, .08
SET WINDOW 1, 80, 1, 2
OPEN #2: screen 0, 1, .08, 1
SET WINDOW 1, 80, 1, 22
BOX LINES 1, 80, 2, 22
! Coordinates of center, window #2
LET X = 40
LET Y = 12

DO  ! main command loop
   WINDOW #1
   LINE INPUT prompt "Command? ": Action$
   ! Prefix with minus sign to erase.
   IF Action$[1:1] = "-" then
      LET Action$ = Ucase$(Action$[2:2])
   ELSE
      LET Action$ = Lcase$(Action$[1:1])
   END IF
   SELECT CASE Action$

   CASE "l"  ! single line between points
        WINDOW #2
        DRAW Line (X, Y)

   CASE "L"  ! erase a line
        WINDOW #2
        ASK COLOR ColorNum
        SET COLOR background
        DRAW Line (X, Y)
        SET COLOR ColorNum

   CASE "b"  ! rectangular box
        WINDOW #2
        DRAW Box (X, Y)

   CASE "B"  ! erase a box
        WINDOW #2
        ASK COLOR ColorNum
        SET COLOR background
```

```
            DRAW Box (X, Y)
            SET COLOR ColorNum

    CASE "t"   ! line of text
            LINE INPUT prompt "Text? ": Text$
            WINDOW #2
            DRAW Text (X, Y, Text$)

    CASE "T"   ! erase text and enclosing box
            WINDOW #2
            ASK COLOR ColorNum
            GET POINT: X, Y  ! point inside box
            FLOOD X, Y
            SET COLOR background
            FLOOD X, Y
            SET COLOR ColorNum

    CASE "h", "H"  ! list the menu
            PRINT "Commands: Line, Box, Text, Help or Quit."
            PRINT "Precede a command with";
            PRINT " a minus sign to erase."

    CASE "q", "Q"  ! go to END SELECT

    CASE else
            PRINT "Commands: Line, Box, Text, Help or Quit."

    END SELECT
LOOP until Action$ = "q"
WINDOW #1
PRINT "Press Return key to erase the screen."
END  ! of main program

PICTURE Set (X, Y)
    ! Set cross-hairs at position X, Y.
    ASK COLOR ColorNum
    PLOT POINTS: X, Y
    SET COLOR background
    PLOT POINTS: X, Y
    SET COLOR ColorNum
END PICTURE  ! Set

SUB Coords (X1, Y1, X2, Y2)
    ! Get coordinates of two points.
    GET POINT: X1, Y1
```

```
        PLOT POINTS: X1, Y1
        GET POINT: X2, Y2
        PLOT POINTS: X2, Y2
    END SUB  ! Coords

    PICTURE Line (X, Y)
        ! Draw line between two points.
        DRAW Set (X, Y)
        CALL Coords (X1, Y1, X2, Y2)
        PLOT LINES: X1,Y1; X2,Y2
        LET X = X2 + 1
        LET Y = Y2 + 1
    END PICTURE  ! Line

    PICTURE Box (X, Y)
        ! Draw a rectangular box.
        DRAW Set (X, Y)
        CALL Coords (X1, Y1, X2, Y2)
        BOX LINES X1, X2, Y1, Y2
        LET X = X1 - 1
        LET Y = Y1 - 1
    END PICTURE  ! Box

    PICTURE Text (X, Y, Text$)
        ! Display a line of text.
        DRAW Set (X, Y)
        GET POINT: X1, Y1
        PLOT TEXT, AT X1, Y1: Text$
        LET X = X1 - 1
        LET Y = Y1 - 1
    END PICTURE  ! Text
```

After opening the graphics and command windows and prompting for a command, the program uses a SELECT CASE statement to execute the command. Most of the work is done in the five subprograms.

The Set picture unit establishes the location in the graphics window where the cross-hairs will appear. The first PLOT POINTS statement establishes a location and colors that location with the existing color. The second PLOT POINTS statement uses background color to make the location invisible. This location then becomes the point where the cross-hairs appear when the next GET POINT statement is executed.

The Coords subroutine unit plot two points, one at location (X1, Y1) and the other at location (X2, Y2). These two points are used by other subprograms for drawing figures.

The Line picture unit first calls the Set picture unit to establish a location where the cross-hairs are displayed. It calls the Coords subroutine to plot the two end points of a line and draws the line with a PLOT LINES statement. It then assigns new values to X and Y, establishing a new coordinate set near one end of the line for the next location of the cross-hairs.

The Box picture unit behaves similarly, establishing a location for cross-hairs and plotting two points. It uses the BOX LINES statement to draw a rectangular box. It assigns new values to X and Y so that the next location of the cross-hairs will be near the lower left corner of the box.

The Text picture unit uses the GET POINT statement to locate a point and the PLOT TEXT statement to write a line of text in the graphics window. The next location of the cross-hairs will be near the first character in the text line.

The commands to erase a line or box are quite simple. The color is changed to background and the line or box is drawn again, effectively erasing it. It is important, of course, that the cross-hairs be used to mark accurately the two ends of the line and the two proper corners of the box.

The command to erase text works a little differently. Before text can be erased, it must be enclosed in a box. The cross-hairs are then placed anywhere inside the box and the mouse button or Return key is pressed. The first FLOOD statement fills the entire box with a solid color, overwriting the text, and then the second FLOOD statement erases the box of solid color. Note that this command can be used to erase any box or the entire window if there is no box.

Many additional commands could be added to this example program to make it a more useful drawing tool. One or two extensions are included among the practice programs.

Summary of Important Points

- A text cursor is not displayed when you are in the graphics mode.
- When in graphics mode, press the Return key or mouse button to return to text mode.
- If you are drawing a geometric figure, you should specify a window coordinate system that conforms to the aspect ratio of your monitor screen.
- You can erase an existing figure by drawing the same figure again using the background color.
- Transformations take place about the center of the coordinate system, not necessarily the center of the figure.

- The Delete Text command of Example Program 12-18 erases a box and any text or other markings within that box.

Common Errors

- Forgetting to run the graphics driver GRAPHICS.COM on a PC before using the PrtScr key to move a graphics image from the screen to an attached printer.

- Trying to display graphics on an old-fashioned PC monochromatic monitor without a graphics card installed.

- Including the SET MODE "GRAPHICS" statement in a Mac program when you want to display output in a small output window.

- Failing to determine and compensate for the screen aspect ratio before drawing a geometric figure.

- Using the BOX KEEP statement to save a large graphics image from a VGA display screen. The image may contain too many pixel bits to fit in the maximum memory available for a string variable. It will probably work on a Mac.

- Rotating a graphics figure without moving the center of coordinates to the desired center of rotation.

- Trying to transform a picture unit containing BOX statements.

Self-Test Questions

1. (a) What is a pixel?

    (b) How many pixels are available in the full-screen graphics window of your monitor?

2. Is graphics supported on a standard IBM color monitor?

3. After you have displayed a figure on a full-screen graphics window, what must you do to return to the normal text screen?

4. What statement causes a program to halt execution for one minute?

5. What statement is used to establish window coordinates?

6. When you refer to the point (5, 10) in a window coordinate system,

    (a) what is the Y coordinate value?

    (b) is it measured horizontally or vertically?

7. (a) Why is it important to know the aspect ratio of a display screen?

    (b) What is the aspect ratio of your own screen?

8. If a monitor has an aspect ratio of 1.5 and the vertical coordinate scale goes from 0 to 80, the horizontal coordinate scale should go from 0 to what value?

9. What are the default coordinates if the entire screen is designated a graphics window?

10. What statement plots a point at location X = 3, Y = 5?

11. What statement draws a line from location (3, 5) to location (10, 10)?

12. Write a statement to draw a square with one corner at location (0, 0) and another corner at location (20, 20).

13. Write a program fragment to erase the square drawn in Question 12.

14. (a) What statement displays the word "READY?" at location (20, 20) on the graphics screen?

    (b) What part of which character is located at point (20, 20)?

15. When drawing a circle with the BOX ELLIPSE statement, how is the location of the circle specified?

16. (a) What statement saves a BOX figure?

    (b) Where is the saved figure stored?

17. What color is usually represented by color number zero?

18. How is an external picture unit called by the calling program unit?

19. (a) What transformation statement rotates a figure 30 degrees clockwise?

    (b) The rotation is about what point?

    (c) What other program statement is required when an angle is specified in degrees?

20. What statement allows a program to use the GRAPHLIB library file?

21. How do you determine where the cross-hairs will be displayed when a GET POINT statement is executed?

Practice Programs

Use the graphics mode. Unless otherwise specified, use a window with a vertical coordinate scale from 0 to 100 and a horizontal coordinate scale from 0 to (100 * A), where A is the aspect ratio of your screen.

1. Display a figure consisting of three square boxes, of side length 10, 20, and 30 units, all centered at the center of the screen.

2. Display a figure consisting of three concentric circles, of radii 10, 20, and 30 units, all centered at the center of the screen.

3. Write a picture unit that draws a circle of radius R with its center at location (X, Y). Pass as parameters the circle radius and the coordinates of the center of the circle. Display an error message if the circle overlaps any of the window boundaries.

    Test your picture unit in a program, using a radius of 30 units and center coordinates of X = 40 units, Y = 40 units. Also test with a radius of 50 units and the same center coordinates.

4. Display a bar graph showing the following information on student enrollment:

Year	Students
1970	13,000
1975	15,000
1980	16,000
1985	16,500

    Use the standard horizontal coordinate scale and a vertical coordinate scale from 0 to 20,000. Each bar should be 10 units wide. Place a label above each bar denoting the year.

5. Enhance the bar graph in Practice Program 4 by drawing a vertical axis with labels for enrollments of 0, 5,000, 10,000, 15,000, and 20,000.

6. The rise and subsequent fall in sales of a new computer company is modeled by the equation

    ```
    Sales(T) = S + (B * Exp(C * T)) - (D * Exp(E * T))
    ```

    where T is the time in years and Exp is the exponential function, one of the standard functions of True BASIC. The coefficient S is the sales rate (units per year) at the beginning of the time period. The coefficients B, C, D, and E are adjustable in order to model different predicted performances. Assume sales of 50,000 units per year and the following coefficient values:

    B = 50   C = 1.10   D = 5   E = 1.37

Use a horizontal coordinate range of -1 to 11, allowing 10 years to be plotted. Use a vertical coordinate range of 10,000 to 100,000, allowing sales of up to 100,000 units per year to be plotted. Define the sales growth function Sales(T) in your program. Assume the beginning year is 1997 and draw a horizontal axis for a 10-year period with each year labeled. Plot sales over this 10-year period or until sales fall to zero. Be sure to use a small enough step in your plotting routine to produce a smooth curve.

7. Write a picture unit to draw axes close to the left edge and bottom edge of the screen. Use a horizontal coordinate range of -1 to 10 and a vertical coordinate range of -10 to 100. Place the intersection of the two axes at the origin of your coordinate system. The X axis runs from 0 to 10; the Y axis from 0 to 100.

    The horizontal axis has ticks (small lines perpendicular to the axis) spaced DeltaX units apart, while the vertical axis has ticks spaced DeltaY units apart. Pass DeltaX and DeltaY as parameters to the picture unit.

    Test this picture unit in a program that displays the graph of sales growth from Example Program 12-4. Use values of DeltaX = 1 and DeltaY = 10.

8. Add two new commands to Example Program 12-18; one to draw a circle in the graphics window, using the Draw Circle (c) command, and one to erase a circle, using the Delete Circle (-c) command. Position the circle by using the cross-hairs first to position its center and then to position a point on its circumference.

    Hint: One way to erase a circle might be to flood it with a solid color and then flood it again with the background color.

CHAPTER 13

Programming with Matrices

13.1   INTRODUCTION

The word *matrix* is another name for an array, normally an array of numbers. Arrays are introduced in Chapter 8 and you learned how to use them when solving problems. You know that FOR loops, either single loops or double-nested loops, are often used to assign values to array elements or to display these elements. All manipulation of arrays ultimately required manipulation of the individual elements.

In this chapter, MAT statements that simplify matrix or array operations are introduced. Matrix arithmetic is also discussed, particularly the addition and subtraction of matrices.

13.2   MAT STATEMENTS

A set of special statements in True BASIC, called *MAT statements*, allows you to manipulate matrices as entities, according to the rules of matrix arithmetic. Manipulating matrices in matrix arithmetic is in many ways similar to manipulating numbers in ordinary arithmetic. MAT statements allow you to manipulate arrays of strings as well as arrays of numbers.

If you are not a mathematician, you may wonder why you should be concerned about matrix arithmetic and the MAT statements. One reason is that MAT statements allow you to do certain things with matrices or arrays, such as changing their size in the middle of a program, that cannot be accomplished in any other way. Another reason is that they allow you to write simpler programs because a single MAT statement can often replace half a dozen ordinary statements.

13.3 READING AND WRITING MATRICES

A matrix is an array and as you know, every array must be dimensioned in a DIM statement before it can be used or referenced in any other program statement. The DIM statement specifies the number of dimensions and the size of each dimension. This size can be specified by a single number or by a lower bound and an upper bound. Most matrices in example programs have a lower bound of one. For example, here are two matrix declarations:

```
DIM Vector(1 to 100)
DIM Transform(3,3)
```

I recommend the first format over the second. MAT statements can also be used with arrays having any legal lower bound and upper bound, such as the following array:

```
DIM Spread(0 to 100, 0 to 50)
```

The MAT INPUT Statement

The fundamental statement used to read matrix values from the keyboard or from a text file is the MAT INPUT statement. This statement reads in values and assigns them to the matrix elements. It assigns the first value to the first element of the first row and continues assigning values in that row, from left to right, until all elements in the row have been assigned values. It then starts assigning values to the elements in the second row and continues in this manner until values have been assigned to all matrix elements. This method of accessing elements and assigning values is often called *odometer order*, meaning that the last index (in this case, the second or column index) varies the fastest.

Here is an example program that reads a matrix:

```
! Example Program 13-1
! Read a matrix from the keyboard.

DIM Ratio(1 to 3, 1 to 2)
PRINT "Type in six element values."
PRINT
MAT INPUT Ratio
PRINT "The matrix has been filled."
END
```

The MAT INPUT statement is similar to the regular INPUT statement. A question mark is displayed to prompt the user when to enter element values. The first number entered is assigned to element Ratio(1,1), the second to element Ratio(1,2), and so forth. Multiple element values, separated by commas, can be entered on the same line.

In this example, six numbers must be entered to fill the array. If you press the Return key before all numbers have been entered, you receive the message "Too few input items. Please add more." and another question mark prompt.

Here is an example of user interaction with the program:

```
Type in six element values on
one line separated by commas.

? 3,4,1,7
Too few input items. Please add more.
? 3,6
The matrix has been filled.
```

Note that if you are using version 3 of True BASIC, the error message "Too few input items. Please reenter input line." is displayed. In this case, you have to reenter all six values.

Compare the simplicity of Example Program 13-1 with the following example using nested FOR loops:

```
! Example Program 13-2
! Read a matrix using nested loops.

DIM Ratio(1 to 3, 1 to 2)
PRINT "Type in six element values,"
PRINT "one after each question mark."
PRINT
FOR Row = 1 to 3
    FOR Col = 1 to 2
        INPUT Ratio(Row, Col)
    NEXT Col
NEXT Row
PRINT "The matrix has been filled."
END
```

It produces similar output:

```
Type in six element values,
one after each question mark.

? 3
? 4
? 1
? 7
? 3
? 6
The matrix has been filled.
```

Both programs accomplish the same task but Example Program 13-1 is considerably shorter and probably easier to understand.

The MAT PRINT Statement

Having entered information into an array, you can use the MAT PRINT statement to display this information on the screen. The MAT PRINT statement displays the element values by rows, in odometer order.

```
! Example Program 13-3
! Read a matrix from the keyboard
! and display it on the screen.

DIM Ratio(1 to 3, 1 to 3)
PRINT "Type in nine element values."
MAT INPUT Ratio
PRINT
PRINT "Here is the resulting matrix."
PRINT
MAT PRINT Ratio
END
```

Element values are displayed one to a print zone, just as if a comma had been placed between the elements in an ordinary PRINT statement. A trailing comma at the end of the MAT PRINT statement produces the same output format. Each time the computer finishes displaying a complete row, the cursor moves to the beginning of the next row. If six single-digit numbers are entered in response to the MAT INPUT statement, here is how the output might appear:

```
Type in nine element values
? 3,4,1,7,3,6,5,-8,4
Here is the resulting matrix.

3            4            1
7            3            6
5            -8           4
```

This example was chosen carefully so that each row fits on the page. If you have a matrix with more columns, you can either reduce the size of the print zone using the SET ZONEWIDTH statement or place a trailing semicolon after the MAT PRINT statement. Here is the program modified by adding a trailing semicolon.

```
! Example Program 13-4
! Read a matrix from the keyboard
! and display it on the screen.
! Add a trailing semicolon to the MAT PRINT statement.

DIM Ratio(1 to 3, 1 to 3)
PRINT "Type in nine element values."
MAT INPUT Ratio
PRINT
PRINT "Here is the resulting matrix."
PRINT
MAT PRINT Ratio;
END
```

The results now look slightly different:

```
Type in nine element values
? 3,4,1,7,3,6,5,-8,4

Here is the resulting matrix.

 3  4  1
 7  3  6
 5 -8  4
```

Redimensioning with the MAT INPUT Statement

A powerful attribute of the MAT INPUT statement is its ability to redimension an array. The number of dimensions cannot be changed, but the size of each dimension can be modified. For example, the statement

```
MAT INPUT Ratio(5 to 8, 8 to 10)
```

changes the size of the Ratio array from 3 by 3 (see Example Program 13-4) to 4 by 3. The following statements are all legal ways of changing the size of the array in our last example:

```
MAT INPUT Ratio(2,2)
MAT INPUT Ratio(1 to 3, 10 to 15)
MAT INPUT Ratio(I, J to K)
```

In the first example, Ratio is redimensioned to an array with two rows and two columns. In the second example, Ratio is redimensioned to an array with three rows, numbered 1 through 3, and six columns, numbered 10 through 15.

The third case is particularly interesting because it redimensions the array on the basis of variable values. These values can be assigned from within the program. In this example, Ratio is redimensioned to an array with I rows, numbered from 1 to I, and (K

- J + 1) columns numbered from J to K. The values stored in I, J, and K are used to redimension the matrix when the MAT INPUT statement is executed.

The MAT INPUT statement has a special form of redimensioning for arrays of one dimension. If a MAT INPUT statement is written as

```
MAT INPUT NumList(?)
```

the array NumList is redimensioned to hold as many numbers as are typed in. **This special form of redimensioning applies only to one-dimensional arrays of numbers.**

Here is an example program using this form of the MAT INPUT statement:

```
! Example Program 13-5
! Use of variable array dimensioning in
! a one-dimensional array.

DIM NumList(1)
PRINT "Type in a list of numbers after the ? prompt."
MAT INPUT NumList(?)
PRINT
PRINT "Number of items in the list is"; Ubound(NumList)
MAT PRINT NumList;
END
```

The size of NumList is set initially to one, knowing that it will be redimensioned later. This program allows a user to type in a sequence of numbers, separated by commas, and the size of the array is adjusted to conform to the number of items entered. The process of entering items terminates when the Return key is pressed. The size of the array is then displayed on the screen and the array itself is printed.

Program output appears as follows:

```
Type in a list of numbers after the ? prompt.
? 1,2,3,4,5,6,7,8,9

Number of items in the list is 9
 1  2  3  4  5  6  7  8  9
```

Other MAT INPUT Statements

The general form of the MAT INPUT statement is

```
MAT INPUT Array1, Array2,...
```

In most cases, a program is easier to use and understand if the MAT INPUT statement is used to enter only a single array, and that is my usual practice.

A prompt can be added to the MAT INPUT statement, using the format

```
MAT INPUT prompt Prompt$: Array1, Array2,...
```

where Prompt$ is any string expression, variable, or constant. This statement displays the prompt and expects the user to enter a sequence of numbers, separated by commas. If all the numbers cannot be entered on a single line, add a trailing comma and the program will respond with a single question mark (?) prompt. You can then continue to enter one or more additional lines, terminating every line except the last line with a trailing comma.

```
! Example Program 13-6
! Demonstrate how multiple lines
! of numbers can be entered.

DIM Ratio(1 to 3, 1 to 3)
MAT INPUT prompt "Enter nine numbers: ": Ratio
PRINT
PRINT "Here is the resulting matrix."
PRINT
MAT PRINT Ratio
END
```

The output results might look as follows:

```
Enter nine numbers: 1,2,3
? 4,5,6,7,8,9

Here is the resulting matrix.

 1  2  3
 4  5  6
 7  8  9
```

If an array has string elements, the MAT LINE INPUT statement is allowed and preferred. Characters are entered into each string element until a carriage return is encountered. The general forms are as follows:

```
MAT LINE INPUT Array1$, Array2$,...
MAT LINE INPUT prompt Prompt$: Array1$, Array2$,...
```

The MAT LINE INPUT PROMPT statement is not very useful, because **it displays the prompt string only for the first item entered**. A single question mark is displayed for each subsequent item (also see the preceding example program). For this reason, you should usually display a line of general input instructions rather than a prompt and then use the plain MAT LINE INPUT statement.

The next example program enters names into an array. Once again the initial size of the array Name$ is set to one. The MAT LINE INPUT statement will accept lines containing commas, such as "John J. Williams, Jr." Note that this statement is used both to redimension the array (by the variable Number in parentheses) and to accept string input.

```
! Example Program 13-7
! Enter names into an array.

DIM Name$(1)
INPUT PROMPT "Number of names to enter? ": Number
PRINT "Enter one name at each ? prompt."
MAT LINE INPUT Name$(Number)
PRINT Number; "names have been entered."
END
```

The following output is produced:

```
Number of names to enter? 3
Enter one name at each ? prompt.
? John
? Betsy
? Linda
 3 names have been entered.
```

The disadvantage of this program is that the user must specify at the beginning how many names will be entered. If you want to enter an unknown number of names into an array, probably the best solution is to dimension the array large enough to hold the maximum number of names and use a special entry to indicate when the last name has been entered. In this case, you must use a loop instead of a MAT statement.

Here is an example:

```
! Example Program 13-8
! Use part of a large array to store names.

DIM Name$(1)
INPUT prompt "Maximum number of names? ": Size
MAT REDIM Name$(Size)
PRINT "After the prompt, press Return key to stop."
LET Count = 1
LET Finished$ = "false"
DO
   LINE INPUT prompt "Name? ": Name$(Count)
   IF Name$(Count) = "" then
     LET Finished$ = "true"
   ELSE
     LET Count = Count + 1
   END IF
```

```
LOOP until Count > 100 or Finished$ = "true"
PRINT (Count - 1); "names have been entered."
END
```

Note that the counter Count is initialized to one and incremented only if a valid name is entered. If you enter a null value for Name$ to stop the entry process, the flag Finished$ is set to true. After exiting the loop, Count will be one larger than the number of names entered and must be decremented by one to equal the actual number of names. Program output looks as follows:

```
Maximum number of names? 20
Press Return key after prompt to stop.
Name? John
Name? Betsy
Name? Linda
Name?
 3 names have been entered.
```

Special redimensioning using the question mark — as demonstrated in a preceding section — is not allowed with the MAT LINE INPUT statement.

The MAT READ Statement

The MAT READ statement is used to read array element values from one or more DATA statements. The general syntax is

```
MAT READ Array1, Array2,...
```

As before, I recommend reading only a single array. The program must contain one or more DATA statements with numeric or string values separated from one another by commas.

If there are more values in the DATA statements than are required by the MAT READ statement, the extra values will be ignored. If there is an insufficient number of values, the error message "Reading past end of data" is displayed.

Here is an example program where only the first four data values are used. The fifth number in the DATA statement is never read.

```
! Example Program 13-9
! Read element values from data statements.

DIM Table(1,1)
PRINT "An array read from DATA statements."
PRINT
MAT READ Table(2,2)
MAT PRINT Table;
```

```
DATA 1,2,3,4,5
END
```

When this program is executed, the following table is displayed:

```
1  2
3  4
```

The MAT READ statement can be used like the MAT INPUT statement to redimension an array.

Other MAT PRINT Statements

The general syntax of the MAT PRINT statement is

```
MAT PRINT Array1, Array2,...
```

This statement first displays Array1, then displays Array2, and so forth. To simplify formatting problems, you should use the MAT PRINT statement to display only a single array.

Commas not only separate the array names — they also specify that the elements in a row be displayed in different print zones.

Another form of the MAT PRINT is

```
MAT PRINT Array1; Array2;...
```

which creates an array whose row elements are separated by only one or two spaces. Note the use of semicolons as separators, specifying that array elements be displayed with only 1 or 2 spaces between them.

It is even possible to use both comma and semicolon separators in the same statement, as follows:

```
MAT PRINT Array1; Array2, Array3;
```

In this case, the elements in the rows of Array1 will be separated by 1 or 2 spaces, those in the rows of Array2 by 16 spaces (or the current print zone width), and those in the rows of Array3 by 1 or 2 spaces. In most cases, however, it is better to display only a single array with each MAT PRINT statement.

A format string, used to control the format of array rows, can be included in the MAT PRINT USING statement. The syntax is

```
MAT PRINT USING Format$: Array1, Array2,...
```

where Format$ is a string constant or variable containing format specifications for displaying the elements in each row.

Here is an example program that displays a two-column array consisting of part numbers and unit prices:

```
! Example Program 13-10
! Display an array of part numbers and prices.

DIM Inventory(1 to 6, 1 to 2)
LET F1$ = "########      #####"
PRINT using F1$: "PART NO.", "PRICE"
PRINT
MAT READ Inventory
LET F2$ = "######      $$$.##"
MAT PRINT using F2$: Inventory

DATA 163151,12.85,177762,33.40,183926,18.75
DATA 205055,7.55,234965,81.60,309835,2.25
END
```

The output looks as follows:

```
PART NO.      PRICE

163151       $12.85
177762       $33.40
183926       $18.75
205055        $7.55
234965       $81.60
309835        $2.25
```

13.4 STORING MATRICES ON FILES

MAT statements can also be used to read matrices from files and to write matrices on files.

The MAT PRINT and MAT INPUT Statements

The general statement to write a matrix on a text file is

```
MAT PRINT #N: Array1, Array2,...
```

This statement writes matrix elements on file #N in the same format that they would be displayed on the screen. The statement has limited usefulness because a file written with this statement cannot be read by a subsequent MAT INPUT statement. You remember that I suggested you write text data files with one item per line and the

MAT PRINT statement violates this principle. Thus the MAT PRINT statement is not used in the example programs that write arrays on text files.

Matrix element values can be read from a text file instead of from the keyboard, provided that they were written on the file in an appropriate format. You can assume one element value per line. The general statements are

```
MAT INPUT #N: Array1, Array2,...
MAT LINE INPUT #N: Array1$, Array2$,...
```

As mentioned earlier, it is usually preferable to read only a single array with either of these statements. The number N is the file or channel number, assigned to a file by the OPEN statement.

In general, the MAT INPUT statement is also of limited usefulness for reading information from sequential text files. You need to know the number of entries in a file so you can dimension an array, read the file entries, and assign them to array elements with a MAT INPUT statement. In order to count the number of entries, you essentially have to go through the file sequentially and read each entry, so you might as well assign its value to an array element at that point. MAT statements are much more useful with record files, as discussed in the following paragraphs.

The MAT WRITE and MAT READ Statements

MAT statements are available to write information on and read information from record files. The statement

```
MAT WRITE #N: Array1, Array2,...
```

writes arrays on a record file, one array element per record. The MAT WRITE statement is usually used with only a single array. The array is written by rows, in odometer order, with element(1,1) being written on the first record, element(1,2) on the second record, and so forth.

The general statement for reading information from a record file is

```
MAT READ #N: Array1, Array2,...
```

and it is also normally used with only a single array.

Here is a simple program to read an array of numbers from DATA statements and write the array on a record file. The record size is set to 8 because the array elements are numbers and each number occupies 8 bytes on a record file.

```
! Example Program 13-11
! Write an array on a record file.

DIM Array(1 to 6)
```

```
INPUT prompt "Name of file? ": FileName$
OPEN #1: name FileName$, create newold
ERASE #1  ! if it already exists
SET #1: RECSIZE 8
MAT READ Array
MAT WRITE #1: Array
CLOSE #1
PRINT "File "; FileName$; " has been written."

DATA 2,5,3,7,5,9
END
```

The preceding program does require that the size of the array and the number of its dimensions be specified, and that these values be compatible with the number of data elements. It produces the following output:

```
Name of file? NUMS.REC
File NUMS.REC has been written.
```

A companion program reads the record file and displays the array:

```
! Example Program 13-12
! Read an array from a record file.

DIM Array(1)
INPUT prompt "Name of file? ": FileName$
OPEN #1: name FileName$
ASK #1: FILESIZE Size
MAT REDIM Array(Size)
MAT READ #1: Array
PRINT
MAT PRINT Array;
END
```

Note in this case that it is not necessary to specify a record size because the file has already been created. A one-dimensional array is assumed. The trailing semicolon in the MAT PRINT statement displays the array in a compact format.

```
Name of file? NUMS.REC

 2  5  3  7  5  9
```

The size of the array can be determined if it is a one-dimensional array, but it is not possible to determine the number of dimensions. The contents of the test file, NUMS.REC, could just as well have been the element values of a 2-by-3 array as a 6-by-1 array

Three points on using MAT statements are worth repeating:

1. I recommend using a single array with each of these statements. The resulting program is simpler and easier to understand.

2. In some cases, MAT statements create the best and simplest program; in other cases, a loop is required. You should use whichever structure is most appropriate.

3. A powerful feature of the MAT statements is their ability to redimension arrays, using a constant, variable, or expression to change the size of any dimension.

13.5   MATRIX ARITHMETIC

A set of mathematical rules exists that allows you to manipulate matrices in much the same way that you manipulate numbers. You can assign a value to a matrix, which means assigning a value to every element of the matrix. You can use the common arithmetic operations of addition, subtraction, multiplication, and division with matrices, but with some restrictions and differences from number arithmetic.

Matrix arithmetic is useful in solving certain scientific and specialized business problems. Some of the simpler operations of matrix arithmetic and their implementation in True BASIC are presented. If you are interested in learning more, I suggest that you read a book on matrix arithmetic like Thomas and Finney, *Calculus and Analytic Geometry*, 7th Edition (Addison-Wesley, 1988).

Matrix Assignments

The element values of one matrix can be assigned to the corresponding elements of another matrix. For example, if both A and B are matrices with two rows and columns, the statement

```
MAT A = B
```

assigns the value of B(1, 1) to A(1, 1), the value of B(1,2) to A(1, 2), and so forth. Here is an example program that demonstrates matrix assignment:

```
! Example program 13-13
! Matrix assignment.

DIM A(2,2), B(2,2)
PRINT "Type in the 4 element values for matrix B."
MAT INPUT B
```

```
MAT A = B
PRINT
PRINT "Here is matrix A after assigning B to A."
PRINT
MAT PRINT A;
END
```

The following output is produced:

```
Type in the element values for matrix B.
? 7,1,-2,8

Here is matrix A after assigning B to A.

 7  1
-2  8
```

You must watch out for one special feature of the matrix assignment statement. The matrix assignment statement can redimension a matrix. Remember that redimensioning can change only the size of a dimension (which it does by changing one or both bounds), not the number of dimensions. The best way to demonstrate this feature is to write the previous example with a different matrix B. Here is the new example program:

```
! Example program 13-14
! Matrix assignment with redimensioning.

DIM A(2,2), B(2,3)
PRINT "Matrix A is 2 x 2, matrix B is 2 x 3."
PRINT "Type in the 6 element values for matrix B."
MAT INPUT B
MAT A = B
PRINT
PRINT "Here is matrix A after assigning B to A."
PRINT
MAT PRINT A;
END
```

Note that matrix B is dimensioned as a 2-by-3 matrix. When you run the program, you have to enter six numbers to assign values to all the elements in B, as shown:

```
Type in the element values for matrix B.
? 7,1,5,-2,8,3

Here is matrix A after assigning B to A.

 7  1  5
-2  8  3
```

The matrix assignment statement (MAT A = B) redimensions matrix A so that it is changed to a 2-by-3 matrix. The program then displays matrix A.

Matrix redimensioning is both a blessing and a curse. The ability to redimension a matrix with the MAT INPUT or MAT READ statements is a powerful and useful feature of True BASIC. Automatic redimensioning in a matrix assignment statement, however, can lead to unexpected results. When assigning the values of one matrix to another, you should make sure that both matrices are of the same size so that redimensioning does not occur.

You can also use the matrix assignment statement to assign the same value to every element in an array. The value can be a constant or the value of a variable or an expression. Here is an example program:

```
! Example Program 13-15
! Assign a value to each array element.

DIM Table$(3,3)
MAT Table$ = ("xxxx")
MAT PRINT Table$
END
```

This program produces the following display:

```
xxxx            xxxx            xxxx
xxxx            xxxx            xxxx
xxxx            xxxx            xxxx
```

The parentheses around "xxxx" are not required in this case, but they are required if the expression on the right side of the assignment statement is anything other than a constant or a simple variable.

Special Matrices and Matrix Properties

There are several special matrices that have not yet been mentioned. The *identity matrix* is a square matrix (same number of rows and columns) with element values of one along the principal diagonal (from upper left corner to lower right corner) and element values of zero elsewhere. This matrix is created by the Idn function.

```
! Example Program 13-16
! Create an identity matrix.

DIM A(3,3)
MAT A = Idn
MAT PRINT A;
END
```

Here is the program output:

```
1  0  0
0  1  0
0  0  1
```

The value of any matrix remains unchanged when it is multiplied by the identity matrix.

The *transpose* of a matrix is that matrix with its rows and columns interchanged. This matrix is created by the Trn function.

```
! Example Program 13-17
! Create the transpose of a matrix.

DIM A(2,3), B(3,2)
MAT READ A
MAT B = Trn(A)
PRINT "Original matrix"
MAT PRINT A;
PRINT "Transpose matrix"
MAT PRINT B;

DATA 2,5,1,3,6,2
END
```

This program produces the following output:

```
Original matrix
 2  5  1
 3  6  2

Transpose matrix
 2  3
 5  6
 1  2
```

Note that the arrays A and B must be properly dimensioned for one to be the transpose of the other.

A square matrix has a value associated with it called its *determinant*. If the determinant of a matrix is zero, there are certain restrictions on how that matrix may be used. The function Det(A) returns the determinant of the matrix A.

```
! Example Program 13-18
! Calculate the determinant of a matrix.

DIM A(3,3)
MAT READ A
PRINT "Matrix A"
MAT PRINT A;
PRINT "Its determinant is "; Det(A)

DATA 2,5,1,3,6,2,2,5,7
END
Program output is shown:
Matrix A
 2  5  1
 3  6  2
 2  5  7

Its determinant is -18
```

Matrix Addition and Subtraction

Adding two matrices means adding the values of the corresponding elements of the two matrices. If B and C are both 2-by-2 matrices, you create the sum matrix A with the statement

```
MAT A = B + C
```

where $A(1, 1) = B(1, 1) + C(1, 1)$, $A(1, 2) = B(1, 2) + C(1, 2)$, and so forth.

Matrices B and C must have the same number of dimensions and each dimension must be of the same size. If needed, matrix A will be redimensioned to the size of B and C, but as in the case of assignment, I recommend avoiding such redimensioning. Here is an example program:

```
! Example Program 13-19
! Matrix addition.

DIM A(2,2), B(2,2), C(2,2)
PRINT "Read matrix B from a DATA statement."
MAT READ B
PRINT "Type in 4 element values for matrix C."
MAT INPUT C
MAT A = B + C
PRINT
PRINT "Matrix B"
MAT PRINT B;
```

```
PRINT "Matrix C"
MAT PRINT C;
PRINT "Matrix A after adding matrices B and C."
MAT PRINT A;

DATA 3,3,3,3
END
```

The following program output is displayed:

```
Read matrix B from a DATA statement.
Type in 4 element values for matrix C.
? 1,2,-3,5

Matrix B
 3  3
 3  3

Matrix C
 1  2
-3  5

Matrix A after adding matrices B and C.
 4  5
 0  8
```

Subtraction is similar to addition, so here is a program that does both addition and subtraction:

```
! Example Program 13-20
! Matrix addition and subtraction.

DIM A(2,2), B(2,2), C(2,2), D(2,2)
PRINT "Read matrices B, C, and D."
MAT READ B, C, D
PRINT "Matrix B"
MAT PRINT B;
PRINT "Matrix C"
MAT PRINT C;
PRINT "Matrix D"
MAT PRINT D;
MAT A = B + C
MAT A = A - D
PRINT "Matrix A = B + C - D."
MAT PRINT A;

DATA 1,2,3,5
```

```
DATA 2,1,1,2
DATA 3,7,1,4
END
```

This program displays the resulting matrix A, as shown:

```
Read matrices B, C, D.
Matrix B
 1  2
 3  5
Matrix C
 2  1
 1  2

Matrix D
 3  7
 1  4

Matrix A = B + C - D
 0 -4
 3  3
```

Note that a single expression like MAT A = B + C - D is not allowed. Only two matrices are permitted on the right side of the MAT expression and thus two MAT statements are needed to accomplish the addition and subtraction. You should check the results yourself by hand or calculator.

Matrix Multiplication and Division

Multiplication of two matrices is allowed only under certain conditions. Division of one matrix by another is not defined, but there is an equivalent process of multiplying one matrix by the inverse of another matrix. These operations really cannot be understood without some background in matrix arithmetic and will not be discussed further.

You should know, however, that True BASIC does have statements for multiplying two matrices and for inverting a matrix. If you need to use either of these operations, consult the previously recommended book on matrix arithmetic and the *True BASIC Reference Manual*.

Multiplying a matrix by a single constant, variable, or expression means multiplying each element of the matrix by the same value. The syntax is

```
MAT A = N * B
```

where N is a constant, variable, or expression and B is a matrix. Note that N must come before B; the statement MAT A = B * N is not allowed. If N is an expression, it must be enclosed in parentheses.

Here is an example program where a list of prices is read from DATA statements and each price is increased by 20 percent — that is, multiplied by 1.2:

```
! Example Program 13-21
! Multiply an array by a constant.

DIM Price(4)
LET Increase = 20  ! percent increase
MAT READ Price
MAT Price = (1 + Increase/100) * Price
MAT PRINT Price
DATA 12.45, 13.95, 8.40, 2.95
END
```

The following results are displayed:

14.94	16.74	10.08	3.54

Summary of Important Points

- Accessing array elements in odometer order means accessing the elements so that the last index varies the fastest. In a two-dimensional array, this means accessing the elements by row, from left to right.

- The MAT INPUT and MAT READ statements assign values to array elements in odometer order.

- Any MAT INPUT or MAT READ statement can be used to redimension an array.

- The MAT PRINT and MAT WRITE statements read values from array elements in odometer order.

- The statement MAT INPUT Array(?) is a special form of redimensioning allowed only with one-dimensional arrays of numeric values.

- The MAT LINE INPUT PROMPT statement displays its prompt only before the first element value is entered, not before subsequent values.

- The MAT PRINT # statement has only limited usefulness because a text file written with this statement cannot be read by a MAT INPUT # statement.

- We recommend using only a single array variable with the MAT INPUT, MAT READ, MAT PRINT, and MAT WRITE statements.

- The matrix assignment statement can be used to redimension an array.

Common Errors

- Reading or writing more than one matrix in a single MAT statement. This is valid but can cause confusion. It is poor programming practice.

- Allowing automatic matrix redimensioning to occur in a MAT assignment statement when you do not want the size of the matrix to change.

- Trying to add two matrices of different sizes, or trying to add more than two matrices in a single MAT statement.

- Using the wrong order of items when multiplying a matrix by a constant. The constant must pre-multiply (be to the left of) the matrix.

Self-Test Questions

1. What is the difference, if any, between a matrix and an array?

2. In what order does the MAT INPUT statement assign values to array elements?

3. What are the differences, if any, between the displays produced by the two following statements?

   ```
   MAT PRINT Array;
   MAT PRINT Array
   ```

4. What is meant by the term "odometer order"?

5. (a) Is MAT INPUT Line$(?) a valid statement?
   (b) Is MAT INPUT Line(?) a valid statement?

6. Given an array dimensioned by DIM Name$(100), does the statement

   ```
   MAT LINE INPUT prompt "Name? ": Name$
   ```

   display the prompt before each name is entered?

7. In what format does the statement

   ```
   MAT PRINT #1: Name$
   ```

   store the elements of Name$ on file #1?

8. In what format does the statement

   ```
   MAT LINE INPUT #1: Name$
   ```

expect to find the individual name values stored in file #1?

9. The statement

    ```
    MAT WRITE #1: Array
    ```

    is used to write an array on what type of file?

10. Are the following statements valid?

    (a)   `MAT A = B + C`

    (b)   `MAT A = B + C + D`

    (c)   `MAT A = B - C + D`

11. In the statement MAT X = Y + Z, must

    (a)   array Y be the same size as array X?

    (b)   array Y be the same size as array Z?

12. If A and B are arrays and N is a simple variable, are these statements allowed?

    (a)   `MAT A = B * N`

    (b)   `MAT A = N * B`

13. What record size is required for a record file designed to store values of numeric variables?

Practice Programs

Use MAT statements wherever possible in these programs.

1. A record file named CLIENTS.REC, with a record length of 40 bytes, contains name strings. These names are stored in the reverse format (last name, first name), with a comma serving as the field separator. Assume no other commas in the string.

    Open the file and determine the number of records. Transfer all names from the file to a redimensioned array. Write a modified array with the names in normal format (first name preceding last name). Display the names in the modified array on the screen.

2. A text file named EXPENSES.DAT contains expense categories (strings) and expense values (numbers), stored one item per line. The first line in the file contains a value representing the number of different expense categories. A sample file might contain the following information:

    3
    Labor
    32248.50

Feed
6742.82
Fertilizer
13840.00

Transfer all items from the file to a redimensioned array with two columns, one for expense categories and the other for expense values. Display an expense report in the following format:

```
Farm Expenses

Labor           $32248.50
Feed            $6742.82
Fertilizer      $13840.00
```

3. A record file named PRICES.REC contains a long list of prices, one per record. Due to inflation, all prices must be increased by 11.4 percent. Modify the file so that it contains the new prices.

4. Modify the PRICES.REC file discussed in Practice Program 3, decreasing all prices by 4.3 percent and adding a handling charge of $2.00 to each price.

5. Sales by division for the current year are shown in the Fig. 13.1:

Division	1st	2nd	3rd	4th
1	3.6	3.7	3.8	3.6
2	1.7	1.5	1.9	2.0
3	5.1	4.8	4.9	5.2
4	1.0	1.0	0.9	1.1
5	8.5	8.5	8.5	8.4
6	5.2	5.4	5.6	5.8

Sales per Quarters (million $)

Figure 13.1   Sales per quarter by division.

Assuming that each division is required to produce an increase of 9 percent in sales next year, calculate and display a revised table of estimated quarterly sales, using the same display format.

Calculate and display the row and column totals for this revised table, with appropriate labels.

6. Libraries are discussed in Chapter 7. Sorting is discussed in Chapter 11. If you have access to the True BASIC Sorting and Searching Toolkit, you might try this problem. It uses the library named SORTLIB.TRC on PCs or SortLib* on Macs. These are both compiled libraries, the source code is in SORTLIB.TRU and SortLib.

CHAPTER
14

An Indexed
Database Program

14.1   INTRODUCTION

This presentation of True BASIC concludes with another database program that brings together many of the concepts and techniques discussed in the previous chapters. You have a chance to examine some points that are different from the example database program in Chapter 9, but there are many areas of similarity. In particular, you are introduced to the concept of separate index files.

14.2   AN INVENTORY DATA FILE

This example program accesses a file of inventory information. The inventory file is a record file, with all information on different inventory parts stored in a record as a fixed-length string of 84 characters or bytes. Each item of information in the record is called a *field* and there are eight fields in each record. These fields are fixed-length substrings of the record string.

If you are using Version 3, you might wonder if the program could be simplified by using a random file. The answer is probably yes but I wanted to use a file structure that would work with all versions of True BASIC. An interesting exercise for an ambitious student would be to solve the problem presented in this chapter using a file with random organization.

In Figure 14.1 we show an outline of the inventory file record, showing the name and length of each field:

Field Name	Length in bytes
Part Number	6
Description	20
Quantity	8
Unit Price	8
Bin Number	4
Reorder Amount	8
Vendor Name	20
Vendor Phone	10
	84

Figure 14.1 Structure of inventory file record.

The part number is used as the primary identifier of a particular part. Because the inventory file is a large file, another file — an index file —is maintained to tell you which record in the inventory file contains the information on a particular part. In this application, the part number field is called the *key field*.

14.3 USING AN INDEX FILE

The index file is another record file with fixed-length records. To understand the concept and use of an index file, remember that one of the fastest ways to search a file or array is a binary search, but this search only works if the file or array is in sorted order. You could sort your inventory file on any field, say, part number, but each time you added a new part, you would have to sort the file again. This is not a fast process because the file is long and the record size is large. Moreover, if you wanted to search for a part by its description, you would have to sort the inventory file again by description.

As an alternative, you can create another file, called an index file, that has small records containing only the part number and the record number. This file can be sorted more quickly than the inventory file. When you search the index file for a part number, you find the inventory file record number for that particular part and you can then access the record directly. The index file gets its name because it is similar to an index in a book — it tells you which record in a file contains the desired information.

An even greater advantage with this type of organization is that you can have more than one index file. In addition to an index file that is sorted by part number, you can maintain another index file containing description and record number, and sorted by description. You can search this second index file for a particular description and find the corresponding record number in the inventory file.

Here is how the information in the part number index file might look, displayed in an expanded form:

Part Number	Record Number
123161	15
202571	7
209115	113
399417	1
576102	23

Figure 14.2 Information in the part number index file.

As you see, you can easily determine the record number for any given part number. The part numbers are in sorted order, but not the record numbers. These record numbers are sometimes called *pointers* because they point to or indicate the record where information is stored for a particular part number.

Because the index file is a smaller file than the inventory file, it is often possible to read the index file into an array in memory and carry out the binary search in memory rather than on disk. This technique produces a much faster search.

14.4   PROGRAM OUTLINE

You should design your program as a menu-driven program. The example program has a main program unit and several procedure units. Only three commands (plus a stop command) are included in the menu and each command is executed from a separate subroutine. Other commands can be added later and are discussed in the practice programs at the end of the chapter.

Here is an outline of the Main program unit:

    name inventory and index files
    open both files
    determine array size and read index file into array
    begin loop
            display the command menu
            select a command: Quit, Edit, List, or Search
            branch to appropriate subprogram
    end loop if command is Quit

The Edit command allows a user to change any field — except the part number — in a specified record. If you don't know the record number, you can use the Search command to find the record number corresponding to a given part number. A part number cannot be edited because a part number change would require sorting the index file again, a complication you should avoid in the first version of this program.

Information is stored in each inventory file record in a packed format to conserve space. *Packing* means storing the individual field strings as closely together as possible in the record. *Unpacking* means extracting the field values from a packed record. The procedures for packing and unpacking records arediscussed later in the chapter.

Here is an outline of the Edit subroutine:

        get record number
        get field number
        if requested, display field names and numbers
        read record from inventory file
        unpack record string
        begin loop
                display old field value
                enter new field value
        end loop when finished editing
        pack record string
        write new record to inventory file
        return to menu

The List command displays the contents of the inventory file. Each record is read, unpacked, and displayed on the screen. The List subroutine outline follows:

        begin loop
                read record from inventory file
                unpack record string
                display record number and record fields
        end loop at end of inventory file
        return to menu

The Search command uses a binary search to look in the index array for the record number corresponding to a specified part number. If the record exists, it is read, unpacked, and displayed. Here is the Search subroutine outline:

        get part number
        search index array for record number
        if record exists
                read record from inventory file
                unpack record string
                display record number
                display record fields

else
          display failure-to-find message
   return to menu

14.5   THE MAIN PROGRAM

Two subroutines, in addition to the command subroutines, are called from the main program. The subroutine OpenFile asks the user for the names of the inventory and index files. Both files are opened using error-trapping routines. This version of the program assumes that both files have already been created and loaded with information. Commands for creating a new file and for adding information to a file are discussed in the Practice Programs at the end of the chapter.

If a file does not exist, the user is asked to try again because the problem may be that the file name was misspelled. If that is not the problem, the user may type in the letter "Q" to abort the program.

The size of the index file is determined and the index file is read into an array named Index$. Note the use of the MAT READ statement to read the file and to redimension the array to the file size.

The subroutine Menu is called next and the menu is displayed. The CASE statement is used to call the selected command subroutine. If an invalid command is entered, an error message is printed and the menu is displayed again.

```
! Example Program 14-1
! Inventory record file with index.

CLEAR
! Open the inventory and index files.
CALL OpenFile ("Name of inventory file? ", #1)
CALL OpenFile ("Name of index file? ", #2)
! Initialize variables and constants.
DIM Index$(1)
ASK #2: FILESIZE Size     ! ask for size of index file
MAT READ #2: Index$(Size) ! store index in an array
LET Indent = 20

DO  ! begin main program loop
   CLEAR
   CALL Menu (Command$, Indent) ! display the menu
   LET Command$ = Ucase$(Command$[1:1])
   SELECT CASE Command$
```

```
        CASE "E"
            CALL Edit (#1, Index$, Size)
        CASE "L"
            CALL List (#1, Index$, Size, Indent)
        CASE "S"
            CALL Search (#1, Index$, Size, Indent)
        CASE "Q"
            ! Quit command, do nothing
        CASE ELSE
            PRINT
            PRINT Tab(Indent); "Please enter E, L, S, or Q."
            PRINT Tab(Indent); "Press any key to continue."
            GET KEY Dummy
    END SELECT
LOOP until Command$ = "Q"
CLOSE #1
CLOSE #2
END  ! of main program

SUB OpenFile (Prompt$, #9)
    ! Open a file or abort the program.
    ! A file cannot have the name "Q".
    DO
        LINE INPUT prompt Prompt$: Fname$
        LET Fname$ = Ucase$(Fname$)
        IF Fname$ = "Q" then STOP ! direct program exit
        LET NoFile$ = "false"
        WHEN error in
            OPEN #9: name Fname$
        USE
            PRINT "File "; Fname$; " does not exist."
            PRINT "Please check spelling and try again";
            PRINT "or type Q to quit. "
            PRINT
            LET NoFile$ = "true"
        END WHEN
    LOOP until NoFile$ = "false"
END SUB  ! OpenFile

SUB Menu (Choice$, Indent)
    ! Display the command menu.
    PRINT Tab(Indent); "    Command Menu"
    PRINT
    PRINT Tab(Indent); "E.....Edit a record"
    PRINT Tab(Indent); "L.....List all records"
```

```
      PRINT Tab(Indent); "S.....Search for a part number"
      PRINT Tab(Indent); "Q.....Quit the program"
      PRINT
      PRINT Tab(Indent); "Your selection.....";
      LINE INPUT prompt "": Choice$
  END SUB  ! Menu
```

14.6 THE EDIT COMMAND

The user is asked to enter a record number that is checked to make sure it is within the allowed range. The inventory file record is read and unpacked. The user is then asked to specify the field number to be edited in this record. Entering a field number of zero produces a display of the field names and associated field numbers.

Only field numbers between 2 and 8 can be edited because field number 1 is the key field — the part number. In each case, the old field value is displayed and a new field value is requested. If the user presses the Return key, the old field value is retained.

The process repeats and the user can change other field values. If a field number of -1 is entered, the process stops. The record is packed again and written back on the inventory file.

Figure 14.3 is a diagram showing a typical file record with each field designated by its field number. Note that the field substrings have varying lengths.

Figure 14.3 *Schematic diagram of a file record.*

You should examine the packing and unpacking process in detail. Each field is stored on the inventory file as a fixed-length substring. The eight substrings are concatenated into a record string of 84 characters. Each field is displayed, in regular string format, as an element of a *string array* named Field$. The Pack subroutine converts the elements of the string array Field$ into a single record string Entry$. The Unpack subroutine converts Entry$ back into the elements of array Field$.

Several functions are used in the Pack and Unpack subroutines. The user-defined function FixLen$(Str$, N) adds trailing blanks to the string Str$. It returns a substring, N characters long, of the resulting string. This function can handle a string of any length. If Str$ is longer than N characters, it is truncated to N characters.

Two new functions for converting between numbers and strings are introduced — in addition to the Str$ and Val functions discussed in Chapter 5. The Num$(N) function converts a number N into an eight-byte string that stores the number in an internal string format. In contrast to the string produced by the Str$ function, **a string produced by the Num$ function cannot be displayed**. The latter string is always exactly eight bytes long, however, and thus allows any number to be stored in an eight-character substring. The complementary function, Num(N$), converts a string of this type back into a regular numeric variable.

For example, if the value of Num$(N) is assigned to the variable N$, then the value of Num(N$) is equal to N.

Looking at the description of your inventory file record, notice that Part Number is always six characters long and is handled as a string. Quantity, Unit Price, and Reorder Amount are all numbers and are stored in the internal string format produced by the Num$ function. They are converted to regular or variable-length strings for display. The two strings Description and Vendor Name have trailing blanks added to create fixed-length strings of 20 characters. You can assume these two strings are originally 20 characters or less in length; if not, they are truncated to 20 characters. Vendor Phone is stored as a string of 10 characters, but displayed as a 12-character string in the format 123-123-1234.

Although you do not use the index file in the Edit subroutine, you should know how it is formatted. The record is 14 characters long and contains two strings. The first six characters are the Part Number, stored as a regular string that is always 6 characters long because part numbers always contain exactly 6 digits. The last eight characters are the record number, stored in the internal string format produced by the Num$ function.

Here is the Edit subroutine with the auxiliary subroutines Pack and Unpack:

```
SUB Edit (#9, Index$(), Size)
    ! Edit a specified record.
    CLEAR
    DIM Field$(8)
    DO
        INPUT prompt "What record number? ": Rec
        IF Rec < 1 or Rec > Size then
            PRINT
            PRINT "Record numbers from 1 to"; Size; "."
            PRINT
        END IF
    LOOP while Rec < 1 or Rec > Size
    SET #9: RECORD Rec ! go to selected record
    READ #9: Entry$    ! and read its contents
```

```
      CALL Unpack (Entry$, Field$)
      PRINT
      PRINT "Enter 0 for a list of record fields."
      PRINT "Enter -1 to stop editing this record."

      ! Select field for editing.
      DO
         PRINT "What field number in record"; Rec;
         INPUT prompt "? ": FieldNum
         SELECT CASE FieldNum
         CASE 0
             PRINT
             PRINT "1.  Part Number"
             PRINT "2.  Description"
             PRINT "3.  Quantity"
             PRINT "4.  Unit Price"
             PRINT "5.  Bin Number"
             PRINT "6.  Reorder Amt."
             PRINT "7.  Vendor Name"
             PRINT "8.  Vendor Phone"
             PRINT
         CASE 1
             PRINT
             PRINT "The part number cannot be edited."
             PRINT
         CASE 2 to 8
             PRINT
             PRINT "Old Value:  "; Field$(FieldNum)
             PRINT "New Value:  ";
             LINE INPUT prompt "": Value$
             IF Value$ <> "" then
                LET Field$(FieldNum) = Value$
             END IF
             PRINT
         CASE  ELSE
             PRINT
             PRINT "Only fields 2 thru 8 can be edited."
             PRINT
         END SELECT
      LOOP until FieldNum < 0
      CALL Pack (Entry$, Field$)
      RESET #9: same    ! go back to beginning of record
      WRITE #9: Entry$ ! and rewrite record
END SUB  ! Edit
```

```
SUB Unpack (Entry$, Field$())
    ! Unpack a packed record.
    LET Field$(1) = Entry$[1:6]
    LET Field$(2) = Trim$(Entry$[7:26])
    LET Field$(3) = Str$(num(Entry$[27:34]))
    LET Field$(4) = Str$(num(Entry$[35:42]))
    LET Field$(5) = Entry$[43:46]
    LET Field$(6) = Str$(num(Entry$[47:54]))
    LET Field$(7) = Trim$(Entry$[55:74])
    LET FirstPart$ = Entry$[75:77] & "-" & Entry$[78:80]
    LET Field$(8) = FirstPart & "-" & Entry$[81:84]
END SUB   ! Unpack

SUB Pack (Entry$, Field$())
    ! Pack an unpacked record.
    DEF FixLen$(Str$, N) = (Str$ & Repeat$(" ", N))[1:N]
    LET Entry$[1:6] = Field$(1)
    LET Entry$[7:26] = FixLen$(Field$(2), 20)
    LET Entry$[27:34] = Num$(Val(Field$(3)))
    LET Entry$[35:42] = Num$(Val(Field$(4)))
    LET Entry$[43:46] = Field$(5)
    LET Entry$[47:54] = Num$(Val(Field$(6)))
    LET Entry$[55:74] = FixLen$(Field$(7), 20)
    LET FirstPart$ = Field$(8)[1:3] & Field$(8)[5:7]
    LET Entry$[75:84] = FirstPart$ & Field$(8)[9:12]
END SUB   ! Pack
```

14.7   THE LIST COMMAND

The List command simply reads each record from the inventory file and displays the record number and the record fields on the screen. It pauses after displaying each record and continues when any key is pressed. It calls a subroutine named PrintRec to display a record, and PrintRec in turn calls the subroutine Unpack to convert the record string to an array of display strings. PrintRec displays both the name of each field and the field value.

```
SUB List (#9, Index$(), Size, Indent)
    ! List the contents of the inventory file.
    CLEAR
    RESET #9: begin
    FOR I = 1 to (Size - 1)
        LET Rec = Num(Index$(I)[7:14])
        CALL PrintRec (#9, Rec, Indent)
```

```
            PRINT "Press any key to continue."
            GET KEY Dummy
        NEXT I

        ! Display the last record.
        LET Rec = Num(Index$(I)[7:14])
        CALL PrintRec (#9, Rec, Indent)
        PRINT "Press any key to return to menu."
        GET KEY Dummy
    END SUB  ! List

    SUB PrintRec (#9, Rec, Indent)
        ! Display a specified record.
        DIM Field$(8)
        SET #9: RECORD Rec
        PRINT "Record"; Rec
        PRINT
        READ #9: Entry$
        CALL Unpack (Entry$, Field$)
        PRINT "Part Number"; Tab(Indent); Field$(1)
        PRINT "Description"; Tab(Indent); Field$(2)
        PRINT "Quantity"; Tab(Indent); Field$(3)
        PRINT "Unit Price"; Tab(Indent); Field$(4)
        PRINT "Bin Number"; Tab(Indent); Field$(5)
        PRINT "Reorder Amt."; Tab(Indent); Field$(6)
        PRINT "Vendor Name"; Tab(Indent); Field$(7)
        PRINT "Vendor Phone"; Tab(Indent); Field$(8)
        PRINT
    END SUB  ! PrintRec
```

14.8   THE SEARCH COMMAND

A primary purpose of this program is to provide a fast way to search for a specified inventory record. The record is specified by part number and the index array is used to determine the corresponding record number. A binary search technique is used to search the index array. This Search procedure is somewhat specialized in the way it handles substrings and so is included as part of the search subroutine instead of as a separate subroutine.

The user enters a part number that must contain six digits. A failure message is displayed if the record for that part number cannot be found. If the record is found, it is displayed with the PrintRec subroutine.

```
SUB Search (#9, Index$(), Size, Indent)
    ! Search for a record using part number index.
    CLEAR
    DO
        INPUT prompt "Part number to find? ": Look$
        IF Len(Look$) <> 6 then
            PRINT
            PRINT "Part number consists of 6 digits."
            PRINT
        END IF
    LOOP until Len(Look$) = 6

    ! Binary search.
    LET Left = 1
    LET Right = Size
    LET Found$ = "false"
    DO
        LET Mid = Round((Left + Right)/2)
        IF Look$ = Index$(Mid)[1:6] then
            LET Result = Num(Index$(Mid)[7:14])
            LET Found$ = "true"
        ELSEIF Look$ > Index$(Mid)[1:6] then
            LET Left = Mid + 1
        ELSE
            LET Right = Mid -1
        END IF
    LOOP until Found$ = "true" or Right < Left
    PRINT
    IF Found$ = "true" then
        CALL PrintRec (#9, Result, Indent)
    ELSE
        PRINT "Part number is not in the file."
    END IF
    PRINT "Press any key to return to menu.";
    GET KEY Dummy
END SUB  ! Search
```

The disk of example programs provided with the book includes both an index file and an inventory file that are designed to be used with this program. The inventory file is named PARTS.DAT and the index file is named XPARTS.DAT. You should run the program with these files. Ways to expand this example program are suggested in several of the practice programs.

Practice Programs

All the practice programs consist of enhancements or modifications to the example database program in this chapter.

1. Write a Delete command subroutine to delete a record from the inventory file. Write a null string on the specified inventory record. This empty record in the inventory file does no harm, although it wastes some space.

    Remove the corresponding entry from the index file (or index array) and adjust that file so there is no empty record. Do you need to sort the index file again?

2. Modify the Delete command to allow a specified range of records to be deleted.

    3.Write an Add command subroutine to add additional records to the inventory file. You should prompt the user with the field name for each field. As minimum error checking, make sure that numeric fields are valid numbers and that the part number contains exactly six digits.

    Ask the user to confirm the accuracy of a complete record before writing it on the file. Add an appropriate entry to the index file for each new inventory record. After you have finished adding records, be sure to sort the index file.

4. Write a Create command subroutine to create a new inventory file. After the inventory file and index file have been opened, call the Add command subroutine to start adding new inventory records.

5. Modify the PrintRec subroutine to allow optional printed reports on an attached printer. Add another parameter to specify whether the report should be displayed or printed. If you use networked printers, send your report to a text file for later printing.

6. Write a Vendor command subroutine to display or print the records of all parts supplied by a specified vendor.

7. Write a Reorder command subroutine to display or print all records of parts whose quantity is less than or equal to the reorder amount. The resulting report might be used as the basis for ordering new stock.

8. Write a CleanUp command subroutine to purge all empty records from the inventory file. You may have to create and sort a new index file.

9. Enhance the Edit command so that all fields including the key field (part number) can be edited. Remember to sort the index file if the key field is changed.

PART 4

Appendices

Specifications and Limits

PC Limits	without 80x87	with 80x87
Accuracy of numbers	14 digits	16 digits
Accuracy of functions (sin, cos, tan, atn, log, exp)	10 digits	16 digits
Smallest positive number (Eps(0))	5.5626846e-309	2.2250739e-308
Largest positive number (Maxnum)	1.7976931e+308	
Maximum string length	65,528 characters	
Maximum number of files open at one time	5 fewer than DOS limit	
Maximum number of dimensions in an array	255	

Mac Limits	without 68881/2	with 68881/2
Accuracy of numbers	14 digits	16 digits
Accuracy of functions (sin, cos, tan, atn, log, exp)	10 digits	16 digits
Smallest positive number (Eps(0))	5.56268e-309	4.94066e-324
Largest positive number (Maxnum)	1.79769e+308	
Maximum string length	16,777,215 characters	
Maximum number of files open at one time	25	
Maximum number of dimensions in an array	255	

True BASIC Limits | **Versions 1 and 2** | **Version 3**

True BASIC Limits	Versions 1 and 2	Version 3
Maximum length of variable names	31 characters	unlimited
Maximum line number or label	999999	
Maximum number of channels open at one time	25	
Maximum ZONEWIDTH	Maxnum	
Default ZONEWIDTH	16 columns	
Maximum MARGIN	Maxnum	

APPENDIX

B

Special Keys

B.1   SPECIAL KEYS FOR PC USERS

Editing Keys

left arrow	moves cursor one character to the left
right arrow	moves cursor one character to the right
tab	moves cursor one word to the right
shift tab	moves cursor one word to the left
up arrow	moves cursor up one line
down arrow	moves cursor down one line
Home	moves cursor to start of the program
End	moves cursor to end of the program
Ctrl left arrow	moves cursor to start of the current line
Ctrl right arrow	moves cursor to end of the current line
PgDn	displays next page in the editing window
PgUp	displays previous page in the editing window
Del	deletes the character under the cursor; if on line tag, deletes the entire line.
backspace	deletes character to left of cursor; if on line tag, joins line to end of previous line
Ctrl End	deletes characters from cursor to end of line
Ctrl Home	deletes word to left of cursor
Ctrl PgUp	deletes word to right of cursor

Editing Keys *(continued)*

Ins	switches between insert and overwrite mode; insert mode: small underline cursor; overwrite mode: large box cursor.
>	on line tag, indents line or marked block
>	on line tag, un-indents line or marked block

Function Keys

F1	moves cursor into the editing window
F2	moves cursor into the command window
F3	finds a word between the cursor and end of program
F4	marks a program line or block of lines; press F4 again to unmark a line or block
F5	copies marked lines from one location to another
F6	moves marked lines from one location to another
F7	undeletes the last item deleted
F8	sets and removes breakpoints
F9	runs the current program
F10	provides help on use of commands

Type HELP or press the F10 key for further information on use of the FIND, MARK, COPY, MOVE, and UNDELETE commands.

B.2 PULL-DOWN MENUS AND SHORTCUT KEYS FOR PC USERS (Version 3)

The File Menu

Command	Shortcut	Function
New	Alt-N	opens a new program file
Open	Alt-O	opens a saved program file
Switch	Alt-L	switches to another open program file
Close	Alt-W	closes an open program file
Save	Alt-S	saves the current program file
Save As	Alt-Z	saves the current program file under a new name
Unsave	Alt-H	deletes a program file from the disk
Print	Alt-P	lists the current file on a printer
Quit	Alt-Q	exits True BASIC

The Edit Menu

Command	Shortcut	Function
Cut	Alt-X	deletes and moves marked text to the clipboard
Copy	Alt-C	copies marked text to the clipboard
Paste	Alt-V	inserts clipboard text ahead of the current text cursor position
Find	Alt-F	looks for a specified word or phrase
Find Again	Alt-G	looks for the next occurrence of the previously found word or phrase
Change	Alt-E	changes a specified word or phrase to another specified word or phrase
Keep	Alt-K	retains only a specified portion of the current program file
Include		inserts a saved file ahead of the current text cursor position
Edit		edits a specified procedure or block of text

The Edit Menu *(continued)*

Command	Shortcut	Function
Select		marks a specified procedure or block of text
Move To	Alt-Y	moves the text cursor to a specified line of text

The Custom Menu

Command	Shortcut	Function
Load		loads a library file into the workspace
Forget		clears all nonessential memory
Script		executes a specified script file
Do		executes a specified preprocessor
Do Format	Alt-D	executes the formatting preprocessor
Do Trace		executes the tracing (debugging) preprocessor

The Run Menu

Command	Shortcut	Function
Run	Alt-R	compiles and runs the current program
Continue		continues running the current program after a breakpoint stop
Breakpoint	Alt-B	inserts a breakpoint at a specified line
Compile	Alt-T	compiles the current program but does not run it

The Options Menu

Command	Function
Toggle FKey Display	displays or hides the expanded split bar
Split at...	moves the split bar to a new position
Hide Menus	hides the menu and scroll bars and suspends mouse support
Double Click Speed	changes the double-click sensitivity of the mouse button

B.3   SPECIAL KEYS FOR MAC USERS

Editing Keys

Most editing on the Mac is done using the Copy, Cut, and Paste commands or their shortcut keys. We list these keys once more.

Cmd-C	copies marked text to the clipboard
Cmd-X	deletes and moves marked text to the clipboard
Cmd-V	inserts clipboard text before the cursor position

Remember that a single click inserts the text cursor at the location of the mouse cursor while a double click marks a word. Any block of program text can be marked or selected by dragging the mouse cursor.

B.4   PULL-DOWN MENUS and SHORTCUT KEYS
for MAC USERS

The File Menu

Command	Shortcut	Function
New	Cmd-N	opens a new program file
Open...	Cmd-O	opens a saved program file
Save	Cmd-S	saves the current program file
Save As	Cmd-Z	saves the current program file under a new name
Unsave	Cmd-H	deletes a program file from the disk
Page Setup...		specifies printing options
Print	Cmd-P	lists the current file on a printer
Quit	Cmd-Q	exits True BASIC

The Edit Menu

Command	Shortcut	Function
Cut	Cmd-X	deletes and moves marked text to the clipboard
Copy	Cmd-C	copies marked text to the clipboard
Paste	Cmd-V	inserts clipboard text ahead of the current text cursor position
Find...	Cmd-F	looks for a specified word or phrase
Find Again	Cmd-G	looks for the next occurrence of the previously found word or phrase
Change...	Cmd-E	changes a specified word or phrase to another specified word or phrase
Keep...	Alt-K	retains only a specified portion of the current program file
Include...		inserts a saved file ahead of the current text cursor position
Edit...		edits a specified procedure or block of text
Select...		marks a specified procedure or block of text
Move To...	Cmd-Y	moves the text cursor to a specified line of text

The Custom Menu

Command	Shortcut	Function
Load...		loads a library file into the workspace
Forget		clears all nonessential memory
Script...		executes a specified script file
Do		executes a specified preprocessor
Do Format	Cmd-D	executes the formatting preprocessor
Do Trace		executes the tracing (debugging) preprocessor

The Run Menu

Command	Shortcut	Function
Run	Cmd-R	compiles and runs the current program
Stop	Cmd-.	interrupts and stops a running program
Pause	Cmd-W	suspends execution of a running program
Continue	Cmd-M	continues running the current program after a breakpoint stop
Breakpoint	Alt-B	inserts a breakpoint at a specified line
Compile	Alt-T	compiles the current program but does not run it

The Windows Menu

Command	Shortcut	Function
Source	Cmd-L	moves the source (editing) window to the front
Set Souce Font...		selects font size for source window
Command	Cmd-J	creates and opens a command window
Close Command	Cmd-U	closes the command window
Set Command Font...		selects font size for command window
Output	Cmd-K	creates and opens an output window
Close Output	Cmd-I	closes the output window
Set Output Font...		selects font size for the output window
Save Output		uses extra memory to save the contents of the output window
Lose Output		does not save contents of output window
Configure...		saves or restores information about window settings

The Help Menu

Command	Function
Help!	introduces the True BASIC help system
Help...	displays a dialog box that allows an individual topic to be selected.
Help Topics	displays a list of available help topics

APPENDIX

C

The ASCII Set of Characters

NAME	DEC	HEX	NAME	DEC	HEX
^@ (null)	0	0	^\	28	1C
^A	1	1	^]	29	1D
^B	2	2	^^	30	1E
^C (break)	3	3	^_	31	1F
^D	4	4	sp (space)	32	20
^E	5	5	!	33	21
^F	6	6	"	34	22
^G (bell)	7	7	#	35	23
^H (backspace)	8	8	$	36	24
^I (tab)	9	9	%	37	25
^J (line feed)	10	A	&	38	26
^K	11	B	` (acute accent)	39	27
^L (form feed)	12	C	(	40	28
^M (return)	13	D	)	41	29
^N	14	E	*	42	2A
^O	15	F	+	43	2B
^P	16	10	, (comma)	44	2C
^Q	17	11	– (minus)	45	2D
^R	18	12	. (period)	46	2E
^S	19	13	/ (forward slash)	47	2F
^T	20	14	0 (zero)	48	30
^U	21	15	1	49	31
^V	22	16	2	50	32
^W	23	17	3	51	33
^X	24	18	4	52	34
^Y	25	19	5	53	35
^Z (end of file)	26	1A	6	54	36
^[(escape)	27	1B	7	55	37

Note: The caret prefix (^) means a control character, for example, ^A means Ctrl-A.

NAME	DEC	HEX	NAME	DEC	HEX
8	56	38	\ (reverse slash)	92	5C
9	57	39	] (bracket right)	93	5D
:	58	3A	^ (caret)	94	5E
;	59	3B	_ (underline)	95	5F
<	60	3C	` (grave accent)	96	60
=	61	3D	a (lowercase)	97	61
>	62	3E	b	98	62
?	63	3F	c	99	63
@	64	40	d	100	64
A (uppercase)	65	41	e	101	65
B	66	42	f	102	66
C	67	43	g	103	67
D	68	44	h	104	68
E	69	45	i	105	69
F	70	46	j	106	6A
G	71	47	k	107	6B
H	72	48	l	108	6C
I	73	49	m	109	6D
J	74	4A	n	110	6E
K	75	4B	o	111	6F
L	76	4C	p	112	70
M	77	4D	q	113	71
N	78	4E	r	114	72
O	79	4F	s	115	73
P	80	50	t	116	74
Q	81	51	u	117	75
R	82	52	v	118	76
S	83	53	w	119	77
T	84	54	x	120	78
U	85	55	y	121	79
V	86	56	z	122	7A
W	87	57	{ (left brace)	123	7B
X	88	58	| (vertical bar)	124	7C
Y	89	59	} (right brace)	125	7D
Z	90	5A	~ (tilde)	126	7E
[(bracket left)	91	5B	DEL (delete)	127	7F

True BASIC
Reserved Words

The following reserved words may not be used as names for variables or procedures in a True BASIC program.

KEYWORDS

ELSE	NOT	PRINT
REM		

RESERVED FUNCTION NAMES

Con	Date	Date$
Exline	Exline$	Extext$
Extype	Extype$	Idn
Maxnum	Nul$	Pi
Rnd	Runtime	Time
Time$	Zer	

Format for Displaying Numbers

True BASIC has a built-in set of formatting rules for displaying numbers. In most cases, numbers are displayed in an appropriate format with no special effort on your part. The rules are given for Version 3 of True BASIC which behaves somewhat differently from Versions 1 and 2.

1. Positive numbers and zero are displayed with a leading space. Negative numbers are displayed with a leading minus sign. All numbers end with a trailing space, even if followed by a semicolon in the PRINT statement.

2. If a number can be represented as an integer with eight or fewer digits (twelve or fewer digits in Versions 1 and 2), it is displayed in integer format.

    ```
    PRINT (7) displays  7
    PRINT (1725) displays  1725
    PRINT (-12345678) displays -12345678
    ```

3. If a number can be represented by eight digits or fewer (six digits or fewer in Versions 1 and 2) preceding a decimal point, it is displayed in decimal format. Digits following the decimal point are rounded so that the total number of digits displayed does not exceed eight. Trailing zeroes after the decimal point and leading zeroes before the decimal point are not displayed.

    ```
    PRINT (1.4) displays  1.4
    PRINT (12345.6789) displays  12345.679
    PRINT (-70410000.57) displays -70410001.
    PRINT (0.00000006) displays  .00000006
    ```

4. In all other cases, a number is displayed in exponential format, with eight digits or fewer (six digits or fewer in Versions 1 and 2) in the *decimal part* before the letter "e". Trailing zeroes after the decimal point in the decimal part are not displayed. The leading digit is between one and nine.

    ```
    PRINT (123456789123456789) displays  1.2345679e+17
    PRINT (0.0000000654321) displays  6.54321e-8
    ```

5. True BASIC rounds numbers to eight significant figures (only six significant figures in Versions 1 and 2), if necessary, before displaying them in exponential notation. For greater display precision, you can use the PRINT USING statement. Remember that True BASIC maintains an internal precision of 14 to 16 significant figures for all numbers.

APPENDIX
F

How To Use The Example Program Disk

I suggest that you make a working copy of the example program disk, using the appropriate method for your particular computer. The original example program disk can then be stored for safekeeping.

F.1 INSTRUCTIONS FOR READING PROGRAM FILES

Example programs for each chapter are stored in separate directories on the example program disk. For instance, programs for Chapter 3 are stored in a directory named CH03. Instructions for using these programs are different for PC and Mac computers.

Users of PCs

To view the programs, put the example program disk in a floppy disk drive, either A or B, and change to that drive by typing the A: or B: command. At the A> or B> prompt, change directories by entering CD \CH03. The command CD means change directory. If you now type in the command DIR, the names of all files in directory CH03 are displayed. For example, the file containing Example Program 3-2 is named EX03-02.TRU. If you want to examine another directory, say, containing the example programs in Chapter 4, enter the commands CD \CH04 and then DIR.

When using True BASIC, you can access any example program on the disk by specifying its path name, a combination of the drive letter, directory name and file name. For example, to load Example Program 3-2 in Chapter 3 with the example program disk in drive A, use the True BASIC command

```
Ok.  Old A:\CH03\EX03-02.TRU
```

As always in True BASIC, the TRU suffix is optional.

Users of Macs

To view and run the programs, put the example program disk in a floppy disk drive and double-click on the icon of that drive. A window of file folders is displayed. Each folder contains example program files for a single chapter. For example, a folder named Chapter 3 contains example program files for Chapter 3.

The easiest way to both view and run an example program on a Mac is to use the True BASIC editor. Start the True BASIC program, as described in Chapter 1, and you should see the editing screen. Select the Open command from the File command menu, as explained in Section 2.9 of Chapter 2. The example program disk should be in a floppy disk drive.

When the Open command is selected, a dialog box appears with a button named Drive. Click on this button with the mouse until the name of the example program disk is selected and displayed. You should see the icons for the chapter folders on that disk. Double-click on the folder for the chapter you want and the icons of the individual example program files in that chapter are displayed. Double-click on the desired example program file to open that example program. A listing of the program appears in the editing window.

For example, to open Example Program 3-2 in Chapter 3, first make sure that the disk named Example Programs is in a floppy disk drive and has been selected. You should then open the folder named Chapter 3 and select the program file named Example Program 3-2.

Once you are satisfied that you have found and opened the correct program, select the Run command from the Run command menu to execute the program.

You can select another program from the same chapter by using the Open command again. The current program disappears when a new program is opened.

F.2   INSTRUCTIONS FOR READING TEXT FILES

The practice programs after Chapter 2 often use text files. These files are stored in the same directories or folders as programs on the example program disk. For example, the test files for practice programs in Chapter 9 are stored in the directory named CH09 or the folder named Chapter 9.

Users of PCs

When using True BASIC, you can access any test file on the example program disk by specifying its path name, a combination of the drive letter, directory name, and file name. For example, the OPEN statement for a text file named TEST.DAT, located in directory CH09 on the disk in drive A, is

```
OPEN #1: name "A:\CHO9\TEST.DAT"
```

You may need to modify the path or file names in your practice programs to conform to your particular situation.

Users of Macs

When using True BASIC, you can access any test file on the example program disk by specifying its path name, a combination of the disk name, folder name, and file name. The disk must, of course, be inserted into a floppy disk drive. For example, the OPEN statement for a text file named Test Data, located in folder Chapter 9 on the disk named Example Programs, is

```
OPEN #1: name &
& "Example Programs:Chapter 9:Test Data"
```

Notice that colons are used as separators, and spaces are allowed in names. Extra spaces before or after the colon separators are not allowed. Because of the length of the path name, ampersands (&) are used to extend the statement over two lines.

F.3 USING THE SUPPLEMENTARY HELP FILES

The Help command in True BASIC only provides help on commands. As I wrote this book, I often found that I needed to look up the exact syntax of a True BASIC statement or refresh my memory on the purpose of a specific function. I decided to create three supplementary help files, place them on the Example Program disk, and ask you to copy them to your True BASIC directory or folder, either on a floppy disk or your hard disk. Here they can be accessed from True BASIC, opening the file using the Old or Open command in the File menu and finding the desired information using the Find command in the Edit menu.

The first file, named STATMENT.TRU, contains information on most of the commonly used True BASIC statements. The spelling of the file name is deliberate, remember the eight-character limit on DOS file names. The second file, named FUNCTION.TRU, contains similar information on True BASIC functions. A more complete list of functions appears in Appendix G. The third file, named TERMS.TRU, contains definitions of computer terminology introduced in this book. These three files should be copied from the Example Program disk to the same directory or folder as True BASIC.

Let's suppose you want to find out more about the function Time$. Access the proper file by entering the following command:

```
Ok. Old FUNCTION
```

With the FUNCTION.TRU file displayed in the source or editing window, use the Find command to find the function named Time$. Information on the use and syntax of that function is displayed. I hope you find these files as useful as I have.

APPENDIX
G

True BASIC
Standard Functions

G.1 MATHEMATICAL FUNCTIONS

Abs(X)
returns the absolute value of X

Ceil(X)
returns the least integer that is greater than or equal to X, equivalent to $-Int(-X)$

Divide(X, Y, Q, R)
a subroutine that divides X by Y, and returns the quotient Q and the remainder R

Eps(X)
returns the smallest number that can be added to X such that the result differs from X

Exp(X)
returns the exponential function of X

Fp(X)
returns the fractional part of X

Int(X)
returns the greatest integer less than or equal to X

Ip(X)
returns the integer part of X

Log(X)
returns the natural logarithm of X

Log2(X)
returns the logarithm of X to the base 2

Log10(X)
returns the logarithm of X to the base 10

Max(X, Y)
returns the maximum value of X and Y

Maxnum
returns the largest positive number in True BASIC (see Appendix A)

Min(X, Y)
returns the minimum value of X and Y

Mod(X, Y)
returns X modulo Y, equivalent to (X - (Y * Int(X/Y)))

Remainder(X, Y)
returns the remainder left after dividing X by Y

Rnd
returns a random number in the range 0 <= Rnd < 1

Round(X)
returns X rounded to an integer

Round(X, N)
returns X rounded to N decimal places

Sgn(X)
returns a value of 1 if X > 0, 0 if X = 0, -1 if X < 0

Sqr(X)
returns the square root of X

Truncate(X, N)
returns X truncated to N decimal places

G.2   TRIGONOMETRIC FUNCTIONS

Acos(X)
returns the arccosine of X

Angle(X, Y)
returns the counterclockwise angle between the X axis and a line from the origin to point (X, Y)

Asin(X)
returns the arcsine of X

Atn(X)
returns the arctangent of X

Cos(X)
returns the cosine of angle X

Cosh(X)
returns the hyperbolic cosine of angle X

Cot(X)
returns the cotangent of angle X

Csc(X)
returns the cosecant of angle X

Deg(X)
converts an angle of X radians to degrees

Pi
returns the value of p (equal to 3.14159...)

Rad(X)
converts an angle of X degrees to radians

Sec(X)
returns the secant of angle X

Sin(X)
returns the sine of angle X

Sinh(X)
returns the hyperbolic sine of angle X

Tan(X)
returns the tangent ot angle X

Tanh(X)
returns the hyperbolic tangent of angle X

G.3 STRING FUNCTIONS

Chr$(N)
returns a character corresponding to the ASCII value N

Cpos(A$, B$, N)
returns the position of the first occurrence of any character of B$ that is in A$, starting at character N in A$ and searching right

Cposr(A$, B$, N)
returns the position of the last occurrence of any character of B$ that is in A$, starting at character N in A$ and searching left

Len(A$)
returns the length of string A$ measured in characters

Lcase$(A$)
changes any uppercase characters in A$ to lowercase

Ltrim$(A$)

trims all leading spaces from A$

MaxLen(A$)

returns the maximum length of the string variable A$

Ncpos(A$, B$, N)

returns the position of the first occurrence of any character of B$ that is not in A$, starting at character N in A$ and searching right

Ncposr(A$, B$, N)

returns the position of the last occurrence of any character of B$ that is not in A$, starting at character N in A$ and searching left

Num(A$)

reverses the action of Num$(N) by restoring the numeric value stored in the string A$

Num$(N)

converts a number N to an internal string representation that cannot be displayed

Ord(A$)

returns the ASCII value of the first character in A$

Pos(A$, B$)

returns the position of the first occurrence of B$ in A$

Pos(A$, B$, N)

returns the position of the first occurrence of B$ in A$, starting at character N in A$ and searching right

Posr(A$, B$, N)

returns the position of the last occurrence of B$ in A$, starting at character N in A$ and searching left

Repeat$(A$, N)

returns a string containing A$ repeated N times

Rtrim$(A$)

trims all trailing spaces from A$

Str$(N)

converts a number N to a string

Trim$(A$)

trims all leading and trailing spaces from A$

Ucase$(A$)

changes any lowercase characters in A$ to uppercase

Using$(F$, V1, V2...)

returns a string containing variables V1, V2,... formatted by F$

Val(A$)

converts string A$ to a number

G.4   DATE and TIME FUNCTIONS

Date
returns the current date in YYDDD format, where DDD is the day of the year and YY is the year of the century

Time
returns the current time measured in seconds since midnight

Date$
returns the current date in YYYYMMDD format

Time$
returns the current time in HH:MM:SS format

G.5   ARRAY and MATRIX FUNCTIONS

Con
returns a numeric array all of whose elements are one, as in the program statement MAT(A) = Con

Det(A)
returns the determinant of the numeric array A

Dot(A, B)
returns the dot product of the one-dimensional numeric arrays A and B

Idn
returns a square numeric array that is an identity matrix, as in the program statement MAT(A) = Idn

Inv(A)
returns the inverse of the square numeric array A

Lbound(A, N)
returns the lower bound in dimension N of array A

Nul$
returns a string array all of whose elements are null strings, as in the statement MAT(A$) = Nul$

Size(A, N)
returns the number of elements in dimension N of array A

Trn(A)
returns the transpose of the numeric array A

Ubound(A, N)
returns the upper bound in dimension N of array A

Zer
returns a numeric array all of whose elements are zeroes, as in the statement MAT(A) = Zer

G.6   MISCELLANEOUS FUNCTIONS

Exline
returns the line number in a program where the most recent error occurred

Exline$
returns a string giving the location in a program where the most recent error occurred

Extext$
returns the error message associated with the most recent error trapped by an error handler

Extype
returns the error number of the most recent error trapped by an error handler

Peek(Addr)
returns a number that is the contents of the memory address in bytes given by Addr

Poke(Addr, Value)
a subroutine that accesses memory location Addr and changes its contents to Value

Tab(N)
moves the printing cursor in a PRINT statement to column N

Tab(Row, Col)
moves the printing cursor in a PRINT statement to row Row and column Col, the printing equivalent of the SET CURSOR Row, Col statement

True BASIC
Run-time Error Codes

Extype	Extext$
1000	Overflow in numeric constant.
1002	Overflow.
1003	Overflow in numeric function.
1004	Overflow in VAL.
1005	Overflow in MAT operation.
1006	Overflow in READ.
1007	Overflow in INPUT (nonfatal).
1008	Overflow in file INPUT.
1009	Overflow in DET or DOT.
1051	String too long.
1052	String too long in MAT.
1053	String too long in READ.
1054	String too long in INPUT (nonfatal).
1105	String too long in file INPUT.
1106	String too long in assignment.
2001	Subscript out of bounds.
3001	Division by zero.
3002	Negative number to non-integral power.
3003	Zero to negative power.
3004	LOG of number <= 0.
3005	SQR of negative number.
3006	MOD and REMAINDER can't have 0 as 2nd argument.
3007	ASIN and ACOS argument must be between 1 and -1.
3008	Can't use ANGLE(0,0).
3009	Can't invert singular matrix.
-3050	Argument for SIN, COS, or TAN too large.
-3051	Argument too large or small for accurate result.
4001	VAL string isn't a proper number.
4002	CHR$ argument must be between 0 and 255.
4003	Improper ORD string.
4004	SIZE index out of range.
4005	TAB column less than 1 (nonfatal).
4006	MARGIN less than zonewidth.

Extype	Extext$
4007	ZONEWIDTH out of range.
4008	LBOUND index out of range.
4009	UBOUND index out of range.
4010	REPEAT$ count < 0.
-4020	Improper NUM string.
4102	Improper TEXT JUSTIFY value (nonfatal).
4301	Mismatched parameters for CHAIN/PROGRAM.
4302	Mismatched dimensions for CHAIN/PROGRAM.
-4501	Error in PLAY string.
5000	Out of memory.
5001	Array too large.
6001	Mismatched array sizes.
6002	DET needs a square matrix.
6003	INV needs a square matrix.
6004	IDN must make a square matrix.
6005	Illegal array bounds.
6101	Mismatched string array sizes.
7001	Channel number must be 1 to 1000.
7002	Can't use #0 here (nonfatal).
7003	Channel is already open.
7004	Channel isn't open.
7051	Record LENGTH <= 0.
7100	Unknown value for OPEN option.
7102	Too many channels open.
7103	File's record size doesn't match OPEN RECSIZE.
7104	Wrong type of file.
7202	Must be RECORD or BYTE for SET RECORD.
7204	Can't use SAME here.
-7250	Can't SET RECSIZE on non-empty RECORD file.
-7251	Must be BYTE file or empty for SET RECSIZE.
-7252	File pointer out of bounds.
7301	Can't ERASE file not opened as OUTIN.
7302	Can't output to INPUT file.
7303	Can't input from OUTPUT file.
7308	Can't PRINT or WRITE to middle of this file.
7312	Can't set ZONEWIDTH or MARGIN for this file.
7313	Can't set ZONEWIDTH or MARGIN for INPUT file.
7317	Can't PRINT to INTERNAL file.
7318	Can't INPUT from INTERNAL file.
7321	Can't SKIP REST on STREAM file.

Extype	Extext$
-7351	Must be BYTE file for READ BYTES.
7401	Channel is not open for TRACE.
7402	Wrong file type for TRACE.
8001	Reading past end of data.
8002	Too few input items (nonfatal).
8003	Too many input items (nonfatal).
8011	Reading past end of file.
8012	Too few data in record.
8013	Too many data in record.
8101	Data item isn't a number.
8102	Badly formed input line (nonfatal).
8103	String given instead of number (nonfatal).
-8104	Data item isn't a string.
8105	Badly formed input line from file.
8201	Badly formed USING string.
8202	No USING item for output.
8203	USING value too large for field (nonfatal).
8208	USING exponent too large for field (nonfatal).
8301	Output item bigger than RECSIZE.
8302	Input item bigger than RECSIZE.
-8304	Must SET RECSIZE before WRITE.
8401	Input timeout.
8402	Timeout value < 0.
-8450	Nested INPUT statements with TIMEOUT clauses.
-8501	Must be TEXT file.
-8502	Must be RECORD or BYTE file.
-8503	Can't use READ or WRITE for TEXT file.
9000	File I/O error.
9001	File is read or write protected.
9002	Trouble using disk or printer.
9003	No such file.
9004	File already exists.
9005	Diskette removed, or wrong diskette.
9006	Disk full.
9007	Too many channels open.
9008	No such directory.
9100	Can't open temporary file.
9101	Can't open PRINTER.
9601	Cursor set out of bounds.
10001	ON index out of range, no ELSE given.

Extype	Extext$
10002	RETURN without GOSUB.
10004	No CASE selected, but no CASE ELSE.
10005	Program not available for CHAIN.
-10006	Exception in CHAINed program.
10007	Break statement encountered.
11000	Can't do graphics on this computer.
-11001	Window minimum = maximum.
-11002	Screen minimum >= maximum.
-11003	Screen bounds must be 0 to 1.
11004	Can't SET WINDOW in picture.
-11005	Channel isn't a window.
-11008	No such color.
11140	No GET MOUSE on this computer

Index

Made in the USA
Monee, IL
31 August 2019